DEVELOPMENT OF

PISTON

AERO

ENGINES

DEVELOPMENT OF
PISTON AERO ENGINES

2ND EDITION

BILL GUNSTON

PATRICK STEPHENS LIMITED
AN IMPRINT OF HAYNES PUBLISHING

This book was first published in 1993
Reprinted in 1994, 1995 and 1996

Second edition published in 1999
Reprinted in 2001, 2006

British Library Cataloguing in Publication Data
A catalogue record for this book is available from the British Library

ISBN 0 7509 4478 1

Patrick Stephens is an imprint of
Haynes Publishing, Sparkford.

Tel: 01963 440635   Fax: 01963 440001
Int. tel: +44 1963 440635   Int.Fax: +44 1963 440001

E-mail: sales@haynes-manuals.co.uk
Web site: http://www.haynes.com

Printed and bound in Great Britain by
J.H. Haynes & Co. Ltd, Sparkford.

Contents

Introduction

I have often written about the remarkable degree to which aviation is prone to the whims of fashion. Another way of looking at the same problem is to note that it is very easy to jump to conclusions which later, and sometimes very much later, are seen to be completely mistaken. Certainly the aviation piston engine has had its fair share of wrong turnings, dead ends and premature dismissals, all because of people jumping to conclusions.

Of course, there were many attempts to build piston engines for aircraft before the Wright brothers, but for practical purposes I think we can say it all began in 1903. At that time the IC (internal combustion) engine was barely 50 years old, and the practical spark-ignition petrol (gasoline) engine precisely 20. Cars, or rather horseless carriages, were such a rarity that they caused a commotion wherever they went. Where they stopped, a crowd gathered—some to admire, far more to jeer and ridicule (at least in Britain). Small wonder that anyone who tried to build a *flying machine* was regarded as a lunatic.

It is beyond question that the aeroplane could not have become an accomplished fact without the IC engine, and by IC I mean the spark-ignition Otto-cycle petrol engine. But there was not much to go on. Cars were increasingly being powered by in-line engines cooled by water, so this kind of engine was picked by many of the earliest aircraft constructors. Indeed, as there was no aero engine industry, the would-be aviator either had to buy an established car, motor cycle or motor boat engine or else make an engine for himself. In the first decade of this century the world centre for aviation, and for advanced technology generally, was Paris. Here in 1907 the Antoinette engines became the first type

ever to be put into production and sold to customers for use in flying machines. These were water-cooled, but in 1908 a radically new type of engine took the world of aviation by storm. This was the Gnome rotary, and for the next 10 years it was made in unprecedented quantities. Then it suddenly faded; instead of being the pinnacle of advanced technology it was regarded as essentially obsolete.

The Gnome, like many other early engines, was air-cooled. The relative merits of direct air cooling and of using the air to cool water in a radiator were fiercely debated. In the early days some builders used water but let it boil away, while in the inter-war years some engines used a closed steam circuit in which the airflow cooled the condensers. Every method had its ardent proponents, and equally vociferous opponents.

There was a similar argument over the in-line engine and the radial. I am a purist and use the term 'in-line' to mean just that: an engine with its cylinders in a straight row. Loosely, it can be used to mean more complicated arrangements, such as the V, X and H, as described later. In the Second World War, such engines were almost non-existent in the USA, Italy and Japan; these countries relied almost exclusively upon the air-cooled radial for all high-power engines. In the starkest contrast, though Britain had powerful radial engines, these were regarded as suitable only for slow and heavy machines and quite useless for fighters. (After we encountered the Fw 190 we changed our minds rather quickly.)

After the Second World War we British jumped to the conclusion that the big high-power piston engine was dead. Apart from a compound gas turbine diesel of extraordinary complexity we gave up development of advanced piston engines, so we played almost no part in a world market of some 65,000 expensive engines. As for air-cooling versus liquid, this seemed to be part of history. From 1945 onwards, the liquid-cooled aero engine almost ceased to exist as an industrial product, and almost all the 600,000-plus examples that littered the belligerent countries were soon reduced to scrap. The only piston engines in really large-scale production after 1958 were the small American air-cooled opposed engines made by Lycoming and Continental. They had no trouble in fighting off any challenge from small turboprops.

But in the 1960s two strange things happened. One was that liquid cooling began to make an unexpected comeback. Even more surprising was that car engines began to be converted for use in aircraft. This process had begun in a big way with the VW 'Beetle', but that engine was a modest air-cooled flat-four. The car engines that began to break into aviation in the 1970 period were Detroit-style, chunky masses of aluminium with water cooling, and rated at 200 hp and more. Everyone had known such engines were cheap, because of the economics of million-plus production, and also very reliable. What few people had realized is that they can be highly competitive on the score of weight. They also tend to run with less noise and vibration than purpose-designed aero engines of equivalent power. People who had spent a lifetime as experts on aero engines began to think that perhaps they didn't know much about the subject.

Of course it takes skill, knowledge, experience and probably some kind of sixth sense to sift the good ideas from the bad or even fraudulent ones. The fact that Whittle utterly failed to get anyone to show any interest in the turbojet for seven years shows that picking the good ideas is not easy. The history of aero engines has always been sprinkled with marvellous new ideas, most of them radical and therefore easy to sell as being far superior to the traditional arrangement which we ascribe to Herr Doktor Otto. I personally know of over 180, and the actual total worldwide is probably around 1,000. Very few have got as far as even running on the bench successfully. Even fewer have flown. Those that have almost made it as commercial products can be counted on the fingers of one hand. But—and this 'but' is a very big one—this does not mean that the very next radical new idea to come along might not sweep away the piston aviation engine as we know it. You just

This book is divided into two parts. Section I attempts to explain how aircraft piston engines work, or worked. I have tried not to make it too much like a dry classroom textbook. Section II outlines the history of the species. Obviously, there is no way one can even mention all the many hundreds of types of engine that have been built. I have deliberately concentrated on engines that were of technical or commercial importance. This has inevitably meant ignoring hundreds of unconventional oddballs.

need that sixth sense to pick it out from among the non-starters.

I am grateful to PSL for suggesting this book. They were spurred to do so by the success of two earlier titles, *World Encyclopaedia of Aero Engines* and *Rolls-Royce Aero Engines*. Those books—whose text and illustrations I have tried to avoid duplicating—were arranged engine by engine. This one is concerned with the principles, and only mentions particular engines where this is necessary. This has not quite been done before. Perhaps the best known general books on piston aero engines are Glenn D. Angle's classic work of 1921 *Aircraft Engine Cyclopedia*, L. J. K. Setright's *The Power to Fly* of 1971, and Herschel Smith's *Aircraft Piston Engines* of 1981, but these concentrated on individual engines. I have assumed that the reader already knows about the more important types of engine, but wants a deeper insight into how they work, and why. An authoritative and masterful work is *The Development of Aircraft Engines and Fuels* by Schlaifer and Heron, published in 1950, but they tended to look at everything from the political angle.

When you are going from engine to engine there are no great problems in trying to present a fair assessment, though I suppose even the most objective author has his likes and dislikes. (I shall never forget Setright's belief that the Napier Sabre was good for 5,500 hp!) On the other hand, when you are trying to explain basic principles it is almost impossible not to let personal opinion creep in. Inevitably, you 'know' that certain ideas worked well while others didn't, and in no time you are using such words as 'better' and 'worse'. On reflection, it may be that such sweeping assessments are not justified. Sometimes particular ideas or design features were never properly tried out, or they were tried out in a half-baked immature form in a very harsh environment.

So I would like to impress upon the reader that liquid cooling is better than air unless it's the other way round, poppet valves are better than sleeve valves (unless . . .), in-lines are better than radials (unless . . .), carburettors are better than direct fuel injection (unless . . .) and the traditional four-stroke Otto engine is better than all alternatives (unless something superior comes along, which it well might).

Bill Gunston
Haslemere, Surrey
1993

SECTION I
HOW IT WORKS

1 Basic principles

Whereas it is common to write books about aeroplanes without explaining how they fly, I do not think I can write this book without explaining how engines work. Of course, many readers will know the basic ideas already, but a lot of even this first chapter is not actually taught in most schools, so I hope it will be useful. I have to assume the reader is interested in aircraft piston engines, but cannot assume he or she even knows the difference between work and power, or between force and pressure. Sorry if this seems boring.

At the risk of losing the reader right at the outset, force, mass and weight are three different things. The most fundamental of the three is mass, which is loosely defined as the amount of matter (or material) in any object. This never changes; a brick has the same mass on the Moon as on the Earth. But weight is the force exerted on an object by gravity. One of Newton's laws says, in effect, 'force equals mass multiplied by acceleration'. Careful measurements have shown that, ignoring air resistance, the acceleration of a falling body near the Earth's surface is 32.2 ft/sec/sec, or 9.81 m/sec/sec. Thus, in old Imperial units, the force that gravity exerts on a mass of 1 lb is 32.2 times the force needed to accelerate the same mass at 1 ft/sec/sec, or 32.2 poundals. This unit is passing out of use, and in metric (or, rather, *Système Internationale*) units, the force gravity exerts on a mass of 1 kg is 9.81 Newtons.

Engineers often use such units as lbf (pounds force) or kgp (kilogrammes puissance), but the preferred unit of force is the Newton. In theory one cannot convert forces to masses, but it will not be too improper if I say that 1 N (Newton) is roughly equal to 0.1 kg, or just under a quarter of a pound. This book is not about jet engines, but it is impossible to measure the power of a jet engine, only its thrust. Such thrust today is usually measured in kN (kilonewtons).

All aircraft engines have to accelerate air rearwards, and thus generate a thrust to pull or push the aircraft along. The piston engine's sole task, apart perhaps from secondary duties such as driving an electric generator or cabin supercharger, is to drive a propeller. This is the crucial intermediary which translates the power of the engine into propulsive thrust. In 1940 the Italians built a kind of jet aeroplane, the Caproni-Campini N1, in which a piston engine drove an air compressor inside the fuselage which blew compressed air out of a nozzle at the back. It was most inefficient, and would have flown much faster if the engine had been connected to a traditional propeller.

What about pressure, work and power? Pressure is defined as force per unit area. We normally use the word in the context of a fluid (ie a gas or a liquid) acting on a solid surface, but we also encounter the idea when two solid surfaces press against each other. There are hundreds of such places inside each piston engine, but often it is not easy to say what the pressure is. Even the finest steel gearwheel changes its shape very slightly under load, and when its teeth come into contact with those of the gearwheel it drives, the teeth actually transmitting the drive very slightly bend and also flatten each other as they slide past. Of course, the deformation (change in shape) is very small, and stays well within what is called the elastic limit of the metal. Thus, as the load comes off, the tooth recovers its original shape. But the point I am making is that as the area of contact is extremely small, a small

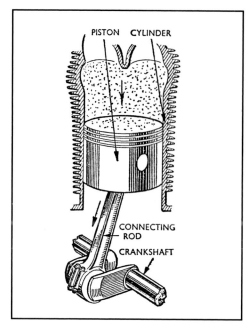

PISTON   CYLINDER

CONNECTING ROD

CRANKSHAFT

Every conventional Otto-type piston engine uses the high pressure of burning gas in the cylinder to drive down a piston, which turns the crankshaft to give a rotary output (Odhams Press).

change has a big effect, and thus it is difficult to determine exactly what the pressure is. Coming down to floor level, the stiletto heels worn by some lady passengers add a significant sum to the price of an airline ticket, because the pressure they exert is far greater than that of anything else on the floor of an airliner, and incidentally much higher than that of a battle tank or any other cargo.

If pressure is force per unit area, then clearly we can multiply the pressure by the area to get the total resultant force. I am sure every reader knows that most piston engines work by generating high pressure in a cylinder to push down a piston. If the peak pressure is 500 lb/sq in and the cylinder diameter (bore) is 6 in, then the area of the top of the piston is 28.2744 sq in and the maximum force exerted on it will be 14,137.2 lb, or more than seven short (2,000 lb) tons.

This force is real enough, but because of the geometry of the engine it will not be the force transmitted by the connecting rod to the crank. It would be if the connecting rod was vertical, as it would be at TDC (top dead centre) or BDC (bottom dead centre). These

happen to be the only places where no amount of pressure in the cylinder can do any good, because the connecting rod's force merely tries to distort the crank, without doing anything to make it turn. The useful work of a piston engine is done when the piston is descending down the cylinder. Then the connecting rod is inclined at an oblique angle. The piston is connected to the rod by a well lubricated pin called a gudgeon pin (known in the USA as a wrist pin). Thus it cannot transmit a rotary force to the con-rod, only a direct pull or push aligned with the length of the rod. This means that the horizontal component of the force in the inclined rod must be balanced by an equal and opposite side force between the piston and the wall of the cylinder.

All over every kind of engine there are places where two or more forces act at a point. The engine designer draws each force as a line of a particular length, in the direction in which the force acts. When he has drawn both forces, he completes the parallelogram and draws the diagonal across it. This is the resultant of the two original forces. To give a graphical idea of resultants, we can suspend three weights from two pulleys. They automatically take up positions such that each force at point O is the resultant of the other two. But in aircraft the problems may be greater. The force transmitted to the airframe by an engine mount is the resultant of part of the engine's weight, a force due to the torque (explained in a moment) imparted to the propeller, a force due to the propeller's thrust, a force due to gyroscopic effects, extra forces caused by bumpy air, forces due to manoeuvres commanded by the pilot and many other things, such as forces caused by the out-of-balance masses thrashing round in the engine. Almost never can an engine be made perfectly balanced. So you can see that the designer always adds a big 'factor of safety' for luck. I studied under a professor of design who said this should really be called a 'factor of ignorance'. We make things stronger and therefore heavier than they perhaps need be because we cannot work out the precise stresses, we are afraid of flaws in the metal, and there is a nagging fear that in one particular aircraft or engine all the parts will be by chance made to the bottom limit of the allowed dimensions, and so will all be weaker than normal.

We just introduced torque. This is the turning effect of a force which acts on something

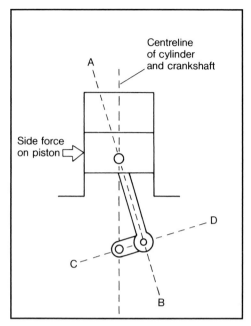

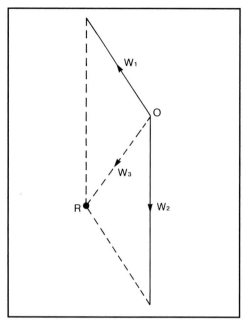

The maximum torque (turning effect) on the crankshaft comes not at mid-stroke but when the connecting rod (line AB) is at 90° to the crankpin (line CD). The unbalanced lateral force has to be reacted by the piston rings against the wall of the cylinder.

Graphical plot of the three forces shown in the previous figure. If we know any two forces acting at a point, and their directions, then by completing the parallelogram we can see their resultant (distance W_3 along direction OR).

The resultant of any two forces is a third force in the same plane. A simple arrangement of weights and pulleys can be used to demonstrate how the angles are governed by the relationship between the forces (see next figure).

that can rotate. The obvious example of such a system in a piston engine is the connecting rod and crank. Torque is equal to the force multiplied by the perpendicular distance from its line of action to the centre of rotation. We saw previously that at TDC and BDC the piston cannot exert any turning effect on the crank. At these times the perpendicular distance from the con-rod's force to the centre of rotation is zero, so torque is also zero. We might at first glance think torque was at a maximum when the piston was half-way down, but in fact—as shown in the diagram above—the peak torque comes earlier when the angle between the con-rod and the crank is 90°. Obviously, we can increase the torque by using a bigger crank and thus increasing the perpendicular distance to the axis of rotation, but this would mean we have to increase the stroke (the distance travelled by the piston from TDC to BDC), which in turn means a taller (or wider, if the cylinders are horizontal) and heavier engine, burning more fuel. We may run into problems of excessive piston speed. You can never get anything for nothing, at least not in engine design. To keep

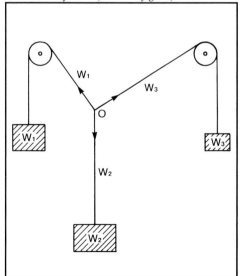

down piston speed we may have to run at lower rpm (revolutions per minute), so if we are not careful we could end up with a bigger and heavier engine that gives *less* power!

When we get to discussing superchargers we are likely to encounter 'moment of inertia'. This is a quality related to torque, and is a measure of how easy or difficult it is to start or stop a body's rotation. Numerically it is equal to the sum of all the masses making up the body multiplied by the square of the distance of each mass from the axis of rotation. For a flat disc $I = mr^2/4$, where m is the disc's mass and r the radius to the edge. Obviously we can increase I by putting more of the mass nearer to the edge, which is why flywheels tend to have thin centres and heavy rims. If we apply torque to a stationary wheel, the torque is equal to I multiplied by angular acceleration. Obviously, a slow-running, single-cylinder engine experiences marked changes in rotational speed; each firing stroke speeds it up, and for the rest of each cycle it is slowing down. Remarkable as it may seem, even a fast-revving aero engine with many cylinders nevertheless also experiences measurable cyclic variations in crankshaft speed, and calculating the result of the different drive torques and the many internal moments of inertia is a job for big computers.

Torque can loosely be thought of as turning effort, and this is the function of levers. Most piston engines have a number of these doing different jobs. For example, there may be rocker arms on the ends of the cylinders which reverse the direction of action of pushrods to drive the valves. Most rockers are simple centre-pivoted levers like see-saws, having no effect (other than adding friction and unwanted moment of inertia) on the magnitude of the force from the pushrod. Other levers are not pivoted at the centre, and they do have an effect on the force. One type, pivoted near the output end, converts a small input force into a much greater output force. Examples are a burglar's jemmy or a tyre lever. The catch is, if you multiply the force by, say, 10, then the output motion will be only one-tenth that at the input. In contrast, we can pivot the lever near the input, in which case we can convert a giant input force into a small output moving through a much greater distance.

We can do something similar with gear-wheels, the difference being that these can impart continuous motion. Of course, with the commonest type of gearwheels the direction of rotation is reversed with each engagement. This is shown in the diagram below, which depicts a gear with 20 teeth (A) meshing with a gear with 100 on a shaft which also carries a gear with 10 teeth meshing with another gear (D) with 100. We can drive either way. If we start by driving gear A we will end up with an output with 50 times the torque (100/20 × 100/10). We say that this gear-train has a mechanical advantage of 50. The catch this time is that the output turns 50

Gears can be used either to increase torque at the expense of speed (rpm), or (by driving D) increase speed at the expense of torque.

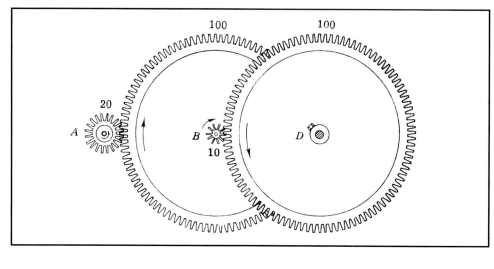

times more slowly than the input, in the ratio 1:50 in fact. This is the kind of arrangement seen in small turboprops, where the engine might turn at 50,000 rpm. With piston engines gear-trains are often needed to drive a lot of accessories, but not often to bring about 50:1 gear ratios. Alternatively, we can start by driving gear D. Then we get a very fast output at A, spinning 50 revs for each rotation of D, but with very poor output torque. Step-up gears are not common in aero piston engines, except to drive superchargers.

Other properties possessed by everything that has any mass are inertia and momentum. Inertia is that property of a body which makes it stay at rest or in steady motion unless acted upon by some outside force. We can imagine a railway locomotive being put aboard a ship by crane. The cables supporting it are flexible, but, because of the inertia of this large mass, we would be hard put to shake the load to and fro. We could, however, start it swinging; but, once we had got a good natural swing going, it would be very difficult to stop, because of its momentum. This is the opposite of inertia, being the tendency of a mass to keep moving once started. Numerically it is equal to MV, the body's mass multiplied by its velocity.

If the velocity is in a straight line, there is no problem so long as the speed is constant. Ignoring such factors as friction and wind resistance, no force need be imparted to the body. But, though they move in straight lines, the pistons in an engine are in anything but steady motion; their speed is accelerated to a maximum, brought to rest and reversed in direction twice in each revolution of the crankshaft. Thus the inertia loads are extremely high, and they have to be handled by a combination of forces exerted by the crankpin and gudgeon pin, compression of the mixture in the combustion space above the piston, and in a small way by friction between the piston rings and the cylinder walls. The crankshaft, like other purely rotary parts, can probably be balanced to eliminate significant inertia forces, but rotary parts are subject to yet another force. Anyone who throws the hammer at the Olympics knows about centripetal force, and the need to apply centrifugal force—until you let go and the hammer flies away. We have seen that everything tends to keep moving in a straight line unless a force is exerted on it, and it is the centrifugal force that makes every atom in a crankshaft, or a propeller, move in a circle. In the case of a point mass moving in a circle, the force is equal to the mass multiplied by the radius multiplied by the square of the angular velocity. This property can cause design problems, but is also made use of in such things as flyweight governors for primitive propeller CSUs (constant-speed units) and in centrifugal separators or filters which remove unwanted particles from lubricating oil.

All the foregoing comes under the general heading of mechanics, and of course mechanical principles govern the design of all engines. But the designer also has to know about a vast subject called thermodynamics, which deals with phenomena involving changes of temperature. All these phenomena are based on the transformation of energy from one form to another. The trouble is that you cannot see energy, nor measure it directly, and it comes in different forms. Some of its forms are electrical, electromagnetic and chemical, but here we are primarily concerned with three forms which are rather simpler to explain. These three are potential, kinetic and heat.

Suppose a chunk of metal falls off the top of a tall building. At the start it has quite a lot of heat energy, because it is not at absolute zero temperature (which we call 0K) but at a normal 'room temperature' which might be 15°C, which is 288K. But we cannot easily make use of that heat energy, because to do so there has to be a 'sink', or region of lower temperature, and this would be hard to find. But our chunk of metal also has a lot of potential energy; the actual amount is Mh where M is its mass and h its height above some datum (such as street level). When the mass falls it is accelerated by gravity, losing height and gaining speed. In other words, it converts potential energy into kinetic energy. As it hits the street it has kinetic energy equal to $0.5MV^2$, where V is its final velocity. Then it hits, and V becomes zero. All the energy is converted into heat. We can simplify things by saying that the falling lump does not touch the building as it falls, we can ignore air resistance (which converts some energy into turbulence which ultimately appears as heat in the air), we can say the object does not bounce, we can ignore the energy dissipated by noise as it hits (which again is dissipated as heat) and we can ignore elastic deformation of the metal or impact damage to the pavement. Making all these simplifying assumptions we can say $Mh = 0.5MV^2$ = the heat energy added during impact.

In other words, while you can convert

energy from one form into another, you cannot—for practical purposes—create it or destroy it. Nuclear and thermonuclear weapons do convert a little matter into a great deal of energy, but we do not use these processes in aircraft engines. The task of a piston engine is to convert the chemical energy available in fuel, which is a form of potential energy, as efficiently as possible into heating a working fluid (99.99 per cent air) and then use this to turn a shaft, and to lose as little energy as possible in the process.

Energy is synonymous with work. Work is defined as force multiplied by the effective distance moved in the direction of the force. Sometimes one has to think a bit, as in calculating the work done by the wind in propelling a yacht whose curved sail is set at an angle to the wind, and mounted on a boat which is travelling in a third (totally different) direction and also slightly slipping sideways through the sea, despite its keel. In piston engines calculations are usually easier. All directions are referred to the axes of the engine, and forces, directions and distances are measurable with great accuracy.

If we lift a weight of 1,000 lb a distance of 1 ft (after much agonizing I decided to use mainly old Imperial measures) we have performed 1,000 ft-lb of work. The weight has acquired 1,000 ft-lb of potential energy. We ignore the small extra work we did overcoming friction in whatever it was we used, such as cables and pulley blocks, or in repeated bending of the cables, which all emerge as heat. By now the reader will have begun to notice that nothing is as simple as it seems, all kinds of energy transfers take place throughout our daily lives, and almost all of them degrade the energy we started with to heat, which is the 'lowest' form of energy. There is a well-known 'law of the conservation of energy'. This repeats that energy cannot be destroyed, but practical machines always output less energy than the input. Consider a piston-engined aeroplane taking off. Most of the energy residing in the petrol (gasoline) is dumped into the atmosphere as heat from the exhaust pipe(s). More is lost in cooling the cylinders, as friction inside the engine, in heating the lubricating oil, in endlessly distorting all the parts of the engine (some of these distortions, such as of valve springs, are obvious), in inefficiently compressing air in a supercharger, in endlessly churning the air and oil vapour inside the engine, in noise, and in many other processes. Not much more than one-quarter of the initial energy actually goes into turning the propeller, which with luck will then convert about 78 per cent of this into propulsive thrust. In other words, the overall propulsive efficiency is less than 20 per cent.

If we specified a new engine merely on the basis of the work it could do, we might end up with an aeroplane that could not fly. We just lifted 1,000 lb through a vertical distance of 1 ft (ie directly against gravity) of 1 ft, but I did not say how long we took to do it. Almost every customer for any kind of engine is interested in its power. Power is the *rate* of doing work, in other words work divided by time. The traditional Imperial unit of power, the horsepower, was defined as 33,000 ft-lb/min, in other words if you lifted a 33,000 lb weight 1 ft in 1 min, that was a rate of working of 1 hp. It was loosely thought of as an output a carthorse could sustain. Of course 1 hp could also lift a 1 lb weight from sea level to 33,000 ft in 1 min, or a 550 lb weight 1 ft in 1 sec. The SI unit for power is the Watt, symbol W. This is defined as 1 Joule (J) per second, and a Joule is 1 Newton-metre per second. In symbols, $1\ W = 1J/s = 1Nm/s$. We met Newtons right at the start; they are roughly 0.1 kg, but we must remember they are units of force, not of mass. For aircraft engines the kilowatt (kW) is a more convenient unit. One horsepower is equal to 745.7 W, or 0.7457 kW. Thus, a Rolls-Royce Merlin can be said to have a take-off power of 1,190 kW or 1,600 hp. But it burns fuel at the rate of 5,410 hp (see diagram).

When we listed the ways in which energy is lost in an installed engine/propeller combination we were actually thinking in terms of loss per unit time, in other words loss of power. Some of these losses, such as elastic distortions and windage losses inside the engine, are constant as long as the engine is running, though they vary sharply with different speeds. (Throughout this book, 'speed' invariably means engine speed in rpm, not aircraft speed in mph.) Other losses grow from zero to a maximum as various items heat up. An obvious instance is the very large loss in cooling the cylinders. In an air-cooled engine this initially involves a transfer of heat from the burning fuel to the mass of metal in the cylinder, cylinder head, valve gear and other parts. As these increase in temperature so does the loss become a steady flow from the burning fuel to the atmospheric air flowing past the engine. With liquid cooling there is a further time delay while the cylinders heat up,

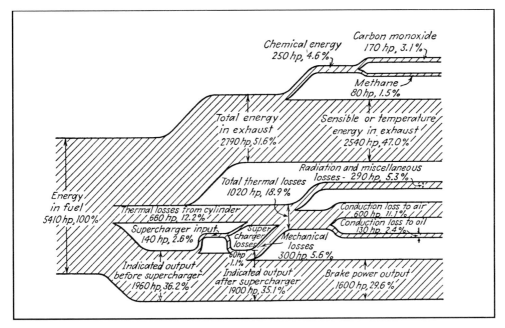

A typical heat balance, or efficiency diagram, for a 1,600 hp aero engine with a gear-driven supercharger of the 1940s. Much more energy is wasted in the exhaust than is used to drive the propeller (SAE paper by Pierce and Welsh).

a thermostatic valve opens, and the liquid coolant starts flowing in a closed circuit conveying the surplus heat to the radiator. As the latter heats up, so does it begin heating up the atmosphere. Virtually all the energy in the fuel eventually ends up as heat in the atmosphere. A wartime raid by 1,000 B-17s or Lancasters might burn over 2,000,000 gallons of fuel. This would release to the atmosphere something like 30,000 million BThU (British Thermal Units), or rather more than 30,000 million kJ (kilojoules). This sounds like, and is, a lot of energy, and every last bit merely heats up the air around us. And the same can be said of every BThU and every kJ of energy burned in every aircraft that has ever flown.

2 Engine cycles

This chapter is really the one that attempts to explain how engines work. Those that follow deal with individual aspects of design, and then the main part of the book tells the story of how piston aircraft engines developed. Before we get on to those topics it is desirable to spell out at least the broad outline of the thermodynamic cycles on which such engines operate.

In another book for PSL, *Plane Speaking*, I ponder on the amazing fact that throughout the nineteenth century the designers of flying machines never thought of using a rocket, or a series of rockets, for propulsion. Such 'engines' were fully developed and had been produced by the thousand for the British Army, notably to the designs of Sir William Congreve. They could be relied upon to give the thrust needed for the short period of flight at which the pioneer aviators were aiming. Instead these visionaries all proposed to use various forms of piston engine, and until the late 1850s the only type available was the steam engine.

The steam engine is called an external combustion engine, because the fuel is burned outside the cylinder. About 100 years ago Charles (later Sir Charles) Parsons invented the steam turbine. Various forms of steam turbine were used in aircraft, but these are outside the scope of this book. In the nineteenth century, however, the dominant engine—used for locomotives, ships and factories—was the reciprocating steam engine. Fuel, usually coal, was burned to heat water in a boiler and turn it into steam at a pressure significantly higher than that of the atmosphere. Atmospheric pressure is about 14.7 lb/sq in. If we say a boiler had a pressure of 50 lb/sq in, which was typical of the mid-nineteenth century, we mean 50 lb/sq in above that of the atmosphere. This is sometimes called 'gauge pressure', because that is what a pressure gauge connected to the boiler would read. The actual pressure would be 64.7 lb/sq in, and at high altitude the gauge pressure would not be far short of this, and the boiler might burst.

Once James Watt, Newcomen, Cugnot and others had shown that various kinds of engine could be driven by steam, dozens, even hundreds, of different forms of steam engine were experimented with. Most involved using the steam to push a piston along a closely fitting cylinder, the piston's linear motion being converted into continuous rotation by a connecting rod driving a crank on a shaft. The shaft preferably had to be at right angles to the axis of the cylinder and arranged to be centred on that axis. In other words, the cylinder had to 'point' exactly at the centre of the crankshaft. This is called the reciprocating type of engine, because the piston reciprocates, or travels to and fro up and down the cylinder.

Once engineers around 200 years ago had learned the basics of such engines they began to make 'double-acting' steam engines. In these, steam is passed first to one side of the piston and then to the other, its admission being governed by some kind of valve driven (by a crank or eccentric) off the crankshaft, so that the steam is always admitted at precisely the right times, and to the correct side of the piston. As noted in Chapter 5, a truly remarkable steam powerplant was created for Sir Hiram Maxim's huge biplane of 1894, but by this time steam for aircraft was on the wane. Only the Besler (Chapter 6) was to make much of an impact in the present century. Refinements such as compounding, in which steam is passed at progressively lower pressure from one cylinder to another, and the use of cut-off, in which a measured amount of steam is allowed to do work by expanding inside the cylinder, have seldom been used in aircraft engines.

Steam engines take a long time to bring to the boil. Moreover, when you add together all the parts, including the furnace and the boiler—as well as either a big water tank or else a condenser to enable the water to be used repeatedly—the bulk and weight almost rule out the engine for aeronautical use. Common sense suggests that an engine installation can be smaller and lighter if the heat of the chemical reaction can be released actually inside the cylinder(s). Such an engine is called an internal combustion or IC engine. IC engines were almost impossible to design until fluid fuels became available, though the principles were understood 200 years ago. Robert Street and Philip Lebon both patented plausible IC engines in the 1790s, and in 1826 Captain Samuel Morey in the USA patented an engine with properly worked out valve gear, a carburettor, electric ignition and water cooling! I do not think he was able to run it, and as noted in Chapter 5 the very first aero piston engines, built by Sir George Cayley in Yorkshire, ran on hot air.

After 1840 patents for IC engines came in a torrent. One landmark was the invention of the four-stroke cycle in 1862. Today we call this the Otto cycle, which is unfair on the actual inventor, Beau de Rochas. Dr Nikolaus Otto began making inefficient and noisy gas engines in 1867, but 11 years later he introduced a much better one. Then in 1883 the same cycle was used by another German, Gottlieb Daimler, to create an engine running on the light oil called petrol. (Fuels are discussed later in this chapter.) Yet another German, Karl Benz, made a somewhat better petrol engine in 1885. These launched the world motor industry, and car engines in turn greatly assisted the development of the first IC engines for aeroplanes. As noted later, in Chapter 5, a somewhat different cycle is named for Dr Rudolf Diesel. Until the Second World War the diesel was widely touted as the coming thing in long-distance aviation, but it had only a small peripheral impact, in the sharpest contrast to its dominance of marine, rail and commercial road transport.

A great engine man, Sir Stanley Hooker, described the four-stroke cycle as having 'one stroke to produce power and three to wear the engine out!' It is the most common heat engine cycle in the world, and is used in most road vehicles in one form or another. But first we might have a look at what we mean by an engine operating cycle. Some engines included in this book are nothing like conventional piston engines in conception, one example being the RC (rotating combustion) engine of which the most common type is the Wankel. Even this has to follow a sensible operating cycle in which a parcel, or enclosed volume, of working fluid is compressed, heated, expanded and allowed to escape. By 'fluid' we invariably mean air, with a trace of some fuel added at an appropriate point in the cycle, usually near the end of the initial compression.

Anyone who has pumped up a bicycle tyre will appreciate that when you compress a fluid it increases in temperature. With vigorous pumping the delivery end of the pump can get almost too hot to hold. With a so-called perfect gas an absolutely universal law is that $PV = RT$, where P is pressure, V is volume, R is a constant (called 'the Gas Constant') and T is the absolute temperature. Clearly, it follows that P, V and T are all interlinked. Common sense tells us that if you reduce V, for example by forcing a piston along a closed cylinder, then you will increase P. For small changes, T may not be greatly affected, but when you compress the parcel of fluid into a very small space then pressure increases enormously, and so does the absolute temperature. We saw in Chapter 1 that absolute temperature uses Celsius degrees but starts at absolute zero, which on the Celsius scale is −273.16°C. On the absolute scale this is 0K, so room temperature, commonly taken as 15°C, is close to 288K. When we come to consider how engines work we must remember that all temperatures are related to the absolute scale, because this has a profound influence on the efficiency an engine can achieve.

Engineers often draw a PV diagram for an engine. For a gas turbine, such as a turbojet, it may not be immediately apparent how you do this, but for a piston engine it is quite straightforward. We could start with a plain closed cylinder in which we had an airtight sliding piston. We start with the piston at the open end, in other words with the maximum volume (A in the diagram). We then push the piston in as far as we can. The PV diagram follows a curve, initially gentle and ending very steep, to point B. At B the air or other fluid is hot. If we immediately let the piston

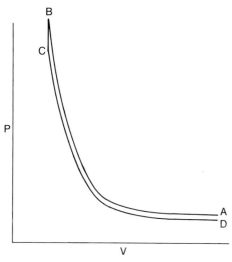

The simplest possible PV (pressure/volume) diagram is that for a parcel of fluid trapped in a closed cylinder by a moving piston. Pushing the piston towards the closed end reduces V and increases P (line AB). Left to cool, the cylinder will radiate heat energy and pressure will fall (BC). Pulling the piston back will eventually cool the fluid below room temperature (CD).

The most efficient possible thermodynamic cycle is that named for Carnot. It is made up of two isothermal (constant temperature) processes (AB, CD) and two adiabatic ones in which no heat is added or lost (BC, DA). This is the only cycle that is perfectly efficient and therefore reversible (ADCBA). It is utterly unattainable in the real world.

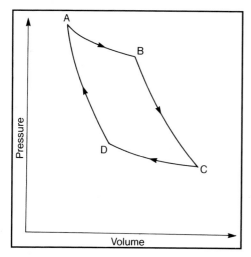

return it would retrace the same line back to A. But if we waited at B for an hour or two, until everything had cooled down, then — in theory, and if there had been no leakage — if we pulled the piston back to the open end the PV curve would start at C, vertically below B, and finish at D. At D the pressure is below atmospheric, and temperature is below room temperature. If we left everything for an hour or two it would return to room temperature and pressure at A.

I don't want to get too deep into classroom stuff, but I cannot avoid bringing in some fundamental ideas that rule the whole of thermodynamics. One is that you can do things to a parcel of working fluid at constant volume. For example, we just let heat escape from B to C, which was a constant-volume change. In most piston engines the combustion of fuel is so rapid that we can almost say the heat is added at constant volume. Alternatively, we can do things at constant pressure. In a diesel engine the fuel is injected over a period, adding heat at (almost) constant pressure, giving a flat top to such an engine's PV diagram. Two other fundamental ideas are isothermal and adiabatic. An adiabatic process is one in which the parcel of fluid is completely insulated against any heat coming in or going out. Our compression AB was almost adiabatic, but then we spoilt it by letting heat leak away from B to C. According to $PV = RT$, in any adiabatic process a compression results in an increase in temperature and an expansion in a decrease. In the real world, adiabatic changes are impossible to achieve, because no matter what we do heat energy will always travel from hot places to colder places. An isothermal process is one that takes place at constant temperature. Again, such a process is difficult to achieve in practice.

All practical thermodynamic cycles fall short of the ideal. An ideal cycle or process is reversible, in that the change could take place in either direction, and indeed could oscillate back and forth indefinitely. A real process cannot do this. For example, we could lose heat from B to C, but we could never make the heat flow back again, from a cooler place to a hotter place. Therefore we can never get anywhere near 100 per cent efficiency. The most efficient thermodynamic cycle possible was described in 1824 by a Frenchman, Nicholas-Léonard-Sadi Carnot. It comprises two perfect adiabatic processes and two isothermal ones, and so is completely reversible. In the forward (clockwise) case, heat is drawn from a hot source and work is done by the hot working fluid during an isothermal expansion AB. Then the supply of heat is cut off and further work is done at the expense of the fluid's thermal energy in an adiabatic expansion BC. Next, a smaller amount of work is done on the cool fluid during an isothermal compression CD. Finally, more work is done in an adiabatic compression DA, ending at the same high temperature at which we started.

Our working fluid must be a perfect gas, which exactly obeys not only $PV = RT$ but also various other laws. I perhaps might repeat that there is no such thing as an absolutely perfect gas, no such thing as a practical adiabatic or isothermal change, and no chance of making an engine run on the Carnot cycle. It is simply the theoretically most efficient thermodynamic cycle possible, and all engine designers try to get somewhere near to it.

Taking for granted such things as cost and reliability, engine designers are interested fundamentally in power and efficiency. The power developed by a piston engine is proportional to the area enclosed by the PV diagram, in other words the area ABCD. With the Carnot cycle the efficiency is also easy to describe. Isothermal AB is at a certain high temperature we can call T_1, while compression CD is at a lower temperature we can call T_2. Thermal efficiency then is numerically equal to $(T_1 - T_2)/T_1$. This doesn't sound too bad until we remember that these temperatures are absolute values, expressed in K. Obviously, there must be a clear upper limit for T_1, and with today's materials this is likely to be around 2,400°C or 4,350°F. Note: this is peak temperature of the working fluid in the cylinder, not the temperature of any metal part, which will be considerably cooler. But what might we expect T_2 to be? Anyone who has watched a typical piston aero engine running with open exhausts, ie with no pipes or ejectors connected to the exhaust ports, will know that the working fluid comes out pretty hot. Many is the time I have watched exhaust pipes glowing bright red despite the bitter cold of the high atmosphere. Suppose the gas leaves the cylinder at 1,465°C or 2,669°F (it is normally hotter). To find the thermal efficiency we first convert all temperatures to absolute K, the upper and lower then becoming 2,673 and 1,738. The result is then $(2,673 - 1,738)/2,673$, which is 35 per cent.

This is a not unreasonable figure for the ideal Carnot cycle. But real engines cannot work on this cycle, because heat is always leaking from hot parts to cold parts. In practice, aero engines actually achieve a thermal efficiency of around 27 per cent. The basic rule of $(T_1 - T_2)/T_1$ makes it clear that, the smaller we can make T_2, the closer we can get to 100 per cent. If we could somehow make our working fluid (exhaust gas) leave the cylinder at absolute zero temperature then we should achieve a thermal efficiency of 100 per cent. In practice this is simply not attainable, we cannot get anywhere near it. For a start, the exhaust cannot be colder than room temperature, which is about 288K. In practice, common sense tells us that if we burn fuel in air in a cylinder to generate gas at 2,400°C, we are hardly going to be able to cool this gas very much by the time it leaves the cylinder a fraction of a second later.

Before moving in to look at real engine thermodynamic cycles, we should not forget that what really matters is the overall working efficiency of the whole engine. This is dependent not only on the difference between the maximum and minimum temperatures of the working fluid in the cylinder, but also on the total energy involved. We can simply express the overall efficiency of the engine as P_s/P_f, where P_s is the actual power transmitted by the output shaft to the propeller and P_f is the power released by burning the fuel. This figure is going to be well below 27 per cent because it takes care of mechanical efficiencies and friction losses, heat lost in cooling systems, power expended in driving accessories, heat lost to the lubricating oil and possibly other factors. As we saw in the previous chapter, with a bit of luck something approaching one-quarter of the power made available by burning the fuel might appear as shaft power at the output. Then we can multiply by perhaps 78 to 80 per cent to get the propulsive efficiency available to the aircraft in the form of propeller thrust, in other words an overall figure of below 20 per cent. Four-fifths of the fuel energy is wasted.

If 20 per cent sounds a poor result, I might comment that so far I have ignored many other factors which all combine to reduce engine performance. Even considering just the basics of what happens to the working fluid, we can note that, no matter whether we use a carburettor or direct injection of fuel into the cylinders, we never get perfect vaporization of the fuel before the mixture is

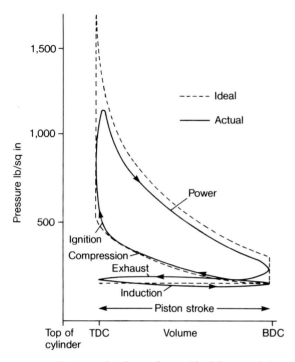

Here we plot the perfect or ideal Otto cycle in a broken line. The induction and exhaust strokes both follow a straight horizontal line exactly at 'room pressure', while the mixture is ignited at the very end of the compression stroke to result in an instantaneous rise in pressure to a peak. Real engines cannot behave like this, and instead follow the full line.

ignited, we never get precisely the optimum fuel/air mixture ratio for each operating condition, and in a multi-cylinder engine (and virtually all aero engines are of this type) we shall have slightly different conditions in all cylinders. For example, some cylinders will run over-weak and others over-rich. Again, the aerodynamic design of the entire inlet system, the cylinder and the exhaust system is always nothing like ideal, yet the working fluid has to move through the engine at high speed. And there are yet further factors which depress a real engine's power and efficiency. For example, on every working cycle every cylinder has to take in a charge of fresh air or mixture, burn it completely and get rid of every molecule of exhaust. This is obviously impossible; there is always some exhaust left inside each cylinder on every operating cycle, which reduces the intake of fresh fluid.

Later in this chapter I must briefly look at

the two-stroke and diesel cycles, but though these have always had their passionate champions they are not important in aircraft propulsion except in the field of microlights and small homebuilts. Probably 99.9 per cent of piston engine flight time is logged on what is generally called the Otto cycle. This is the best-known of the four-stroke cycles, so-called because the piston makes four strokes (movements along the cylinder) in each working cycle. The cylinder has some form of inlet valve which periodically opens to admit air or petrol/air mixture and then closes. It also has an exhaust valve which periodically opens to let the hot exhaust gas escape. The theoretical Otto cycle begins with the piston at TDC and the inlet valve open. The piston then moves down the cylinder to BDC, drawing in fresh mixture (or, in a direct injection engine, a charge of fresh air to which fuel is added separately). This is called the induction or inlet stroke. Somewhere near—probably just after—BDC the inlet valve closes. Thus, when the piston moves back along the cylinder the air or mixture is trapped, and so it is compressed and gets hot. This is called the compression stroke. Near TDC, with both valves still closed, the mixture is ignited, usually by a hot spark. It burns extremely swiftly (but in proper running certainly does not explode), and the pressure and temperature quickly reach very high values, driving the piston back down the cylinder on what is called the power stroke. Near BDC the exhaust valve opens, and the hot gas escapes from the cylinder being forced out by the fourth stroke of the piston, called the exhaust stroke. Then the cycle begins again.

An advantage of the four-stroke cycle is that it is methodical and painstaking. One complete stroke is devoted to induction of the fresh charge of fluid, and another complete stroke to getting rid (this is called scavenging) of the exhaust gas. Yet this same feature is a source of weakness. A steam locomotive gets four power strokes out of every four strokes of the piston: they are all power strokes. In contrast, the seemingly more modern aircraft engine gets only one power stroke per four strokes of the piston, and this not only means that for three-quarters of the time each cylinder is not giving power but consuming it, but it also makes the output intermittent, magnifying the fluctuation in torque in the crankshaft and tending to demand a large number of cylinders in order to get a smooth output.

As noted earlier, it was Beau de Rochas who described the four-stroke cycle, but Dr Otto who put it to use. The pure Otto cycle is, of course, just as theoretical and unattainable as the Carnot cycle, but in this case we can get very near it. If we could create a perfect engine, with perfect fuel, we might achieve it in every detail. The ideal Otto cycle consists of an induction stroke at constant P (the lowest pressure in the cycle), followed by an adiabatic compression stroke, the instantaneous addition of all the heat from the fuel (ie at constant V), a perfect adiabatic power stroke and finally a perfect exhaust stroke at the same constant pressure P. A real Otto cycle falls short of this for several reasons, and I have superimposed a typical real cycle diagram on an ideal one. For one thing, real valves do not open fully and close fully instantaneously; they take time to open and close, so they must start opening early and finish closing late. In fact the valve timing of a real engine is nothing like the TDC/BDC of the ideal cycle. The working fluid has inertia, and it takes time to start it accelerating through a valve aperture; once moving through a valve, it will wish to continue, drawing whatever other fluid is available after it. The fuel does not all burn instantaneously. Even the most perfect mixture take time for the flame front to travel across it, so the spark has to be timed early, before TDC, and the burning will continue well after TDC. Thus the addition of heat is not isovolumetric (at constant V), but results in a curve starting on the compression stroke and finishing on the power stroke. Heat is lost through the cylinder head and walls, and through all other parts, so the compression and, especially, the expansion strokes are not adiabatic. And the inlet and exhaust strokes do not appear as superimposed horizontal lines at minimum P, because the induction stroke sucks the working fluid in at well below ambient pressure (we'll ignore supercharge-boosted engines for the moment) and the exhaust has to be pushed out against atmospheric pressure to overcome the losses through the ports and piping.

Having said all that, the PV diagram for a real Otto-cycle engine is nothing to be ashamed of. Bearing in mind that the power is proportional to the area enclosed by the big loop (minus the much smaller area enclosed by the exhaust/induction loop), the departures from the ideal PV diagram are quite modest. To give a rough idea of where the heat energy from the fuel goes, about 27 per cent is obtained as useful work at the propeller shaft, about 35 per cent is lost in cooling the cylinders, oil and other parts, about 33 per cent is lost in the exhaust and about 5 per cent is expended in friction, internal windage and driving the accessories.

In determining engine power a key factor is MEP (mean effective pressure), in other words a measure of the average gas pressure acting on the piston. It is possible to measure this directly, by attaching an instrument called an indicator via a pipe to the combustion space. This traces out an indicator diagram, which is a PV diagram, and by measuring the area of this it is possible to calculate the IMEP (indicated MEP). From this it is necessary to subtract losses due to friction within the engine. Typically the mechanical efficiency might be around 95 per cent, so we multiply IMEP by this value, or whatever we have measured on the actual engine, and the result is BMEP (brake MEP). From this we can get bhp (brake horsepower) by multiplying BMEP by the swept volume (measured in compatible units, such as cubic inches) and rpm and (for a four-stroke engine) dividing by 792,000. The resulting value can then be compared with the bhp calculated from measuring torque on a brake dynamometer at different rpm. Early engines had a BMEP around 60 lb/ sq in, early Gipsy engines reached 120, and a few specially boosted engines (in 1945, and in modern Unlimited racers) can hit about 450. A typical figure for a modern high-performance engine for general aviation would be 200–250.

It is obvious that the piston cannot travel the whole length of its cylinder. There has to be room at the top for the compressed mixture, and this is called the combustion space or clearance volume. As noted later, it can be a simple shape like a slice of the cylinder, but far more often it has a complicated form more like a hollow pyramid. But obviously the volume actually traced out by the moving piston, between TDC and BDC, is a perfect cylinder. Its volume is called the swept volume (because it is 'swept' by the moving piston on each stroke) or capacity or, in the USA, displacement. Most of us are familiar with this parameter with cars and motor cycles, because it gives a rough idea of the engine's 'size' and potential power. Numerically it is equal to $0.7854D^2LN$, where D is the cylinder diameter (bore), L the length of piston travel (stroke) and N the number of cylinders, the answer coming out in cubic inches or litres depending on what units we used to measure the cylinder dimensions. ($0.7854D^2$ is the area of each piston on which the gas pressure acts.)

We have seen that the compression of the charge by the ascending piston is essentially adiabatic. According to $PV = RT$ the charge gets much hotter because of the compression; in the diesel type of engine it is deliberately compressed so much that the oil fuel burns the instant it is sprayed in. With spark ignition engines the compression is much less, but we still want it to be as high as possible. This is because the ideal efficiency of an Otto engine—indeed, of any conventional reciprocating IC engine—is equal to $1 - 1/r^{\gamma-1}$, where r is the compression ratio and γ is the ratio of the specific heats of the working fluid (taken as air) at constant pressure and constant volume. We need not bother much about γ, but numerically it is about 1.41. We naturally want our efficiency to be as close to 1 as possible, so we want the quantity we must subtract from 1 to be as small as possible,

An indicator measures the pressure inside the cylinder throughout an engine's operating cycle. This shows all the basic parts of a four-stroke engine, together with a typical indicator diagram. Gears from the crankshaft turn cams to open and close the valves (one valve only shown) (McGraw-Hill).

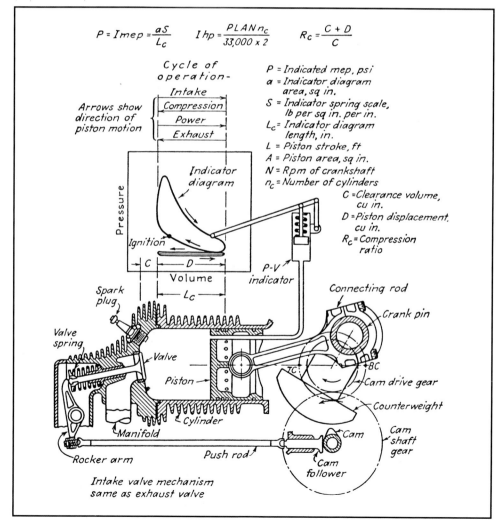

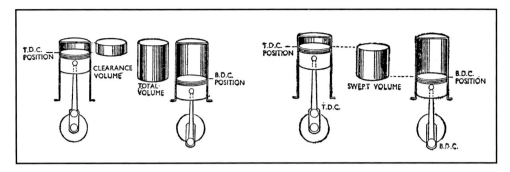

At TDC (top dead centre) there is bound to be a small space for the compressed mixture (the clearance volume). At BDC (bottom dead centre) the space inside the cylinder is the total volume. The difference between the two is called the swept volume or capacity, usually measured in cc (or litres) or cubic inches. It gives a general idea of an engine's power (Odhams Press).

which means making r as high as the engine can stand. Limits on r are set by mechanical strength, but far more severely by dissipating excess heat from the cylinder head (the closed end of the cylinder) and by the problem of detonation, as described later in this chapter.

We can consider three different volumes inside the cylinder, which we can call (author's notation, adopted for simplicity) V_t, V_c and V_s. V_t is the total volume inside the cylinder at BDC, and it is equal to V_s (the swept volume or capacity) added to V_c (the clearance volume left at TDC). We call V_t/V_c the compression ratio, which we have already given the symbol r. The relationship $PV = RT$ makes it impossible to relate the pressure in the cylinder directly to the position of the piston, but obviously the bigger we make r the greater is the pressure before the charge is ignited. In the earliest IC aero engines r was typically about 5. Today many piston engines are still being made with r set at 6.4, examples being air-cooled in-line and radial engines of the former Soviet Union, Poland and Czechoslovakia. However, the wish to increase efficiency has led to a general wish to increase r, and it is remarkable that, after sticking at around 6 for 80 years, r has now shot up to around 10.5 in many of the newer engines.

At this point we can turn to discuss other cycles, such as the two-stroke and the diesel. We might also take note that virtually all IC aero engines are single-acting. In other words, the cylinder has only one closed end in which combustion takes place. It would be perfectly straightforward to sketch a double-acting engine, like a steam locomotive. One obvious

change, compared with today's engines, is that the piston would have to be rigidly attached to a piston rod sliding in a gas-tight hole in the end of the double-ended cylinder nearest to the crankshaft. The free end of this rod would then be linked to the crankpin by the connecting rod. Various designers have tried to make double-ended IC engines, and in a few cases, notably with large low-rated stationary engines burning gas or oil, they have achieved success. I think it is fair to predict that nobody will ever make a successful double-acting piston aero engine. There is no law against it, and readers are invited to try, but nobody has done it so far. And this is tough, because in theory you get a smoother engine, with twice as many firing strokes per revolution, and something like double the power for only a modest increase in weight.

Of course, the advocates of the two-stroke would also claim to offer something like double the power, and certainly precisely twice as many firing strokes per revolution, as in the common type of engine. In practice, few things are as simple as they appear to be at first sight, and the fact that—except in the smallest sizes—only a small proportion of aero engines are two-strokes shows that there is another side to this particular coin. To get through the four operations of induction, compression, power and exhaust in just two strokes—one movement of the piston down the cylinder and one movement back—clearly calls for clever design; indeed it may seem to be impossible. We have to use the upward travel of the piston for compression and the downward stroke for power, so we are faced

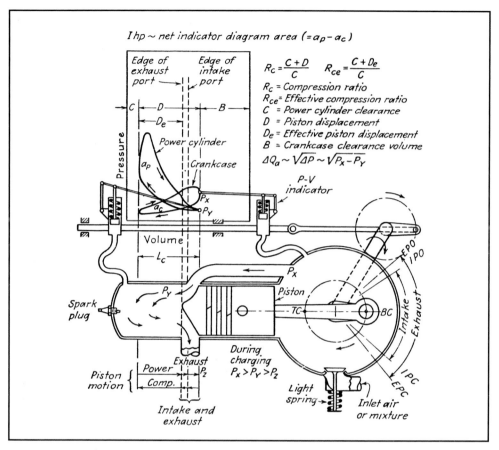

Designers have always thought they ought to do better than have one power stroke in every four strokes. The two-stroke engine gets one power stroke in every two, ie every downstroke is a power stroke. It loses out in the difficulty of clearing out the exhaust and bringing in a good fresh charge of mixture (McGraw-Hill).

with the task of carrying out induction and exhaust in a very brief time interval, and simultaneously, while the piston is near BDC!

To accomplish this, nearly all two-stroke engines use some form of external compression to pressurize the incoming charge before it reaches the cylinder, so that, as the exhaust escapes from one side of the cylinder under its own residual pressure, the fresh mixture can rush in on the other side. Almost always, ports are cut in the cylinder walls near BDC, so that as these are uncovered by the piston near the bottom of its stroke the exhaust can escape and the fresh charge come in. We want the two fluid masses to mix as little as possible, so usually we give the piston a humped top to direct the fresh mixture up to the top of

the cylinder. The simplest way of providing pre-compression is to admit the fresh air or mixture first to the crankcase, where it is automatically compressed by the downgoing piston. But aero engines tend to have several cylinders, and at once we have problems dividing the crankcase into separate compartments for each cylinder. With opposed cylinders, which is one of the most popular arrangements for GA (general aviation) engines, this idea breaks down completely. In any case, with multiple cylinders there are considerable difficulties in supplying the correct mixture via the crankcase to all cylinders. One answer is direct injection, and another is to forget about crankcase compression and add an external supercharger. Such a blower can conveniently be driven by an exhaust gas turbine (ie, we can use a turbocharger), because in a two-stroke engine the exhaust gas has high residual energy. On the other hand, the last thing we want to do is place obstructions in the way of the hot exhaust gas leaving the cylinder. Thus, we can forgo the advantage of not needing any valve gear and add exhaust valves. Indeed, one attractive new two-stroke (a diesel), the Merlyn, has four exhaust valves per cylinder! This helps to get the exhaust out of the way quickly, while the fresh charge comes in under high pressure.

Two-strokes are certainly by no means dead in the world of aviation, and if anything diesels are becoming increasingly important. I have many memories of proponents of the diesel, 40 and more years ago, stridently campaigning for what they claimed to be a better kind of engine for aeroplanes. None of them ever got anywhere, though the Junkers company did achieve quite useful sales with an unusual species of two-stroke diesel which used opposed pistons moving towards and away from each other in very long cylinders with two crankshafts along the top and bottom of the engine. This arrangement gave quite good results (see Chapter 6), but even here these engines were never more than also-rans. After the Second World War Napier put a lot of effort into remarkable two-stroke diesel compound engines (see Chapter 7), but these could not compete with the swiftly growing attractiveness of gas turbines.

Via the two-stroke I have found myself discussing the diesel without first outlining its operating cycle. Whether it is a two-stroke or four-stroke, the true diesel is a compression-ignition engine. Strongly, and thus heavily, constructed, it draws in pure air and compresses it (AB) much more than in spark-ignition engines. Early diesels were designed to r of about 12, giving a pressure at TDC of about 500 lb/sq in. Modern diesel aero engines operate with r of 17 or 18, which makes the air (at B, before any fuel has been burned) considerably hotter than the turbine entry temperature in Whittle's first turbojet!

Somewhere very close to TDC a fuel injector starts to spray fuel into the cylinder. As explained later, the fuel system of a diesel engine has to be extremely precise. It has to inject exactly the correct quantity of fuel, at exactly the correct rate, and do so against the very high pressure of the 'red hot' air in the cylinder. The fuel starts burning as soon as it leaves the injector, but the fine spray continues while the piston moves away from TDC

and starts travelling down the cylinder (BC). The rate of fuel injection is such that, despite the downward travel of the piston, the pressure in the cylinder stays at the same very high value as at TDC. Then, at a predetermined point (C), the fuel supply is cut off. From there onwards the piston continues with the power stroke as in other engines, following close to the line of adiabatic expansion (CD). Near the end of the power stroke (D) the exhaust valve opens (this description applies to a four-stroke diesel). Thus, the four-stroke diesel cycle resembles that of a spark-ignition engine except for the much greater compression and for the addition of heat from the burning fuel not at constant volume (or very near to it) but at constant pressure, over a much longer period. This alters the shape of the PV diagram.

Diesels have many advantages. Their oil fuel tends to be cheaper, and some would claim it is safer to use. There is no problem of

In a diesel engine pure air is taken into the cylinder and compressed very highly (AB). Compression ratio (V_t/V_c) might be 15 or more. Then fuel is sprayed in at a controlled rate such that pressure is held at the maximum value as the piston begins its descent (BC).

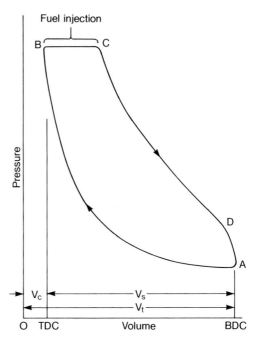

detonation (described later). Perhaps the greatest single advantage is that, mainly because of the higher value of *r*, the efficiency is greater and thus the fuel consumption less, for any given power output. With dramatic rises in the price of petroleum fuels this factor has tended to come to the fore, and accounts for the recent enhanced interest in diesels for light aircraft. Other possible advantages for diesels include the absence of an ignition system and perhaps the absence of valve gear. On the other hand, most diesels are inevitably heavier than equivalent spark-ignition engines. Because their chief moving parts have to be strong and massive it is difficult to achieve high rpm, and another likely drawback is the need for a turbosupercharger or some other kind of blower to scavenge the cylinders of burned gas. Traditionally the diesel has also suffered from being heavy and ponderous. Even Junkers, the greatest exponent of diesel aero engines, calculated that such engines were uncompetitive for flights shorter than about five hours' duration, when the fuel saved might outweigh the greater engine weight. Today, however, quite remarkable high-speed diesels exist which appear to be little if at all heavier than any other piston engines, as described in Chapter 8.

A few more general requirements can be listed which apply to all aero engines. Weight is obviously important, and for some aircraft designs it is the total weight of engines plus fuel which is important. In other words there is no point in saving 500 lb in total installed engine weight if this choice means an increase of 1,000 lb in the fuel required for a given flight. Put another way, if we know we are going to have to make very long flights, it may pay to use a heavy and complicated engine in order to achieve better sfc (specific fuel consumption, the rate at which fuel is burned for a given power output) and thus achieve an overall saving in take-off weight, and also in cost per flight.

Drag is another obvious factor. When around 1910 early aviators were thrilled to get airborne at all, nobody thought much about it; at least, it was of minor importance. Even in the 1920s drag, which can very loosely be called wind resistance, was often almost ignored. Both in-line and radial engines were simply bolted on to the aircraft and left in the open air. Gradually, as aircraft designers learned how to build cantilever monoplanes, without bracing struts or wires, speeds began to increase considerably. From that time on,

almost every engine was installed with some thought to minimizing drag, which in the case of liquid-cooled engines included paying attention to the radiator. Nowhere was the process more effective than in the case of air-cooled radial engines, where instead of offering an ungainly shape – called by aerodynamicists a 'bluff-body' – they were enclosed in a tight cowling in such a way that overall drag was often zero, thrust from the heated cooling air more than countering drag from other causes.

In most cases an aero engine has to work in any attitude, and possibly even under severe negative g. An oft-told story is how RAF fighter pilots in the Battle of Britain frequently found themselves at a severe disadvantage in that the float-chamber carburettor of the Merlin II or III could not function under negative g (Chapter 7).

Of course, it goes without saying that engines have to operate over a wide range of ambient temperatures, the atmosphere at high altitude being generally colder than a Siberian winter. They have to be as perfectly balanced as possible, because the last thing the pilot or aircraft designer wants is a collection of heavy masses which, rotating or oscillating, threaten to tear the engine out of the airframe. The aircraft engine must also be able to spend most of its life at quite high power settings. Whereas the average power developed by a car engine over a typical year is around 22 per cent of the maximum, the corresponding figure for an aero engine is unlikely to be less than 50 per cent and might exceed 60 per cent. Despite this, reliability has to be of the highest order. In the early days, prior to about 1925, reliability was by modern standards appalling. I had an uncle who by 1930 had made 14 airline flights – with famous carriers such as Imperial, Sabena and KLM – and experienced five forced landings, in each case through engine failure. This is discussed in later chapters.

This is a book about engines, but I ought to say a little about such related topics as fuels and propellers. Some reciprocating engines are very tolerant of different kinds of fuel. I personally have since 1960 believed that the Stirling engine, a four-stroke reciprocating engine, has been very near to a big breakthrough, including use in aviation. The Dutch Philips Research Labs have run Stirlings on all common petroleum fuels and also on everything from crude petroleum, black and sticky, to salad oil! Indeed one of Dr Diesel's early experimental engines was even designed to run on finely divided coal dust! In contrast, aircraft piston engines have in the main been cosseted with a diet of petrol (gasoline) specially tailored to such engines and produced to tightly controlled specifications. But the specifications have changed dramatically.

As explained in more detail in subsequent chapters, the piston aero engine needs a fuel system and an induction system. The former supplies fuel under pressure, at exactly the rate needed by the engine rpm, altitude and power output. The induction system does the same with the necessary air supply. Until recently most engines used a carburettor to mix the fuel with the incoming air, so much of the induction system actually handled the highly combustible mixture. Typically this is 93 per cent air and 7 per cent petrol by weight, while the ratio by volume is in the order of 9,000:1. The fuel in the mixture is not in the form of droplets, or ought not to be, but in the form of invisible vapour. Though we would be immediately aware of its presence, by smell, the mixture fed to the cylinders is very close to being pure air.

Nevertheless, the tiny fraction of fuel vapour is what gives the engine its power. Hydrocarbon fuels based on petroleum are so taken for granted that it may seem strange to enquire why this should be the case. We naturally want a fuel that is readily available in large quantities at an affordable price. It should be an easily pumped liquid, not prone to thickening or freezing, safe to handle, and non-toxic. It must release the greatest possible heat energy per unit mass or volume. (In short-range light aircraft the question does not arise, but in many cases the limiting factor is the weight of fuel and in others the problem is its volume.) The fuel must be stable, even if left in the tanks for a long period, yet must burn extremely rapidly when mixed with air. Typically, the time that elapses between injection of liquid fuel into the carburettor and combustion in the cylinder, about 1 ft away, is about 1/16 sec, and in a direct-injection engine complete vaporization may have to be accomplished in less than 0.001 sec. Any fuel left in the form of droplets will not only fail to make its contribution of heat energy but may also damage the engine. So the fuel must be extremely volatile, even at very low temperatures, though we do not want the fuel to boil – vaporize – on its way from the tank to the engine.

As explained in later chapters, designers took a long time to develop streamlined radial installations. By 1944 designers knew more about how to do it, for example in the Hawker Fury.

In the earliest days of aviation, refineries of crude petroleum were being built all over the world. Their products were kerosene, for all forms of heating and lighting, and a smaller amount of fuel oil for steam boilers and various industrial processes. These, the first petroleum products, were produced by distillation. At the bottom end of the fractionating column one could get heavy lubricating oils. At the top came the light fractions, called gasolines (petrol). To us it seems amazing that these liquids had only a very small market, and were either burned at refinery stacks or poured into any handy river! Very gradually after 1890, the world population of cars began to open up a market for gasoline, and it began to be sold from retail 'filling stations'. In 1903 the Wrights bought a can or two from a boatyard at Elizabeth City, not far from Kitty Hawk. This gasoline almost certainly was refined by Standard Oil at Baltimore, from Pennsylvanian crude. It had an octane number of about 38, but neither this measure nor its significance were known at that time.

You could say no two samples of fuel are alike. Crude from one oilfield differs sharply from crude from another, and even the crude from a single well naturally changes as the level falls, rather like sucking a complex milk shake through a straw. A major constituent is bound to be paraffins, the proper term for petroleum fractions in which each molecule comprises a straight chain of interlinked carbon atoms, each joined to a hydrogen atom on each side. The simplest paraffin, and thus the lightest and most volatile, is methane, a single carbon with four hydrogens around it (CH_4); it is a gas at room temperature and pressure, and is today being considered as a useful fuel in its own right. Other fractions are more complex, comprising olefins, aromatics and naphthenes with different kinds of branched or ring-like molecular structures. The possible combinations of these, plus other trace chemicals, are for practical purposes innumerable.

In 1903 nobody had heard of the phenomenon of detonation—also called knocking or pinking—but it is one of the basic hazards of the Otto-type engine. The Wrights found their 1903 engine would start off giving about 16 hp, but would fairly quickly overheat and fall away in power to about 12 hp. With a compression ratio of 4.4 it is possible that 38 octane petrol would indeed cause detonation and overheating, but this is a mere guess. In their 1905 engine the Wrights reduced the compression ratio to 4, and appear to have suffered no more from overheating and power loss. Not a lot happened for the next 10 years, apart from automobile 'filling stations' proliferating all over the globe. (In 1903 there were just three in Africa, one each in Algiers, Cairo and Cape Town!) The proportion used in aeroplanes increased sharply after the outbreak of the First World War in August 1914, almost all the big tonnage used by Britain and France coming from highly aromatic petrols refined from crudes from the Dutch East Indies. In April 1917 the USA entered the war, and—to the relief of the hard-pressed British and French—quickly supplied shiploads of petrol refined from American crudes. There was immediate severe engine trouble, with overheating, loss of power and mechanical failures. (Only much later was it realized that, while the East Indies petrols had an octane number of about 70, the US supplies had an octane number of 45 to 55. What this means is explained later.) This spurred research into detonation, and how fuels can be improved to avoid it.

Someone discovered that adding 20 per cent benzol (benzene) to the American fuel eliminated the problem. Benzene (C_6H_6, the simplest of the ring-shaped aromatic molecules) was produced by distilling coal tar. The Royal Aircraft Factory (today the Royal Aerospace Establishment) at Farnborough had begun research into fuels in 1915, and in 1917 began an urgent investigation into what actually happened when fuel burned in a cylinder. This classic work, by Professor A. H. Gibson, laid down many of the basic principles governing an engine's performance. Gibson knew that in 1906 a pioneer researcher, Hopkinson, had drawn attention to the possibility of pre-ignition or detonation (without using the latter term), but he was unable to detect the problem by ear because of the deafening noise of the propwash and open exhaust of the test engines. (It would have been simple to use a single-cylinder engine driving a silent dynamometer brake and with the exhaust piped outside the testbed.) Gibson judged the engine was detonating when cylinder heads glowed bright red!

It was not until 1919, just after the war, that the Shell company Asiatic Petroleum engaged a distinguished engineer, H. R. (later Sir Harry) Ricardo, to research the whole problem of fuels and engines. In 1923 Ricardo published a classic book, *The Internal Combustion Engine*, in which he explained, 'When the rate of temperature rise due to compression by the burning portion of the charge exceeds, by a certain margin, that at which it can get rid of its heat by conduction, convection or other means, the remaining portion ignites spontaneously throughout its whole bulk, thus setting up an explosion wave which strikes the walls of the cylinder with a hammer-like blow and, reacting in its turn, compresses afresh the portion first ignited. This further raises the temperature of that portion, and with it the temperature of any isolated or partially insulated objects in its vicinity, thus ultimately giving rise to pre-ignition.' The combination of excessive temperature and intense shock waves is very destructive.

Ricardo continued to investigate, and very gradually the understanding percolated down to the engine designers that detonation can set an absolute limit on engine performance. Together with two physicists whose names will be instantly known to anyone interested in British aviation technology prior to 1950, Henry T. Tizard and David R. Pye, Ricardo laid down basic guidelines. One of these was that the chemical composition, and especially the molecular structure, of the fuel had a profound effect on engine performance. Another was that if a fuel could be made more resistant to detonation, the engine compression ratio could be increased, and its power and efficiency could thus be greatly improved. But by 1921 the crucial investigation was going on in the USA, by sheer chance in the town made

Schematic molecular structures of some basic constituents of hydrocarbon fuels: (a) methane, CH_4, simplest of the paraffin series; (b) n-heptane, C_7H_{16}; (c) iso-octane, or 2,2,4 tri-methyl pentane, or C_8H_{18}; (d) benzene, C_6H_6.

famous by the Wright brothers, Dayton, Ohio.

A General Motors subsidiary, Dayton Engineering Labs (Delco), was having trouble with kerosene-fuelled generator sets. These used a battery ignition system designed for cars by a GM engineer, Charles F. Kettering, and these were thought to be the cause. Kettering defensively wondered if the problem might not lie in the fuel. He enlisted the help of Thomas Midgley, assisted by Thomas A. Boyd, and managed to get GM to fund a major research programme. Very quickly they confirmed that detonation in an engine was related to its compression ratio, and also to the molecular structure of the fuel. But what next? One vague theory was that knocking was promoted by the intense radiation from the flame front as it spread out like an expanding sphere centred on the spark plug. They wondered if the problem might be eased by making the gas more opaque, thereby greatly reducing the radiant heat. Midgley and Boyd began screening no fewer than 30,000 organometallic compounds, hundreds of which were added to separate specimens of fuel and tested in their special Delco-Lite engine with interchangeable heads for varying the compression ratio. On 9 December 1921 they tested a compound with the formula $Pb(C_2H_5)_4$. It proved to have an incredible ability to improve a fuel's anti-knock qualities. Almost overnight, TEL (tetraethyl lead) became an important additive to aviation fuel—and, much later, to ordinary automotive petrols. Without it the power of engines in the Second World War would have been reduced by up to 50 per cent.

The US Army Air Service began testing leaded fuel in 1922. Very soon the engines were fouled by deposits of lead oxide, and exhaust-valve seats were burning out. Discouraged, the Army gave up, but Midgley and Boyd eventually found a suitable scavenging agent. They added a trace of ethylene dibromide, causing the formation of lead bromide which, having much lower melting and boiling points than the lead oxide, carried the lead away in the exhaust. In late 1926 the US Navy picked up where the Army had left off, and began using leaded fuel to test its new Wasp engine. After the aircraft tanks had been filled, the TEL was added in the ratio 3 cc—less than a teaspoon—per US gallon. This was an inconvenient and risky procedure, which also meant that parts of the fuel in the tank had no lead and other parts had a high concentration. Later, leaded fuels were produced at the refinery.

As a general rule, if you cannot measure what you are doing, your work is not scientific. So far, though valuable discoveries had been made, the whole subject of fuels and detonation remained unquantifiable. Much of it was wrapped up in a mumbo-jumbo of toluene numbers, aniline numbers, HUCRs (highest useful compression ratios) and other measures, none of which was precise nor could be translated into any other measures. In 1924 Standard Oil (NJ) and General Motors had formed a joint subsidiary called Ethyl Gasoline Corporation. Its research director, Graham Edgar, concentrated on anti-knock fuels and discovered—contrary to what Ricardo had stated—that some of the paraffin series, the straight-chain molecules as mentioned earlier, had excellent anti-knock qualities. After much research Edgar confirmed that one paraffin hydrocarbon, n-heptane (n means normal, in other words, with just a row of single hydrogen atoms along each side) would detonate under almost any conditions. For engines, it was a disaster! In contrast, iso-octane, one of the branched-chain paraffins, had the highest anti-knock quality of any pure fuel he could find. Iso-octane has the simple formula C_8H_{18}, but is more correctly written 2,2,4 trimethyl pentane (see diagram); in other words it is pentane (a chain of five carbon atoms) with the hydrogen atoms at locations 2, 2 and 4 replaced by methyl (CH_3) groups. Both fuels are pure compounds, and thus absolutely precisely repeatable, and so Edgar could use them as the basis for a scale of 'knock rating' that would be as precise and enduring as the Celsius scale of temperature. He simply called n-heptane 0 and iso-octane 100. This 'octane' scale has been used ever since.

Gradually workers all over the world began to understand the importance of a fuel's anti-knock rating. At the US Army's Wright Field Samuel D. Heron—who will appear again in this book—demonstrated that while benzol ceased to be useful in the new breed of supercharged radials, TEL was vital. He educated the Army and, with Edgar, helped the Army issue a new specification for aviation fuel in 1930 which actually prescribed an octane rating: 87. (At the same time F. R. Banks was brewing special fuels to help the RAF win the Schneider Trophy, as noted in Chapter 6, but these had no relevance to normal flying.) In the early 1930s three famous pilots—J. H. 'Jimmy' Doolittle, Edwin E. Aldrin and Frank D. Klein—got the US Army and major airlines to aim at fuel of 100 octane rating, and also persuaded oil companies to produce it. The method initially adopted was hydrogenation, in which hydrogen is combined with the base stock in the presence of a catalyst such as finely divided nickel. Shell introduced hydrogenation at St Louis and Standard Oil at Baton Rouge, though at first the scale of operations was small.

Heron set up tests at the Wright Field powerplant laboratory in which an R-1340 Wasp was first run on unleaded gasoline of 55/60 octane, and then on new fuels of 92 and 98 octane. He then left to join Ethyl, Captain Frank Klein taking his place. Klein showed that the Wasp engine could give 550 hp on the 'cooking' fuel, 720 hp on 92 octane and no less than 900 hp on fuel containing 8 cc/gal of TEL, raising octane rating to about 98. He then carried out tests in the air, using the Wasp-powered Boeing YP-29. Accurate figures were already in for this one-off prototype on 92 octane. Klein demonstrated that, with 98 grade fuel, its level speed was increased (depending on height) by 7 to 11 per cent, rate of climb increased by 40 per cent and take-off run reduced by 30 per cent. By the end of 1935 the US Army had established precise specifications for fuels of 65 and 92 octane, and was writing that for 100 grade, of which 300,000 US gal had been delivered by Standard Oil (later renamed Esso, then Exxon) by December 1935. From 1 January 1938 100 octane was the standard fuel of US Army combat aircraft.

Amazingly, nothing was done to produce such fuel in Britain, even though in 1935 Dr S. F. Birch of Anglo-Iranian at their Sunbury laboratories had discovered an alkylation process which almost trebled the yield of 100 octane from any base feedstock. Instead, the British Air Ministry was content to import the vital fuel from the USA, and in fact Bristol and Rolls-Royce discovered important variations in the response of different sample fuels when tested under rich-mixture conditions. Cutting a complex story short, much research led to the publication of different PNs (performance numbers, the term for octane ratings in excess of 100) for weak and rich mixture. For example, from 1942 '100 octane' was universally described as 100/130 grade, 130 being the rich-mixture response. The importance of this fuel to the RAF in the Battle of Britain cannot be overstated (see Chapter 7).

Wartime pressures accelerated the demand

Capt Frank Klein used the Boeing YP-29 fighter prototype, powered by a Pratt & Whitney R-1340 Wasp, to carry out the first tests of 100-octane fuel in 1934.

for ever higher performance, and from the start the Boeing 345, later designated B-29, was planned to use even more knock-resistant fuel in its R-3350 engines. The result was specification AN-F-33 of July 1944 describing fuel with 4.6 cc/gal of TEL and almost double the amount of alkylate as compared with 100/130. This fuel was rated at PNs of 115/145. Previously US aviation gasolines had been coloured blue, but with the profusion of grades different dyes were added to make 80/87 octane red, 91/98 blue, 100/130 green, 108/135 (introduced in 1949) brown and 115/145 purple. The highest grades formed a significant fraction of the total production of aviation gasoline (petrol) at the end of the Second World War, when the total reached an amazing 30,300,000 US gallons per day. It then swiftly fell to below 6,000,000, before climbing again during the Berlin airlift and the Korean War.

In 1957 production peaked once more at 17,200,000 US gal/day, the high grades being needed for such engines as the R-2800 Double Wasp, R-4360 Wasp Major, R-3350 Cyclone and Turbo-Compound, Hercules and ASh-82. The 108/135, which was 115/145 with TEL content reduced from 4.6 to 3.0 cc/gal, was withdrawn in 1966, the few remaining highly rated big engines either switching to 115/145 or being derated. Those that are left today are all cleared to operate on 100LL, which together with ordinary car fuels—commonly called Mogas or autogas, and with a rating of about 92—are the only gasolines available today for aircraft. Consumption by aircraft piston engines fell away to 5 million gal/day in 1970 and has since halved, but the past year or two has shown a tendency to increase, despite the body-blow to light aviation dealt by US product-liability legislation. The basic fuel today is 100/130 with the TEL content reduced from 3.5/4.0 to only 2.0 cc/US gal, to eliminate plug fouling and exhaust-valve deterioration in older engines. Hence the designation 100LL, from low-lead. It is blue in colour.

There is just one more aspect of the basic engine cycle to be outlined in this chapter. All IC engines operate by arranging for a succession of chemical reactions to take place in their cylinders. If we go into really fine detail these reactions are complicated, because they involve a large number of elements and compounds which initially were present in the atmosphere, fuel, lubricating oil, perhaps the injection of an anti-detonant liquid and possibly even parts of the engine or such extraneous matter as ingested birds! But it is permissible to simplify the reaction to: fuel + air = exhaust. Making a further assumption that a fair average composition for all the different hydrocarbon fractions that make up a typical Avgas is C_8H_{18}, we can write the equation in proper notation:

$$2C_8H_{18} + 25O_2 = 16CO_2 + 18H_2O$$

Leaving out the numbers, fuel + oxygen = carbon dioxide + water. This has been the most basic chemical equation of almost every IC engine. We cannot see or smell the carbon dioxide, and it has the advantage of being chemically inert. During the Second World War it was common—and very sensible—practice in the Soviet Union to pipe a proportion of the cooled exhaust into the space above the fuel in the aircraft tanks, so that incendiary bullets or cannon shells could not cause an explosion. Carbon dioxide is dangerous to humans only in high concentration, when its presence excludes oxygen (we produce it in our breath). In contrast, if the engine runs with inadequate air the above equation is changed to: fuel + a little oxygen = carbon monoxide + hydrogen. Carbon monoxide, CO, is lethal to humans.

Any chemist will appreciate that, for any given fuel, there is only one chemically ideal fuel/air ratio. We call this the stoichiometric ratio, and in typical petrol engines it is around 1:15.2 (1 lb or kg of fuel to 15.2 lb or kg of

An approximate graph showing the total world production of aviation petrols (gasolines or Avgas) over the past 80 years. The trend today is fairly static.

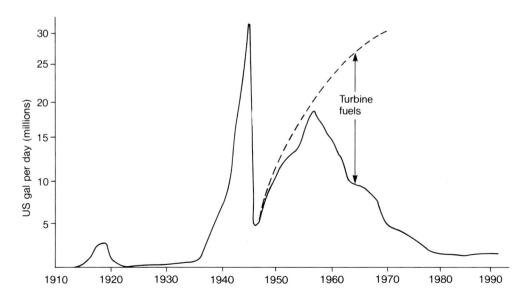

air); in volumetric terms the ratio is in the region of 1:9,000, as we saw earlier. But maximum power will be developed at a richer ratio, perhaps 1:13 by mass, while the best economy (flying for range, for example) may require a leaner (weaker) mixture such as 1:18.

Note that the exhaust of an engine running with sufficient oxygen always contains water. You can see the stuff dripping from your car exhaust on a frosty morning, along with clouds of steam. At high altitude the water very quickly changes from vapour to ice crystals. These are visible and, often, persistent. They betray the presence of high-flying aircraft by forming 'condensation trails'. In the Second World War the exhaust from huge armadas of B-17s and B-24s, already rather cooler than normal by being expanded through a turbosupercharger, often formed contrails covering hundreds of square miles. Sometimes contrails do not disperse, but persist as natural cloud.

To complete this chapter I should add a note on propellers. Unlike marine propellers, all successful aircraft propellers have been identical in form, with blades acting as miniature wings arranged radially at 90° around the axis of rotation. Designers use the word 'station' to describe positions from the hub to the tip (and they use the same word to describe positions from nose to tail of a fuselage or from the centreline to a wing-tip). At any given blade station the cross-section through the blade has an aerofoil profile similar to that of a wing. Often it is the simple flat-bottomed profile called Clark Y. It is obvious, however, that the profile varies from the tip in towards the root.

There are several reasons for this. One is that the air speed and angle of attack—the angle at which the air meets the blade—vary over a wide range, and also change greatly depending upon whether the aircraft is at rest with the engine idling, taking off at maximum rpm or cruising at high forward speed. Even with the aircraft parked, the propeller still draws through it a large airflow. One should never stand anywhere near the front of an operating propeller, but one can judge the strength of the airflow by standing in the slipstream to the rear. It is this acceleration of a large mass of air which generates the thrust, and, with the aircraft at rest, for a given fuel flow a propeller generates higher thrust than any form of turbojet or turbofan engine. It makes little difference whether the shaft

power to drive the propeller is furnished by a turboprop or piston engine.

I have no intention of going deeply into propeller design, because it is complicated. Each blade has an exceedingly tough existence, suffering a torque force from the engine, a centrifugal force which keeps it attached to the hub, a twisting force which tries to rotate the blade in the hub and a thrust force which pulls (or pushes) the aeroplane along. The thrust corresponds to the lift generated by a wing, and the torque component corresponds to a wing's drag. In addition to these forces the blade suffers powerful gyroscopic and vibration loads, the former being greatly magnified during manoeuvres.

The relative wind at each station is made up of two components, one along the axis of rotation—which is usually almost aligned with both the axis of the fuselage and the direction of travel—and the other at right angles to this in the plane of the propeller disc. The former is loosely taken to be the aircraft speed V, and the latter the tangential speed $2\pi rn$, where $2\pi r$ is the circumference at station (radius) r and n is the rotational speed. If we measure r in ft, then we should measure V in ft/sec and n in rps (revolutions per second). Obviously, as r varies from zero to a maximum at the tip, so does the tangential speed. Since V is the same all along the blade we are faced with the problem of making the blade twisted so that the pitch (loosely, the setting of the blade) is extremely coarse at the root and fine at the tip. With a simple propeller this means the angle of attack of the inner part of each blade with the aircraft at rest will be above the stalling angle, and these parts will give little if any thrust. As the aircraft accelerates during its take-off run, the increasing V will reduce the angle of attack until the whole propeller is unstalled and giving its full thrust.

However, the setting of the blades is ideal for one air speed only. Designers can plot propeller efficiency against air speed. One propeller may give high thrust on take-off, peak in efficiency at $V = 176$ ft/sec (120 mph) and then fall away sharply. Another can be designed to peak in efficiency at 352 ft/sec (240 mph), but its coarse pitch will give very poor thrust on take-off. The Fairey-Reed propeller designed for the Supermarine S.6B racing seaplane of 1931 was designed for peak thrust and efficiency at 587 ft/sec (644 km/h/ 400 mph). This resulted in pitch so coarse that on take-off almost the entire propeller was stalled, merely churning 'a hole' in the air;

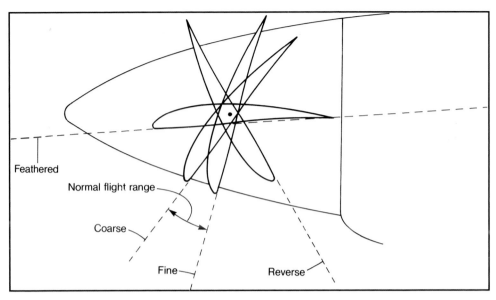

Today's propellers may have a pitch range of 120° or more, ranging from the feathered position (following engine failure) to reverse (for use after landing). In between come the normal flight settings.

gradually, as the seaplane picked up speed, so did the thrust build up, but the take-off was very long, and, for various reasons, exceedingly tricky.

The obvious answer was a variable-pitch propeller. Such a propeller can be set to fine pitch on take-off and coarse pitch in high-speed flight. Geoffrey de Havilland described such a design in *Flight* for 12 March 1910. Early examples, in 1918–21, were clumsy and unreliable, and usually offered a choice of two pitches only. By the late 1930s much-improved hubs had been developed, with hydraulic or electric actuation of the blades, and with a CSU (constant-speed unit) to adjust the setting automatically over a wide range, depending on V and n (rpm). Most VP (variable-pitch) or CS (constant-speed) propellers operate over a range of pitch angle (commonly measured at $r = 75$ per cent of tip radius) from 10° to 30° or 35°. A feathering propeller can be set to an ultra-coarse angle at which, in the absence of drive torque, the propeller remains stationary. With no input torque, the propeller acts as a windmill, and in a positive (normal) setting this would give high drag and also, by driving the failed engine, risk causing further damage. In the feathered setting the inner portions of the twisted blades try to drive the propeller one way, and the outer portions try to drive it in

the opposite direction, the two torques exactly cancelling out. In the reverse-pitch position the blades are turned right round so that the blade acts like a wing inverted, rather inefficiently generating 'lift' in the opposite direction. Thus, with the propeller pitch lever in *reverse*, when the pilot opens the throttle the propeller acts as a powerful brake. (Note: the direction of rotation never alters.)

Early propellers were assembled from laminates (thin sheets or plies) of wood, and as the grain had to run from tip to tip to resist the enormous centrifugal force the propellers had two blades. Towards the root the blade became extremely thick, for strength, and ceased to have an aerofoil profile. A four-blade propeller tended to be two two-bladers assembled at 90°. When I was a small boy I was interested to find the latest aircraft having three-blade propellers. These were of metal, with blades inserted into a strong steel hub, and the extra blade helped absorb the increasing power of engines. The process continued. The Spitfire I entered service with a two-blade wooden propeller, and in 1940 was greatly improved by receiving a propeller with three variable-pitch blades governed by a CSU. Of course, the pilot retained a lever giving him direct control of the CSU datum setting. Before landing, he had to be sure to select *fine*, so that, should he have to overshoot, the engine would give high power and the propeller maximum thrust. If he forgot, the engine n would be far below the desired 3,000 rpm, and the propeller efficiency very poor, and he would almost certainly 'fall out of the sky'. In 1942 the Spitfire IX received a four-blade propeller to absorb the increased power (especially at high altitude) of the Merlin 61 and its successors. In 1944 the Spitfire XIV had to have a five-blade propeller to translate the power of the Griffon 65 engine into thrust whilst still keeping within the strict limits on propeller diameter imposed by the Spitfire's modest ground clearance. In 1945 later Griffons even drove contraprops, a six-blade unit made up of two three-blade propellers rotating in opposite directions. This naturally demanded a more complex drive gearbox on the engine, but had the advantage of eliminating the previous piloting difficulties caused by the drive torque and spiral slipstream on take-off.

I have now mentioned gearboxes. Today at least half the piston engines in use have direct drive, the propeller running at the same speed as the crankshaft. Sometimes better results are achieved by using a larger propeller running at reduced speed, with a reduction gearbox enabling the engine to run at high n to generate the greatest possible power. The very first successful aeroplane, built by the Wrights in 1903, had a single engine with

The simplest aircraft still have solid propellers, either of aluminium alloy or laminated wood. Larger propellers have hollow blades, and these cross-sections show some of the contrasting methods of construction (HamStan).

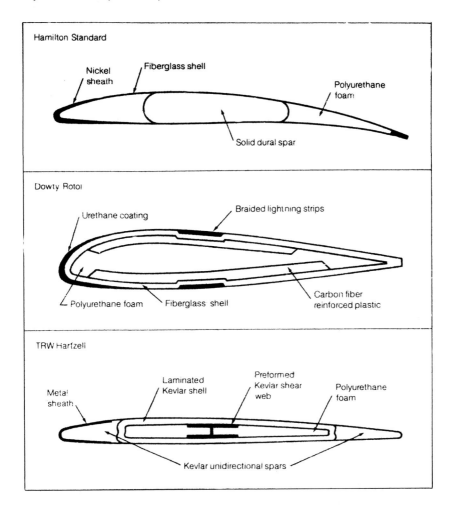

chain drives to two pusher propellers. These chains geared the propellers down in the ratio 23:8, and also made them turn in opposite directions, both excellent choices. Geared drives are discussed in Chapter 4.

Very few propellers have had a single blade, but at least three individuals have promoted single-blade types. These have the blade balanced by a weight on the opposite side of the hub. The best-known pattern was the Everel, flown on a Piper Cub in 1933. At the other end of the scale, today the latest high-power propellers have as many as six blades, to absorb the power at low rotational speed and thus minimize noise, but these are driven by turboprops. Propfans have even more blades.

Today many propellers are still made from laminates of wood. They are relatively cheap and aerodynamically efficient, but tend to be heavy and difficult to repair. From the early 1920s many blades were forged in solid aluminium or Duralumin, and these far outnumbered all other types in the Second World War, where their ease of repair (after belly landings, for example) was a major advantage. By 1945 new 'paddle-blade' propellers were in production, because at speeds over 350 mph it is usually preferable to maintain the maximum blade chord all the way to the tip. Some of these blades were made from two thin steel sheets formed to the correct aerofoil profile and welded together around the edges. Today many propellers are made of GRP (glass fibre reinforced plastics), sometimes with a metal strip along the leading edge to resist erosion. The inboard portion is often of good acrofoil profile to help cool the engine and provide maximum ram effect at the inlet.

3 Engine design I

In this chapter I can turn to the hardware of actual engines. It seems reasonable to try to follow through the trip made by the air as it is captured from the atmosphere, passes through the engine and finally is returned to the atmosphere. The subheadings for this chapter could be listed as inlet systems and carburettors, valve gear, cylinders and pistons, ignition, crankshafts and camshafts, and lubrication. This leaves cooling, superchargers and installations for the next chapter.

Inlet systems are a crucial part of what we today would call the 'breathing' of an engine. This is just as important to an engine as it is to people. If you can't breathe well, your power output takes a nosedive. But in the earliest aero engines this was seldom appreciated. If you look at the route traversed by any air unfortunate enough to get sucked into a Gnome rotary you might wonder that any managed to reach the cylinders (Chapter 5). On the other hand, with most early engines there was hardly any 'inlet system' at all. The air was just sucked into the carburettor, through a short pipe which often faced backwards!

Today it is taken for granted that the engine designer wishes to wring as much power out of his engine as possible, within the limits imposed by the available materials and the need for reliability. Other things being equal, power is directly proportional to the rate at which the air passes through the engine (not just the speed of flow but the mass per unit time). One could equally say that power is directly proportional to the rate at which the fuel is burned. For any given operating condition the fuel/air mixture ratio should ideally be one fixed value, so airflow and fuel flow will be directly related. We have seen that, in

terms of volume flow, the airflow is about 9,000 times greater than the fuel flow, a figure worth remembering. Accordingly, there is seldom any problem or limitation imposed by piping the fuel—though high precision is needed in controlling it—but there are nearly always problems in handling the far greater flow of air.

Anyone who studies aerodynamics, or hydrodynamics for that matter, will know that you will get poor results if you just suck air into the open end of a pipe. A little thought will show that most of the molecules of gas will have to swing in a curved path round the sharp lip of the tube. Their momentum will carry them round towards the middle of the tube. Only the centre of the tube will draw in air at high speed, the outer parts being stagnant. A much better intake is a tube whose inlet has the form of a wide bell-mouth. This allows the air to curve in round a large radius, filling the whole tube with high-speed air.

But we can do even better by making the inlet face forwards. Then we can take advantage of the aircraft's own speed. Our inlet can still 'suck', but, instead of having to accelerate each molecule from rest, they are already rushing at high speed towards the inlet. This is called the ram effect, and in the late 1920s designers (of aircraft rather than of engines) began to take full advantage of it. Numerically the dynamic pressure, the pressure generated in an open-ended tube facing forwards, in which each molecule of air is brought to rest, is equal to $\frac{1}{2}\varrho V^2$, where ϱ is air density and V is air speed. Note that the ram pressure is proportional to the square of the speed; in other words at 480 km/h (300 mph) it is 9 times as great as at 160 km/h (100 mph). To give an

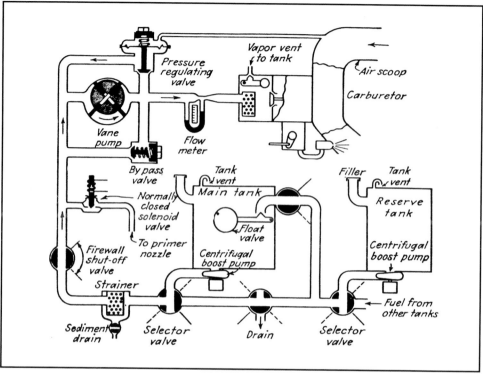

Schematic diagram of a simple fuel system. Prior to starting the engine, the solenoid valve admits fuel from an electrically driven primer pump. The vane pump is driven by the engine (McGraw-Hill)

idea of the magnitude of ram pressure, at 100 mph at sea level it will be about 0.18 lb/sq in (5 in of water), whereas at 300 mph it will be 1.63 lb/sq in (45 in). In a real inlet duct the values will be slightly less.

Bearing in mind always that to get more power you want to get more air into the engine, it is natural to place the air inlet in the full slipstream of the propeller. Thus, even at the start of take-off the air speed into the inlet may be 500 ft/sec (over 563 km/h/350 mph). The duct then enlarges, trading velocity for pressure, so that after curving round to the carburettor the V may be a mere 100 ft/sec. In the carburettor, described next, it may speed up to 250 ft/sec, before falling to below 200 ft/sec in the inlet manifold feeding the cylinders. I will cover such things as protecting the inlet against icing and sand or dust in the next chapter.

We now have a hurricane of fresh air coming in. How do we mix it with just the right amount of fuel? In nearly all the earliest engines the answer was a device called a car-

burettor. This is supplied with both ingredients, and its job is to mix them to give the correct (ie near-stoichiometric) fuel/air ratio, and with the fuel vaporized. First we have to design an aircraft fuel system. In a light aircraft this can be simple. You need a tank, with a gravity (overhead) filler, with a secure cap, and an air vent (which needs some thought in aerobatic machines). Then you need a supply pipe, with an on/off cock, a filter and, probably, a branch leading into the cockpit so that the pilot can prime the engine prior to starting by working a small hand pump for the specified number of strokes. This usually squirts a spray of neat fuel into the inlet manifold or even direct into the cylinders to facilitate starting from cold. From the filter the fuel pipe goes to the carburettor. In simple aircraft the fuel is fed by having an adequate head of fuel between the high-mounted tank and the engine. If the fuel tank cannot be significantly higher than the engine then a tank booster pump is needed. In addition, you need two more: a so-called 'wobble

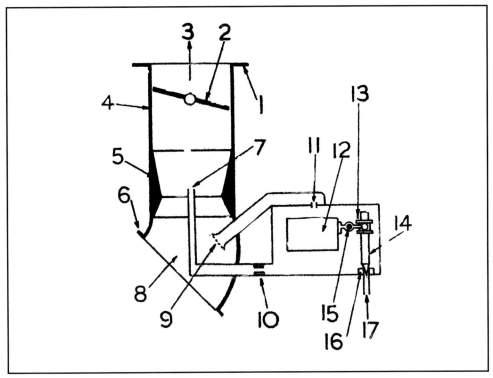

The parts of a simple float-chamber carburettor: (1) engine connecting flange; (2) throttle (shown closed); (3) mixture to engine; (4) choke tube or throttle bore; (5) choke; (6) air intake flange; (7) fuel jet; (8) incoming air; (9) pressure balance tube; (10) main jet; (11) float-chamber vent; (12) float; (13) needle collar; (14) needle valve; (15) float pivot; (16) needle seat; (17) fuel connection.

pump' worked by the pilot during the starting procedure, and a pump, usually of the rotary vane type, driven by the engine while it is running. These pumps are upstream of the carburettor, and it is necessary to insert a pressure-relief valve in a bypass line to avoid problems of over-delivery.

We have already seen that aircraft piston-engine fuels are extremely volatile. Even at sea level they continuously keep evaporating, and at high altitude the process becomes very rapid. It is made even faster by a pump sucking the fuel up from a low tank to a high engine. The last thing we want is for the fuel in the pipe to turn to vapour, because then it would all stay in the tank, the pump churning ineffectively. The only sure answer is to pressurize the fuel line so that it is kept under adequate positive pressure at all times. This is invariably done by fitting the booster pump in the bottom of the tank, where the fuel is drawn off. This pump is usually of the centri-fugal type, driven electrically. Of course, the fuel system of an aircraft designed for aerobatic flight, or high-altitude flight, is much more complex. The fighters of 1945 typically had as many as 300 separate items in their fuel systems.

So now we have properly controlled flows of fuel and air being supplied to the engine. They are combined in the carburettor, and this is an ideal example of a device which is simple in concept but often extremely complicated when you study a real example. The basic idea rests on the fact that, if you speed up a fluid flow by making a tube narrower at some point, its pressure falls. This is explained in another PSL book, *Faster than Sound*. So a simple carburettor has a streamlined constriction, called a choke tube, in the large pipe through which the air passes. If you then feed the fuel along a small-bore pipe terminating in an open end in the centre of the choke tube, the reduced air pressure will suck the fuel out.

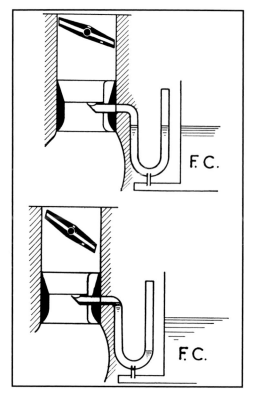

A simple carburettor with the engine inoperative (throttle closed). The fuel in the U-tube is at the same level as in the float chamber FC. In the second drawing the engine is running, with the throttle slightly open. Fuel is being sucked out of the jet by the reduced pressure in the choke tube (Hobson).

The beauty of the idea is that, very roughly, over a useful range of conditions, changes in the intake airflow will automatically result in a corresponding change in the depression in the choke, and thus in a corresponding change in the flow of fuel. Thus we keep the correct mixture strength, and vaporize the fuel.

First we have to arrange for a suitable control of the fuel as it arrives at the carburettor. The traditional arrangement is to pipe it into a float chamber close beside the choke tube. This chamber contains a float, either made of material of very low density or else hollow. As the fuel first comes in, pushing air out of the chamber through a small hole in the top, the float rises and in so doing drives a rocker arm which pushes down a needle valve in the fuel inlet. When the chamber is full, the needle valve is seated to shut off the supply of fuel. In normal running the needle valve is just slightly open, holding the fuel in the chamber at the full level and matching the rate at which it is drawn off into the choke tube.

Thus the fuel is held at a constant level, which is chosen to be just below the level of the open end of the jet delivery tube. As the incoming air passes at high speed through the choke tube, the partial vacuum draws a fine spray of fuel out of the pipe. The actual rate at which the fuel is delivered is metered by placing a precisely made constriction, called the jet, in the pipe as it leaves the float chamber. The carburettor can be of the updraught or downdraught type, depending on which way the air flows through the choke tube. Thus, the ram air inlet can be above the engine or underneath (or in some other location, such as the leading edge of the wing). In a downdraught carburettor the fuel jet pipe can be horizontal, projecting radially into the choke tube, with the end cut off at an angle to avoid any ram effect such as an upward-facing pipe would experience. In an updraught carburettor it can simply point upwards.

Somewhere in the air passage, usually downstream of the choke tube, is inserted the throttle. This is a flat valve, circular if the pipe is of circular section, able to rotate on bearings at each side. Edge on, it hardly constricts the flow; this is the 'full throttle' position, and from here it can rotate through up to 90° (usually about 85°) until it closes off the airflow entirely. This valve is under the direct control of the pilot. Such a basic carburettor would work, after a fashion, but inventors love to make things better.

One of the first things they did was to arrange for the fuel to be drawn out of the float chamber through a vertical tube or well, and to place inside this a second, slightly smaller tube with a row of holes perforating it from top to bottom. This inner tube, called the diffuser, was sealed into the carburettor at the top, and an air inlet was added to admit air to the space in the fuel well surrounding the diffuser. At the start this space would be full of fuel. As the engine began operating, the depression in the choke tube would draw not only fuel but also air into the diffuser tube, so that the jet delivery pipe in the choke tube would receive not neat liquid fuel but a fine fuel/air emulsion, which would evaporate completely in the choke tube. As the throttle opened, the increasing suction would lower the level of fuel in the diffuser tube, until eventually all the holes were uncovered, supplying the right airflow to match the maximum flow of fuel. Without the diffuser the mixture would tend to become too rich at full throttle, and the jet of liquid fuel coming out of the jet delivery tube would not all vaporize in the fraction of a second before reaching the cylinders.

This is just the beginning. Designers soon added special arrangements for feeding a fine spray of fuel with the engine idling, when flow velocity through the choke tube was insufficient to create a usable depression. Then extra air passages had to be added to take care of high-altitude conditions, when the velocity through the choke tube would be the same as at sea level, creating the same depression and trying to draw off the same flow of fuel, while the actual mass flow of air (in lb/min, for example) might have been cut by more than half. Then an accelerator pump was added, to provide a sudden extra flow of fuel to speed up the engine whenever the throttle was suddenly banged wide open. This pump was in the form of a cylinder, full of fuel, with a plunger connected directly to the throttle linkage. Opening the throttle forced the plunger a corresponding way down the cylinder to force the fuel straight into the choke tube.

By the late 1920s various forms of automatic servo device were being added to maintain the desired mixture ratio at all altitudes without the pilot needing to make adjustments. These all used stacks of aneroid capsules, thin corrugated metal bellows as used in barometers and also in simple airspeed indicators. It is straightforward to devise a servo system in which the linear motion generated by the expansion and contraction of the capsule stack (caused by changes in atmospheric pressure) is used to move a hydraulic spool valve which admits oil to one side or the other of a piston connected to the mixture control lever. A similar arrangement is used in automatic boost control, as noted later. Altogether, 50 years ago the float-chamber carburettor had reached a high degree of refinement; but it still suffered from shortcomings. One of the most serious was outlined in Chapter 2: such carburettors cannot work under negative g, and so are unsuitable for fighters and other aerobatic aircraft. Another problem is that it is extremely difficult to supply exactly the right amount of the correct mixture to each cylinder. Arising out of the two foregoing problems, the engine may be prone to backfiring, in which a flame travels

through the inlet manifold full of unburned mixture back from a cylinder to the carburettor. This can be very dangerous, and flame traps have to be inserted in the inlet manifolds. Inevitably, these cause drag and thus reduce power.

A further serious drawback is that the choke tube contains two things that depress the temperature of the airflow: a venturi and evaporating fuel. If you plunge your hand into petrol and then expose it to a gale your hand will almost freeze. The intense cold of the choke tube may cause the evaporated petrol to condense on the cold wall of the tube, thus playing havoc with mixture strength. Worse, any moisture in the incoming air can cause extremely rapid build-up of ice, sufficient to block off the airflow to the engine completely in less than a minute. Many carburettors are heated by lubricating oil or even exhaust gas. But today there are many kinds of injection carburettor which solve or avoid most of the problems.

Such carburettors eliminate the float chamber, and usually the choke tube, and instead measure the airflow and use the result to

Here we have a slightly more complicated carburettor, with the engine at full throttle. Air is being sucked in through the holes in the diffuser tube, so that what comes out of the jet delivery tube is a fine fuel/air emulsion (Odhams Press).

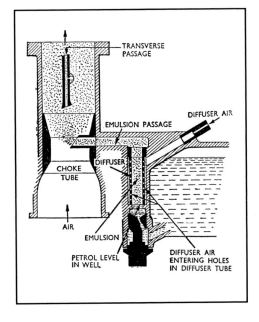

meter a bulk (liquid) supply of fuel which can then be sprayed in at a suitable location. One of the best-known of the early injection carburettors, important at the end of the Second World War, was the Bendix-Stromberg. This feeds ram pressure from small inlets in the induction-pipe airstream to one side of a diaphragm, and suction from a powerful venturi to the other side. The diaphragm thus moves, driving a poppet valve in the fuel regulator open or closed. Fuel is pumped through this valve at a rate broadly proportional to air mass flow. The fuel flow is further corrected by various needle valves, and by a stack of capsules in an altitude mixture control unit. The fuel reaches the spray nozzle at about 5 lb/sq in, sufficient for almost complete vaporization within a few inches. This still causes intense cooling of the resulting mixture, but there is unlikely to be a serious problem. The fuel is injected downstream of the throttle, and if any ice does form it is unlikely

to find anywhere to adhere to, especially as the mixture is approaching parts of the engine that are quite hot.

During the Second World War, engineers at the SU carburettor company and at Rolls-Royce and Bristol developed so-called speed/density carburettors. These became standard on the Merlin and other important engines. They did away with the obstruction imposed by the choke tube, and instead measured the difference in pressure between the inlet and exhaust manifolds and the charge temperature, the two measures giving its density. The fuel was then supplied to a spray nozzle at the eye of the supercharger. The fuel pump was of the multi-plunger swashplate type. Its speed was matched to that of the engine, and the angle of the swashplate was determined by the pressure difference (tending to increase flow) and the temperature (tending to reduce it). Later Rolls-Royce devised a simple arrangement in which a plain

Nearly all high-power engines from 1944 onwards used injection-type carburettors (or direct injection into the cylinders). The Bendix-Stromberg was the most common carburettor, which metered the fuel flow by balancing the difference in air pressures (A/B) against the difference in fuel pressures (C/D). The fuel was sprayed in downstream of the throttle to reduce icing problems (McGraw-Hill).

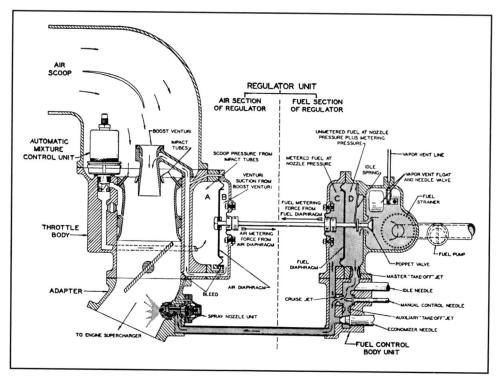

gear-type pump supplied fuel at constant pressure to two jets in parallel. The area of one jet was controlled by a needle positioned by a pressure-difference capsule and the other by a needle positioned by a thermometer, while a third control was driven by a centrifugal governor giving a speed input. Several modern carburettors follow similar principles.

Many modern engines inject the fuel directly into each cylinder. The original Wright engine could be said to have a primitive form of direct injection, and this was certainly a feature of the Antoinette of 1904. Subsequently the lighter and simpler carburettor ruled supreme, except in diesel engines, despite prolonged efforts in the USA by Marvel, Bosch and Eclipse. Ultimately, in 1940, the Eclipse (by then part of Bendix) achieved success, initially on the big Wright R-3350 Cyclone 18. But it might never have got there had not the Germans shown what could be done. Development of diesel engines, including many for aircraft, gave the Germans plenty of experience, notably in solving the problems of precision manufacture. To squirt a microscopic dose of fuel into each cylinder in turn, so that the engine not only runs properly but also achieves minimum fuel consumption, is a severe challenge. This is partly because the injection pressure has to be about 500 lb/sq in and partly because the amount of fuel injected in each dose is almost vanishingly small (for a 240 hp engine about 0.0002 lb or 0.0077 cu in, smaller than a grain of sugar). Manufacturing tolerances have to be in the order of five millionths of an inch, never previously called for in any branch of engineering.

In view of this it is surely remarkable that both Daimler-Benz and Junkers chose in 1933 to develop direct fuel injection for their next generation of high-power spark-ignition engines. These ran on the bench in 1935, and by 1937 were coming into production as the DB 601 and Jumo 211. Both had 12 cylinders, and so had a 12-cylinder injection pump between the inverted blocks of cylinders. The main contractor for the fuel system of both engines was Bosch. Each pump group was made like a fine watch, with complex anti-backlash linkages giving a precise stroke to the tiny plungers feeding the cylinders, the original input timing being by a camshaft. Inputs varying the stroke were provided by sensors measuring altitude and boost pressure, to give fuel delivery proportional to charge density. The measured doses were

Diesel experience enabled the Germans to adopt direct injection in their spark-ignition engines before the Second World War. This is the Bosch 12-cylinder injection pump underneath a Jumo 211, between the cylinder blocks. The plungers and drives had to be made with watch-like precision.

delivered to nozzles flush with the cylinder wall, with three radial spray holes. Injection began at 99°–104° before TDC, depending on the engine and throttle opening, and always finished at TDC. Of course, the injected fuel would not start to burn until ignited by the spark.

Today direct injection is almost as popular in piston aero engines of over 200 hp as all the different forms of carburettor combined. Increasingly, manufacturers are turning to electronics. You still have to have high-precision pumps, but they are becoming controlled by small circuit boards sensitive to an increasing number of relevant factors. Electronic control can take care of more variables than before, and do so more precisely, 'and more frequently. Fuel control signals are sent out at least twice per revolution of the crankshaft, giving near-instant response to variations in operating conditions without any pilot workload. This is discussed further in Chapter 8.

So far we have controlled the flow of air into the engine, which (as the throttle) also serves as the pilot's direct control over power output. But we now need a system of valves in order to admit air or mixture to each cylinder in turn at the correct times and subsequently to enable the exhaust gas to escape. Such valves have to be opened and closed very

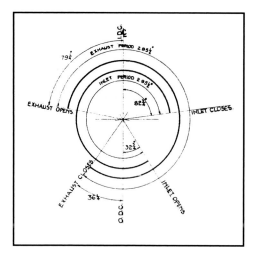

Valve timing diagram for a Gipsy Major II. As it is an inverted engine, TDC becomes ODC (outer dead centre) and BDC becomes IDC (inner). Real valve timing is nothing like what one might expect (see text).

accurately, in order to adhere precisely to the ideal timing diagram (the graphical plot of when each valve opens and closes, related to crankshaft position). They naturally have to be gas-tight when closed, even against very high pressure differences, yet must impose the smallest possible restriction on flow when open. Not least, they suffer the harshest environment of any part of the engine. In early engines they were responsible for more engine failures than any other component.

There are many types, but almost all today's engines (and over 90 per cent of those in the past) have used some form of poppet valve. Nearly all the rest have used a totally different species, the sleeve valve. Whichever type is used, there must be one route by which mixture enters the cylinder and another through which the exhaust escapes. At first glance it would appear obvious that the inlet should open at TDC and stay open through 180° to BDC, and that (after the compression and power strokes) the exhaust should open at BDC and close after 180° at TDC. As noted earlier, in practice it is not like this at all. It takes time to accelerate anything from rest, even a parcel of air or hot gas. The incoming mixture progresses along the inlet manifold in a succession of jerks, jumping forward each time some is admitted to the cylinder. When each charge arrives at the inlet valve it has to

come to rest. Then, as the valve opens, the mixture has to accelerate, and this takes time. Exactly the same is true in trying to get rid of the exhaust. Moreover, once started, the flow keeps going until the valve closes and seals the path off. Thus, real timing diagrams are nothing like the apparent ideal. I picked the Gipsy Major for two reasons: it is typical, and also, being an inverted engine, the diagram is 'upside down'. To avoid misunderstanding it is usual with such engines to replace TDC by ODC (outer) and BDC by IDC (inner). Thus, when we look at such a timing diagram, we must remember the cylinder head is at the bottom and the crankshaft at the top. Far from being 180° each, both the inlet and exhaust periods are 295.5°! For one period of 69° and another of 162° both valves are open (but not wide open) together!

Poppet valves are in principle a disc on the end of a rod, like a mushroom. When closed they are seated on the circular rim of a valve port in or near the top of the cylinder combustion space. From this circular port a pipe is connected, either to bring fresh air or mixture to the inlet valve or to convey exhaust gas away from the exhaust valve. Everything possible must be done to streamline the flow, remove constrictions and improve the engine's breathing qualities. For this reason it is quite common to have more than just the two valves, and high-performance engines often have two inlet and two exhaust valves per cylinder. There are countless variations, and early engines often had side-valve cylinders (so-called F-head or L-head), in which the valve stems are upright and parallel beside the cylinder, operating in ports which are off to one side. Today almost all piston aero engines have some form of overhead valve in which the valves are beyond the cylinder head and point towards the crown of the piston.

Valves are driven in unison with the crankshaft by some form of valve gear. A few engines have poppet valves which are positively controlled at all times, being driven in both directions to close or open. Far more often, the valves are driven in the open direction only, against the force of strong springs which tend always to keep them closed. Coil springs are today almost universal, and often two or even three are used for each valve, one inside the other, in case one should break. The operating conditions of every valve may be imagined. At 3,000 rpm each valve slams on to its extremely hard seat 25 times per second. In between each of these violent closures it is subjected to the full combustion pressure in the cylinder, which for a valve of 51 mm (2 in) diameter means a force of some 1,588 kg (3,500 lb). All this in an intermittent environment of white-hot gas, so that even the inlet valve will settle down at metal temperatures ranging from 320°C at the edge to about 440°C nearer the centre. For the exhaust valve conditions are far worse. Not even the best austenitic steel could stand up to the duty for long, were it not for the fact that the valve is specially designed to conduct the intense heating away from the head.

The only possible way to do this is to make the valve stem hollow and partially fill it with some material which can absorb a lot of heat per unit volume (not quite the same thing as specific heat, which is per unit mass) and which is a liquid at the valve's operating temperature. The material naturally must remain stable without the slightest chemical reaction with the metal even over many years. Workers at Farnborough tried mercury as early as 1912, but this metal does not wet the steel and so heat energy finds it difficult to transfer from the steel to the mercury. The answer, in which both Heron and Edgar played a part, was to put a little sodium into the valve. Though highly reactive, in the

atmosphere, this metal is stable inside the valve and, sloshing about from one end to the other under the impulses of the valve's own rapid movements, conducts heat at a very high rate from the head to radiate from the stem. Even so, the valve head operates at a bright-red temperature, hottest around the edge. The cylinder barrel or block, surrounding the steel liner, is usually aluminium or aluminium alloy, and so is the cylinder head. Into each exhaust port opening is fitted a carefully ground ring of Stellite, one of the hardest and most wear-resistant alloys known. This valve seat is shrunk by immersion in liquid nitrogen, so that after fitting it expands tightly into the bulk metal of the head. Even in hundreds of hours of operation there must be no warping or other distortion of the valve or seat. The slightest gap will immediately grow, as white-hot gas escapes through it on each firing stroke, causing rapid failure of the valve at that point.

To operate the common type of poppet valve an intermittent push is needed on the end of the valve stem at carefully chosen times in each four-stroke cycle. Each of the repeated pushes opens the valve, the stem sliding in a precision-made guide tube, usually of soft, low-friction phosphor-bronze, which fits tightly (a so-called push-fit) into the

Early engines usually had side valves (left), but for many years the overhead valve (right) has been almost universal. Overhead valves can be operated via long pushrods and rockers, as shown, or by an overhead camshaft (Odhams Press).

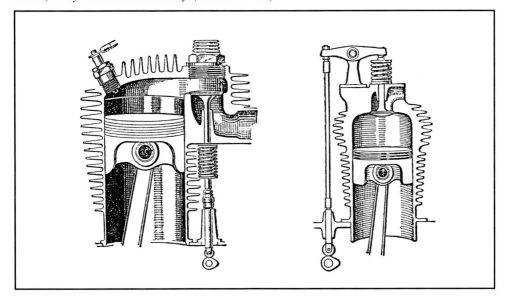

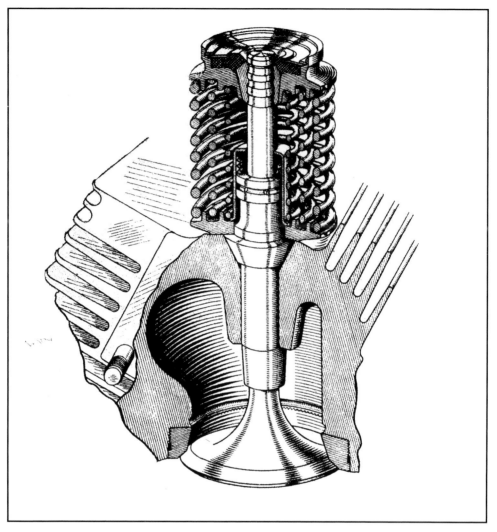

Poppet valves are invariably slammed shut by at least two coil springs, the head being carefully ground to fit exactly against a very hard Stellite seating ring inserted into the light-alloy head. This is a valve in a Bristol Pegasus (1935–45).

cylinder head. The pushes are generated by cams of suitable profile, mounted on a shaft or ring geared to the crankshaft. An in-line or opposed engine normally has camshafts (one Second World War engine, made by Chrysler, had camshafts with 32 cams in one row), whereas a radial has either a lot of short camshafts or, more often, a large-diameter cam ring fitting around the periphery of the crankcase. The exact profile of the cams is of crucial importance. As the cam rotates, the profile bears against a tappet on the end of the pushrod which opens the valve. Some tappets are just flat ends, some smooth curved ends, and some free-running rollers. Whatever happens, the tappet must always remain in contact with the face of the cam, with minimum friction or wear despite the high operating speeds. To show the criticality of cam profiles, reliability of the Bristol Jupiter was greatly improved by a seemingly trivial change to the way the cam ring was made, the design profile remaining unchanged.

As noted, almost all modern engines have overhead valves. The common way of driving these is for the push rods to drive one end of a rocker arm pivoted to the top of the cylinder head. The other end of the rocker pushes on the end of the valve stem. Invariably provisions are made for rigging the valve gear, to adjust the clearances and avoid either excessive tightness or any significant gap appearing despite the different expansion and contraction of the hot cylinder and cool valve gear. Today the entire valve gear is usually enclosed to retain oil or grease lubrication and keep out dirt.

From the earliest days of IC engines inventors tried to perfect a system of valves based on concentric sleeves interposed between the piston and the cylinder, with ports cut in the walls. At last, after 10 years of costly effort, the monosleeve (originally patented by Burt and McCollum) was perfected by A. H. R. (later Sir Roy) Fedden at Bristol, and used for a succession of high-power air-cooled radials. His objectives were to obtain smoother valve gear with larger ports and thus better breathing, to eliminate highly visible loss of oil, and in particular to devise valve gear for radial engines with two rows of cylinders. Fedden was reluctant to depart from using four valves per cylinder, yet he could find no elegant way of designing valve gear for a two-row radial, and he had to use two or more rows in order to go well beyond 1,000 hp, which in the early 1930s he could see was going to be necessary.

What happened is outlined in Chapter 7. Eventually superb sleeve-valve engines were developed, and the same technology was adopted by other companies, but all the effort was perhaps unnecessary. The most important high-power engines after the Second World War had two poppet valves per cylinder, and the same is true of almost every four-stroke aero engine today.

Beyond doubt, the design of the cylinder is the key to creating a good piston aero engine. All the rest is simple by comparison. Today most engines are of fairly low power, typically of less than 300 hp, and by far the most common arrangement is to use two, four or six cylinders mounted horizontally opposite each other. This gives a good compromise between such conflicting factors as cost, weight, balance of the moving parts, even drive torque and many other variables. So at this point, as we turn to cylinder design, we can also look at the basic layout of the engine. We can also note that the engines built in the all-time record numbers have had several quite different arrangements, so it is fair to conclude that the good and bad features of each configuration all come out roughly equal.

Many of the earliest engines followed car practice and had four or six water-cooled cylinders arranged upright in a straight line. Such engines powered almost every aircraft of the Central Powers in the First World War. In contrast, the Allies used water-cooled V-8s and V-12s, air-cooled V-6s and V-8s, water-cooled radials and also large numbers of the completely novel rotary species in which the crankshaft was fixed to the aircraft and the propeller was fixed to the spinning engine. These types are discussed in Chapter 5.

In the inter-war years designers learned how to enclose in-line and V engines in a streamlined cowling, with a nice pointed propeller spinner in front. This looked far preferable to the flat-fronted radial engines, even when the latter had been improved by fitting first Townend-ring cowls and later long-chord

Also taken from the Pegasus, a typical radial-engine cam drive. The crankshaft drives via serrations on the sleeve whose outer teeth drive the layshaft gear. Just visible behind this is the small pinion which, via the internal ring of teeth, drives the cam drum at one-eighth crankshaft speed. Note: the crankshaft sleeve rotates freely inside the cam sleeve (McGraw-Hill).

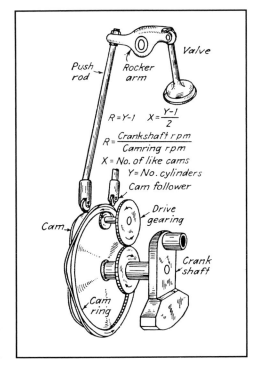

Valve

Push rod

Rocker arm

$$R = Y-1 \qquad X = \frac{Y-1}{2}$$

$$R = \frac{Crankshaft\ rpm}{Camring\ rpm}$$

X = No. of like cams
Y = No. cylinders
Cam follower

Drive gearing

Cam

Crank shaft

Cam ring

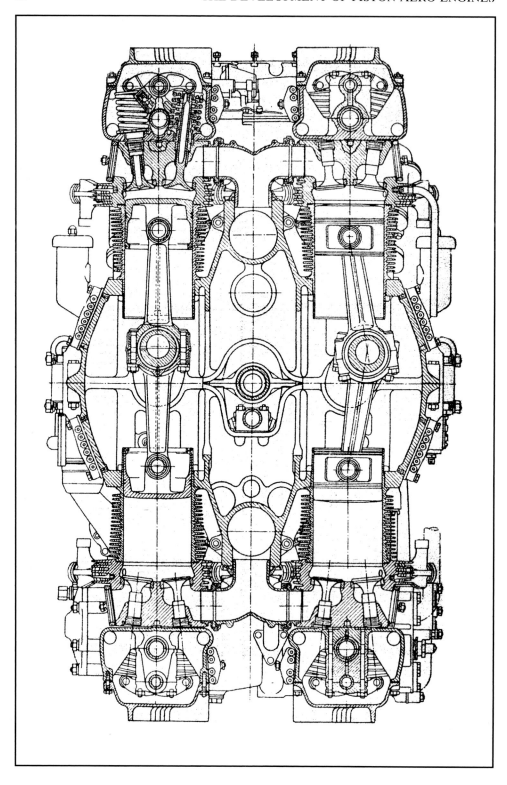

cowls with adjustable cooling-air exits (Chapter 6). The dominance of liquid-cooled V engines in the Schneider Trophy races accentuated the belief that air-cooled radials were useless for fast aircraft, such as fighters. When in 1941 the Italians replaced the radial engines of their fighters by German inverted-V liquid-cooled engines it was regarded in Britain as the obvious thing to do. One editor wrote, 'The wonder is that they ever imagined they could produce good fighters powered by bulky drag-producing motors.'

In aviation it is easy to jump to conclusions which are later seen to have been mistaken. In fact a properly installed air-cooled radial could be fully competitive with any other kind of piston engine. In Chapter 7 it is explained that the re-engined Italian fighters were faster than their predecessors because 840 hp radials had been replaced by liquid-cooled engines of 1,475 hp. The British Fury, Soviet La-5 and Japanese Ki-100 were examples of fighters originally designed with liquid-cooled engines which were greatly improved by being re-engined with an air-cooled radial. Like poppet versus sleeve valves, the answer to the question, 'Which is better, the liquid-cooled V or the air-cooled radial?' is certainly, 'Yes, definitely one or the other.'

In the mid-1930s Frank Halford, a famous freelance designer, was busy creating engines for Napier. He produced the Rapier and Dagger, which each had four parallel banks of upright air-cooled cylinders, and then went on to the Sabre, which had four horizontal banks of liquid-cooled cylinders with sleeve valves. What distinguished all these engines was their large number of small cylinders. For example, the 955 hp Dagger had 24 cylinders with 48 valves, whereas the Wright Cyclone developed up to 1,525 hp with only nine cylinders and 18 valves! Other things being equal, the fewer parts there are in an engine the better. Twice as many parts is likely to mean twice the price, twice the maintenance man-hours

Opposite Cross-section through a Napier Dagger, showing the four banks of air-cooled cylinders, each with two plugs and two valves yet adding up to only 16.84 litres (1,207 cu in). Halford thought the complication worthwhile in order to make the parts small and thus run at 4,200 rpm, but the RAF found servicing Daggers such a non-stop business that the Dagger-engined Hereford bomber was quickly withdrawn.

and twice as many things to go wrong. Like most things in engineering, the design of a piston engine is a compromise between conflicting factors, and the best answer is usually a moderate solution in between the possible extremes.

The advantages of having the smallest number of cylinders are self-evident, so what are the drawbacks? One is that, with only one firing stroke out of every four, the impulses driving the crankshaft would be infrequent, giving rise to severe vibration resembling that of a cement mixer or dump truck. In a high-power engine the cylinders would have to be very large, worsening the vibration and cyclic stresses throughout the engine and necessitating extremely massive construction. There is a clear upper limit to cylinder size. When the mixture is ignited, the flame front travels through it at high speed, in the range of 200-400 ft/sec, but this begins to appear slow when it is remembered that at 3,000 rpm the whole chemical energy of the fuel must be released in not much more than one-thousandth of a second (assuming combustion occupies 20°-25° of crankshaft travel). Even with two spark plugs located on opposite sides of the combustion space the mixture cannot be sufficiently burned in the available time if cylinder diameter is significantly more than 152 mm (6 in).

Accepting this, we may try to keep the engine simple by making the stroke very long. In fact, in early engines the stroke was often as long as 178 mm (7 in), even when the bore was not much more than 102 mm (4 in). Naturally for any given engine rotational speed, the linear piston speed near mid-stroke must be proportional to the stroke. Quite apart from considerations of wear, the inertia forces acting on the crankpin and gudgeon pin are increased by a long stroke, and there are many other structural and gas-flow problems. Shortening the stroke and then increasing the engine rpm may make some problems worse; for example, reciprocating inertial forces are proportional to stroke but also proportional to the *square* of the rotational speed. Despite this, as in automotive (road vehicle) engines, the trend has for 70 years been in favour of shorter strokes and higher rotational speed.

This book cannot pretent to be a textbook of design. There are plenty of those, and even these major works (most of which are out of date) cannot fully describe the interplay of the enormous number of conflicting factors which influence the designer. The historical record shows that you can get the same performance and reliability from engines as completely different as, for example, the Merlin, Twin Wasp and Hercules. On the other hand, seemingly trivial changes in detail design can multiply the life of a part by 10,000 times or more. At least, this used to be the case, when designers lacked the sheer arithmetical power to calculate all the stresses in every part in every operating condition, and then repeat the calculations for dozens or even hundreds of designs or alloys changed only very slightly. Today computers make the task almost simple. The designer can draw a connecting rod on a graphic display and watch the variation in stresses as he makes very small alterations to the pin diameters, the rod cross-sections and, most important of all, the way the rod blends into the little and big ends (the little end being that pinned to the piston by the gudgeon pin and the big end being that attached to the pin on the crankshaft).

Even using a modern high-power computer and graphic display it is less simple to play off one engine configuration against another. We make things easier by following fashion. Almost every modern engine designer knows what sort of thing he has in mind before he begins. Not many engines start with the proverbial clean sheet of paper. Most are to be the product of a company which already has a reputation for a particular species of engine, which today is usually of the flat or horizontally-opposed type. We are fortunate that there are also many smaller companies whose engines are of in-line, inverted, V, W (fan), X or radial types, while there is also a sprinkling of two-strokes, diesels, and two-stroke diesels. The fact that all have what appear to be competitive specifications suggests that there is little to choose between one basic configuration and another. Many ideas that seemed to be good at the time never came to anything. For example, once aircraft designers had learned how to create really streamlined aeroplanes, around 1930, several engine designers pushed the idea of the engine with horizontally opposed cylinders which could be buried inside the wing, with almost no drag. This idea never caught on, and the only aircraft with buried engines to be built in quantity (the B-36) had very large conventional radial engines. Among the prototypes with buried engines were the Brabazon, big enough to bury any kind of engine, and the Beech 34 Twin Quad, which was one of the very few to make use of shallow engines inside a thin wing.

My own view is that the Beech 34, for example, gained little from its buried engines, and this subject is discussed further in the next chapter. As for basic engine layout, there is certainly little to choose between air and liquid cooling, or between poppet and sleeve valves. The optimum number of cylinders naturally varies to some degree with the power. Nobody would build a 1,000 hp twin, but two cylinders is no problem at under 50 hp, especially as the rpm may be high. Dozens of designers have seen advantages in lots of cylinders, and in the Second World War there were several high-power engines with more than 24 cylinders, including the Lycoming XR-7755 (36) and Wright R-2160 (42)! These engines were the result of a desperate search for extremely high power, and we are fortunate that the gas turbine matured just in time to save us from having to change 84 or even 168 plugs per engine. At the other end of the scale the Wright R-1820 Cyclone was developed to give 1,525 hp with nine cylinders, and today's Merlyn diesel puts out a brochure figure of 650 hp from only three. My personal view is that, with the piston engine now unlikely to find a market much above 500 hp, 200 hp per cylinder is too much.

One of the surprises is that whereas the radial type of engine was absolutely dominant in the twilight years of the large high-power engine, today such engines are very rare (Chapter 8). This is strange, because the radial appears to make better use of the available material than any other configuration, and to be simpler and lighter than alternative arrangements. For example, the single-row radial has all its cylinders driving on one crankpin, and in fact the engine appears to consist of little but cylinders. In contrast, the in-line, V or opposed engine has a long and heavy crankshaft housed inside a large crankcase. And for an air-cooled engine the radial would seem obviously preferable to any engine whose cylinders were arranged one behind the other.

I have emphasized how crucial to engine performance is the design of the cylinder. In the earliest aero engines the anti-knock value of the fuel was extremely low—nobody had heard of such a measure, but it was actually in

Opposite *Some basic engine configurations. The in-line engines are seen from the side and the rest from the front. There are other arrangements, such as the inverted in-line and the X.*

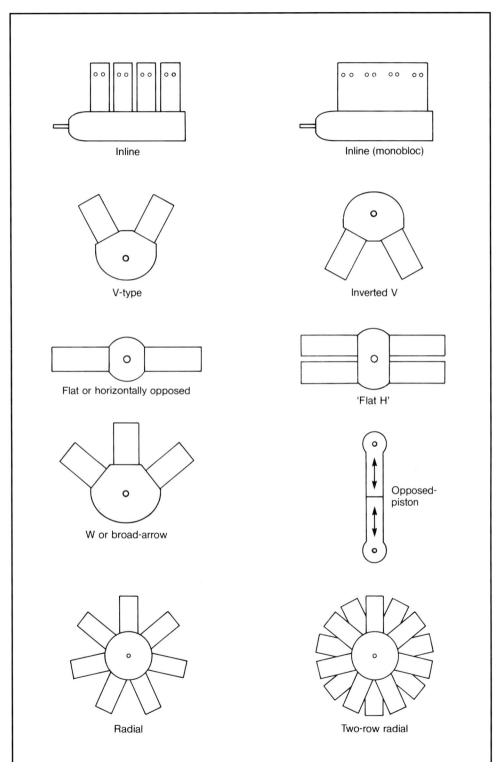

Inline

Inline (monobloc)

V-type

Inverted V

Flat or horizontally opposed

'Flat H'

W or broad-arrow

Opposed-piston

Radial

Two-row radial

Development of air-cooled cylinders is to some degree reflected in the total area of the metal fins through which heat could be transferred to the airflow. The Jaguar cylinder (left) of 1922 was very good for its day (the connection between the two plug bosses is for the gas-starter pipe). Yet the cylinder of the 1950 Wright Cyclone (above) has more than nine times the fin area (McGraw-Hill).

the range 32 to 50 – but the temperatures reached in the cylinder were not far short of what they might be today. Indeed the heat rejected in the exhaust, and the exhaust temperature, could be even higher than in modern engines. To dissipate the surplus heat direct to the atmosphere was almost impossible. A few designers realized that you have to make it as easy as possible for the heat to flow from the hottest to the cooler places, and to provide the maximum area where hot metal is in contact with cooling air or water. They knew that it is essential never to make the hottest part, such as the cylinder head, into an island connected only by thin gauges of metal, but all this had to be reconciled with the need to make the engine light, carry the operating stresses and be capable of repeatable and economic manufacture with the available tools and techniques.

An engine designer of around 1900 would have been envious of the deep and close finning on air-cooled cylinders of high-power engines of 50 years later. In round figures, a 1950 cylinder could have 150 times as much area through which the heat could be transferred to the cooling air! By contrast, early air-cooled cylinders looked rather crude, and it is no wonder that most of them tended to overheat. Water-cooled car engines of the 1905-10 era invariably had cylinder blocks of cast iron so heavy as to rule them out for any aeronautical use, but with the Antoinette engine (Chapter 5) success was achieved with much lighter individual cylinders, each made as a thin-walled iron tube, closed at one end and carefully machined internally. Around this was then electrolytically deposited an even thinner outer shell of copper to form a jacket filled with cooling water. This was

The Antoinette V-8, in production in 1907, had separate iron cylinders on to which a thin jacket of copper was deposited through which water was circulated by the pump at the front. Note the separate head held by six studs, with a plug in the centre and, at the top, the pocket to which petrol was piped to form a small pool from which a spray was drawn off on each induction stroke. The vertical black pipes are exhausts.

almost the only reliable and effective alternative to the purely air-cooled cylinders of the rotary engines until in 1915 Hispano-Suiza showed what could be done with cylinder blocks cast in aluminium, with steel liners to the cylinders.

Subsequently almost all cylinders have been made of aluminium or aluminium alloy, with steel liners to stand up to the high temperature and the wear of the sliding piston rings. As noted earlier, bronze or phosphorbronze tubes are inserted to carry the valves, and hard Stellite rings are used as valve seats. The edges of the valve head and seat are carefully ground to the same, or almost the same,

angle (for example, Bristol poppet-valve heads were ground to 91° included angle and the seats to 90°).

Like cylinders, pistons were originally of cast iron. Before the First World War at least three designers of car engines, including W. O. Bentley, began fitting aluminium pistons. Bentley soon had satisfactory aero engine pistons of the same material. This was remarkable, because previously nobody had believed that the light metal could withstand the high temperatures. Bentley reasoned correctly that, with good design, the extremely good heat conductivity of aluminium would keep down the peak temperatures to manage-

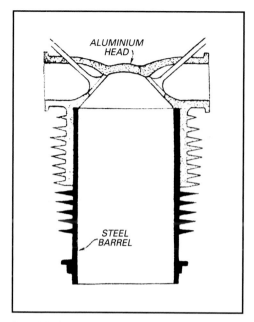

ALUMINIUM
HEAD

STEEL
BARREL

Simplified diagram showing typical air-cooled cylinder construction. One valve would be inlet, the other exhaust.

able limits. Since 1920 aluminium and its alloys have dominated cylinder and piston design, most modern pistons being of materials similar to Y-alloy, an aluminium alloy containing 4 per cent copper and smaller amounts of iron, silicon, nickel, magnesium and titanium. A very similar alloy was chosen to build Concorde. The piston crown typically operates at 260°C–320°C (500°–610°F).

Another advantage of aluminium alloy for pistons is light weight. This is important in reducing inertia stresses in what are the fastest-moving parts in the whole engine (except for the rim of a supercharger impeller). But the low-density metal is relatively soft, and it would wear particularly rapidly along a sharp edge. The earliest IC engines merely machined the piston to be the best possible running fit in the cylinder, hoping that both components would expand equally as they became hot. By 1895 it had become common practice to machine a groove near the top of the (then cast iron) piston and fit into it a ring of hard springy steel, which would always slide in contact with the cylinder wall. Some designers, such as Manly (Chapter 5), had already adopted multi-ring arrangements similar to those used today. The top

ring is always a compression ring of wedge section. This ring provides the chief gas-tight seal between the piston and cylinder. Its operating environment is severe, and the slightly tapered section is designed not to stick in its groove around the piston. Below it are at least two further rings, which like the first have their free ends ground at a diagonal angle so that, when in place, they butt together to make an almost gas-tight joint. Near the bottom of the piston, round what is called the piston skirt, is an oil control ring. This is ground to a rectangular section with sharp 90° corners. Its purpose is to prevent excessive amounts of lubricating oil being pumped by the piston into the combustion space, where it would burn.

The combustion space is the heart of any IC engine. We have already seen that in aero engines it is usually rather like a flat cone. The base, the top of the piston, is usually flat. Sometimes the top of the piston is hollowed out, and forms most or even all of the combustion space when the piston is at TDC, there being no room above it. More often the mixture is compressed in a space above the piston, bounded by the inside of the cylinder head (which can be conical or curved) and sometimes a very short length of cylinder liner. In a few engines the piston comes right up to the underside of the head, so that recesses must be provided in the otherwise flat crown to accommodate open valve(s) on the exhaust stroke (see drawing of Emdair, page 186).

In the earliest aero engines the designer was usually reluctant to use a separate head. The combination of very high pressure and high temperature made the achievement of a reliable joint a real challenge, and there had been so many cases of cylinders exploding and heads flying off, even with massive car and motor cycle engines, that most designers elected to make the cylinder open at the bottom only. The designer then had either to add water-cooling jackets or, if he was bold enough to adopt air cooling, a so-called poultice head. This comprised a cap of cast aluminium incorporating cooling fins, fitted as closely as possible over the end of the cylinder. The poultice contained the guides for the valves, but their seats were machined in the steel end of the cylinder. Obviously, the poultice head was bad design. The flow of heat had to get through the steel wall of the cylinder, get across the air gap (and no matter how accurate the manufacture there were always bound to be air gaps, in both the cold

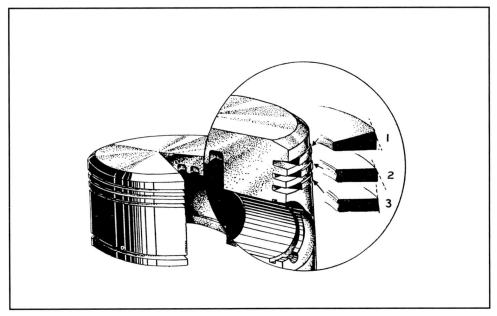

Typical piston with rings shown magnified. 1 is the compression ring, the wedge section having less tendency to stick in its groove. 2 is an intermediate ring. 3 is the scraper ring, the scraped oil escaping through holes into the inside of the piston (Allison).

and hot condition) and then flow through the bulk aluminium to get to the fins.

Many different forms of cylinder construction could be seen, even prior to 1914, including crude attempts to make air-cooled cylinders of aluminium. The one that was to become almost universal was first seen on the Siddeley Puma (Chapter 5). Unlike the BHP, from which it was derived, this in-line water-cooled engine had an aluminium cylinder block containing steel liners. Each liner had a short length of thread at the top, which was screwed into the aluminium head. The liners were completely open at the top, and the head accordingly contained not only the valve guides, at a large angle to each other matching the V-shape of the head, but also the seats. Today almost all engines have aluminium-alloy cylinder barrels with steel liners screwed into an aluminium-alloy head.

Crankcases often are, or are made up of, the largest single parts of the engine. Despite this they have to be extremely strong and rigid, for they are the structural basis of the whole engine. They carry the bearings for the crankshaft and propeller shaft, and reduction gear if fitted. They are the foundation to which the cylinders are attached. Almost always the crankcase also provides the attach-ments for the accessories and almost every-thing else, as well as the trunnions or feet on which the engine is itself mounted in the airframe.

Crankcases could well be made from CFRP (carbon fibre reinforced plastics) or various other classes of composite material. There would certainly be a saving in weight, but not in price. When composites have replaced metal in such structures as aircraft fins (stabilizers) there has been a saving in price as well as in weight, because the number of parts has been reduced by perhaps 95 per cent, with a corresponding reduction in assembly and labour costs. This gain cannot be realized if the metal part is already a single casting. Various small parts subject to neither high temperature nor high stress can often be made in GFRP (glass fibre reinforced plastics), with a reduction in weight and cost. Such parts include inlet manifolds and even rocker-box covers. On the whole the piston engine is not a good subject for composite materials, unlike airframes.

Having got the mixture inside the cylinder and being compressed by the rising piston, we then have to ignite it. In a diesel engine, and (with distressing results) in some of the over-boosted engines specially 'tweaked' to race at

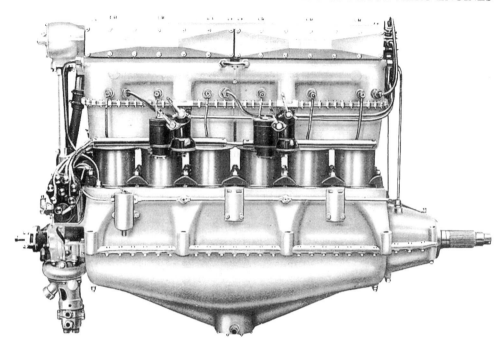

The 240-hp Siddeley Puma was one of the first engines to have steel liners screwed into an aluminium upper block, with water cooling passages.

Reno, the heat of compression does it all by itself. In ordinary engines we have to use some other means to bring the compressed mixture at some point to a temperature in excess of 425°C (800°F), and to do so at precisely the right instant in each operating cycle. Since the Wright brothers this means has been electrical. The Wrights used the make-and-break method, which in 1903 was very important for cars and motor cycle. To make an electric arc (spark) jump the gap between two electrodes you need a high potential difference between the electrodes, in the order of 10 kV (10,000 volts) or more. But if you start with two electrodes in contact and then separate them, you can get an arc with quite low voltages. As the electrodes come apart, the low-voltage current jumps the microscopic gap as it opens up. This ionizes the air along the path taken by the arc, making it simple for the arc to continue to jump across as the gap becomes larger. The external circuit could hardly be simpler, comprising a battery or DC generator (12 V would be ample), plus a simple induction coil to boost the voltage. (This coil was often used only for starting, and was left on the ground.) The problem was that the make/break points inside the combustion chamber had to be driven mechanically, which meant that a push/pull or rotary (cam) drive had to pass through a gas-tight hole in the

chamber wall. This more than anything else confined simple low-tension ignition to engines in which combustion pressures and rpm were unambitious.

Apart from the diesels, virtually every piston aero engine today uses high-tension ignition. Such a system must generate a voltage sufficiently high to jump the gap of 0.25–1.0 mm (0.01–0.04 in) between the electrodes of a spark plug. Most readers will be familiar with plugs, but may not know of the prolonged battle it took to find suitable insulators (Chapter 6), suitable material for the electrodes and points, and a suitable way to screen the high-tension plug leads (the cables carrying the high-tension current to the plugs) with carefully earthed conductive wire braiding to eliminate the severe radio interference that otherwise resulted.

For 80 years designers have chosen either of two forms of HT (high-tension) ignition systems. In one, more common on cars, a battery continuously feeds the relatively small number of turns in the primary winding of an induction coil. An engine-driven interrupter

repeatedly breaks the circuit, causing an HT impulse to flow from the thousands of turns of the induction coil's secondary winding. The HT pulses are fed by a rotating distributor to each cylinder in the correct sequence. The other scheme, more common in aero engines, is to use a magneto. This is simply a compact electrical machine which combines everything needed to produce the HT pulses in one package. Major components include a rotor driven by the engine which spins between the poles of a magnet or primary coil (the rotor can be a wire-wound armature, a metal-laminate multi-pole inductor or a multi-pole magnet), a secondary winding with turns of thousands of fine wire, a contact-breaker which makes and breaks the primary circuit (as in coil ignition), a condenser (to stop wear caused by arcing at the contact-breaker points), and a distributor to feed the HT pulses to the plugs. Today a third type of ignition system is rapidly gaining ground. The electronic or transistorized species use a simple coil to generate the HT current, and then a compact solid-state circuit board to govern the distribution and timing according to measurements of rpm, manifold pressure and intake air temperature.

In the early days of aviation, ignition systems vied with valve gear as the cause of most of the frequent engine failures. Whereas with the LT (low-tension) circuits the problem is maintaining good contacts and electrical continuity, with the HT the problem is insulation. Flying through rain tended to provide the HT with a perfect path to earth without having to jump any plug gaps. Accordingly, as well as trying to make ignition systems weatherproof, engine designers gradually decided to fit dual (completely duplicated) ignition systems, right down to having two plugs in each cylinder, and to demonstrate that the engine would run equally well on either. In the Second World War about a million pilots learned to run up to about 1,000 rpm before take-off and then switch off each HT circuit in turn. The resulting 'mag drop' should not have been more than 50 or at the outside 100 rpm, caused by the slightly longer

Section of a typical plug (for Bristol radial engines of 1935–45) showing the central steel electrode surrounded by platinum-iridium points. The plug is fed with HT pulses by a hermetically sealed cable surrounded by wire-braid radio screening (Bristol).

time taken to get the mixture burned using one plug only. If either ignition system was faulty, the engine would possibly backfire and certainly stop firing. Switching the other 'mag' back on again would cause a massive backfire and the resumption of running. You did not take off with one HT circuit inoperative. Today dual ignition is mandatory for all certificated engines for manned aircraft.

In an ideal engine the mixture would be ignited at TDC and would all burn completely and instantaneously. What actually happens is that the spark jumps the gap, heating the compressed mixture in the immediate vicinity to the point at which it begins to burn, and there is then a significant delay before the mixture really starts burning, with a travelling flame front. This flame front then takes a further appreciable time to travel through the entire bulk of the mixture and leave nothing unburned. All this time, the piston is moving. We want to get the highest possible pressure throughout the power stroke, so we have to time the spark well before the piston reaches TDC. In fact, we want to be able to vary the timing. The elapsed time needed to burn the

mixture varies only very slightly with engine speed; thus, when the engine is idling, the crankshaft may turn through 5° while the mixture is burning, whereas at full power it may turn through as much as 55°. Thus, at idling speed the ignition can be retarded, perhaps so that the spark occurs 6° before TDC, whereas at full power the ignition timing must be advanced, though there are many exceptions to this rule. For 50 years almost all engines have had an advance/retard mechanism built into the ignition system, for example by driving each magneto via a coupling containing centrifugal weights operating on cams. Other timing systems operate by changes in induction-manifold pressure, and the latest are, of course, fully electronic, the variation in timing being just another factor controlled by a small solid-state box fed with measurements of all the engine variables.

We now have the correct mixture being fed into the cylinder, compressed and ignited at the correct times. The downgoing piston drives a connecting rod which turns the crankshaft. These are among the strongest and most expensive parts of the engine. I have heard of

Simplified magneto-type ignition system for a seven-cylinder engine. The armature pole shoes (not shown), which generate the current, and the cam and distributor rotor are all driven from the engine (BTH).

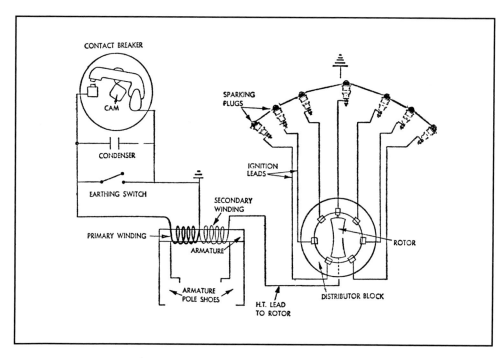

Y-alloy and even aluminium con-rods, but for all practical purposes con-rods, crankshafts and camshafts are all forged in some high-tensile steel, typically one with 1.9 per cent nickel, 0.75 per cent chromium, 0.7 per cent manganese, 0.25 per cent molybdenum and 0.37 per cent carbon. One cannot worry too much about weight here; what is needed is sheer strength and very long fatigue life within tight limitations on available volume. Of course, everything possible is done to minimize weight; for example, you will seldom, if ever, see a con-rod with a square or rectangular cross-section. Such components, like the shafts, are machined all over, and the con-rod ends up with an H-section. As noted earlier, seemingly insignificant changes to the precise shape of the rod can make all the difference between satisfactory life and fatigue failure within the first hour.

An in-line engine has simple rods, and the designer has merely to achieve the best compromise between cylinder spacing (determined by cylinder diameter), crank-web thickness and crankpin stress. In every such engine of my acquaintance the small end is continuous, the gudgeon pin being threaded through it, and the big end made in two parts which are clamped round the crankpin by bolts. In a V or opposed engine the designer has more choice. He can use fork-and-blade rods, in which the cylinders along one side drive narrow 'blade' rods whose big ends fit between the split forked big ends of the rods on the other side (see DB 601 con-rod drawing). Or he can use master rods along one side with enlarged big ends providing bearings for the small big ends of slave rods along the other. Or he can adopt the answer seen in most modern lightplane engines and make the cylinders not actually opposite each other, so that each drives a plain rod on its own crankpin. In the Porsche PFM 3200 there are only three 'pots' on each side, but the crankshaft has six crankpins and eight bearings (there's an extra bearing at the front).

A single-row radial has only one crankpin. One of the cylinders drives a master rod with a giant big end which drives the crankpin. All the other cylinders have simple slave, or articulated, or link, rods pin-jointed to bearings around the big end of the master. To balance the rotating parts the two webs which hold the crankpin are extended on the opposite side of the crankshaft to carry counterweights. Sometimes these are just fixed to the crankshaft, or forged integral to it; in other engines

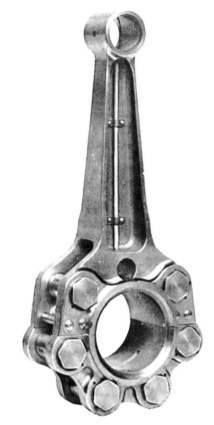

A typical radial-engine master rod: one of the two inside a Hispano-Suiza 14AA (Type 79) a French 1,100 hp engine of 1937. Note the six pins for the six link rods for the other cylinders of the same row, and the pipe taking oil from the crankpin to the gudgeon pin.

they are attached by pins or links so that they can swing relative to the shaft, or they incorporate loose rollers which, swinging to and fro in holes in the counterweights, are forced to move towards the axis of rotation of the shaft. Often quite complex arrangements are needed to damp out different orders of vibration.

This is the case even with a two-row radial, in which the two crankpins are at 180° and might be thought to balance each other out. The same is true of an opposed engine, with cranks at 180°, or a multi-crank in-line or V engine in which they are usually spaced at 120°. Everything possible is done to make the inertia forces and the rotating couples balance each other out.

The subject of vibration and balance is an

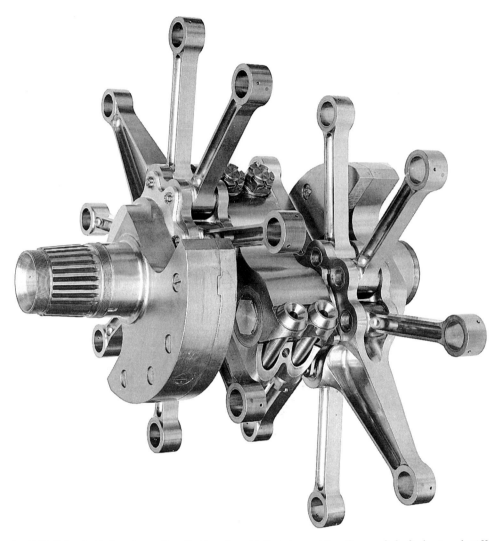

In 1932 Bristol chief engineer Roy Fedden thought that, by making the crankshaft short and stiff, his 16-cylinder Hydra (photo page 151) would not need a centre bearing (he was wrong). The two crankpins are secured by twin pinch-bolts.

enormous one. Every part of the engine is to some degree flexible, and everything bends, stretches or twists, not only in the primary way (which usually means with frequency N or N_1, which means crankshaft rotating frequency), but also in secondary and even tertiary harmonics, and in other ways which combine engine speed with the natural frequency of the part. As the second harmonic is just double the crankshaft frequency it cannot be eliminated or even reduced by counterweights rotating with the crankshaft. In our computerized age it ought to be possible to design an engine so that it runs smoothly the first time it is started. In the past, engines were actually put into production which, if they were not bolted down, would leap about. That is not what the designer of a light airframe appreciates.

We have already seen that certain engine configurations are more or less inherently balanced. Opposed engines are almost perfect. Radials are also very good, except that the large centripetal force acting outward along the crankpin is difficult to balance for all harmonics by weights on the opposite side. In any case, the radial must have an odd number of cylinders (preferably five, seven or nine per row), and a very important related factor which I have not mentioned previously is firing order. Take a simple four-in-line, such as a Gipsy or many car engines. It would be possible to design this so that the cylinders fired in the sequence 12341, but, bearing in mind that each cylinder fires once on every two revolutions of the crankshaft, this would result in a terrible engine! Every four-in-line I have ever heard of has the two cranks in the middle arranged at 180° to those on the ends, and the valve gear and ignition arranged to give the firing order 13421. Likewise, the almost universal firing order for a six-in-line is 1536241, though, as explained earlier, the strange dynamics of the Gipsy Queen were thought best served by 1246531! As for radials, a seven-cylinder will have the firing order 1357 (on the first revolution of the crankshaft) 246 (on the second). If you designed an eight-cylinder radial the sequence wouldn't work.

The last subject to be outlined in this chapter is lubrication. A few engines, including the two-strokes, run on a mixture of between 20 and 50 parts of petrol to one of lubricating oil. Most of this species have no separate lubrication system. Other engines could not run for more than a few seconds without proper lubrication. The oil used in smaller GA (general aviation) engines is often identical to that used in cars, such as SAE 20–50. Big engines, such as the Double Wasp, use SAE 50. The oil is essential for interposing a film between metal parts which slide over each other. It also provides essential cooling for several parts of the engine, notably gears transmitting high power.

In a car the bulk oil is normally stored in the engine sump, but most aero engines have a separate tank, mounted on the engine or, more often, on the airframe. From here the oil is piped to the main pressure pump, invariably of the intermeshing-gear type, which sends the main flow at high pressure to passages bored through the crankshaft. From here it escapes via the main and big end bearings. Usually these are of the plain type, the crankshaft and crankpin(s) revolving inside relatively soft bearing shells of white metal or phosphor bronze. Oil is pumped to each bearing from inside the crankshaft, and thence through holes in the soft shell where it emerges from a diagonal groove to form a fine film, the dynamics of the bearing being arranged so that the continuously replenished film never lets the metal surfaces touch each other. In some engines the big end and/or main bearings are of the needle roller type. These too need an oil supply, both for lubrication and for cooling. The oil escapes from the open ends of the bearing shells and is flung off the periphery of the moving parts at high speed. The result is that the interior of the crankcase is filled with oil mist, and the walls, and in particular the lower parts of the cylinders and the undersides of the pistons, are covered in oil. Probably the most crucial remaining parts are the gudgeon (piston) pins. Though it would be possible to provide these with positive pressure feed through holes drilled along the con-rods (or by pipes, see A.12 drawing), they are normally lubricated by the

In V-type engines the designer may elect to use fork-and-blade connecting rods. One example was the Daimler-Benz DB 601, shown here with the cap of the blade (or plain) rod disconnected. An unusual feature of this engine was that the crankpin was driven by three rings of roller bearings.

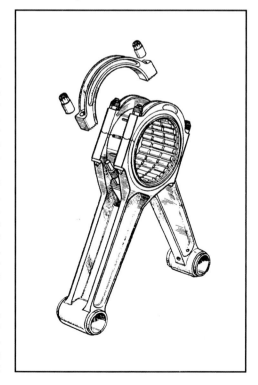

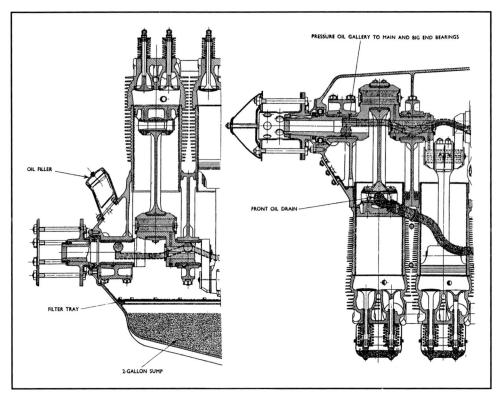

*The original DH Gipsy was an upright engine (*left*), with a sump full of oil. When, in late 1929, the engine was inverted, no wet sump was possible. Instead pressure oil was fed to the crankshaft, collecting round the cylinder skirts to be returned to the external tank (*right*).*

same splash feed as other interior items. Hot oil is collected in the sump, from which it is continuously sucked out by scavenge pumps and returned to the tank.

Several filters are inserted in the circuit, usually one between the tank and the pressure pump and another as the scavenge oil enters the tank. There must also be an oil cooler, even though the hot scavenge oil is often cooled by being used to heat the carburettor and possibly other parts. The oil radiator can be cooled by ram air, or by the fuel flowing to the engine. Many engines have various forms of pressure relief valve. For example oil at full pump pressure, of from 50 to 200 lb/sq in depending on engine type, may be needed to change the pitch of the propeller, especially for emergency feathering. A second supply, set by spring-loaded valves at some value near 50 lb/sq in, will be the main flow piped to the crankshaft. A third flow, set by another valve at only 8 lb/sq in or thereabouts, will be piped to the camshaft, valve gear, reduction gear and accessory drives. In most early engines various parts, such as valve rockers, had to be periodically lubricated by hand by a grease gun. Such attention is as far as possible eliminated in modern engines.

Another thing that designers have tried to eliminate is warming up. Never a feature of jet or turboprop engines, warming up was needed with early piston engines because, especially in winter, cold oil was so thick that the engine pressure circuits were not always able to supply a satisfactory film to the metal/metal rubbing parts. Thus, starting the engine and taking off at once risked seizure. In 1937 Bristol introduced a system which made warming up unnecessary. The high-pressure oil was arranged to be able to pass through a restrictor valve and thence return to the tank. Thick, cold oil would not pass easily through the restrictor, allowing pressure to the main bearings to increase and also opening a fresh supply to spray the interior of the crankcase.

4 Engine design II

In the previous chapter we studied most of the problems encountered in arranging for the air and fuel to reach the cylinder in the correct proportions and at the right time, there to be ignited. In this chapter—the last to deal with generalized design problems—we look deeper at the problem of cooling the cylinders, and go on to consider cowlings, superchargers, exhaust systems, the propeller drive, accessories and the engine's installation in the airframe.

Cooling is one of the most important factors in the design of the cylinder. The problem is greatly accentuated because of man's failure so far to invent a thermodynamic cycle that could be called efficient. We have seen that aircraft piston engines have a thermal efficiency in the region of 25 to 27 per cent. In other words, to develop a power at the piston of 100 hp a cylinder has to release heat from the burning mixture at the rate of about 400 hp. The greater the fraction of the chemical (heat) energy in the fuel that we can turn into useful work, the less is our problem of keeping the cylinder acceptably cool. This problem is clearly greatest when the engine is running at maximum power. On the other hand, at maximum power the fraction of total fuel heat that has to be dissipated by the cooling system is a minimum, typically about 33 per cent. When the engine is idling the fraction can reach 70 per cent, but it is 70 per cent of a very much smaller total. Of course, this ignores external effects, such as the much greater slipstream (propwash) velocity at full power, which increases the cooling capacity of air and liquid cooling systems alike.

The need to cool the engine is obvious; or is it? Some readers, familiar with gas-turbine engines, may ponder on the fact that today's high-pressure turbine blades can operate for many thousands of hours under far greater stress than any cylinder and in a gas temperature greater than anything in most piston engines. Moreover, the turbine blade is continuously subjected to this temperature, instead of having three cooling cycles in between each hot one. There are several answers to this. One is that each HP blade in a modern fighter or wide-body engine costs as much as the complete engine of a typical light plane. Both on the score of material cost and manufacturing cost the GA (general aviation) cylinder is in a different league—it has to be. Secondly, the turbine blade is retained by a fir-tree root slotted into its disc, but otherwise touches nothing but the white hot gas. In the cylinder there is contact with moving metal in the form of the piston and valve gear, and actual metal-to-metal contact has to be avoided by interposing a film of oil. These factors dictate a maximum cylinder temperature something like 1,000°C cooler than the TET (turbine entry temperature) of the jet engine. Quite apart from this, the HP blade is deep inside the engine (or should be)!, whereas a glowing cylinder would pose an obvious fire risk.

The two most fundamental choices to be taken by the designer—assuming he or she is so fortunate as to have a free hand, with no preconceived ideas—are the engine's basic configuration and the method of cooling to be adopted. To some degree the two are interlinked. There have been quite a few high-power V engines with air-cooled cylinders, but they made no impact to compare with those that had liquid cooling. Even more to the point, since the First World War I can hardly think of a single water-cooled radial.

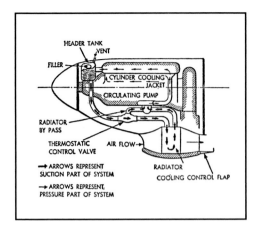

Schematic diagram of a liquid cooling system. Water, water/glycol or some other mix, is stored in the header tank and pumped round the closed system by a pump mounted somewhere low down on the engine. When the cylinder jackets have heated the liquid sufficiently, a thermostat opens a valve to pass a proportion of the flow through the radiator. The flow through the radiator and the radiator flap position are adjusted depending on engine power, airspeed and altitude (RR).

Development of air cooling of cylinders is shown actual size by (a) 1911 Renault fins, (b) 1938 Pegasus, (c) 1944 Wright W-type inserted cylinder-barrel fins.

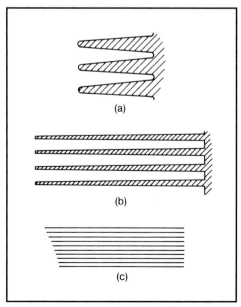

The performance of the cooling system depends greatly on the detail design. Over 80 years ago water cooling was not very different in principle from what we can do today. You need a pump to pump fresh cool water through jackets surrounding the cylinders. The heat escapes through the thin iron (later steel) cylinder wall straight into the fast-flowing water, which conveys it away to a radiator where it is transferred to the atmosphere. We can't do much better today, though we can make the circuit run hotter and use a smaller radiator. In the sharpest contrast, if you compare a modern air-cooled cylinder with one from 80 years ago the differences are startling. I commented earlier that a cylinder of 1950 (that of the Cyclone 7BA) had 150 times as much fin area with which to dissipate the heat as one of similar capacity dating from 1910 (Renault). As the temperature of the burning charge has always stayed pretty much the same, one could deduce that the air-cooled cylinder has made fantastic progress.

Put another way, if air-cooling made any sense in 1908, and could be made to work, then by 1950 it must have been so much better that the seemingly complicated and heavy choice of cooling by water or ethylene glycol would never have stood a chance. This is especially the case when it is remembered that the efficiency of a cooling system depends on the rate at which it can handle unwanted heat, measured in terms of J or BThU, per unit area of cylinder wall per unit time. In a typical air-cooled cylinder the difference in temperature between the cooling fins and the passing airflow is seldom less than 250°C, even in the tropics, whereas with water the difference is seldom greater than 80°C. All these factors favour air-cooling, quite apart from such obvious additional considerations as the bulk, weight and drag of the cooling water, piping and large radiator, and the difficulty of avoiding any leaks. Yet, as explained in the final chapter, liquid cooling is if anything making a come-back.

The water or other liquid in a liquid-cooled engine does at least interpose a buffer between the source of heat and the highly stressed parts. In contrast, air cooling depends critically upon keeping the air flowing past the cylinders. At least with aeroplanes the engine was usually in the slipstream from the propeller, or else in the air being sucked into a pusher propeller. Many of the earliest aero engines were derived from motor cycle designs where it was quite possible for the engine to run with no airflow round it at all, other than that induced by convection. Despite the propeller, several early engines were prone to severe overheating whenever they were run on the ground. Indeed, some were so badly cooled that they even over-heated in flight. On 25 July 1909 Louis Blériot was getting ready to ditch in the Channel when he flew into a shower of rain. This cooled down his overheated Anzani, and he was able to reach Dover, and gain everlasting fame.

Of course, if you try you can overheat almost any engine. With a liquid-cooled engine, you can sometimes override thermostatic controls and steadfastly keep radiator shutters closed when climbing at high power and low air speed. With air-cooled engines you can leave cooling shutters or gills closed when running on the ground. In 1944 I flew in Albemarles, powered by Hercules sleeve-valve radials. They had been designed as high-speed bombers, but instead were being used to tow Horsa gliders (which were much bigger than the tug). The result was that instead of cruising at about 350 hp per engine at 6,096 m (20,000 ft) at 386 km/h (240 mph), the engines were cruising at 1,200 hp at 305 m

(1,000 ft) at 161 km/h (100 mph). On each (mercifully short) trip the cylinder-head temperature would rise alarmingly. After landing, clouds of oil smoke would rise like a pillar above each engine. At Brize Norton one could sometimes see 40 or more smoke pillars at once. Obviously, on turning the Albemarle (and the Hercules-engined Stirling and Hali-fax) into a tug, the engine should have been given better cooling, with a fan. Fan cooling is discussed in Chapter 7.

To some degree, adding a fan (which in modern engines goes hand in hand with com-plete ducted control of the cooling air) enables air-cooling to be used with an engine of any configuration. Even without such a forced-draught system, designers today have a free choice of liquid or air-cooling with any chosen engine layout—within the limitations of fashion, as noted earlier. Of course, the fact that aircraft piston engines today seldom extend to powers above 500 hp tends to restrict the range of likely configurations, with few modern engines having more than six cylinders.

Except in microlights and similar low-per-formance aircraft, all modern engines are carefully enclosed in a cowling. With liquid

Today the most important liquid-cooled engines are produced by Teledyne Continental. Only the head is cooled, the barrel being kept at a reasonable temperature by the piston oil squirt. These engines are discussed later in this chapter. Note: 250°F is 121°C and 270°F is 132°C.

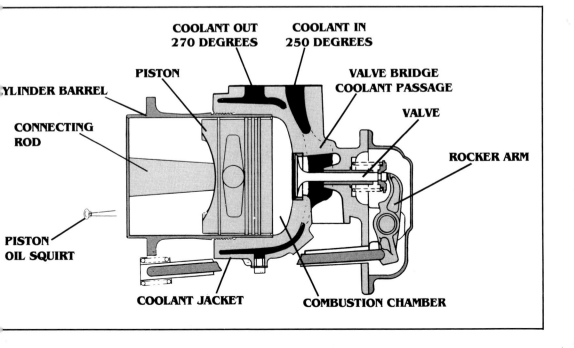

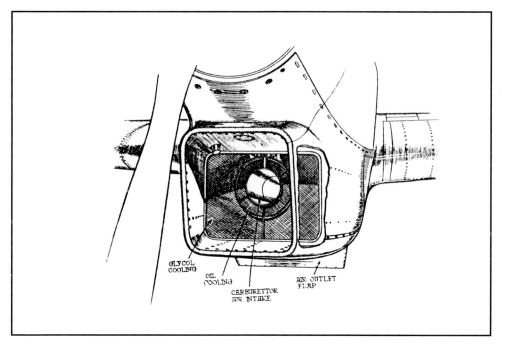

There are countless ways in which a radiator can be arranged. In the Hawker Henley dive-bomber of 1937 pure glycol was used, passed through a single cooling matrix under the engine. In the centre was the ring-type oil radiator, through the centre of which passed the ram air to the engine (Temple Press).

cooling it is possible to place the heat exchanger (radiator) anywhere in the aircraft. Thus, the cowling could be completely enclosed, although almost always it contains a ram intake to feed the air needed for combustion in the cylinders. This is commonly called a 'carb-air inlet', though of course there may be no carburettor, and a better term is the 'induction-air inlet'. In most of the growing crop of liquid-cooled engines the cowling is sealed except for a single ram inlet which serves ducts to the engine or turbosupercharger, to the radiator and to the oil cooler. There are obvious advantages in locating both these heat exchangers as near to the engine as possible. Usually the pilot can control airflow through the radiators by means of shutters. As explained later, in some installations the addition of heat to the cooling airflow can be made to give dragless cooling, or even positive thrust.

With air-cooling the cowling usually has larger openings at both front and rear, arranged to achieve the greatest possible airflow past the cylinders with the minimum pressure drop. As far as possible the front (inlet) openings are directly forward-facing, in the full slipstream of the propeller, though with many lightplane propellers the inner portions of the blades are relatively inefficient. With opposed engines, which today are in the majority, the cooling air is usually taken in through an approximately rectangular inlet on each side of the spinner, the flow entering the cowling above the centrelines of the cylinders. The latter are boxed in by close-fitting baffles (flat sheets) along the sides, over the heads, and at the rear, so that to escape the air has to pass down around the finned cylinders. Thus it reaches the lower half of the cowling, which has exit openings to atmosphere. In-line engines, such as the Gipsy, invariably have the inlet offset to one side of the centre line, and the main exit from the cowling on the opposite side. Radials invariably have a simple annular entry around the spinner. The exit may be via a similar peripheral ring, if necessary controlled by gills, or through one or more slot openings in the sides of the fuselage. A few agricultural aircraft, concerned with utility rather than performance, leave their radial engine completely uncowled, just as it

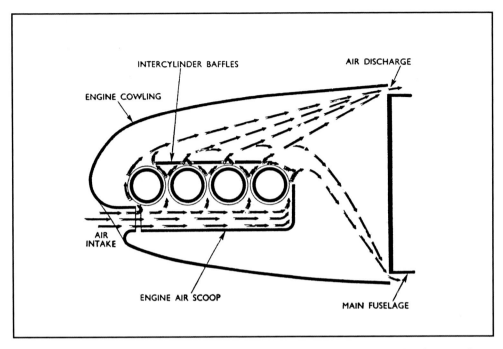

Though it specifically applies to the de Havilland Gipsy engines of 1927–50, this diagram shows the basic principle followed in all air-cooled engines. The air is rammed in on one side of the cylinders only, and guided through the cooling fins by baffles before being sucked out by the slipstream (DH Engines).

would have been in aircraft 60 years ago.

I have been careful to refer to 'liquid cooling'. Of course, the most common cooling liquid is water, but not all liquid-cooling engines use it. Indeed, in the early days of aviation the fuel itself was sometimes used as a cooling medium, the engine running on an over-rich mixture. Several thousand Renault and RAF (Royal Aircraft Factory) engines in the First World War were ostensibly air-cooled, but their sustained operation depended upon holding the mixture strength at about 13 per cent fuel by weight. Any attempt to weaken the mixture nearer to the stoichiometric value of about 7 per cent would result in increasingly severe overheating, to the point where parts of the cylinders would be seen to be glowing dull red at night. This wasteful use of fuel was acceptable in an age when fuel was cheap, and environmental issues had not been given a thought.

After the First World War several liquid cooling media were experimented with in an attempt to find something that remained liquid at temperatures significantly greater than 100°C. We have seen how, in seeking

ways to cool exhaust valves, the best heat-transfer medium was judged to be molten sodium. In the 1960s, to generate auxiliary power in space, heat-transfer systems were designed using a eutectic mixture of sodium and potassium, or lithium, or mercury (as vapour). With such coolants the cylinder could run much hotter, the coolant system would weigh less and the radiator, at perhaps 650°C, would be much smaller and capable of giving ramjet-style thrust. I will leave today's private owners to ponder on the prospects for such exotic coolants.

In fact, water is an outstandingly good cooling medium, with extremely high ability to transfer heat. Its only real shortcoming is that it boils at 100°C at sea level, and at even lower temperatures at higher altitudes. It is possible to push up the boiling temperature by keeping the entire cooling circuit under pressure. Many of the final types of high-power liquid-cooled engines used a mixture of water plus about 30 per cent ethylene glycol, the latter being simply an antifreeze additive, as in cars. At a pressure of 40 lb/sq in such a mixture could circulate at 130°C. Alternative schemes,

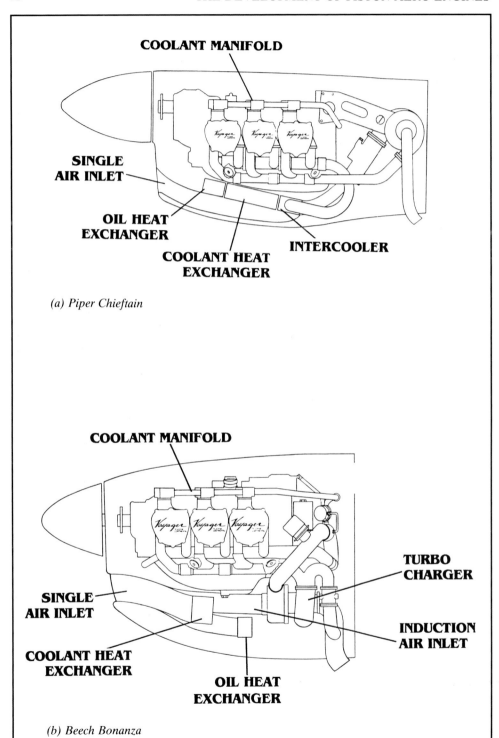

COOLANT MANIFOLD

SINGLE AIR INLET

OIL HEAT EXCHANGER

COOLANT HEAT EXCHANGER

INTERCOOLER

(a) Piper Chieftain

COOLANT MANIFOLD

SINGLE AIR INLET

COOLANT HEAT EXCHANGER

OIL HEAT EXCHANGER

TURBO CHARGER

INDUCTION AIR INLET

(b) Beech Bonanza

discussed later, included the use of pure ethylene glycol, at ambient pressure, and so-called evaporative cooling in which the circuit is filled with water which is allowed to boil, the steam being converted back into water in a condenser which, being flush with the aircraft skin, offered little or no drag. Today an Austrian, Oskar Westermayer, is busy rebuilding Continental O-200 engines with cylinder heads cooled by pure ethylene glycol (see chapter 8), with increased compression ratio. Among the advantages he claims about 25 per cent reduced fuel consumption.

In my view the debate between air and liquid cooling will continue into the next century. The fact that today air-cooling has about 99.9 per cent of the market ought not to influence us too greatly. As I explain in Chapter 8, TCM (Teledyne Continental Motors) are convinced that liquid cooling can result in superior overall efficiency, and in the long term will probably become the preferred answer. The Rutan/Yeager team did not do this argument any harm when they picked a liquid-cooled engine to push their Voyager non-stop around the world in December 1986.

Today's TCM engines are discussed in the final chapter, but I think it is appropriate to talk about the basic pros and cons in this chapter, as well. Most people would say that it seems obvious that if you can reject your unwanted heat direct to atmosphere via the metal/air boundary of cylinder cooling fins, then this must result in the simplest and cheapest engine. On 19 April 1945, when they had cancelled their big liquid-cooled engines and committed their piston-engine future entirely to traditional air-cooled radials, Pratt & Whitney issued a long and hard-hitting treatise explaining that liquid cooling was nonsense. Basically, it argued that, whichever method was adopted, you had to reject the heat to the passing airflow anyway, so why bother with complicated pipes full of liquid?

Opposite Two current installations of TCM liquid-cooled engines show quite different arrangements. The geared Voyager GT-550 in the Piper Chieftain (a) has all the coolers arranged in a flat row through which ram air passes upwards, with a branch at the rear to feed the sideways-on turbo. The T-550 in the Bonanza (b) has direct drive, which puts the engine relatively higher and makes room underneath for separate pipes to the vertical coolers and for a turbo under the engine.

With a bit of further thought we can see it is not quite so simple, and the liquid-cooled engine installation of the 1990s seems to me to be very convincing, especially in aircraft where speed is important—in other words, the arguments do not apply with the same force to agricultural aircraft.

We have already seen, and it is repeated in Chapter 8, that liquid cooling makes life easier for the cylinder. Temperatures cannot fluctuate violently, and the overall result is an engine which will perform more efficiently and last longer. When TCM first offered what is now called the Voyager series of engines they were quickly selected by Boeing to power the huge HALE (high-altitude long-endurance) Condor. This remotely piloted vehicle, used for electronic intelligence, has since 1985 set totally new standards for both altitude and flight endurance. TCM claim that liquid cooling not only makes possible higher altitude capability and reduced fuel consumption but also longer life and extended TBO. As for installed drag, RAM Aircraft would say, if you do it right then you can beat any air-cooled installation. A photograph shows the beautiful enclosed cowling over the Voyager GT-550 engines of the Cessna 414AW, while a diagram shows the simple cooling circuit. The 60/40 mix of Prestone (glycol) and water is stored in a 10 litre (2.7 gal) (football-size) tank behind the engine, and cooled by a flush radiator, as big as a large book, inside the extended tail of the nacelle (Chapter 8). The result is superior performance.

In the previous chapter we traced the path of the induction air and fuel into the combustion space. In one method the fuel was injected 'at the eye of the supercharger', but we have not discussed the question of supercharging at all. As its name suggests, a supercharger is an air pump whose purpose is to pump a bigger charge of air or mixture into the cylinders on each induction stroke. In a few cases it is used to boost the power output at sea level or at other low altitudes, just as in some high-performance cars. Far more often its purpose is to sustain power output as the aircraft climbs to high altitude. An unsupercharged, or 'unblown', engine falls off in power in proportion to the decreasing pressure of the atmosphere, which in such an engine determines the mass of charge taken into each cylinder on each induction stroke. Thus, in a simple engine, performance falls away with height until at 6,096 m (20,000 ft) the available power is half that at sea level.

Today's liquid-cooled engines are aesthetically beautiful. The Cessna 414AW installation starts with a BlackMac McCauley propeller, faired into a cowl which is sealed except for a ventral duct for induction air to the turbo and small flush inlets for the oil cooler and intercooler. In the front of the cowl is a landing light.

In the Cessna 414AW, typical of the latest practice, the glycol/water mix is cooled in a radiator mounted flat in an extended nacelle extension aft of the wing. Air enters through inlets above the wing and passes through the radiator downwards.

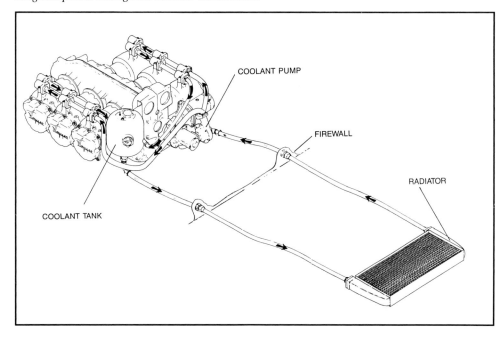

COOLANT PUMP

FIREWALL

RADIATOR

COOLANT TANK

The dominant type of supercharger has always been the centrifugal. This has an impeller which rotates at very high speed inside a close-fitting casing. The essential feature of the impeller is that it consists of a series of radial vanes with their flat faces set at 90° to their direction of motion. Early impellers had nothing else, but later types backed the vanes with a disc and added curved guide vanes at the root (hub) to assist the air to flow smoothly into the spaces between the vanes. These spaces constitute channels in which the air is forced to rotate at the high speed of the impeller, which accelerates it both tangentially and, under centripetal force, outwards. It thus leaves the edge of the impeller at very high speed and in a direction determined by the tangential and radial components. High speed means low pressure, so the high-velocity air is passed through a diffuser surrounding the impeller. This comprises a ring of curved vanes so arranged that the air passages between them diverge. Thus, as the air passes through the diffuser, its high velocity is traded for high pressure.

Most superchargers are driven mechanically, by means of step-up gears from the rear end of the crankshaft. In early superchargers trouble was experienced with failures of the drive shaft or stripping of the gear teeth. There were two causes. One was that the rigidity of the drive multiplied the inevitable slight fluctuations in crankshaft speed, some of which occur as the result of the firing of individual cylinders on each crankshaft revolution. The cure here was to insert a spring-drive coupling (a familiar device in power transmissions for over a century) in which the drive torque is transmitted through several (typically six) coil springs, inserted between drive spokes and driven spokes, which easily accommodate the small angular movements. The other source of trouble was that to achieve a useful pressure rise centrifugal impellers have to operate at a very high tip speed. There are obvious severe limitations on diameter, so the only answer is to drive the supercharger at very high speed. Typically, the drive gears multiply crankshaft speed by about 7 in a large engine and 11 in a small one, the latter figure equating to an impeller speed of perhaps 30,000 rpm. Thus, the stored energy and angular momentum of the impeller is enormous. Should the pilot suddenly close the throttle from full power, a rigid train of gears would be grossly overloaded as the impeller speed is violently reduced. The

answer here is to take the drive through (typically three) intermediate gears incorporating centrifugal clutches. These resemble a drum-type car brake. Centrifugal force keeps clutch blocks pressed against the inner faces of either the peripheral gear ring or side plates. Closing the throttle eases the pressure slightly and allows the outer part of the intermediate gear, and the impeller, to over-run and slow down gently. If the engine is suddenly shut down and stopped, the supercharger can be heard still spinning.

Superchargers in low-altitude racing engines are relatively simple, and the main problem is ensuring that the cylinders do not part company with the crankcase. In contrast, most superchargers in aero engines are there in order to try to maintain high power at high altitude. They are not fitted in order to increase power at ground level, and so a special 'boost control' is fitted to protect the engine. Boost pressure is the difference between ambient atmospheric pressure and the pressure in the supercharger delivery manifold feeding the cylinders. Boost can be negative, but at high throttle openings could be as great as 25 lb/sq in, expressed in US engines as 80 in Hg (80 inches of mercury) and in German engines as 1.7 ata (1.7 times local

Superchargers can make a fantastic difference to power at high altitudes. An unsupercharged Rolls-Royce Merlin would have put out about 200 hp at 10,668 m (35,000 ft). The Merlin III (Hurricane I) gave about 400 hp at this height, but the two-stage supercharger of the Merlin 61 (Spitfire VIII) increased power to 825 hp!

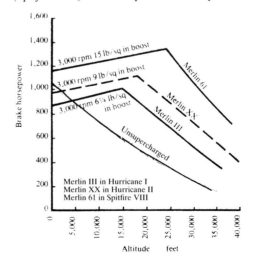

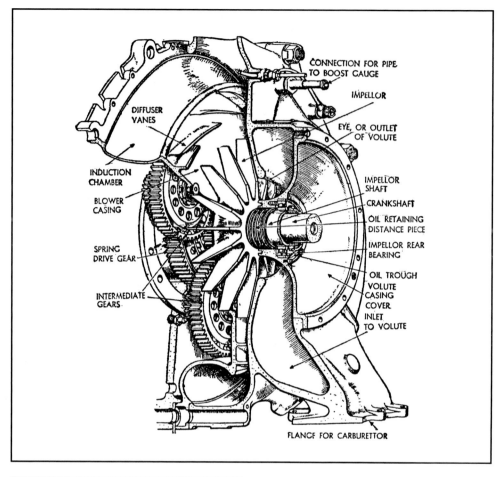

CONNECTION FOR PIPE
TO BOOST GAUGE

IMPELLOR

DIFFUSER
VANES

EYE, OR OUTLET
OF VOLUTE

INDUCTION
CHAMBER

IMPELLOR
SHAFT

BLOWER
CASING

CRANKSHAFT

OIL RETAINING
DISTANCE PIECE

IMPELLOR REAR
BEARING

SPRING
DRIVE GEAR

OIL TROUGH

VOLUTE
CASING
COVER

INTERMEDIATE
GEARS

INLET
TO VOLUTE

FLANGE FOR CARBURETTOR

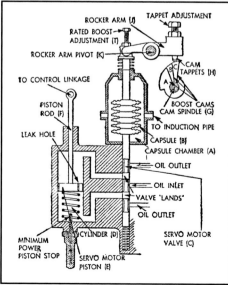

ROCKER ARM (J)   TAPPET ADJUSTMENT

RATED BOOST
ADJUSTMENT (T)

ROCKER ARM PIVOT (K)

CAM
TAPPETS (H)

TO CONTROL LINKAGE

BOOST CAMS
CAM SPINDLE (G)

PISTON
ROD (F)

TO INDUCTION PIPE

LEAK HOLE

CAPSULE (B)

CAPSULE CHAMBER (A)

OIL OUTLET

OIL INLET

VALVE 'LANDS'

OIL OUTLET

MINIMUM
POWER
PISTON STOP

CYLINDER (D)

SERVO MOTOR
VALVE (C)

SERVO MOTOR
PISTON (E)

Above *Cutaway of the supercharger of a Pegasus radial engine, showing how the impeller is driven via a spring gear and friction-clutch intermediate gears. Rotating anti-clockwise, seen from this side, the high-speed impeller delivers the compressed air out between the diffuser vanes* (Odhams Press).

Left *Schematic diagram of a standard British boost control, in which the 'fixed' end of the aneroid capsule was positioned by one of three cams. Upward movement of the piston opened the throttle* (H. M. Hobson).

atmospheric pressure). The boost control is a typical pressure-sensitive device comprising a stack of aneroid capsules whose expansion and contraction determine the position of a high-precision spool valve. This valve feeds a fluid, usually high-pressure engine oil, to a piston connected to the throttle linkage. The other end of the aneroid stack (that not connected to the valve) can simply be fixed to the capsule chamber. More often it is positioned by a rocker arm whose position is determined by three cams on a shaft rotated by the pilot's throttle linkage. With the throttle closed, the rocker arm bears on the lowest cam position. Opening the throttle rotates the cams to bring each in turn into its highest position, the first giving maximum cruising boost, the second rated boost and the third take-off or combat boost.

Take-off or combat boost results in the highest power of which the engine is capable. It is invariably available only for a limited period, such as five minutes. It combines maximum boost pressure with maximum rpm, and almost always calls for the carburettor or fuel-injection system to supply additional fuel, over and above that needed for the extra power, to give an unusually rich mixture. This avoids detonation and helps to cool the cylinders. Some engines have a water-injection system, which is also called into play by selecting this maximum power setting. Even better results are achieved by injecting a mixture of water and from 25 per cent to 75 per cent of methyl alcohol (methanol), the latter serving chiefly as an antifreeze. Water injec-

tion avoids the rapid fuel consumption and carbon deposition of over-rich mixture, and gives far greater potential power increase. With a typical weak mixture the knock-limited indicated MEP in one US engine was just over 140 lb/sq in. Enriching the fuel to a fuel/air ratio of 10 per cent enabled the IMEP to be increased to 200 lb/sq in, but adding 0.25 lb water plus 0.25 lb methanol per 1 lb of fuel enabled IMEP to reach no less than 280 lb/sq in! Thus, compared with normal running, the full-throttle power was doubled.

After take-off the pilot has to throttle back; the maximum continuous power corresponds to rated boost, also called maximum climbing boost. This is usually the same as maximum WM (weak-mixture) power. As the aircraft climbs, so the atmospheric pressure falls, and so does the ambient temperature. Both effects are favourable. The falling pressure means that there is less back-pressure on the exhaust, while the falling temperature means that air density for a given pressure increases. Thus, as the automatic boost control is maintaining the boost pressure set by the pilot, the supercharger can pump in more mixture to the cylinders. Accordingly, with the pilot's controls untouched, the power keeps rising with altitude, which is the opposite of what

Schematic diagram of a two-speed supercharger drive. Oil pressure locks either the left or right clutch plate against the central disc in the casing, taking the drive through either the large pinion (low, or M, gear) or the small pinion (high, or S, gear) (Bristol).

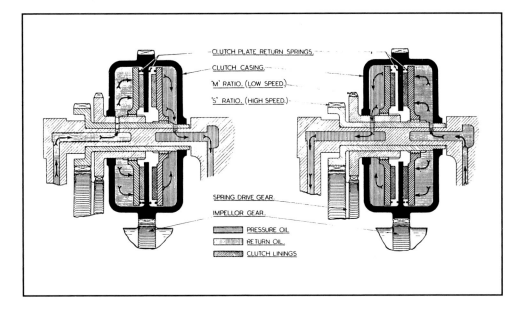

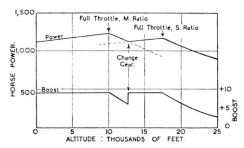

Variation of boost pressure and power with altitude for an engine with a two-speed super-charger. Of course, the pilot's instruments show him boost and rpm only (Air Ministry).

would happen with an unsupercharged engine.

Of course, there comes an altitude at which the supercharger can no longer maintain the original induction-pipe pressure. This height is called the rated altitude, and (except for take-off) this is the point at which the engine gives its greatest power. Further increase in height will result in progressively falling output, unless the supercharger has a two-speed drive. In a typical arrangement the three intermediate gears, which otherwise would house centrifugal clutches as previously described, instead house double-acting hydraulic clutches. These transmit the drive through either of two different-size pinions meshing with corresponding gears round the edge of the spring drive. When oil pressure is supplied to one side of each clutch the impeller rotates at the low ratio, called M-gear, the other gears being unable to drive. Switching the oil pressure to the other side disconnects the M-gears and transfers the drive to the high-ratio or S-gear drive. The gear change may be triggered barometrically or directly by a cockpit lever. The author's wartime *Pilot's Notes* say the change from M to S gear 'should not be made until there has been a drop in boost pressure from 2 to 5 lb/sq in . . . The change should be made at the height at which the engine gives the same power in either ratio. At the same boost and rpm the engine gives less power in S gear, because driving the supercharger consumes more power, and the supercharger heats the charge more, and so less weight of mixture is drawn in at each stroke.' An accompanying graph shows the variation of full-throttle power and boost with altitude, at given rpm, for a particular engine with a two-speed supercharger.

A few engines even had three-speed supercharger drives. Obviously the ideal would be an infinitely variable transmission, and this was adopted by several manufacturers, notably Daimler-Benz in the Second World War. Their drive bore a family resemblance to the 'fluid flywheel' used on Daimler cars between the wars. Oil was pumped along a passage (A in the drawing) in the drive shaft, to emerge through radial holes B. Centrifugal force caused the oil to travel radially out at high speed until it encountered the curved ends of passages C, which directed it into corresponding inter-vane passages in D. The high-speed oil acted on the vanes of D like a turbine, driving D round in the same direction. Exactly the same arrangement was duplicated on the other side of the central driving member, so balancing the end-thrust. By controlling the oil supply the drive could be varied from zero up to an almost 'solid' drive, with only about 2 per cent slip. As noted in Chapter 7, these engines were unusual in that the drive shaft was transverse, the impeller being on one side of the engine. In most superchargers the axis of rotation is aligned with the crankshaft.

There is a totally different form of supercharger drive, which eliminates gears and enables the supercharger to be located anywhere on the engine, or even elsewhere in the aircraft. This is the turbosupercharger, and today it is more common than geared types, and its history goes back to 1906 (Chapter 5). Basically, the exhaust from the engine is used to drive a turbine which is directly connected to the supercharger. The 'turbo' has many eminently desirable features. Its only problem was that, in the first 40 years of this century, it was extremely difficult to make a turbine that could operate reliably in a working fluid of white-hot exhaust gas. It was precisely the same problem as that faced by the builders of early jet engines.

Provided one can solve this problem, the turbo forms an almost ideal adjunct to the piston engine, for any customer who considers the dramatically improved performance at high altitude is worth the extra bulk, weight and cost of the turbo itself, and of pressurization of the aircraft. I doubt if anyone would install a turbo in order to boost power at sea level, because at low levels it accomplishes little. Whereas an ordinary supercharger's output is linked to the speed of the crankshaft, the turbo's output depends solely on the pressure difference between the gas in the exhaust pipe and the ambient atmosphere. This is a minimum at sea level, so the turbo's

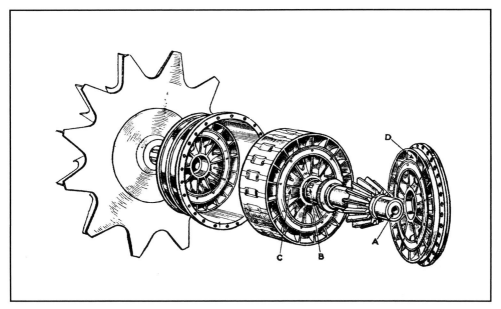

Many high-power German engines incorporated an infinitely variable hydraulic drive to the supercharger, which at low level could disconnect the drive entirely. As described in the text, this was the drive on the Daimler-Benz DB 601A.

Schematic diagram of the induction system of an engine equipped with both a turbosupercharger and a mechanically driven internal supercharger. Such installations were seen on the B-17, B-24 and B-29 bombers in the Second World War.

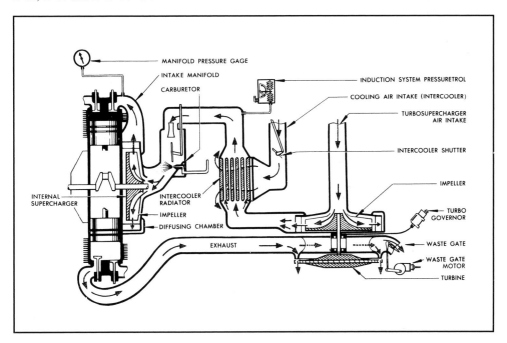

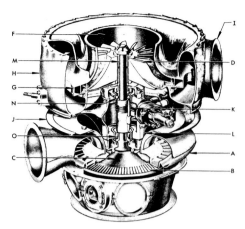

Cutaway of the General Electric BH4 turbo as used on the B-50 and Stratocruiser: (A) nozzle box; (B) turbine buckets (blades); (C) turbine wheel; (D) impeller; (F) air inlet; (G) diffuser; (H) casing; (I) air delivery; (J) baffle ring distributing cooling air; (K) lube-oil pump; (L) pump casing; (M) main shaft; (N) upper ball-bearing; (O) lower roller bearing. At the left is the exhaust pipe connection.

performance will also be a minimum. As the aircraft climbs, however, this pressure difference grows even greater. The power developed by the turbine rises in exact proportion, so the supercharger is able to maintain the pressure in the induction manifold close to that at sea level. In turn, this means that the pressure in the exhaust manifold also remains close to the sea-level value, automatically increasing the power of the turbine to maintain engine power very near the sea-level value up to a high altitude. Eventually the turbo governor senses that turbine rpm is on the allowable limit. Beyond this rated altitude the power inevitably falls as in other engines. There are many incidental advantages. There are no problems with sudden torsional shocks or fluctuations in engine speed, and the turbo forms a natural exhaust silencer and flame damper.

A critical factor is the design of the exhaust manifold, and the nozzle box which directs the hot gas on to the turbine. The whole assembly must be gas-tight, even under considerable pressure, aerodynamically efficient and lagged to give a cool exterior. The high pressure is needed because the turbine is of the blow-down or impulse type. The pressurized exhaust gas in the nozzle box is allowed to expand through the ring of nozzle guide vanes, emerging at much lower pressure but at very high velocity. The high-velocity flow impinging on the buckets (blades) drives the turbine. Usually a valve called a waste gate is incorporated in the nozzle box or exhaust manifold. At low altitudes some or all of the exhaust is allowed to escape through the waste gate. As altitude is increased, the gate is progressively closed. This not only forces more gas through the turbine but it also increases the pressure in the exhaust manifold, and thus the power of the turbo.

The engine has to be specially designed to operate with high exhaust back-pressures. As noted later, many designers avoided turbos because they were worried about cylinder overheating or sleeve distortion. On the other hand, this back-pressure has almost no effect on engine power. The piston finishes its exhaust stroke with a pressure remaining in the cylinder of about 85 lb/sq in (200 in Hg). Thus, when the exhaust valve is opened, the pressure ratio across it is at least 6, far above the critical value. Consequently, the pressure downstream has no effect on the rate at which the gas escapes from the cylinder. Moreover, in real engines the valve timing is different from the theoretical ideal. At BDC the exhaust valve is already partially open, and before the engine has to expend work in positively pumping out exhaust against the back pressure more than 75 per cent has already escaped. Thus, three-quarters of the turbo gas is obtained at no cost in crankshaft power, only the remaining quarter having to be pumped out. The net result is that the turbine gas horsepower is four to five times as great as the power taken from the engine in pumping against back pressure. Even with a turbine efficiency as poor as 65 per cent the turbo still recovers two to three times the lost crankshaft power.

Almost always, the large turbocharged engines of the Second World War delivered the air through an intercooler (and possibly a carburettor) to a second supercharger driven from the crankshaft. Today's turbocharged engines for general aviation hardly ever have an additional mechanically driven supercharger. Almost always, the basic engine is unsupercharged and the turbo is an optional addition. But there are still several interesting forms of supercharging which can be briefly mentioned here, though they are discussed in more detail in later chapters. There have always been clear limits on impeller tip speed, though over the years these limits have been progressively raised, so the only way to achieve greater compression of the induction air has been to use a forward-facing ram intake feeding two impellers in series. Sometimes the engine installation featured two superchargers, one external and the second internal: for example, the wartime American P-38 and P-47 fighters had turbosuperchargers from 3 m (10 ft) to 6 m (20 ft) behind the engine, the compressed air then being piped to an internal supercharger driven off the crankshaft. In an alternative scheme the engine's internal supercharger was given two stages, the first physically larger than the second, both turning on the same shaft (see Twin Wasp supercharger, next chapter). In either scheme an intercooler, cooled by air or liquid, was needed to reduce the temperature of the air before it reached the engine. It may seem foolish deliberately to reject energy (heat) to the atmosphere, but hot air has lower density, and engine power is directly related to the flow of air through the engine measured not by volume but by mass. Strictly, most of the intercoolers were really aftercoolers, because they were downstream of both compression stages. Aftercooling achieves the greatest reduction in inlet manifold temperature, whereas intercooling (between stages) reduces the power needed to drive the superchargers.

Obviously, as in everything in engineering, the design of the engine inlet system is a compromise between conflicting factors. Today almost all piston-engined aircraft stay mostly below 3,048 m (10,000 ft), and are normally aspirated (ie they have no supercharger). Fitting superchargers driven by the crankshaft or the exhaust gas gives greater altitude performance, but makes the engine installation bulkier, heavier and more costly, both to buy and to operate. But in days gone by, the wartime demand to fly higher than the competition resulted in some aircraft in which a complete separate engine was carried merely to drive a high-capacity supercharger! During the First World War many types of German heavy bomber were fitted with extra engines purely to drive superchargers feeding air to the main engines. This seems an odd idea, but it was resurrected in German aircraft of the Second World War and is described in Chapter 7. One can argue inconclusively about whether or not this is a good idea. Of course, it would be pointless unless the objective was to increase ceiling at the expense of everything else.

Having got the engine running, we have to connect it to the propeller. In most of today's engines the connection could hardly be simpler. The front of the crankshaft is simply extended forwards and fitted to receive the

The unusual installation of the Allison engine in the P-38 Lightning: (A) oil cooler inlets; (B) intercooler inlet; (C) main radiator; (D) engine air inlet (via turbosupercharger E); (F) turbo cooling inlets; (G) cockpit heater inlet; (H) cooling and ventilating inlet.

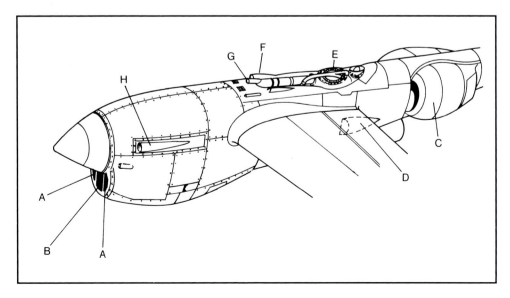

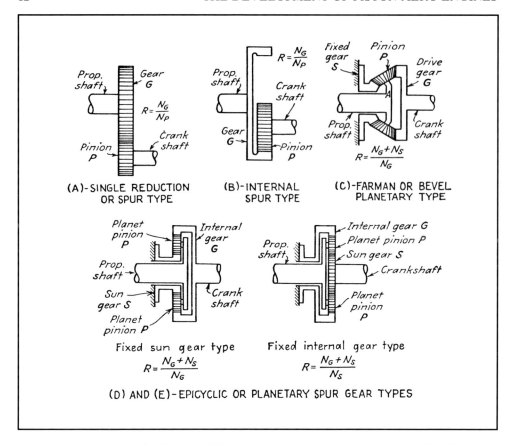

The five chief types of reduction gear. The commonest are simple spur gears and the Farman or bevel type (McGraw-Hill).

hub of the propeller. This is called a direct drive. The crankshaft will already be precisely located in the engine by the main bearings, but these are not designed to carry large end-loads such as the thrust of a propeller. In aircraft with braking propellers, able to be set in reverse pitch, the thrust on the shaft can be in either direction. The answer is to add a thrust bearing, usually close to the propeller. This is almost always a quite large ball bearing, transmitting the thrust from a raised land or flange on the propeller shaft straight to the front of the crankcase.

There is absolutely no reason why the ideal engine speed should also be the ideal propeller speed. In fact, where turboprops are concerned, the ideal engine speed is likely to be from 10 to 30 times as fast as that of the propeller. The remarkable thing is that so many piston engines, especially today, get away with a direct drive. Of course, one could make

a propeller turn at any speed, but we are interested in obtaining useful thrust with high efficiency. We can perhaps obtain this with quite a small propeller with many blades, turning at high rpm (say, 2,500), but we would probably get the same thrust with much higher efficiency, and with far less noise, from a propeller with half as many blades, turning at half the speed, but with 50 per cent greater diameter. Note that 50 per cent greater diameter means 2.25 times the disc area, and thrust is proportional not to diameter but to disc area.

Back in 1903 the Wrights recognized the need to match the speeds of their engine and propellers. For the next 10 years few people bothered, and tens of thousands of propellers worked quite well at the same speed (about 1,200–1,500 rpm) as the engines. Even the very largest and most powerful engines, such as the Fiat A.14 and Wright T-4, managed with direct drive, because the propeller could be given four blades instead of two, and increased in diameter without running into problems of excessive speed at the tips. The need to keep tip speed well below the speed of sound is fully explained in another PSL book, *Faster than Sound*. It was during the 1920s that the general progress of engine design raised crankshaft speeds to the 2,000–2,500 rpm level, enabling any given size of engine to give much greater power. In turn, the greater power tended to call for a bigger propeller, and faster engines and bigger propellers demanded a reduction gearbox. Once test pilots were given geared engines they went into ecstasies. One US Army pilot reached 300 m (1,000 ft) before another pilot in an identical aircraft, but with a direct-drive engine, had left the ground.

A sketch shows five common forms of geared drive. At first glance it might be thought that almost all geared engines would use plain spur gears. The drawbacks of this type of gear are that it imposes high stresses on the crankcase, and also on the gears themselves because all the power is transmitted through one tooth contact. It also offsets the propeller above or below the crankshaft, and this can be an advantage or a disadvantage in such matters as total installed drag, propeller ground clearance, pilot view and the ability to fit a gun to fire through the propeller hub. An offset propeller can prevent uniform cooling of a radial engine, though such engines have been built in some numbers (for example, the British Pobjoys). The more complex gearboxes all have various advantages, for example in reducing crankcase stress and in splitting the drive along a number of intermediate pinions. Belts, especially toothed ones, have come into fashion since 1960. For powers below 500 hp, and especially for modern microlight engines, the broad toothed belt or multiple V-belt drive is today becoming more common than a geared drive (Chapter 8).

Some designers of early engines hit on the seemingly neat idea of driving the propeller not off the crankshaft but off the camshaft, which in most four-stroke engines rotates just half as fast. Of course, the camshaft had to be strengthened and provided with thrust bearings. It also had to be fitted to accept the hub of the propeller. In early engines the propeller was usually carved from laminates of wood. The hub was drilled down the centre and then drilled to accept a ring of bolts which clamped

circular steel plates or flanges at front and rear. The rear plate was welded to a central tube which was keyed or splined to the propeller shaft on the engine. This assembly helped to hold the highly stressed laminations together, as well as transmitting the drive. Similar arrangements, often with a light spinner to reduce drag, are seen on microlights and lightplanes to this day. With metal propellers the hub could be splined direct to the engine propeller shaft. Much effort was expended in devising standard shafts, so that every suitable propeller could be made to fit. Alternatively the propeller is sometimes simply attached by a ring of bolts to the front face of a driving flange on the engine. Sometimes this flange has numerous radial splines, or teeth, which mate with the back of the propeller to transmit the torque. With controllable-pitch propellers the hollow shaft usually carries oil pipelines, electric cables or a mechanical linkage.

Getting rid of the exhaust has occasionally

Hispano-Suiza pioneered the moteur canon *in which a large gun fired through the hub of the propeller of a geared V-type engine. In the Second World War the idea was used chiefly in the Soviet Union.*

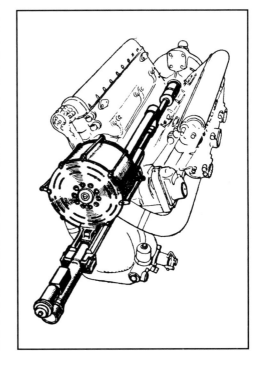

posed problems. Wherever possible, early designers merely let the hot gas pass direct from the cylinder to atmosphere. This is deafeningly noisy and can pose a fire hazard, and it was not long before some kind of exhaust pipe was thought a good idea. Of course, the exhaust could be piped away only in static engines, which until after 1920 were almost exclusively of the in-line or V type. The pipe might go straight to the rear or almost straight upwards, the stack often ending 6 ft above the cylinders in order to direct the hot gas above the upper wing (photo page 146). Engines of X or W (broad-arrow) form sometimes posed difficult problems, and even the simple Merlin in one installation (Mosquito) caused a little difficulty (Chapter 7). Radials usually had mere short stubs, but once various kinds of surrounding cowling were added these had to be extended. The commonest answer was to join the stubs into a ring discharging in one or possibly two pipes underneath (Gladiator). In 1932 Bristol began to introduce exhaust collector manifolds forming the leading edge of the cowling. These could be seen to be of a different material (nickel-plated stainless iron) from the aluminium cowling. With a nine-cylinder engine, 18 short pipes fed the

The hub for a large propeller of the type used in 1914–30. The propeller, made of multiple wood laminations, was drilled to accept the ring of drive bolts which also clamped it between the large discs.

gas to the ring, from which a single pipe (in a few cases, two) took it away past the outside of the cowl. In 1936 it was realized that this ring was heating the air passing through the cowling to cool the engine, and an aluminium shroud was added, the air being drawn through by suction round the leading edge.

BMW used this leading-edge suction to draw air through the oil cooler which, together with the oil tank, formed the armoured leading edge of the installed BMW 801. This outstanding engine, however, grouped its exhaust into 14 separate stacks discharging at the rear. Whereas in the 1930s almost every manufacturer in the world, other than Bristol, installed radial engines with a collector ring behind the engine, discharging through a single short pipe directed downwards or sideways, by 1945 it had been realized that the exhausts could assist flow through the cowling and add to propulsive thrust. Thus in the Hawker Fury (page 31) Bristol dropped the front manifold and instead led the gas to 18 pipes discharging to the rear from a recessed slit in each side of the rear of the cowling. About a year later, in 1946, Convair designed the Models 110 and 240 transports, the first of the Convair-Liners, with the exhaust from each Double Wasp engine piped aft to a venturi constriction where the high-velocity gas drew in almost double the airflow through the cowling that could be achieved otherwise. The air/gas mix, in the ratio of about 5:1, finally left through twin nozzles behind the trailing edge which gave forward thrust.

In 1934 several companies had begun to experiment with the exhaust from in-line and, particularly, V engines, to see whether useful thrust could be gained. By 1937 Rolls-Royce had succeeded in developing so-called ejector exhausts which at full throttle added about 150 hp to the available propulsive power. Each took the exhaust from two cylinders and directed it back in a pipe of C-section, like a fishtail bent around a tube. Reluctance to lose this thrust was one reason why Rolls-Royce never fitted a turbo to the Merlin. Later marks of this engine had a different exhaust system, with a separate short expanding pipe from each cylinder. A restored Hurricane with such pipes looks—and is—quite wrong.

Aircraft intended to fly military missions at night required exhaust flame dampers. With V-type engines the simplest answer was to add a surrounding shroud to screen the exhaust stubs. These were prominent on many

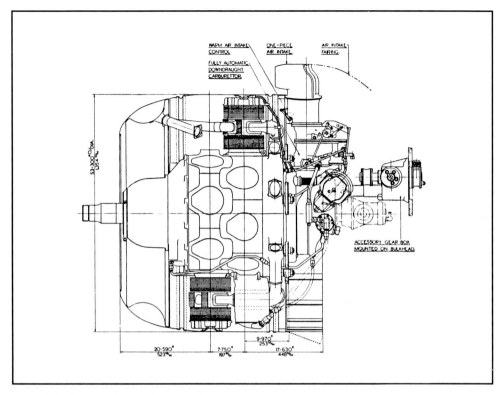

One of the first installation diagrams for the Bristol Hercules sleeve-valve radial in 1938. An inlet above the cowling admitted ram air to the downdraught carburettor. The cowling fitted tightly around the whole engine, curving inwards at the front to give 'forwards lift', the cooling air being controlled by gills at the rear. Mixture was fed from behind, exhaust being piped to a collector ring inside the front of the cowling. Note: many cylinders are omitted for clarity (Bristol).

Mosquitoes and Lancasters, while on Bf 110G night fighters the shroud became a heavy high-drag assembly with two widely spaced inlets, each of 300 mm (1 ft) diameter, to feed cooling air into a giant pipe leading back over the wing! British bombers and night fighters powered by the Hercules radial had a single long pipe with a closed end, the gas escaping through rows of (typically a total of 36) small aft-facing exits. BMW's answer on the 801 engine, for example, as fitted to many Do 217s, was to end each of the 14 exhaust pipes in a stack of five closely spaced flat fishtails. As noted earlier, aircraft fitted with turbo-superchargers almost never emitted visible flames.

Early aero engines were started by simply 'swinging the propeller'. This was hard work, and potentially dangerous, especially as with a tractor installation the person turning the propeller had to stand immediately in front of it.

As aircraft became more sophisticated they incorporated cockpit handpumps with which the pilot could prime the engine with a spray of neat fuel. The number of strokes of this pump depended on whether the engine was cold or had recently been run, on the ambient temperature, and possibly on other factors. While the engine was being primed, ground crew would pull the propeller through several blades—say, at least one revolution—to shear through the oil films, which in winter could be viscous and offer high drag, and to ensure that the danger of hydraulicing could not occur. Also known as hydraulic shock, this problem could be met with radial or inverted engines, in which oil or fuel might drain down into one or more cylinders and, being incompressible, either stop the engine from turning or force off a cylinder head. The cure was to remove a plug from the suspected cylinder(s) and let the liquid drain away.

Such aircraft as the Lancaster II or, seen here, Messerschmitt Bf 110G night fighter accepted a substantial reduction in performance in order to avoid showing exhaust flames or hot metal at night. The author calculated this Bf 110G-4/R-1 would have been nearly 64 km/h (40 mph) faster at 6,096 m (20,000 ft) with simple ejector exhausts.

When all was ready the pilot would check that his ignition switch(es) was in the *off* position, and call to his helper 'Switches off'. In fact, in many ignition systems, the *off* position meant that the switch was closed, but we need not go into that. The pilot would then call 'Petrol on, throttle closed'. If the aircraft had brakes, which was very rare until the 1930s, he would also tell the helper that these were on. The helper would then pull through one or two blades, whereupon the pilot would flick the ignition switches and call 'Switches on, contact!'—or the equivalent in his own language. The engine might fire, but usually the helper would need to pull through one or two more blades. As soon as the engine fired he would stand clear.

By the First World War engines were getting bigger, and compression ratios were rising, until swinging propellers was very difficult indeed. It was not uncommon to see three men gripping each other's wrists all adding their pull to the unfortunate mechanic pulling the propeller. So B. C. Hucks devised a self-contained mobile starting system. This was based on a car, or car chassis, the Ford T being the most common. On to this was built a pair of A frames carrying a shaft at about the height of a typical propeller hub. The rear of the shaft carried a large pulley driven by a belt from the vehicle's engine, when the drive was engaged by the driver. The front of the shaft

could be adjusted up or down to enable driving dogs to engage with corresponding sockets on the front of the propeller. Of course, the inclination of the shaft seldom matched that of the (tail-down) aircraft, but with such a crude drive system this did not matter. Hucks starters were used worldwide from before the First World War until 1935, and in some countries, including the Soviet Union, into the 1940s.

This method could not be used with large aircraft. Some of these were laboriously started by ropes thrown over the propeller blades, and the problems may be imagined. With engines which were both large and geared, such as the Rolls-Royce Eagle, the torque needed at the propeller was well beyond anything readily applied by mechanics, so hand turning gear was added. By this time special booster magnetos were also in use, and starting a Handley Page bomber in 1918 involved careful co-operation between the pilot, working the primer, throttle, hand-drive starting magneto and hand-turning engagement clutch, and the mechanic(s) who laboriously turned the engine by means of large handles.

Some of the biggest bombers and flying boats had engines more than 6 m (20 ft) above the ground or water. Several people invented improved ways of starting, the most significant being that of Major Norman at the RAE at Farnborough. He devised a practical gas system, energized by a small trolley-mounted flat-twin engine. One cylinder provided power, while the other pumped a fuel-rich mixture to the engine to be started. The mixture was supplied to each cylinder in turn, at a pressure high enough to make the engine rotate. The ignition was then switched on, firing the rich mixture and starting the engine. One drawback was that the aircraft had to be equipped with small-diameter piping leading from the ground socket to each cylinder of each engine, and with a selector cock feeding each engine in turn of a multi-engine aircraft. Another drawback was that each pipe terminated at a non-return valve which projected into the cylinder combustion space, and this uncooled projecting valve promoted the onset of detonation when the engine was running.

In 1920 Roy Fedden, lately of Cosmos and by now of Bristol, designed a gas starting system which eliminated almost all the RAE method's faults. In early 1922 he was able to install such a system in a Handley Page transport fitted with Jupiter engines (Chapter 6),

A Hucks starter is offered up to the AS Lynx of an Avro 504N of Cambridge UAS in 1932.

and over the next decade it became a widely used system with many foreign licensed versions or copies. But by the 1930s aircraft were beginning to be equipped with auxiliary power systems, especially electric. Previously the only electric systems had been to supply radio and navigation lights, the total power of perhaps 200 W being provided by a lead/acid battery charged by a small windmill generator. After 1930 the main engines began to be equipped to drive a generator, enabling the available power to reach 1 kW or more. This was enough to drive flaps, retractable landing gear and many other services, including an electric starter on each engine.

The electric starter swept away all the previous problems, but it still presented the designer with choices. For one thing, a clutch had to be interposed between the starter and the engine which could connect the two together only when needed. This clutch system had to be unidirectional, so that when the engine fired it did not violently try to drive the starter. To convert the high speed of the motor into the high torque needed to turn the engine a reduction gear was needed. The drive gears also had to incorporate an input from hand-turning gear, rotated by a hand crank inserted through a hole in the cowling (sometimes one crank on each side of the engine), to start the engine in emergencies, or when batteries were flat, or to unstick viscous oil films in Arctic conditions.

Such an electric starter is called direct-cranking, and it is the most common type in general aviation today. An alternative form is the inertia starter. Here, hand cranks or a relatively small electric motor are used to speed up a heavy flywheel. Perhaps 1,000

times the author listened to the rising whine of the flywheel of a Harvard's Wasp engine, as he held down the heel end of a foot rocking lever (treadle). At full rpm, which might take 10 seconds to achieve, he would press down the toe end of the pedal, switching off the current but engaging the flywheel with the crankshaft. A spring clutch took up the shock, and the Wasp would be running in two or three seconds. Hand-cranking a flywheel was hard work, because the crank(s) drove via step-up gears to accelerate the flywheel to some 12,000 rpm.

In 1936 a totally new kind of starter came into use on Jumo 205 diesels, followed later by high-power engines for naval aircraft, and quickly spreading into land-based air forces. This was the cartridge or combustion starter. The energy in such a starter is supplied by the extremely rapid combustion of solid-fuel grains in what looks like a giant shotgun cartridge. This is loaded into a breech—which, to save time in hectic action, can sometimes take up to five cartridges—which is connected by a pipe to the starter mounted on the engine. When the pilot presses the starter button, the cartridge is fired, immediately feeding gas along the pipe under a pressure of at least 2,000 lb/sq in. This enters the starter unit, driving a piston down a cylinder against a spring. The piston drives a ball-screwjack, which, by means of opposite-rotation threads linked by anti-friction ball-bearings, converts the piston's linear movement into rotation. This rotation is imparted to the engine via a multi-tooth dog connection. The power transmitted is so great that, even though the output may be less than one complete rotation, the engine's own inertia will keep it rotating through several further turns of the crankshaft, during which it will fire and start running. A cartridge starter is self-contained, and thus useful at forward airstrips where there is no electric power, or on a crowded carrier deck. It is lighter than the massive electric starter that would otherwise be needed for high-power engines, but the engine has to be specially strengthened to accept the enormous input torque. The cartridges were too expensive to appeal to civil operators.

Cartridge starters use brute force to overcome the high torque needed to spin the crankshaft of a high-compression engine

whose oil may be at sub-zero temperature. Early engines used vegetable oils exclusively, castor oil being by far the most popular. This is an excellent lubricant, but between the wars it was progressively replaced by mineral oils derived from petroleum. The latter could be made available in much greater quantities, and to precise specifications. Another advantage was that mineral oils have a shelf life measured in years, whereas the vegetable oils deteriorate. With mineral oils different grades could be provided for summer and winter, but starting in sub-zero temperatures still posed problems. To this day, it is largely because of the lubricating oil that piston engines are

Bristol was one of the pioneers of the gas starter, which was especially useful on very large aircraft whose propellers could not easily be turned from the ground. High-pressure air fed through a fuel atomiser supplied a rich mixture to each cylinder in the correct firing sequence, at a pressure high enough to rotate the engine. Meanwhile the pilot twirled the handle of a starter magneto to fire each charge (Odhams Press).

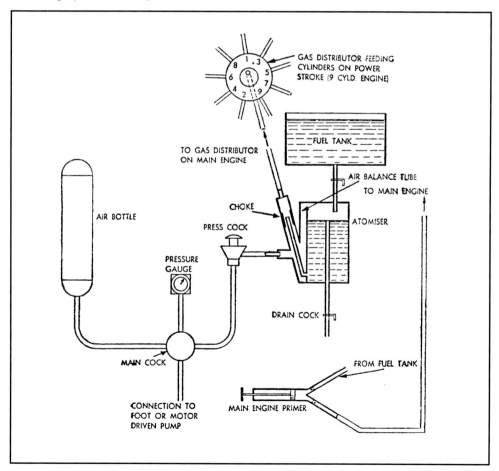

warmed up between starting and take-off. Clearly this was an undesirable handicap for defending fighters faced with incoming enemies, and various schemes were adopted to enable fighters to 'scramble' immediately. Bristol's HIOP (high initial oil pressure) was mentioned earlier. Some engines were equipped to recirculate hot oil even when the aircraft was parked. Another scheme was oil dilution by the fuel. About four minutes

before shutting down the engine after a sortie the pilot would switch on the dilution system, allowing petrol to flow through a metering jet into the oil feed to the engine. The proportion might be 15 per cent, any excess quickly evaporating. The resulting thinned oil facilitated starting and distribution of the lubricant throughout the engines, even after standing several days in Arctic conditions. The pilot could take off the moment he

In 1918 few engines drove anything except the propeller, a fuel or oil pump and the tachometer. How things had changed by 1938 is shown by this view of the accessories on the back of a Bristol Pegasus XVIII (engine itself not shown): (1) HP fuel pump; (2) spare drive; (3) constant-speed propeller governor; (4) LP air compressor; (5) electric generator; (6) electric/hand starter; (7) starter handle connection; (8) dual fuel pump; (9) HP air compressor; (10) tachometer; (11) oil feed; (12) oil feed filter; (13) oil pressure connection; (14) mag/carb interconnect; (15) bypass to oil tank; (16) HIOP (high initial oil pressure) to crankcase; (17) engine oil pump; (18) double contact-breaker magneto (each side). Most would also have driven a hydraulic pump (Bristol).

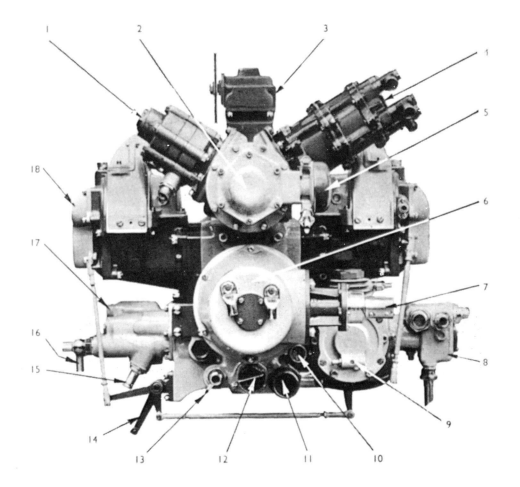

obtained a normal oil-pressure reading.

It will by now be obvious that, even in the first 40 years of aeroplane flight, piston engines became quite complex. I am sure many readers, who would regard a Seafire 47 or P-47D as brutishly simple compared with modern aircraft, were surprised at the comment that their fuel systems contained 'some 300 components'. In this count I regard a tank booster pump, for example, as one component, even though it may have 80 or more parts. So installing the engine in the airframe became a major design problem. It was necessary to take into account the thrust axis of the propeller, the forces (thrust, torque, weight and vibration) imparted to the airframe, the need for accessibility and easy removal, the total installed drag, and the multitude of connections needed with the fuel and oil systems, possibly with water or some other boosting liquid, with radiators and oil coolers, with doping and priming systems, with anything up to a dozen cockpit controls (some of them critically adjusted to perhaps one-hundredth of an inch without backlash) and with all the aircraft accessory systems.

Early engines drove nothing but the propeller and items confined to the engine itself, such as magnetos and pumps for fuel, oil and water. By the 1930s engines were driving electric generators, hydraulic pumps (for flaps, landing gear and gun turrets, for example), vacuum pumps (for blind-flying instruments), air compressor (for various services including brakes), propeller CSU (constant-speed unit), tachometer (transmitting rpm to the cockpit) and, in agricultural aircraft, an additional mechanical or hydraulic drive to a remote pump for spraying or driving a dusting system. In aerobatic aircraft the entire installation, including all tankage, must be designed for sustained operation under negative g.

One has only to look at photographs of early aircraft to appreciate that aerodynamic drag played a minor role in the design of the engine installation. This is discussed in the next chapter, where the point is also made that early multi-engined aircraft tended to use their engines in tandem push/pull pairs. By 1920 many engines were being installed on the nose of a large fuselage. Such engines were often completely out in the open, and in others were buried inside the airframe. In either case the useful thrust was appreciably reduced by the drag of the fuselage immediately behind the propeller. In a few cases the engine and its mounting structure was hinged

to the fuselage so that, for maintenance access, the whole installation could be swung open like a gate. This was particularly the case with radial engines.

Such engines tended to have higher installed drag than water-cooled types, especially after the Curtiss D-12 had shown how streamlined a water-cooled engine could be made to look. In 1926 H. C. H. Townend, a British aerodynamicist, perfected a ring cowling which became public knowledge in 1929 as the Townend Ring. It was basically a narrow-chord wing wrapped in a circle around a radial engine, improving the uniformity of cooling and, by generating a lift force in the forward direction, reducing drag by an average of 11 per cent. At the same time the US National Advisory Committee for Aeronautics (NACA) was carrying out its first tests with the newly built Propeller Research Tunnel, and a systematic programme for reducing the drag of air-cooled radials led to the design of a cowling rather more advanced than Townend's, in that it began as a curved lifting (ie, forward-pulling) section but continued as a tight drum surrounding the engine and extending back to meet the fuselage or nacelle, leaving a narrow peripheral gap for the escape of the cooling air. The NACA cowling was first fitted to the Wright R-790 engine of a Curtiss AT-5A. It immediately increased speed from 118 to 137 mph. Without the cowling this would have required the engine power to be increased from 220 to 303 hp, with a corresponding increase in fuel consumption.

The news spread like wildfire, and by 1933 radial cowlings were being fitted with pilot-controlled gills to control the flow of cooling air for maintenance of the correct cylinder-head temperature with minimum drag. The NACA was surprised to find that cowling the wing engines of a Fokker F.VII/3m reduced drag only very slightly. Further tunnel research showed that the wing engines were in the position of maximum drag, several feet below the wing. The NACA noted, 'The standard design of the period was to support the engines above or below the wing on a strutted structure whose dimensions were determined by eye, rather than by any aerodynamic considerations.' It was found that if the engine was moved up so that it could be faired into the leading edge of the wing, then drag would be approximately halved.

Thus, during the 1930s, ignorant aircraft design was progressively replaced by design

This Curtiss AT-5A, a trainer member of the P-1 Hawk family, was the first aircraft to fly with the NACA cowling, later to become universal. The NACA report for 1928 said the cowling had the same effect as increasing the power of the Wright R-790–1 engine from 220 to 303 hp!

based on quantitative knowledge, for example of drag. Tandem push/pull nacelles disappeared, to be replaced by engines faired into the leading edge. Occasionally drag came out below prediction, notably in the Lancaster where the engines (unlike those of the early versions of Halifax) were in exceptionally clean cowlings mounted so low that the top of the cowling was aligned with the leading edge. Less obvious was the enormous amount of research that went into reducing the weight and drag of a Merlin cooling system by over 50 per cent between 1935 and 1940. In the Mosquito the same engine was cooled by radiators of a wide but shallow form fitted into the leading edge of the wing. This gave extremely low drag. In the Mustang the Allison and later the Packard-built Merlin were cooled by different forms of radiator installed in a duct inside the rear fuselage. This duct was profiled to act as a diffuser, with a ram inlet, a divergent entry, a large radiator causing low pressure-drop, and a convergent aft section with a controllable flap. Drag of this installation was always extremely low, and in some conditions the later installations, such as that of the P-51H, could give forward thrust.

Thus, by 1935 the installations of both air-cooled and liquid-cooled engines had been transformed. The incentive to achieve better installations came from the revolution in airframe structures, which replaced high-drag strutted biplanes by all-metal cantilever monoplanes. This removed the previous limitation on speed and greatly emphasized the need for low-drag powerplants. Some of the most ambitious installations would have buried the engines in the wing, with cooling airflow rammed in through inlets in the leading edge. Few of these were built, examples including the Convair B-36 (with pusher engines) and Bristol Brabazon (with coupled pairs of engines driving the separate halves of coaxial tractor propellers). De Havilland sought minimum drag in the D.H.91 Albatross by installing air-cooled engines in cowlings through which air was ducted from ram inlets in the leading edge, passing inwards past the cylinders to escape underneath. In the Soviet Union Petlyakov designed the Pe-8 (ANT-42) heavy bomber with very deep inboard nacelles housing the coolant radiators for both the inboard and outboard engines, but this accomplished little except to add to the plumbing.

The harsh conditions of the Soviet Union remind one that the installation must also guard against the possibility of icing or of ingesting sand, dirt or other foreign matter. Obviously, most kinds of filter would obstruct the inlet airflow and reduce performance. Almost all solid particles that could cause damage can be removed by making the air flow round a sharp bend. The air sweeps round the bend while the solid material tends to carry on under its own momentum in an almost straight line, enabling it to be extracted. Alternatively, large filter panels causing little pressure drop can be used, either hinged or with doors in the inlet so that the air is filtered only when necessary. Icing is normally prevented by circulating hot engine oil around the carburettor or by adding hot air from a muff around the exhaust pipes, again with a valve so that this is done only when icing threatens. A diagram shows a typical wartime Pratt & Whitney downdraught inlet, as fitted to R-2800 engines of the Martin B-26 Marauder.

When the RAF and Luftwaffe were being rapidly expanded in the late 1930s, both their supporting industries hit on the idea of equipping engines of different types as completely dressed and cowled 'power eggs' with standardized accessories, controls, pipe connections and airframe pick-up points. In Britain one of the first was the Merlin XX powerplant developed jointly by Rolls-Royce and Morris Motors, the latter having carried out a large amount of the work on improved cooling systems. Thanks to this self-contained power package, Avro were able to produce the Lancaster, because neither they nor Rolls-Royce had spare manpower to design a new Merlin installation. As it had been designed to fit the Hercules nacelle in the Beaufighter,

Avro returned the compliment and bolted Hercules engines on to 300 Lancasters. In the same way several German aircraft, such as the Do 217 and Ju 88, came off the production line with either air-cooled radials or liquid-cooled engines. In the case of the Ju 88 the coolant radiators were of an annular shape fitted around the front of a circular cowling, making the liquid-cooled engines look like radials anyway!

For 80 years virtually all installations have placed the engine ahead of a fire-resistant firewall. This is usually thin sheet steel, but an alternative was asbestos sandwiched between sheets of aluminium. All pipes and cables passing through the firewall were themselves protected, and fuel and oil lines could be shut off on the side remote from the engine. Inside the cowling the engine's likely fire sources could be sprayed from extinguisher bottles, commonly filled with methyl bromide (CH_3Br), triggered by an overheat sensor, or by a crash switch (inertia or deformation) or by a protected red button in the cockpit, often next to the feathering buttons.

Ahead of the firewall the engine is enclosed in hinged or quickly removable cowling panels, secured by patented fasteners. The engine may be carried by a structure welded from steel tubes, and this almost always incorporates anti-vibration links which are usually of rubber or similar flexible material. Sometimes the vibration-damping mounts are between the airframe and the engine mount-

Front-line aircraft have to be able to operate in harsh environments. In the USAAF attack bombers, provision had to be made to counter sand or dirt ingestion or icing of the inlet duct. The R-2800 engine often had the duct inside the cowling, as here (Pratt & Whitney).

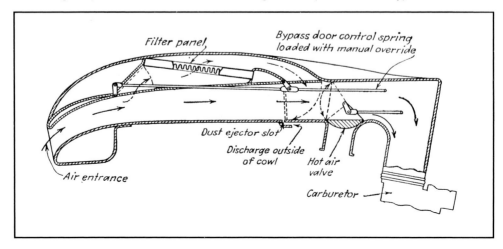

Rolls-Royce and Morris Motors, working day and night, developed a standard package for the Merlin engine which incorporated a brilliantly compact and light radiator. It enabled the Merlin to be quickly fitted to the Beaufighter II, as seen here with suppressed exhausts for night fighting, and later made possible the Lancaster.

The Germans were also good at standardization. The installation of the Jumo 211 inverted-V liquid-cooled engine in the Ju 88 featured a circular cowling with a circular radiator on the front, the top segment being the oil cooler. While such an installation was easily bolted on to different types of aircraft, the Ju 88 was later easily converted to BMW 801 radial engines.

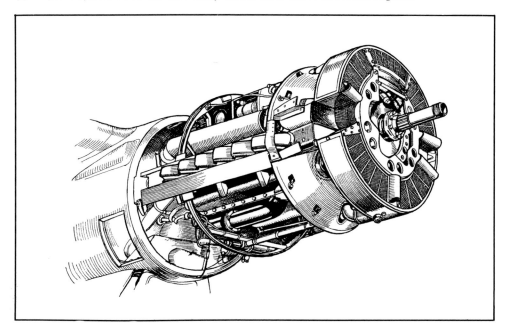

ing structure, but they are usually between the mounting structure and the engine. The complete mounting system has to be designed as an integrated whole, to accept all the loads from the engine and propeller and to permit limited movements, some linear and others of an angular nature, by correctly arranging the location and axis of each vibration damper. Some installations carry the engine in a stressed-skin extension of the airframe, while others use a pair of large forgings in a low-density alloy such as Elektron magnesium alloy, an example being the DB 601.

After 1945 even the largest engines became enclosed in so-called petal cowlings. Instead of being composed of several removable panels, these cowlings were designed to be hinged open in such a way as to expose the engine completely. Typically the cowling would be made in left and right halves which were themselves arranged to hinge open into upper and lower portions, while remaining attached to the airframe. Once open, the large petals had to be braced against wind loads by locking them open with stays. This gave perfect all-round access for maintenance. In some helicopters the engine was mounted at an angle in the extreme nose, near ground level, and again fully exposed by opening left and right doors, which formed the nose of the helicopter. Of course, all such large cowling panels have to be securely locked closed by various kinds of patented latch.

Today's lightplanes usually have an engine installation designed with computer help to combine the best features of strength, light weight, accessibility and low drag. In most cases the cowling is of glass fibre reinforced plastic material, even if the rest of the airframe is metal, because this is easy to mould in complex shapes and is relatively cheap. It is no worse than thin aluminium in resisting bird strikes, and perhaps the only significant disadvantage is that the relatively soft material can be badly eroded by hail. A particular feature of modern installations (except in agricultural aircraft) is their beautiful aerodynamic design, the cowling enclosing the engine completely, with no unsightly joints or gaps and, often, a complete absence of auxiliary inlets.

SECTION II
HOW ENGINES DEVELOPED

5 The dawn of powered flight

When the first aviators sought engines with which to power their flying machines they did so in a world of rapid and exciting progress. Within the previous 20 years, say from 1885 to 1905, a whole range of new inventions had become, if not commonplace, at least firmly established. Among them were the motor car, motor cycle and tricycle, speedboat, hydroplane, steam-turbine ship and airship. All needed an engine giving more power, in relation to weight and bulk, than anything seen previously.

This book is primarily concerned with aeroplanes, but I cannot ignore airships. Their original name was dirigible, the French word meaning steerable (which a balloon is not). The very first manned powered flight took place on 24 September 1852 when Henri Giffard's airship rose from the Paris Hippodrome (racecourse). Giffard's single-cylinder steam engine drove a propeller measuring 3.4 m (11 ft) at about 150 rpm. It was said to give 3 hp and to weigh 160 kg (352 lb). Perhaps wisely, it was slung about 12 m (40 ft) below the envelope to avoid igniting the hydrogen with sparks. On this first flight Giffard landed safely at Trappes, 27 km (17 miles) to the west, but his craft was so slow that the slightest breeze would have removed the 'dirigibility'. Giffard tried unsuccessfully to find an engine that was light enough yet more powerful. Later he wished to build a huge airship with a steam plant weighing 30 tonnes!

Though little known in other countries, several interesting airships were built in Czarist Russia. One of the most impressive was O. S. Kostovich's *Rossiya* of 1887, which had the first petrol engine ever to fly. A remarkable spark-ignition four-stroke, it weighed 240 kg (529 lb) complete, and was reputed to develop 80 hp. It had eight large, water-cooled cylinders arranged in opposed pairs which fired together to preserve balance. The connecting rods drove the overhead crankshaft via large rocking levers like a James Watt beam engine! Chains drove an intermediate shaft and the valve camshaft. Just 10 years later Gabriel-Iona, a Frenchman, designed a three-cylinder compound steam engine for the airship *Lebed*. The boiler burned kerosene, and the basic engine weighed 450 kg (992 lb) and was said to give 52 hp. On one end of the crankshaft was a large pulley which via a very

Strange in appearance, in fact the engine of Kostovich's airship was a remarkable achievement for 1887. It was probably the world's first petrol engine to have eight cylinders (N. A. Eastaway).

Probably the second steam engine to fly was this three-cylinder compound engine made by Gabriel-Iona for a Russian airship (N. A. Eastaway).

long belt transmitted the drive to the airship's slow-turning propeller.

The aeroplane made even more severe demands on high power/weight ratio, and moreover demanded constant high power. All the other vehicles, including airships, could 'cruise' at quite a modest throttle setting, such as 50 per cent power (though nobody in those days actually measured it), whereas the primitive flying machines could only just get their wheels off the ground if the engine was at full power, and running well. If the pilot was heavier than normal or the engine misfiring only slightly, flight was often impossible. This demand for continuous maximum power was severe, but there were a few mitigating factors. Getting into the air was an end in itself, and until after 1908 the duration of the flight was of relatively minor importance. And the proud owner might be delighted to dismantle, inspect, oil and reassemble his engine after every flight.

I said at the start of this book that, for practical purposes, powered aviation began with the Wrights. But in the world of science and engineering nobody starts from a vacuum, or the proverbial clean sheet of paper. There is always someone who has done something like it previously. We know that in about the year AD 50 Hero of Alexandria drew plans of an engine driven by steam reaction jets, but I

have no doubt someone else had pre-dated him. Beside jet propulsion the piston engine seems a step backward, but it was probably the only practical engine in the nineteenth century.

It is easy to see the shortcomings and design faults of early engines, but we must never forget that since the dawn of time mankind has never been able to do better than 'the state of the art' allows. Each designer of an early engine knew only what had been done before; indeed, all too often he was ignorant of it. For example, one of the greatest pioneers, Lawrence Hargrave, toiled in Australia almost totally isolated from the designs and achievements of others. Despite this, in the 1880s he not only devised the double boxkite, which 20 years later was to show European aviators how to build a stable aeroplane, but he also designed, built and tested remarkable engines driven by long but light cylinders of compressed air. In his 1889 engine the air was cunningly fed in exact proportions to three cylinders spaced at 120°. These rotated around a fixed crank, and each cylinder was mounted on one blade of a three-blade propeller.

Hargrave recognized that, in the context of his times, all that was needed was power for a minute or so. Today that would be inadequate for Qantas flying non-stop from Australia to London, but the early aviators were not bothered about endurance or range. It is for this reason that we can see that so many of them decided on unnecessarily complicated and indeed clumsy powerplants. For example, in 1990 the whole of France celebrated the fabulous centenary of '*Le premier pilote du monde*' (the first pilot in the world). The organizing committee was virtually a *Who's Who* of every person in French public life. For a year the name of Clément Ader was made to ring round the world, because he was supposed to have flown his aeroplane *Eole* on 9 October 1890. What actually happened was that this contraption did get daylight under its wheels for what some observers considered to be a distance of 50 m (164 ft). Had he actually flown, he would have crashed, because *Eole* was totally deficient in means of control. Yet he fitted it with a furnace, boiler, steam engine and even a condenser so that the water could be recirculated! With hindsight, we can see that the effort expended on this propulsion installation should have been devoted to the problem of how to fly.

Other would-be aviators who used steam

engines included the Russian Aleksandr Mozhaiski and the American (later naturalized Englishman) Sir Hiram Maxim. Mozhaiski's monoplane had one tractor and two pusher propellers, and in 1884 is reputed to have made a brief hop down a ramp, its boiler pouring black smoke. Maxim's gigantic biplane had a boiler fuelled by naphtha which supplied steam at 320 lb/sq in (double the pressure of contemporary locomotive boilers) to amazing compound engines each of which weighed only 141 kg (310 lb) yet developed 180 hp. In 1894 this vast machine, with the wing area of a B-52, showed that it could lift off and fly; but it was restrained by a railed track. Had it been allowed to climb away I doubt that it could have been controlled, but with smoke and steam trailing behind it it would have been a memorable sight.

There were many other steam, hot-air and even petrol engines planned for aircraft prior to 1900. The only engines that really flew, however, were powered models, notably those of Tatin in 1879 and of Langley in 1896. Frenchman Victor Tatin's model had a modern configuration, with two propellers on the leading edge of a cantilever monoplane wing and a tail at the back. The fuselage was a cylinder of compressed air. American Samuel Pierpont Langley decided the best arrangement was to use tandem wings of almost equal size. His No.5 model was powered by a small steam engine driving twin pusher screws, and it made many good flights of almost a mile.

Langley would have left it at that, but in 1898 he was asked by the US government to build a full-size 'aerodrome' (as he called his models). He adhered to the same configuration, and asked Stephen M. Balzer to supply the engine. Balzer had built a pioneer rotary engine for a car of 1894. This engine was a spark-ignition four-stroke with three air-cooled cylinders. His derived aero engine weighed 49 kg (108 lb) and was said to give 12 hp, but it never proved reliable. Langley thereupon asked Charles M. Manly, his assistant and test pilot, to see if he could do better. The result was a truly remarkable engine, which appears to have worked reliably and whose ratio of power to weight was not surpassed for about another 10 years. Indeed, the so-called Manly-Balzer engine was a brilliant achievement, which unfortunately was installed in an unsuccessful flying machine.

It was properly called by the names of both engineers because a Balzer engine was used as the basis, but when Manly had finished it was

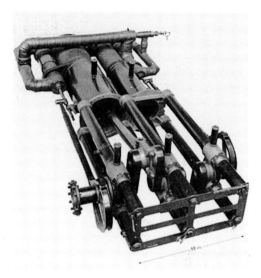

Maxim's gigantic biplane of 1894 was powered by two of these amazingly advanced steam engines, which (ignoring the boiler) had a weight/power ratio of only 0.78 kg (1.72 lb)/hp! Equally remarkably, nothing exploded.

something totally different, and also dramatically better than anything previously available. At first glance it looked like a five-spoked wheel, because of the peripheral fuel/air supply pipe. It was a static radial, with five water-cooled cylinders of 127 mm (5 in) bore and 140 mm (5.5 in) stroke, giving a swept volume of 8,850 cc (540 cu in). Every part was designed and made with the utmost care. Indeed, Manly had to do almost everything himself, the best machine shops asserting that his demands were impossible. Each cylinder was spun from flat steel plate 1/16 in (1.6 mm) thick, the main portion having to be precisely circular and straight yet integral with the domed head. Into this was inserted a cast-iron liner, machined to the same 1/16 in thickness and so accurately made that it was a shrink fit. Then Manly had to cut the inlet/exhaust port in the top of the cylinder, weld on the valve box to this port and also weld on the steel water jacket, with a thickness of 1/50 in (0.5 mm) around the top of the cylinder.

The light thin-walled cast-iron pistons rode on four rings and were of brilliant design. One drove a master rod while the four others drove slave rods with their big ends pinned to bronze slippers held against the master big end by coned rings screwed on at each end. Manly invented an efficient surface carburettor filled

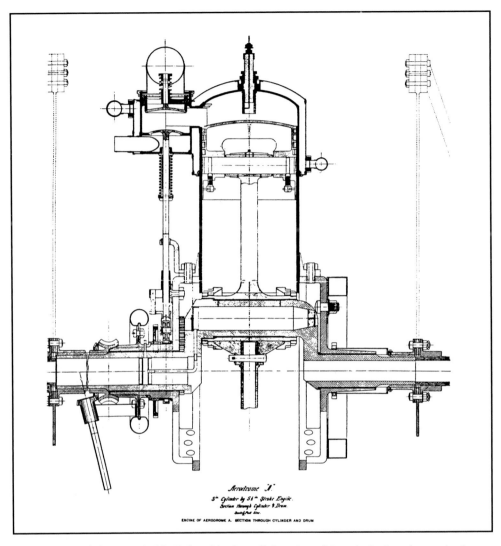

Cross-section of the remarkable Balzer-Manly radial engine of Langley's Aerodrome A, drawn through the top cylinder. This cylinder had the master big end, whose cap, along with the slippers of the four other rods, was held by the coned rings slipped over each end of the crankpin (Smithsonian).

with balls of porous wood which presented an evaporative surface of possibly hundreds of square feet to the high-velocity air flowing through the chamber and into the annular manifold. The inlet valves were simply spring-loaded, while the exhaust valves were driven by a cam drum just as in almost all subsequent radial aero engines. Manly was certainly one of the pioneers—if not the originator—of the modern ignition system with a high-tension coil and distributor feeding plugs which even

had platinum electrodes. Of course, Manly then had to create all the auxiliaries, such as the various pumps, do all the testing, design the installation and the drive to the two pusher propellers, and then fly the 'aerodrome'.

What Setright calls 'this jewel of an engine' made many runs of up to 10 hours' duration at full power, giving 52 hp at 950 rpm. Its weight is given as 56.7 kg (125 lb) in one source, 62 kg (137 lb) in another, 82 kg (180 lb) in another

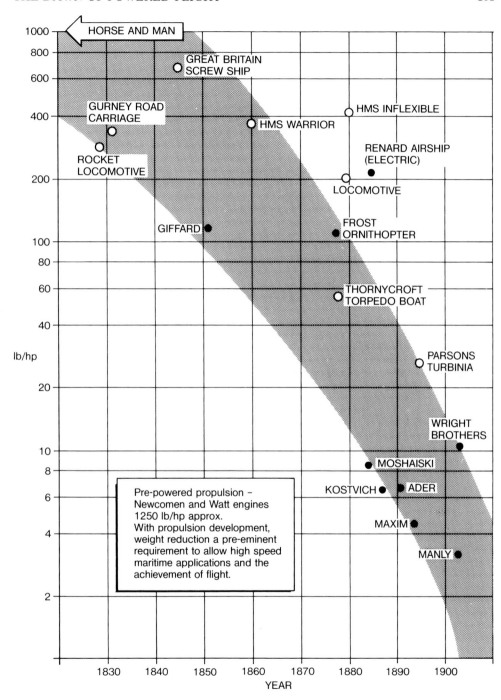

Generalized plot on a logarithmic vertical scale showing how during the nineteenth century man's engines were developed from almost nothing. The weight/power ratio in lb/hp is that for the whole power plant, which in the case of steam engines includes the boiler (but not fuel). Air vehicles are shown solid black.

and 94 kg (207.5 lb) (with cooling water) in another. There is no doubt that the bare engine really did weigh only 56.7 kg (125 lb), giving a power/weight ratio of 2.4 lb/hp. Similar ratios were common among aero engines, especially those of around 52 hp, from 1920 up to the present day. When one considers the extremely limited range of materials Manly had to work with, and the absence of anything resembling a modern high-precision machine shop, his achievement really looks almost superhuman. Sadly, he permanently damaged his eyesight brazing on the ports and water jackets, and then almost drowned on the second attempted flight of 'Aerodrome A' on 8 December 1903.

When that happened, the Wrights were about to test their own first powered Flyer. But before turning to them it is worth taking a further broad look at the overall scene. Langley was fortunate to have almost unlimited funds and a helper in a million. Most would-be aviators had to try to buy an existing engine, and those available were to various degrees unsuitable. We have seen how the first vehicles with IC engines were built in 1884–6 by Benz and Daimler. Their engines had very modest BMEP and a speed of around 600 rpm, and even by 1900 the resulting car engines seldom exceeded 750 rpm. As a result the engine power/weight ratio was so poor that these pioneer engines were useless for aviation. For example, in 1900 Austrian

Wilhelm Kress sought an engine for his giant seaplane, which had three monoplane wings in tandem. He needed 35 hp, and calculated he could lift a 240 kg (530 lb) engine. The lightest 35-hp engine Daimler could provide weighed 381 kg (840 lb). Kress's machine was wrecked when, making a sharp turn when taxiing, this ponderous engine tore loose.

Salvation lay in Count de Dion. Helped by the discovery that the Otto patents were not valid in France, he teamed up with Georges Bouton and in 1895 produced the first of a series of air-cooled engines running at 1,800 rpm. The high speed enabled them to set a completely new level of power/weight ratio, though some of the de Dion type engines were unimpressive. I am thinking especially of the first aero engine used by the little Brazilian, Alberto Santos-Dumont. He was one of the first customers for a de Dion Bouton tricycle, and for his first airship, in 1898, he used an odd de Dion engine with two cylinders in tandem. It was reckoned to give 3 hp, yet it weighed 36 kg (80 lb).

Early in this century airships were almost as important as aeroplanes. Because of their potentially much greater endurance, the airship was sometimes better off with a heavy engine if its fuel efficiency was better than that of a light one. In a paper by John Hempson (IMechE/Newcomen Soc) the following figures are given as an example:

Dirigible

	Air-cooled	Water-cooled
Engine	250 lb	600 lb
Fuel (20 hr at 50 per cent power)	1,100 lb	650 lb
Total weight	1,350 lb	1,250 lb

Aeroplane

	Air-cooled	Water-cooled
Engine	250 lb	600 lb
Fuel (4 hr at 80 per cent power)	304 lb	176 lb
Total weight	554 lb	776 lb

Thus, when one considers engine(s)-plus-fuel weight it may well pay to use an engine that is heavier but more fuel-efficient. This is a dominant consideration today in the choice of engines for everything from a fighter to a wide-body.

Hempson's figures were based on engines of 100 hp, and his weights for the air-cooled and water-cooled engines were fairly

representative. We have already seen that the choice of how to cool the cylinders has been perhaps the biggest single point to be decided throughout the entire history of the piston aero engine. In the first 10 years of this century there was a distinct preference for water-cooled engines, with the notable exception of rotary types as described later. Most of the air-cooled species were inadequate in power

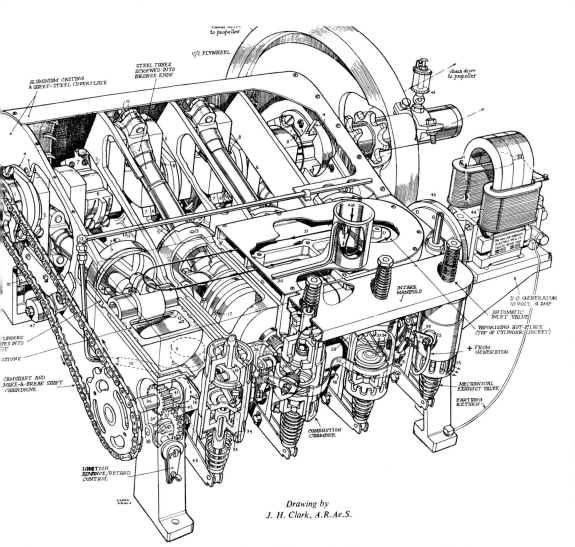

Drawing by
J. H. Clark, A.R.Ae.S.

Even Washington's Smithsonian accepts the 'Clark drawing' of the engine of the 1903 Wright Flyer as the standard reference. (1/2) bearing caps in one piece with plate (3) screwed over key-shaped hole (4) in ends of crankcase; (5) hole as (4) but in intermediate ribs; (6) white-metal bearings screwed to inter-rib halves (7); (8) splash/drip bearing oil; (9) oil return from pools in crankcase via gallery (10) to pump (11); (12) oil from pump via rubber tube (13) giving drip feed to cylinders; (14) pump gear; (15) big-end nuts/shims/lockstrip; (16) gudgeon-pin lock; (17) piston-ring retainer pegs; (18) cylinder liner screwed into jacket; (19) air inlet; (20) fuel pipe; (21) fuel evaporates on hot top of water jacket; (22) sparking plug, comprising positive electrode (23) and make/break contact (24); (25) make-/break lever driven by lever (26) via bearing (27) screwed into neck (28) with springs (29/30) all rocked by 'cam' (31) on shaft (38);

(32) busbar feeding voltage to positive electrodes; (33) retaining rings; (34) sealing disc; (35) exhaust ports; (36) camshaft driving valves and also (11) via (14); (37) spring-loaded sliding pinion driving make/break shaft (38) via peg in inclined slot (39); (40) cam pushes (37) to alter valve timing; (41) cams drive exhaust valves via rollers (42) on rockers (43); (44) floating coils; (45) friction drive off flywheel; (46) sight-feed lubricator; (47) hardwood chain tensioner (Temple Press).

and had other shortcomings, though the first British aeroplane designer, A. V. Roe, flew successfully on only 6 hp provided by a JAP motor cycle engine. At this time cars, like aircraft, were in their infancy, and it was a little early to form rigid opinions. Already, however, the view was taking shape that 'all the best motors [cars] have water-cooled engines'. Another chronicler observed, 'Air-cooled engines are fitted to the cheaper style of motors.' This view certainly persisted; despite the success of the VW Beetle, it has endured up to the present day. This inevitably exerted a psychological effect on aviators until the mid-1920s. Beyond that time such engines as the Jupiter and Wasp, and in the smaller sizes the Gipsy, swept away any prejudice against air cooling.

Until 1906 the available engines were so unattractive that most aircraft designers either tried to get special engines built or, if they could not afford that, they tried to make their own. Had he not most unfortunately been killed, the Englishman Percy Pilcher would almost certainly have beaten the Wrights as the first to fly an aeroplane. Unlike almost all his contemporaries, he already knew how to fly. In 1899, when he suffered his fatal crash, he had almost finished building his first powered machine, with a simple in-line oil engine. Thus, it was left to the bicycle makers from Ohio, Wilbur and Orville Wright, to succeed where so many had failed. They succeeded simply by thinking rationally about the problems and solving them one by one in a methodical way. For example, like Pilcher, they saw that virtually all other builders of flying machines had got the cart before the horse. They were engaged in building often quite complicated flying machines in the strange belief that they could then merely climb aboard and fly. The Wrights saw that, like any pilots, they first had to learn how to fly.

Accordingly they spent from August 1899 until 1903 flying various test rigs, models and then manned gliders in order to discover the problems of controlled flight and then solve them. By 1903 they knew how to fly; all they had to add was a propulsion system. After finding nothing on the market that was remotely suitable, they designed their own engine, and it was manufactured entirely 'in house', mainly by their mechanic Charlie Taylor. To anyone who had just studied the Manly engine the 1903 Wright engine would appear at the least pedestrian, if not positively crude. Having said that, it was designed and built for perhaps 5 per cent of the cost of Manly's (ie Langley's), it was workmanlike and reliable, and it did all that was asked of it.

It was broadly like some 1903 car engines, in being a four-stroke four-in-line, with water cooling. On the other hand, the cylinders were horizontal, and the weight was dramatically reduced by casting the crankcase—the largest single part—in aluminium. I have read 13 different weights for this engine, ranging from 54 kg to 109 kg (120 lb to 240 lb). I believe the best figure to be 69 kg (152 lb) for the bare engine, and about 79 kg (174 lb) including the radiator and piping (but no water). The typically clear pen drawing by J. H. Clark shows all the main details. C/I is Clark's not obvious abbreviation for cast iron. Nobody would quarrel with machining the cylinders in this material; Manly's cylinders were an amazing *tour de force* which I suggest yielded a lot of scrap. The Wright con-rods were another example of simple design, although Taylor had little choice but to machine the crankshaft and camshaft from solid steel. In fact there were two camshafts. One drove the exhaust valves, which were pushed upwards into the underside of a drum-like valve box which was threaded on across the cylinder head and made gas-tight by a gasket. The inlet valves, which were identical, were of the automatic spring-loaded type, pulled open by cylinder suction. The second camshaft provided the blows which repeatedly opened and closed the ignition make-and-break points inside the combustion space. The cutaway shows the chain drive to the main camshaft and the gears to the make-and-break shaft, which incorporated a neat means of varying the spark timing. The advance/retard handcrank and a needle valve in the fuel supply from the tank were adjusted before take-off. In the air there was no means of control other than turning off the fuel cock. Even with this off the engine would run for several more seconds, because the supply of fuel was allowed to drip on to the top of the water jacket surrounding the cylinders. Here it rapidly evaporated, the mixture being drawn off into the four inlet valves along one side each time they opened. There was no need for a throttle, the brothers rightly deciding that full throttle would be needed all the time.

This historic engine is probably very much like what anyone might build today if they had little money and only the simplest tools. It is easy to dismiss it as crude: for example, the wooden roller to tension the chain, the uncontrolled carburation and the deafening exhausts blowing straight out a few inches from the fabric of the lower wing. The brothers' philosophy was expressed by Taylor, who said the first engine 'had no carbureter, no spark plugs, not much of anything . . . but it worked'. Bore and stroke were both 102 mm (4 in), giving a capacity of 3,296 cc

(201 cu in). It was bolted by its four rather massive feet to two ribs of the 1903 Flyer, to the right of the centre line, the weight being balanced by the prone pilot on the left. At the rear of the engine were the flywheel and two pinions driving the propeller chains, one chain being twisted into a figure '8' to make the propellers handed (driven in opposite directions). With the pilot settled in place, the fuel cock was turned on and the engine was started by the other brother turning a propeller. The pilot then adjusted the ignition until rpm were at maximum, typically 1,100–1,200, at which time the power was around 16 hp, the MEP being 49–53. The brothers first ran the engine at Dayton in February 1903, and apart from the natural thrill they must have felt they were impressed at its smooth running.

Its shortcomings were quite deliberate. Despite the fact that they put platinum points on the make-and-break electrodes, which suggested that they were hoping to run for hundreds of hours, the rest of the design choices were what you might call pragmatic. Anything not essential was left out. Today there are differences of opinion on precisely what was included and what was not, but I have no doubt whatever that on 17 December 1903 the engine had no water pump and no lubricating oil pump, even though both are shown in various drawings, and some descriptions refer to both as if they had been fitted. The water jackets merely surrounded the cylinder barrels, and the hottest parts—the heads and valve boxes—were uncooled. The inevitable result is that the hot parts got hotter and hotter and the water would probably eventually have boiled. Heating of the intake air reduced its density, so that after about one minute of full-throttle running the power fell to about 12 hp. Even this was sufficient to give the correct propeller speed, and it is a lasting pity that the brothers never made their planned longer flights to the Coastguard station on the afternoon of 17 December. Certainly the engine could have given adequate power for five minutes or more.

Subsequently the Wrights did all the things one might have expected. They made their later engines upright, with better cooling, and with pumps for fuel, oil and water. Cylinder design was altered to feature separate water-cooled heads, the assembly being held to the crankcase by long studs. Simple carburettors were introduced, together with high-tension magneto ignition. Typical of the later Wright engines was the 6–60 (six cylinders, 60 hp) of 1913. This had a capacity of 6,658 cc (406 cu in). With an MEP of typically 80–85, the 6–60 gave 60–65 hp at 1,500 rpm, though Orville Wright once measured 74 hp at 1,560 rpm. But by this time many other builders had caught up. Wilbur had died in 1912, and the last of the original Wright (brothers) engines was produced in 1915.

Indeed, the brothers never regarded their engines as more than adjuncts to their aeroplanes. There was never any attempt to set up a production line of engines for sale. The only place an aviator could go to buy a Wright engine was the Paris firm of Bariquand et Marré. This company carried out a series of modifications to the Wright engines, many of which angered the brothers (though they made good engineering sense). Some Europeans, especially in France, were incen-

The Wrights followed the classic 1903 engine with a series of others which in 1906 resulted in this upright engine of 4,372 cc (266.8 cu in) capacity, rated at 30 hp at 1,300 rpm and weight 99 kg (218 lb). The automatic inlet valves and rocker-driven exhaust valves seated directly in the top of the cast-iron cylinder on which was shrunk the cast-aluminium water jacket. There was still no carburettor, fuel being metered by pump to a warm air manifold. Here the crankcase side panel has been removed to reveal the camshaft, on which are also worm drives for the petrol and oil pumps (UTC Archive).

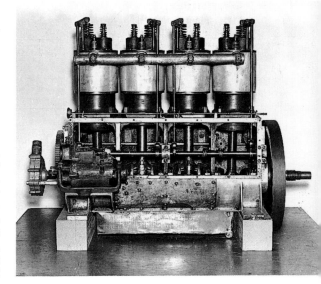

sed at the success of the country boys from Ohio. All kinds of arguments were brought to bear to prove that they had not flown, or not flown when they claimed. Robert Esnault-Pelterie made a totally wrong copy of an early Wright glider, and when it would not fly properly he proclaimed that the Wrights were lying charlatans. In July 1907 the Wrights sent a Flyer III(mod) to Europe. It lay at Le Havre for a year, but eventually Wilbur was able to go to France and put it together. On 8 August 1908 he made a short flight of less than two minutes' duration, but in that time staggered all who watched. For the first time it was impressed on the many aviators present that an aeroplane must be controlled. Yet later the Voisins claimed that his flights were possible only because he had used 'a French engine, made in France', overlooking the fact that the Bariquand et Marré was a Wright engine made under licence!

Gabriel Voisin's deplorable autobiography makes it clear that he, and not the Wrights nor any of his many French contemporaries, single-handedly carried out all the development and perfection of the powered aeroplane, in 1905–10. Strangely, he did not claim also to have pioneered aero engines, which in 1905–07 in France were available from Buchet, Serpollet (weak engines burning carbonic-acid gas), Dutheuil-Chalmers and Esnault-Pelterie, the latter being marketed as REP. A Danish aviator, J. C. H. Ellehammer, made his own engines, with three and later with five cylinders. None of these was of lasting importance, and so the bulk of the market was won by another engine which, like those of the Wrights, was specially designed for lightweight applications. It became of great importance, and then faded from the scene before the First World War. This engine was the Antoinette.

Antoinette was the name of the daughter of Jules Gastambide, chairman of a versatile company named Société Antoinette. His chief partners were Louis Mengin and Leon Levavasseur, and of the latter Charles Gibbs-Smith wrote, 'He remained an artist in whatever he did.' Originally an electrical and marine engineer, he was the mainspring behind Société Antoinette, among other things designing speedboats, flying machines and their engines. His famous V-8 engine was on the drawing board in 1902, to power fast boats, mainly for rich sportsmen on the Riviera. By 1904 it was in production. Levavasseur put one into a bird-like

monoplane, which failed to fly. This did not alter the fact that here was an engine that could enable Europe's wealth of would-be aviators actually to fly, and by the time this market opened up, in 1906, the engine had already been fully proven in motorboats. Subsequently, Hempson wrote, 'The first flights of almost all European pioneers were made with its aid.'

All Antoinettes followed the same general principles. The Société Antoinette had ample resources, so Levavasseur was able to design a perfect engine, uncompromised by limitations in development cost or manufacturing facilities. All the early production were V-8s, but later amazing derivatives appeared with 16 and even 32 cylinders! Santos-Dumont's strange tail-first biplane *14bis*, which between 13 September and 12 November 1906 made what are generally regarded as the first aeroplane flights in Europe, was initially powered by the 24 hp Antoinette, with cylinders of only 80 mm (3.15 in) bore and stroke to give 3,214 cc (196 cu in) capacity, which was priced at £328, appreciably more than the cost of established (but much cruder and heavier) car engines of similar power. Soon the *14bis*, and at least 100 other aircraft, were fitted with the 50-hp version, with bore of 110 mm (4.33 in) and stroke of 105 mm (4.13 in), which was keenly priced at £480. Over the three years from 1906 these engines were developed to run at higher rpm, and with slightly higher MEP, so that they were able to give 32–35 and 67–70 hp, respectively.

In some respects the Antoinette differed from almost all that had gone before. The crankcase was a beautiful machined casting in aluminium, rather in the shape of a house with a tall V-roof, the sloping upper surfaces carrying the eight separate cylinders in banks 90° apart. In the original Antoinette each cylinder comprised a cast iron barrel and separate bolted-on head, with a surrounding water jacket of electrolytically deposited copper. When clean and polished the beautiful appearance of these engines may be imagined. Fuel was fed by a variable-stroke pump direct to a storage pocket in the head of each cylinder, from where it was drawn in a fine spray on each opening of the adjacent automatic inlet valve. This was the first time the argument was heard that aero engines were better (or worse) off with carburettors. Levavasseur did not claim any saving in weight or complexity, but did claim 'more reliable carburation under all conditions'.

The cylinders in the two banks were not quite opposite each other, so that two identical connecting rods could drive side-by-side on each crankpin. An unusual feature was that, by pushing or pulling a knob on one end of the camshaft, the engine could be made to run in either direction. The weakest features were probably the fuel system, because the fine copper pipes bringing the fuel to the vibrating cylinders tended to crack and break (for example, putting Latham into the Channel, so that Blériot made the first crossing), and the cooling system. The latter was of the evaporative type, the water inside the copper jackets being allowed to boil. In early installations the steam was allowed to boil away, but from the Antoinette IV (9 October 1908) onwards these beautiful dragonfly-like monoplanes reused their cooling water with the aid of huge aluminium condensers bolted along each side of the fuselage. Each condenser comprised a bank of numerous (usually 40) tubes running 4 m (14 ft) from beside the engine to just aft of the cockpit behind the wing. These were the most graceful aircraft of their day, their chief shortcoming being the direct drive to a crude propeller with spoon-like blades of curved aluminium sheet riveted to a central tube.

In 1908 (or earlier) Levavasseur added a flat-four (horizontally opposed) engine, using the larger-size cylinder. It was rated at 25 hp and had a gigantic box-like aluminium crankcase. One was bought by Ya. M. Gakkel for his Gakkel I of 1909 and Gakkel II of the following year. The actual engine is in the Soviet air force Monino museum. The main top cover (if it ever existed) is removed, revealing the huge ball-bearing big ends. A Russian engine of 1908 was the water-cooled V-4 by S. V. Grizodubov, flown in his Wright-type biplane. The engine has some Wright features, though it had a carburettor feeding mixture through a large aluminium manifold. This also survives at Monino.

In the United States a rival to the Wrights emerged in the form of Glenn Curtiss. Like the Wrights he began with cycles, and then motor cycles, and it is worth noting that his world record motor cycle speed of 209.3 km/h (136.3 mph) set on 23 January 1907 was not beaten on the ground until 1911 and not officially in the air until 1917! In 1904 he slightly modified one of his air-cooled V-twin bike engines to power a small airship. In 1907 he was a founder member of the AEA (Aerial Experiment Association), for which he provided engines. The first were air-cooled V-8s which were essentially a row of four of his established V-twin motor cycle engines. Called the B-8, these were neat 40-hp engines with quite small cylinders (92 mm bore, 83 mm stroke, 4,395 cc) ($3\frac{5}{8}$ in bore and $3\frac{1}{4}$ in stroke, 268 cu in), each machined from a single steel forging with a plain barrel and finned head, all held down by four long tie-bolts. Curtiss followed with a water-cooled four-in-line, with cylinders of 127 mm (5 in) bore and stroke, and brazed copper water jackets, of 30 hp. Then he doubled this up to produce a V-8 conservatively rated at 50 hp, and it was this engine that enabled him to walk off with the two chief speed prizes at the world's first great aviation meeting, at Reims in August 1909. A

The placard on this exhibit in the VVS Museum at Monino states that it is the Antoinette flat-four used by Gakkel in 1909. Utterly unlike previous Antoinettes, it is closely similar to the 1909 Darracq. It may have been misidentified (N. A. Eastaway).

Fiat's first aero engine, the SA 8/75, was built in 1908 using experience gained with racing cars. An air-cooled V-8, it had a carburettor on top feeding inlet manifolds behind the valve pushrods. At the front gears drove the camshaft and twin magnetos.

year later Curtiss produced the OX-5, a V-8 with smaller cylinders (102 mm bore, 127 mm stroke, 8,249 cc) (4 in bore, 5 in stroke, 503 cu in) with the water jackets changed to Monel high-nickel alloy. The overhead valves were arranged transversely across each cylinder, the inlet pushrod being inside the tubular exhaust pushrod. Weighing about 181 kg (400 lb) and rated at 90 hp at 1,400 rpm, these were undistinguished engines. Tens of thousands were made during the first World War, appalling quality control resulting in poor reliability which killed many pupil pilots.

In Italy Fiat was already an established car builder when the SA 8/75 aero engine was completed in 1908. An air-cooled V-8, it was rated at 50 hp and weighed 68 kg (150 lb) not including its surrounding circular cowling in which it was mounted by large transverse

tubes passing through trunnions in the ends of the aluminium crankcase. The cast-iron cylinders were held down by long tie-rods, and had overhead inlet and exhaust valves driven from a central camshaft, and dual ignition. It simply lacked the ability to transfer heat to the air, and overheated badly. In 1912 Fiat tested a basically similar engine with water cooling, and during the First World War all production was focused on water-cooled engines, as noted later.

The French Renault firm built its first aero engine at the same time as Fiat, and with a somewhat similar design, but with what is called an F-type head, in which the one-piece cast-iron cylinder is extended sideways at the top to provide a chamber for a direct-driven inlet valve and a rocker-driven overhead exhaust valve, the two valves being in line and opposite each other. In the end of the projecting chamber was the plug. The propeller was driven off the camshaft, at half crankshaft speed, and the rear end of the crankshaft drove a cooling fan. Despite this the Renault overheated, and so apart from being very heavy for its power it also had to be cooled by burning an over-rich mixture. The only things to be said for these unimpressive engines were that they were fairly reliable and could be installed as a tractor or pusher, yet many thousands were made. When in 1912 the Royal Aircraft Factory at Farnborough decided there had to be a British aero engine it used the Renault as the basis for the RAF.1A, from which larger and better designs followed during the war.

Another who launched into the field with an air-cooled engine in 1908 was Alessandro Anzani. Like Curtiss, a motor cycle engineer, he chose the W or fan configuration with three air-cooled cylinders spaced at 60°. The vertical cylinder had a master rod, to which were pinned the link rods from the other two. An F-head was used, but the reverse of the Renault with the inlet valve on top. This initial model became famous because Louis Blériot fitted one to his No XI monoplane, in place of one of Esnault-Pelterie's indifferent REP engines, immediately before flying the Channel on 25 July 1909. It proved to be just another feeble and unreliable engine, and had it not been for a providential shower of rain it would have overheated and put Blériot 'in the drink'. Subsequently Anzani produced so many different engines, one of them a four-row radial with 20 cylinders, that he never carried out any proper development. Most had inadequate breathing through small valves, and were limited by the basic shortcomings of the cast-iron air-cooled cylinder.

Some Anzanis had one or more rings of holes drilled around the cylinder barrel at such a level that they were uncovered by the piston near BDC. These holes enabled exhaust gas to escape and so unloaded the hot and highly stressed exhaust valve. As in two-strokes, they sometimes let in fresh air, to cool the piston crown. Such holes were seen in some ENV engines (English water-cooled V-8 engines made in France) and in many other marques, perforated Antoinettes even having pilot control over the apertures. S. F. Cody, the first man to fly an aeroplane in Britain, at one time used a British Green, a well-made but pedestrian water-cooled four-in-line, and claimed to have increased its power from 60 to 70 hp by perforating the base of the cylinders. A great engineer, Laurence Pomeroy, considered such holes merely ruined oil control and idling, as well as making engines even noisier.

Early in this century it was extremely difficult to make a good air-cooled cylinder. Many builders therefore turned to water cooling, but—apart from the bulk, weight and vulnerability of the radiator and piping—they found it hard to devise a practical and reliable form of cooling jacket. The Antoinette and ENV were examples of engines with copper jackets deposited electrolytically. The Buchet six-in-line had its cylinders cast in three pairs, each pair being surrounded by an outline box framework to which watertight metal sheet covers were then screwed. The Wolseley V-8 again had cylinders cast in pairs, each pair having a sheet aluminium jacket screwed directly to the casting. The Green had individual steel cylinders around which removable copper drum jackets were clamped at the top. The bottom of each jacket was sealed by a large ring of black rubber. This was partly vulcanized by the hot cylinder, but the outer part in contact with the copper was claimed to remain soft and maintain a good seal.

Special mention may be made of the New Engine, often called the NEC from New Engine Company. This was advertised from 1909 as two-cylinder 15–20 hp, four-cylinder 35–40 hp and six-cylinder 50–60 hp. It was the only two-stroke to be of much importance in the early days of aviation. NEC claimed 'a gain of 80 per cent in power as compared with any four-cycle engine of the same cylinder dimensions'. The most common aero version was a water-cooled four-in-line. These engines had a Roots-type blower to blast fresh air through the cylinders to ensure good scavenging while the piston was below mid-stroke, uncovering the inlet and exhaust ports. A typical NEC full-throttle speed was 1,500 rpm, which for 1910 was exceptional. Another feature was the way, just before the piston closed off the inlet, a very rich mixture was introduced. This rapidly mixed with the swirling fresh air already in the cylinder to give the desired final mixture, which was compressed to 80 lb/sq in (ratio about 5.5) before being fired. The New Engine was one of the remarkably few two-strokes to look like succeeding in the aviation market. It is not easy to see why the two-stroke never made it. There is naturally a strong inclination to follow the choices of the general herd, especially if your life depends on it, and the NEC was always regarded as an oddball. Such factors as weight, higher fuel consumption and greater noise can be dismissed as of little significance. NEC stressed the simplicity of their engines— 'no poppet valves, no sliding sleeves, no compression in the crankcase or separate cylinders . . .'—while the American author Herschel Smith puts their failure down to complexity!

So far we have studied numerous engines which came on the aviation market in 1908. In the same year the first production examples were made of an engine which was destined to sell by the thousand, and to dominate aviation until war broke out in 1914. Then, in developed versions made by many companies, it provided a large proportion of the horsepower of the Allied air forces. This remarkable engine was the Gnome rotary.

The Société des Moteurs Gnome was a long-established Parisian engineering works run by the Seguin family. Around 1905

Laurent Seguin told his elder brother Louis he thought the time was right to design 'a rotative motor for the developing field of aviation . . . weighing a kilo per horsepower'. The two brothers did the design jointly. There is no doubt that Laurent had from the outset envisaged a rotary engine, in which the crankshaft is fixed and the radial cylinders revolve around it. Such engines had been used in cars and motor cycles, but not in aviation. It is interesting to see that, having the proverbial clean sheet of paper, the brothers chose to produce such an engine. The Musée de l'Air has a Gnome five-cylinder radial (not rotary) with geared drive, thought to date from 1906. This looked like an aero engine, but was apparently used in a high-speed boat. Certainly we know of no derived Gnome radial.

Using an almost identical design of cylinder, the first rotary engines were made in 1908. They had five cylinders and produced 30–35 hp. Very few were made, one being

Cross-section in the plane through one cylinder of the classic '50 Gnome' of 1909–10. The mounting is the plate in the centre which holds the crankshaft around which the engine rotates on the large ball bearings. The hollow crankshaft is continued far to the right to serve as the air inlet, incorporating the carburettor. Mixture escapes from the crankcase through the valve in the crown of the piston.

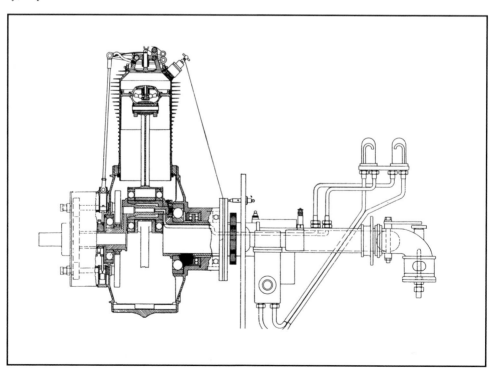

used by Roger Ravaud to power his unsuccessful hydroplane at Monaco in June 1909. The first production Gnomes, for aeroplanes, had seven cylinders, of 110 mm (4.33 in) bore and 120 mm (4.72 in) stroke (7,980 cc/487 cu in), rated at 50 hp at 1,200 rpm. The first to fly appears to have been bought by Louis Paulhan and flown in his Voisin on 16 June 1909. Two months later Paulhan went to the great competitive meeting at Reims. There he was incensed to find that his rival Henry Farman had received the stewards' permission to remove his unreliable Belgian four-in-line Vivinus and substitute a newly purchased Gnome. Despite protestations, Farman's change of engine was pronounced perfectly legal. With it he won the Grand Prix de Distance on 27 August and the Prix des Passagers the following day! At this time about half the world's aviation market was centred on Paris, and news of the Gnome spread like wildfire. Deliveries of Gnome aero engines proved the point: 1908, 3; 1909, 35; 1910, 400; 1911, 800; 1912, 1,000; 1913, 1,400. This exceeded the combined total of all other engines.

Every Gnome was made 'like a watch', the ruling material being nickel steel, and they were therefore expensive. The '50 Gnome' cost £520, compared with £280 for the 50-hp Vivinus, £365 for the 60 hp Green and £480 for the 50 hp Antoinette. Compared with the Antoinette, you did not seem to get much for your money. The five radial cylinders looked extremely clean, and the only other parts comprised a tube at the back with a carburettor and magneto. It was a remarkable achievement, quite unlike all rival engines. It was such a sweeping commercial success because, properly managed, it provided the reliable, lightweight power that aviators everywhere were seeking.

Not least of the odd features was that the engine was always mounted behind the propeller. Thus, in the numerous pusher installations, the propeller was between the engine and the aircraft! In all cases the entire powerplant was carried by a long tube projecting from the centre line. This tube was an extension of the crankshaft. The open end was the air inlet. Here there was either a simple fuel spray or a crude manually controlled carburettor. This fed a rich mixture straight out of the open crankpin into the crankcase. The mixture was made over-rich to avoid crankcase explosions, though these were not unknown. From the crankcase the mixture escaped through valves in the crowns of the pistons, which were drawn open by suction on the induction stroke when the exhaust valve in the end of the cylinder was closed. The valve in each piston was of the poppet type, balanced by pivoted weights and loaded by pairs of coil springs so that, despite centrifugal force, they remained closed except during induction. The mixture was fired by a plug fed from a magneto on the main mounting plate, the exhaust escaping direct to atmosphere through the mass-balanced valves driven by pushrods running round a cam ring.

Altogether, the Gnome filled the need of the pre-1910 era. The fact that the whole engine rotated made it smooth-running. A contributor to *Flight* in 1913 began a poem with 'Give me the hum of a fifty Gnome . . .', though most observers likened its sound to a buzz. In the days when to fly at all was an achievement, the Gnome's drawbacks were secondary. These drawbacks were many. No engine could be safely allowed to run as long as 20 hours before being stripped and overhauled, invariably with a few parts needing replacement. The rich mixture flooding through the crankcase would have swept away normal lubrication, so a copious supply of oil had to be fed in all the time the engine was running. This oil passed up through the pistons and so was burned. Accordingly the oil had to be miscible with the fuel and burn cleanly to leave no ash, and the obvious choice was castor oil. As oil consumption was generally at least 30 per cent as high as consumption of fuel (which itself was used inefficiently) it followed that a very rich oil-loaded exhaust streamed from the running engine like a Catherine wheel. Everything downstream soon became covered in a film of oil, and for this reason engines in tractor installations were surrounded by a cowling, open underneath to let everything drip out. An hour's running typically cost 45p for fuel but 75p for oil!

A more serious fault was the lack of any proper control. Again, this was no problem in 1909: pilots wanted full throttle. A simple flap valve controlled the air supply, and the engine would be started with this at a setting known to give good idling. With the engine spinning, the air valve would then be opened wide. Firing would cease, but the engine's inertia would keep it turning while the fuel valve was opened until firing picked up again, at once giving full power. Helpers would let go of the tail and the machine would take off. Subsequently the only control the pilot would

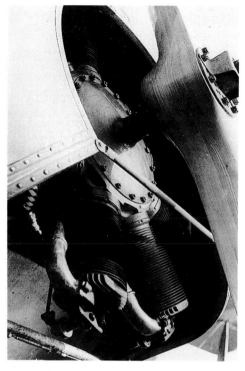

Castor oil poured in a cloud from the early rotaries, so if they were ahead of the cockpit they were surrounded by a cowling, open at the bottom to let the oil drip out. This is the Le Rhône in Vivian Bellamy's Avro 504K replica.

have would be by cutting out the ignition, invariably by a button—called a blip switch—on top of the control column. Another shortcoming was the inherent weakness of the valves in the hottest part of the pistons. In the pre-war era professional aviators had their Gnomes dismantled after every flight to check these valves, and also that their springs were all set to equal tension so that all cylinders received the same charge.

After the Gnome achieved fame in August 1909 things happened fast. The original engines had only one piston ring, but very soon the pistons were given two rings plus a top ring made of thin bronze, called the obturator ring, which could flex to the shape of the cylinder and provide a seal even if the thin-walled (1.5 mm) cylinder distorted. New models appeared, with seven or nine cylinders in different sizes, with Greek names (oddly, in the sequence Omega, Alpha, Beta and Delta), followed by the Lambda and a smaller number of derived two-row 14-cylinder

engines of which the most powerful was the Delta-Delta of 200 hp. The exhaust-valve pushrods were driven by four cam rings. Foreign licensees were numerous, though not all found a market.

The Seguins were not the sort to rest on their laurels, and they strove to eliminate the weak design features. One of the obvious ones was the valve in the piston, and in late 1912 production began of the Gnome Mono (*monosoupape*, single valve). This had conventional pistons, but a ring of apertures around the lower part of each cylinder. At the end of the power stroke these were uncovered by the piston having travelled past them. The exhaust valve opened early, allowing most of the exhaust to escape and ensuring that, by the time the inlet ports were open, pressure in the cylinder was so low that little exhaust would pass into the crankcase to cause contamination (no explosion was likely, because of the richness of the crankcase mixture). The upgoing piston would expel the rest of the exhaust, and on its downward travel it would suck in fresh air through the still-open exhaust valve. The latter would shut when the piston was about one-third of the way down.

The piston's continued descent would cause a partial vacuum in the cylinder, so that the moment the inlet ports were uncovered the rich mixture would rush in and mix with the fresh air. Thus there were similarities to two-strokes, though the Mono remained a four-stroke engine. Perhaps surprisingly its MEP was higher than that of most other rotaries, though specific fuel consumption was even worse. During the war the most numerous model of all the Gnome rotaries was the Mono B2, with nine cylinders of 110 mm (4.33 in) bore and 150 mm (5.9 in) stroke (12,841 cc/783 cu in), rated at 100 hp but normally giving slightly more. As a substantial amount of air entered via the exhaust valve there was little point in throttling the hollow crankshaft inlet, so a limited degree of control of power—which was found essential for forma-tion flying—was made possible by adjusting the fuel flow.

Several companies managed to devise rotaries sufficiently different from the original Gnome to circumvent the Seguin patents. The most important were those of Pierre Clerget (1911) and Louis Verdet, trading as Société Le Rhône (1912). The Clerget was certainly an improvement on the Gnome, having a better cylinder with deep fins all the way down, conventional overhead inlet and exhaust valves worked by separate pushrods (with pipes taking the carburetted mixture to the inlet valves), and what may have been the first aluminium pistons in an aero engine. Almost all also had dual ignition, the plugs being side-by-side in the side of the head near the exhaust valve. The 130-hp Clerget 9B, made by Gwynnes of Hammersmith, London, was the most common engine of the Sopwith Camel despite its high price of £907.50. Occa-sional failure of the flexible obturator ring caused severe overheating, and to try to solve this the Admiralty asked Lieutenant W. O. Bentley (already an established car designer) to try modifications. He produced a suc-cession which culminated in the outstanding BR.1 (Bentley Rotary), with aluminium cylinders with shrunk-in cast iron liners, aluminium pistons and a steel head held down by four long bolts. This was rated at 150 hp for a price of £605. Bentley went on to design the BR.2 with cylinders enlarged to 140 mm (5.5 in) bore and 180 mm (7.1 in) stroke (24,961 cc/1,522 cu in), weighing 224 kg (493 lb). It was nominally 200 hp at 1,300 rpm, though in October 1917 the prototype gave a reliable 234 hp. This was the pinnacle of the rotary engine.

The Le Rhône differed from the Gnome in many ways, some features being curious. The cylinders were of steel, but with a pressed-in cast-iron liner. In the flat head were inlet and exhaust valves, but these were driven by a single rocker pivoted in both directions by a lever and push-pull rod. Compression could be varied by selecting the number of turns that the cylinder was screwed into the crankcase, so the radial inlet manifolds incorporated tele-scopic inserts. Strangest of all, the master rod had a big end in the form of two rings forming the outer race of two large ball-bearings on the crankpin. The inner, facing sides of these rings were machined to leave three concentric grooves, in which ran the curved bronze slip-pers which formed the ends of the other eight rods. When the assembly was put together the

Left The pinnacle of the Gnome rotary series was the 240 hp BB18c, with 18 Mono-type cylinders.

Below Even more important than the original Gnome was the Monosoupape. Air still entered through the long hollow crankshaft, into which the fuel was metered, but it could reach the combustion space via inlet ports round the cylinder skirt. More air entered through the exhaust valve.

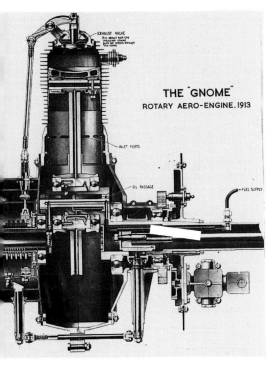

THE "GNOME"
ROTARY AERO-ENGINE. 1913

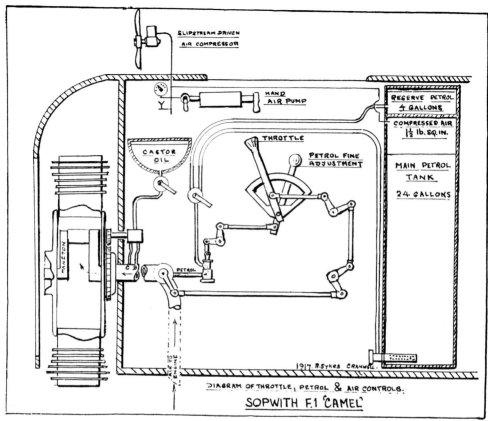

DIAGRAM OF THROTTLE, PETROL & AIR CONTROLS.

SOPWITH F.1 'CAMEL'

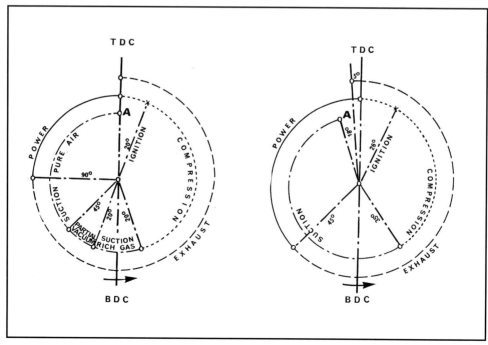

curved slippers were held between the facing grooved tracks. The result eliminated the inequalities in piston acceleration that result from a conventional arrangement of master and slave rods, and the Le Rhône was a particularly smooth-running engine.

In 1914 the German firm Siemens und Halske produced a rotary with cylinders of basically Clerget type. Its unique feature was that the fixed mount at the rear carried an epicyclic differential gearbox which drove the crankshaft in one direction and the rest of the engine in the opposite direction. Thus, high power could be generated at 1,600 rpm but with a propeller rpm of only 800, and greatly reduced windage losses from the spinning cylinders. The most important models, in the ShIII series, were unusual in having 11 cylinders in one row.

Two further engines in the Soviet Monino museum are of interest. One, designed by A. G. Ufimtsev for his No 2 Spheroplan circular-winged machine, was known as the ADU-4 (aviation engine Ufimtsev No. 4), and was claimed to produce 60 hp for a weight of only 58 kg (127.8 lb). An air-cooled rotary, its machined steel cylinders were not fixed to any crankcase, but were free to pivot at the head end to a framework of steel straps which held the engine together. Thus, the con-rods were fixed to the pistons, which always remained aligned with the crankpin. Even stranger, there were six cylinders. An accompanying sketch shows why such a number is undesirable. Engine A fires its six cylinders in sequence, but then has to wait one whole revolution without power. Engine B fires 1352461, which again involves most irregular

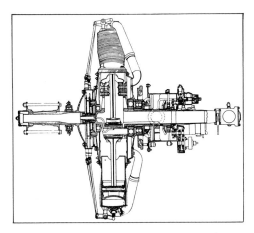

Section through the 1917 11-cylinder Siemens und Halske, of 160 hp. Large bevel gears (concentric dotted rings) just behind the mounting made the crankshaft turn one way and the engine/propeller in the opposite direction! Like the Le Rhône, the Siemens fed mixture through external pipes to the cylinder head.

running. Engine C, with seven cylinders, can follow the sequence 13572461, all intervals being identical. The other Russian engine looked odd, because of its huge crankcase and reduction gear, but it was otherwise more like a marine engine. It is hard to believe it gave 180 hp for a weight of only 164 kg (361.5 lb)! The seven cylinders were completely encased in pressed copper water jackets which were sealed by the bolted square-sided rings which held the cylinders to large ribbed platforms projecting from the crankcase. The 'constructor' of this 1914 engine was A. Nesterov, not to be confused with the aircraft designer and pilot P. N. Nesterov.

Most aircraft in Czarist Russia had imported engines, including Salmsons. These were the only really successful water-cooled radials. From the start in January 1912 the Salmsons featured the Swiss Canton-Unné drive, in which all (usually nine) con-rods were identical, all having their (small) big ends pinned to a cage around the crankpin. The cage and crankpin were joined by a set of epicyclic gears, so that the cage could transmit the drive without itself rotating. Each cylinder was enveloped in a ribbed water jacket and had twin pushrods to the valves, whose springs were of the hairpin type to reduce engine diameter. Some Salmsons had the crankshaft vertical or transverse, with a 90°

Above left This sketch by Cadet R. Sykes at RFC Station Cranwell in 1917 shows that a Camel pilot had quite a lot of engine management to do. The systems shown would not have differed much even though the Camel could be powered by the Clerget, Le Rhône, Gnome Mono or BR.1.

Left Timing diagrams for the 100 hp Gnome Mono (left) and '80 Le Rhône' (right). The totally different timing emphasizes the marked difference between these great mass-produced rotaries. The Gnome weighed 136 kg (300 lb) and burned 38 l (10 gal) fuel and 7.57 l (2 gal) oil per hour. The Le Rhône actually delivered 93 hp, weighed 109 kg (240 lb) and had the much lower consumption of 23 l (6 gal) and 3.785 l (1 gal) respectively.

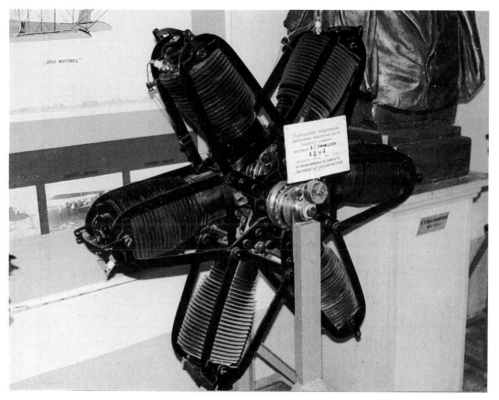

Much less ordinary than it appears at first sight, Ufimtsev's ADU-4 had swinging cylinders pivoted at their outer ends! (N. A. Eastaway).

Sketches explaining why a radial should have seven cylinders rather than six (see text). Readers can draw their own sketches to work out firing sequences with other numbers of cylinders.

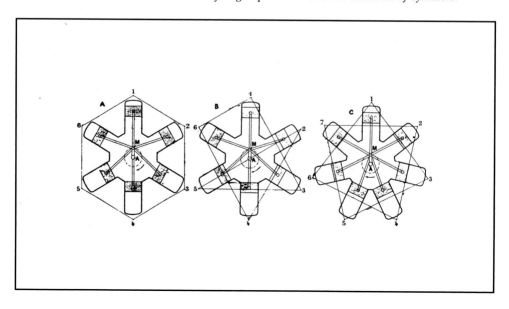

Though odd in appearance, Nesterov's 1914 water-cooled radial was fairly conventional (N. A. Eastaway).

bevel drive to the horizontal propeller shaft.

Another favourite engine of the Russians in the pre-war era was the Argus. This Berlin firm made four-in-line water-cooled car engines from 1902, and derived aero engines from 1906. By 1910 most had six separate iron cylinders with copper jackets, and vertical overhead valves each with its own pushrod. In late 1910 it was joined by the prototype of an engine called the Austro-Daimler, which followed generally similar principles. The difference was that its designer, Ferdinand Porsche, already showed the prowess that he was to display with VW and Porsche cars. From the start there were versions with four and six cylinders, and an oft-told story is how S. F. Cody bought one of the latter in 1912 and fitted it to his much-rebuilt third aircraft and walked off with the £5,000 first prize at the British Military Aeroplane Trials. His aircraft was an obsolete monstrosity, utterly useless as equipment for the urgently begging RFC, but its completely reliable 120 hp carried all before it. The Austro-Daimler cylinder had a bore of 130 mm (5.1 in) and the long stroke of 175 mm (6.9 in), giving a capacity (six cylinders) of 13.9 litres (848 cu in). The modest speed of 1,200 rpm kept piston speed from being excessive, and breathing was outstanding, with enormous inclined overhead valves driven via a single push/pull rod beside each cylinder. It was a very tall engine, and the jackets covered only the upper part of each cylinder. On the other hand the hottest parts, such as the exhaust valve region, were carefully cooled. The inlet valve and its seat could be unscrewed, which in turn allowed the exhaust valve to be removed with the cylinder still in place. The massive crankshaft ran in seven main bearings, and was slightly offset from the centre line to give smoother running. In early 1914 the electro-formed copper jackets were replaced by sheet steel welded in place. Reliable and efficient, these engines are generally regarded as the inspiration—some have said the prototypes—of the many thousands of engines made for the German and Austro-

Hungarian aircraft during the war, by Mercedes, Benz, BMW, Hiero and others.

It was certainly the prototype for the very important series of six-in-lines produced in Britain. These began with the Austro-Daimler made under licence by Beardmore, who fitted dual ignition and twin carburettors, and then raised the power to 160 hp mainly by increasing the bore to 142 mm (5.59 in). Frank Halford then developed it into the Galloway-built BHP. This had bigger cylinders of totally different design, with a screwed steel liner, flat iron head and surrounding sheet steel jacket. An offset overhead camshaft drove three valves per cylinder, one large inlet and two smaller exhaust. In June 1916, the first BHP reached 250 hp at 1,500 rpm. In turn this was the starting point for the Siddeley Puma, with what could be called the modern style of water-cooled cylinder in which the six steel liners were inserted into a single block of cast aluminium, the liner having a short threaded portion at the top to secure the aluminium head. Many problems, notably porosity of the cast blocks and burning of the exhaust valves, forced the Puma to be derated from the planned 300 hp to 240. It was to be about 1930 before the aluminium casting industry could guarantee perfect products.

During the war the most numerous German engine was the Mercedes. Inspired by the Austro-Daimler, these engines nevertheless showed significant differences. The cylinder barrel and head were machined steel forgings screwed together, the head then having the valve pockets, guides and ports, and twin plug bosses, all welded on. The slightly inclined valves were driven by an overhead camshaft with a lever at the rear which enabled it to move axially to reduce compression for easy engine starting. Though excellent engines, they were conservatively rated and thus appeared heavy. The most powerful, the D IVa with 160 × 180 mm (6.3 × 7.09 in) cylinders (21.7 litres/1,323 cu in), was rated at 260 hp at 1,400 rpm and had a dry weight of 425 kg (936 lb).

The Mercedes cylinder greatly influenced the design of the Rolls-Royce Eagle in Britain and the Liberty in the USA. The former, at first simply called 'the 200-hp engine', was

Opposite The 1912 Austro-Daimler can fairly be regarded as the ancestor of all the water-cooled six-in-lines which powered German and Austro-Hungarian aircraft of the First World War.

designed in 1914. Royce chose the V-12 configuration, with a wet-sump aluminium crankcase and epicyclic reduction gear to the propeller. Each cylinder was machined from a single steel forging, complete with the head. The steel jackets and the inlet and exhaust ports were then welded on, and the assembly attached to the crankcase by four bolts in the corners of the flanged base. An overhead camshaft operated the single inlet and exhaust valves of the cylinders of each bank. The initial Eagle, of 20.32 litre (1,240 cu in) capacity, was quickly cleared at 250 hp, and subsequent versions gave up to 375 hp, with aluminium pistons with improved rings and various arrangements of carburettors and magnetos. All had left and right cylinders opposite each other, those of one bank (which it was depended on whether the engine was left or right-handed, tractor or pusher) having master rods and the other bank having slave or link rods.

In the United States a profusion of builders made generally undistinguished engines. After Curtiss the most important marque was the Hall-Scott, and by 1913 E. J. Hall had achieved quite a good 127 mm × 178 mm (5 in × 7 in) cylinder of 'Mercedes' type steel construction, with overhead camshaft. In great haste he and Jesse Vincent of Packard designed the Liberty V-12 in five days in the summer of 1917, using virtually the same cylinder. The first Liberty was actually a V-8, and there were other forms, but the V-12, nominally of 400 hp and of 27 litre (1,649 cu in) capacity, was overwhelmingly the most important. To decrease width the banks were spaced at only 45°, and another unusual feature was coil ignition, as in most cars.

Generally similar cylinders were used in Fiat's wartime six-in-lines, notably the A 12 family. These had the same 160 mm × 180 mm (6.3 in × 7.09 in) cylinder size as the Mercedes D IVa, but were lighter and gave 300 or even 325 hp. They had two inlet and two exhaust valves per cylinder, and an odd feature was that special high-viscosity oil was packed around the camshaft, renewed during flight by the pilot pumping it from a small topping-up tank. Another refinement was that the gudgeon pins were lubricated under pressure via pipes clipped to the con-rods. Twelve even larger cylinders (170 mm × 210 mm, 57.2 litres/6.7 in × 8.26 in, 3,490 cu in) were used for the giant Fiat A 14, at 725 hp the most powerful engine produced in quantity by 1918.

Designed in a frantic hurry, the Liberty V-12 was the right engine at the right time, and examples built in 1918 served in the US Army and the RAF until after 1933. Note how the valves were driven by short rockers from an enclosed overhead camshaft.

Fiat went on to produce many more engines, always in competition with Isotta-Fraschini. The latter produced numerous engines with iron cylinders cast in pairs, culminating in the impressive V 5 eight-in-line of 1915. Two years later came the important V 6, a six-in-line with separate steel cylinders, with steel jackets secured by small screws. On top of each pair of cylinders was bolted an aluminium casting containing the enclosed valve gear, including the ports for the vertical inlet and exhaust valves on the engine centreline. The crankshaft had only four bearings, but the main drawback of the 250/275-hp V 6 was its height of almost 1.016 m (40 in), which in single-tractor aircraft meant a poor forward view for the pilot.

Later Isotta-Fraschini used nothing but monobloc (cast in one piece) aluminium heads. But two engineers were by 1913 starting to scheme aero engines in which the entire cylinder block was a single aluminium casting. These men were Marc Birkigt, a Swiss, and Charles B. Kirkham, an American. Kirkham worked with Curtiss, and the result was the Curtiss K-12 of 1916. A neat V-12, it was potentially a great engine, running at the unprecedented speed of 2,500 rpm and thus

able to give 400 hp despite having a capacity of only 18,778 cc (1,145 cu in). It became the D-12 (see Chapter 6). Birkigt set up his factory in Barcelona to make cars, the company being named Hispano-Suiza (Spanish-Swiss). In 1915 he produced his first aero engine, in a workshop in Paris. Production began a year later, after solving many problems, and by 1918 derived engines were being made by 23 licensees! S. D. Heron commented that Birkigt initially 'showed little knowledge of either cylinder or valve cooling', but in most respects the Hispano pointed the way to the future.

The original engine was a water-cooled V-8 with cylinders 120 mm × 130 mm, 11,775 cc (4.72 × 5.12 in, 718 cu in). It was rated at 150 hp at 1,400 rpm, and had a dry weight of 202 kg (445 lb). Each cylinder was machined from a forging in carbon steel. The flat top incorporated seats for the two valves, which were arranged in line with the crankshaft. At the top of each side were drilled the threaded bosses for the two plugs, arranged at 90° to the valves. The entire upper part of each cylinder, about 70 per cent of its total length, was threaded, so that it could be screwed into the monobloc cast aluminium cylinder block.

Casting was then an inexact art, and to avoid an impossibly high scrap rate from porosity each block was coated with black stove enamel by a special process. The direct contact over the whole working length ensured rapid heat transfer from the thin steel cylinder wall to the water in the passages cast in the block. As each block was completed, the four cylinders were adjusted by rotating them until their bottom faces were precisely in line. Then the block was attached to studs on the crankcase by a ring of nuts around the flanged base of each cylinder.

The two blocks were 90° apart. In most V-type engines the angle was 60°, and in the Liberty only 45°. Birkigt could see that choosing 90° was not going to cause problems from excessive width; the SPAD and SE.5a prove that he was right. The big angle made his engine more rigid. In separate-cylinder engines all the rigidity has to be provided by the crankcase, which accordingly has to be thick-walled and massive. Birkigt's cast blocks of cylinders enormously increased rigidity, and the wide angle enhanced it further, enabling the crankcase to be much lighter. The wide angle also left room between the blocks for the duplex (twin-choke) carburettor and the hot-water jacketed induction manifold. Above each inlet port was a kind of funnel, with a hand cock. These were used to squirt in petrol to prime the engine before starting (though experienced front-line pilots usually squirted through the exhaust stubs and then pulled the propeller backwards to suck in). The same cocks were used before shutting down for the night to pour in a little kerosene so that the castor oil did not gum up the piston rings, thus facilitating starting.

An important advance in the Hispano was that the cylinder blocks were extended upwards to enclose the valve gear. A bevel shaft at the back of each block drove the overhead camshaft which ran in three gun-metal bearings. It drove the valves directly, not via any intermediate lever (which was another unusual improvement). On the end of each valve stem was a threaded extension ending in a hard steel disc. This disc was actually impacted by the cam, and clearance was adjusted by screwing the disc in or out, it having serrations which locked on the similarly serrated cap on top of the springs. Each valve oscillated in a guide of cast iron, screwed into the aluminium, and could operate with either of its two concentric coil springs broken.

All these were features that became virtu-ally standard in all engines, but the main machinery had some unusual features. The pistons were aluminium castings, not forgings, and they drove tubular con-rods. The main rod had a white-metalled big end which bore over the whole surface of the crankpin. Its outer shoulders were themselves white metalled, and these were driven by the forked big end of the opposite rod, whose bridged cap allowed the main rod to move freely. Auxiliary drives were at the rear, one of the most crucial being the pump which at 80 to 120 lb/sq in forced lubricating oil along internal galleries throughout the engine. (There was just one external copper pipe which fed oil to the front bearing of the camshaft.) The main bearings varied according to engine type. The

Fiat made 13,260 A 12 engines. Note the enormous inlet manifold and water pipe from the pump underneath, the valve gear reminiscent of the Liberty, and the oil pipe linking the big end to the gudgeon pin.

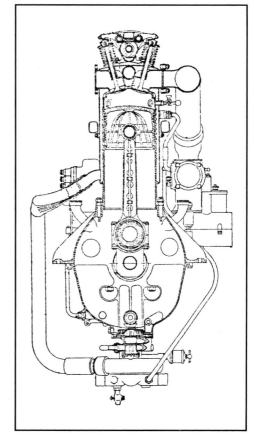

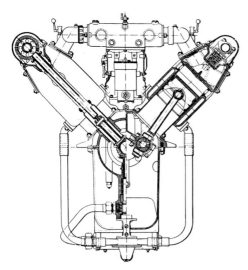

Cross-sections between and through cylinders of a Wolseley W 4B Adder, the British-built version of the 200/220-hp geared Hispano-Suiza V-8. Very important in the First World War, these engines led to over 100,000 Klimov V-12s in the Second World War.

cross-section shows a common 200-hp geared version. These raised the propeller shaft, so that in a few aircraft a cannon could fire through the hub of the propeller. Most geared versions had no fewer than ten ball-bearings (five double bearings) for the propeller shaft and front end of the crankshaft. The crankshaft had three plain bearings between the

cranks and a large ball bearing at the rear end.

During the First World War nearly 50,000 Hispanos were made, most of them of 200/220 hp but going up to 300 hp. They were in many ways outstanding, and when well managed were very reliable. One advantage was their compactness, the length of the geared engines being further reduced by locating the propeller-shaft gear between the cylinder blocks. In contrast, German fighter pilots had the choice between a 200-odd hp six-in-line about 2 m (6 ft) long which made aircraft clumsy, or a compact rotary of about half the power. Most of the serious faults of the Hispano stemmed from hasty wartime production, when engine life was unimportant. Trying to keep a surviving SE.5a flying in Britain has proved a major task. Such aircraft were built to last just a few hours at the front line. Nobody expected them to fly for over 70 years. Problems have included the fact that over a period castor oil turns into a tenacious varnish which locks everything solid. The original reduction gears, always a weak feature, have been replaced by superb new gears designed by apprentices at the RAE Farnborough, with a modern tooth form and better materials. The valve gear was redesigned to eliminate the smack as the harsh-profile cam impacted on the disc, and thus in turn to eliminate cracking of the guides caused by the resulting side loads. The locking slot at the bottom of each valve stem had square corners, promoting a fatigue crack in a very short time. New valves were made with a slot with a radiused bottom. Such details are today instinctive, but were unknown 75 years ago.

6 Between the World Wars

During 1919–39, between the First and Second World Wars, other wars took place all over the world. These conflicts had a significant effect on the development of aircraft engines. So too did various air races, notably the international seaplane races for the Schneider Trophy, and after 1930 there was increased competitive pressure for better engines to power civil airliners.

By 1919, to be able to fly was no longer an end in itself. Aero engines had become commercial products, and the customers wanted sustained high power and high reliability. In order to achieve this, it was normal to strip, inspect and rebuild engines at intervals seldom greater than 100 hours and possibly less than 50. This was possible because of the low cost of manpower. The cost of fuel was also a minor consideration, though of course specific fuel consumption was of importance in a very few aircraft in that it determined how far the aircraft could fly without refuelling. Range was by modern standards very short. To fly from (for example) London to Athens meant three or even four intermediate stops to refuel. Another factor which eased the problems was that only very few aircraft were concerned with flight performance, but it was during this 20-year period that designers learned the importance of the installation of the engine. The progress made was enormous, and perhaps greater than in the subsequent half-century.

The point has been made repeatedly that by far the most difficult, and most important, task in the development of the piston aero engine was the design of the cylinder. Probably 90 per cent of the engines produced prior to 1919 had cylinders which were extremely poor by modern standards. Where water-cooled cylinders were concerned Kirkham in the USA and Birkigt in Europe pioneered the use of thin steel cylinders screwed into a monobloc aluminium head-casting linking a whole row of cylinders in one rigid unit. The air-cooled cylinder was in some ways more difficult, and in 1915–16 Britain's Royal Aircraft Factory carried out the first systematic research anywhere in the world on such cylinders. The principals in this work were Professor A. H. Gibson and Samuel D. Heron. By late 1916 they had laid down basic principles, the three main ones of which were: the head should be aluminium, since this metal conducts heat faster than the same mass of any other metal; the head should be a single piece of metal, because joints cannot be maintained in perfect thermal contact; and the heat should be able to escape from the largest possible fin area after travelling the shortest possible distance along a path with the greatest possible cross-section area.

These principles were first used in September 1916 in the design of a completely new engine, the Raf 8, which was to lead to an important engine of the 1920s. At the end of the war a technically illiterate Government purchasing machine had committed the British fighting services to an engine that proved to be unusable. This engine, the ABC Dragonfly air-cooled radial, is instructive in that one can compare its original cylinder with that designed for it at Farnborough in late 1918. The difference is startling. The original head had no provision for cooling at all. But even with a good cylinder this engine remained deeply faulted, and was soon abandoned. In contrast, there was nothing fundamentally wrong with the Raf 8, and in January 1917 Farnborough's chief engineer,

Major F. M. Green, moved to the Siddeley Deasy Car Co, later renamed Armstrong Siddeley Motors, with (among other things) a remit to continue development of this promising air-cooled radial. Its cylinders were similar to those designed to help the Dragonfly.

The Raf 8 had 14 cylinders of 127 mm (5 in) bore and stroke (22,534 cc/1,374 cu in), arranged in two rows. At this time many radials had large numbers of cylinders arranged in other ways. For example, the Smith Static of 1914 (a fine engine, especially for that period) had 10 cylinders in a single row but with the con-rods offset and bearing alternatively on the two crankpins of a two-throw crankshaft. Roy Fedden's Cosmos Mercury of 1917 likewise had a two-throw crankshaft, but its 14 cylinders were arranged in a helix (spiral), with seven thin con-rods working side-by-side on each crankpin. In contrast, the Raf 8 had what became the almost universal arrangement. The cylinders were arranged with a front row of seven, all in the same plane, and an identical rear row. One cylinder in each row drove a master rod with a big end made in two parts which could

be bolted together over one of the two crankpins of the one-piece crankshaft. The other six cylinders of each row drove articulated or link rods. Though in many ways outstanding, this engine needed a lot of development. One of its remarkable features was that the rear end of the crankshaft was geared up to drive a small supercharger. The drives were soon fitted with centrifugal clutches, but to avoid costly development the supercharger was replaced in 1921 by a simple fan driven at crankshaft speed merely to improve mixture distribution. By this time the engine was named Jaguar, and it gave about 300 hp. This was a conservative rating, and even after 1922, when the stroke was lengthened to 140 mm (5.5 in) (capacity 24,797 cc/1,512 cu in), the rating remained 300 hp at 1,500 rpm, though by 1924 it had risen to 385 hp at 1,700 rpm. It found a large market in aircraft for the RAF, Fleet Air Arm and Imperial Airways.

In 1918 Roy Fedden, seeing how completely the Ministry of Munitions had decided to standardize on the Dragonfly, decided to design a bigger nine-cylinder radial with the ultimate objective of 500 hp. He was (rightly)

One of the oft-told stories of aviation is how the British Government committed its aircraft industry in 1918 to the Dragonfly, an engine incapable of being used. Here we see cross-sections through the Dragonfly cylinder (left) and through that designed at Farnborough to replace it (right), which was similar to that of the Raf 8.

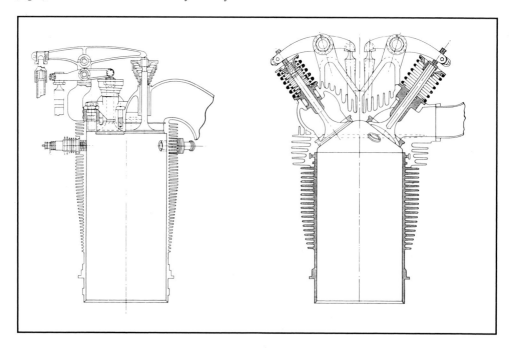

convinced that a single-row, air-cooled radial represented the simplest and cheapest answer to the problem of designing an engine of this power, which was the highest that appeared to be demanded for the immediate future. There were many engines of greater power, as will be described later, but for all practical purposes 500 hp took care of every normal (ie non-racing) military and civil application until 1930. Thus Fedden's thinking was sound. Inevitably a nine-cylinder, single-row engine had a bigger frontal area than one with 14 smaller cylinders in two rows, but with aircraft speeds typically around 161 km/h (100 mph) this made little difference.

Fedden's big engine, named the Jupiter, first ran on 29 October 1918. It was a predictably sound design, though with hindsight one can see some doubtful features. Bore and stroke were 146 mm and 191 mm (5.75 in and 7.5 in) respectively, giving the substantial capacity of 28,749 cc (1,753 cu in). These cylinders were machined from steel forgings. Fedden knew that Farnborough had shown the best head to be solid aluminium, but he was afraid of the problem of attaching such a head to the steel barrel. In any case, he was not convinced such a head really transmitted heat better. Accordingly he made the steel cylinder closed at the top, providing a seat for the valves. He was aware of the size of the cylinder and the probability that future engines would run at much higher rpm, and to obtain good breathing he fitted four valves (two inlet, two exhaust) to each cylinder. These were of course overhead, and parallel to the cylinder axis, driven by two pushrods up the front of the cylinder with tappets acted on by front and rear cam rings driven at one-eighth crankshaft speed in the reverse direction. On top of each cylinder, and containing the valve gear, was an aluminium 'poultice head' held tightly down to the end of the steel cylinder by studs and set screws, with Invar packing sleeves under the nuts to maintain— or attempt to maintain—good thermal contact despite the different expansion of the steel and aluminium.

Anyone who can get hold of a copy of my biography of Fedden, *By Jupiter*, will soon see that he had an unrivalled urge to work—as he would have said, 'night and day'. Thanks to his leadership, development of the Jupiter was relentless, so that after 1926 the Jaguar could no longer compete. Obviously he never ceased to increase the fin area on the cylinder barrel and head. The crankcase, a two-piece aluminium casting, was replaced by a tougher and lighter drop forging, split into front and rear halves united by nine long bolts which projected through the rear cover to mount the engine to the airframe. The original design of a one-piece crankshaft, necessitating a split master rod bolted over the crankpin, was replaced by a solid big end threaded over the crankpin of a two-piece crankshaft. The end of the crankpin was not splined or keyed, but merely held tight by a bolt which squeezed the split ends of the web. A major boost was the purchase of a licence in 1921 by the French Gnome-Rhône company (the firm formed by a merger in 1914), and in 1926 they in turn licensed Bristol to use the Farman-type epicyclic reduction gear, the resulting increase in rpm (from around 1,750 to 2,200) not only increasing power but also solving vibration problems. Early Jupiters had a triplex carburettor whose three choke tubes fed to points 120° apart in a circular gallery around the rear of the crankcase containing a curious spiral guide which, it was said, gave precisely equal mixture distribution to the nine cylinders. This was eventually replaced by a conventional inlet manifold, and in any case Jupiters were available from 1927 with a supercharger of particularly good design. The last major change, clearly overdue in 1929, was to replace the poultice head by a forged aluminium head screwed and shrunk on to an open-ended steel barrel.

These developments turned the Jupiter into perhaps the world's most reliable engine, with power increased from around 380 hp to well over 500. Even the latter was a conservative figure, because a special short-stroke version built for the 1927 Schneider Trophy race gave 960 hp. This was the first of the Mercury family, unrelated to the 1917 engine of that name. In the 1930s continued relentless development—mainly in the nature of detail design refinements, combined with better materials and petrol of 87 and then 100 octane—resulted in the Mercury giving 995 hp in regular RAF service, while the Jupiter was developed into the Pegasus which exceeded 1,000 hp, still on the original size of cylinder.

As described later, Bristol progressively abandoned these fine engines in order to concentrate on engines with sleeve valves. By 1930, 10 years after the formation of Bristol's Engine Department, the Jupiter was well on the way to becoming the engine of the world. A 1929 issue of the French *L'Aéro* had banner headlines '*SCANDALE JUPITER*' because the British-designed Gnome-Rhône engine powered over 80 per cent of the military and commercial aircraft at the Paris airshow. By that time there were 17 foreign licensees, and Jupiters had flown in 262 different types of aircraft.

Predictably, Gnome-Rhône had been seeking a way to evade the terms of the licence, and increasingly they just ignored it. In October 1927 they called the latest GR Jupiter the Mistral, and ceased to pay royalties. A year later they produced the Mistral Major, or GR14K, a 14-cylinder, two-row engine. Fedden's insistence on four valves per cylinder made it almost impossible for him to design a two-row engine with elegant valve gear. Gnome-Rhône side-stepped the problem by using just two large valves per cylinder. This made the valve gear almost simple, and by 1932 the GR14K had become an important family at powers up to 900 hp, which

Fedden's nine-cylinder engines could not then rival. It was partly to overcome the valve gear problem that Fedden turned to sleeves.

In the 1930s GR beat Bristol in licensing many countries to build their (Bristol-derived) engines. They also produced neat two-row engines of amazingly small diameter, such as the 950 mm (37.4 in) 14M Mars, but this, and the rival Hispano-Suiza 14AB, were simply not powerful enough to produce effective warplanes for the Second World War. What was more interesting was that Alfa-Romeo in Italy and Nakajima in Japan did build two-row engines with four-valve cylinders, and complicated valve gear, though they were not of great importance. With the benefit of hindsight one can see that, despite the excellence of Fedden's engines, he did not have to choose four valves and he did not have to develop sleeve valves either. To see the proof

With the rear wheelcase removed the Bristol Jupiter's supercharger is exposed. This 1927 supercharger had a modest steel impeller with curved inlet guide vanes. Around it can be seen the diffuser vanes which guided the mixture into the nine induction pipes. The Jupiter was developed into the Pegasus (see p. 76).

Cross-section through a cylinder of a Bristol Pegasus. This descended from the poultice-head Jupiter via the Jupiter with a screwed-on forged head. The Pegasus cylinder was refined in detail and had greater fin area. The joint ring (inset) was soft copper (Odhams Press).

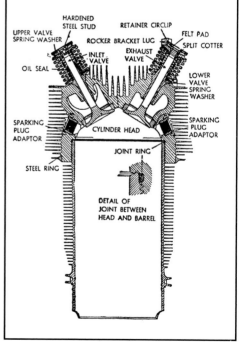

Cutaway Mikulin AM-34RN, a great Soviet V-12 of 1933. Note the double overhead camshafts to drive the four valves of each cylinder, and the massive double-helical reduction gear just visible at the right (N. A. Eastaway).

one need look no further than the USA, where Wright and then Pratt & Whitney came from behind to become the leading suppliers of high-power engines to the world.

They did this entirely with radial engines with air-cooled cylinders with two valves, but first we should look at the alternative type of engine. Such water-cooled V-12s as the Liberty, Rolls-Royce Eagle and Condor, BMW VI and various Fiat and Isotta-Fraschini types all continued in use through the 1920s, even though they had traditional separate cylinders. But such engines were on the way out. In the Soviet Union A. A. Mikulin managed the production of the M-17, a licensed BMW VI of which over 22,000 were made (compared with 9,200 of the original German engine). He progressively introduced improvements, and by 1930 was allowed to use his own initials in the AM-30. This was further developed into a family of AM-34s which, whilst retaining the original 160 mm × 190 mm (6.29 in × 7.48 in) cylinder, more than doubled the power to 1,275 hp. During the Second World War the same 46.7 litre (2,850 cu in) engine culminated in the AM-47 at 3,100 hp. How to go from around 500 hp to 3,100 is worth examining in some detail. The

first thing Mikulin did was replace separate cylinders by steel liners in aluminium blocks. He also fitted four valves per cylinder, each directly actuated so that each block had two camshafts. The more powerful versions also had an excellent supercharger and a massive spur reduction gear with double-helical 'herringbone' teeth.

In April 1917 Napier in England ran the prototype of the Lion. Designed by A. J. Rowledge, this was a water-cooled engine with 12 cylinders, of 140 mm × 130 mm (5.5 in × 5.125 in) bore and stroke (23,960 cc/1,461 cu in) arranged in W or 'broad arrow' configuration. Each row of four steel cylinders had traditional steel water jackets welded on, each cylinder then being spigoted into the crankcase and bolted through flanges at the base. On top were beautiful monobloc cast-aluminium heads in one piece for each row, secured by screwing in the steel valve seats which were flanged within the flat tops of the cylinders. Each cylinder had four valves driven by two overhead camshafts. The centre block had vertical master rods to which the link rods from the other cylinders were pinned. (A cross-section appears in *World Encyclopaedia of Aero Engines*.) It was an

The Napier Lion V was a bomber version (eg, Vickers Virginia), with direct spur reduction gear. It gave 460 hp at 2,000 rpm.

excellent basic design, well-balanced, rigid and smooth-running, but having no parents and no offspring it made no impact on history. Most Lions gave 450 to 550 hp at a little over 2,000 rpm, but by almost doubling the speed to a remarkable 3,900 rpm, and compression ratio from 5.8 to 10, Schneider Trophy engines gave up to 1,400 hp.

Rival engines were made by Curtiss. As noted in the previous chapter, Charles B. Kirkham produced an outstanding water-cooled V-12 in 1916, the K-12. In its crankcase and six-cylinder blocks, all three cast together as a single piece, it pushed the art of casting aluminium beyond the capability of the period, and there were also problems with the reduction gear and the fact that the crankshaft needed seven bearings. Nevertheless, Arthur Nutt (Kirkham's successor as chief engineer) strove to rectify deficiencies and succeeded in qualifying a much better engine, the D-12, in 1922. This quickly became very important, and in both its original and enlarged 22,960 cc (1,400 cu in) forms it won two Schneider Trophy races and set seven world speed records. Even in racing trim it only gave about 488 hp, but Curtiss took the trouble to install it in a streamlined way, with a pointed propeller spinner leading into the smooth and tight-fitting cowling. In 1926 Curtiss began producing a further enlargement, the 25,420 cc (1,550 cu in) Conqueror, of 575 hp. This was virtually the only remaining water-cooled engine in the USA, but, despite being made in large numbers for the Army and airlines, at powers up to 650 hp, it faded rapidly after 1932, being replaced by air-cooled radials. Its final application was as the V-1570–61, with turbo-supercharger, giving the Consolidated PB-2A a speed of 441 km/h (274 mph) at 7,620 m

(25,000 ft), compared with 343 km/h (213 mph) at sea level. This was probably the fastest combat aircraft in the world in 1934.

When Richard Fairey saw D-12 installations he immediately purchased a licence, and used his Fairey Felix version in the Fox high-speed bomber (much faster than any RAF fighter). But the British Air Ministry did not want another engine builder, and used the experience to spur dormant Rolls-Royce into designing a new engine. Rowledge (ex-Napier) and Sir Henry Royce schemed a remarkably advanced X-16 engine, with the four cast blocks of small 114 mm × 121 mm (4.5 in × 4.75 in) cylinders all spaced at 90°. The prototype was already running when 'the Old Man' ordered a fresh start on a conventional V-12, with cylinders 127 mm × 140 mm (5.0 in × 5.5 in) (21,254 cc/1,296 cu in), slightly greater capacity than the X-16. This ran at the end of 1926 as the F, later named Kestrel. It launched Rolls-Royce into the business of designing modern aero engines, and incidentally proved a considerable commercial success.

Having been most competently designed in 1926 the Kestrel was basically more modern than the Curtiss engines, and was better able to stand up to competition from air-cooled radials. At sea level the advantage lay with the air-cooled engine, which almost always had a much lower installed weight and, by being short, enhanced fighter manoeuvrability. As noted later, the installation was becoming increasingly important. At altitude, the air-cooled engine quickly became deficient in cooling; put another way, if it was made to deliver high power it overheated. Moreover, it was unable in the early 1930s to handle a high degree of supercharging; in a liquid-cooled engine the mixture could be compressed to a considerably higher pressure and temperature without causing detonation. To show some results in practice, in 1933 the Boeing P-26A (air-cooled Wasp H) reached 378 km/h (235 mph) but needed 12 minutes to climb to 6,096 m (20,000 ft); the Gloster Gauntlet (air-cooled Mercury) reached 373 km/h (232 mph) and needed 9 minutes to climb to 6,096 m (20,000 ft); the Hawker Fury II (water-cooled Kestrel) could only reach 354 km/h (220 mph) but could climb to 6,096 m (20,000 ft) in 8.64 minutes. This was because of the better ability of the water-cooled engine to maintain power at high altitude.

In the period immediately following the First World War there were no high-power, air-cooled engines in the United States, and an adverse economic climate, with a glut of wartime engines and near-zero budgets for any form of aviation. But in 1921 Wright ran the R-1, very like a short-stroke Jupiter. This petered out, as did several other designs, although the J-5 Whirlwind, a 220-hp nine-cylinder radial of 1925, did a great deal for aviation in May 1927 by keeping going for over 33 hours to take Lindbergh to Paris, despite exposed valve gear and unimpressive cylinder-head cooling. In 1924–5 Wright's president, chief engineer and chief designer all left to form Pratt & Whitney Aircraft. Wright struggled on, and not only improved the Whirlwind but also designed a succession of larger engines which led to the R-1750 (an early example of the US designation system

Cross-section (No 5 cylinder, looking aft) through a typical supercharged Rolls-Royce Kestrel. Note the end-pivot valve rockers, and good inlet aerodynamics.

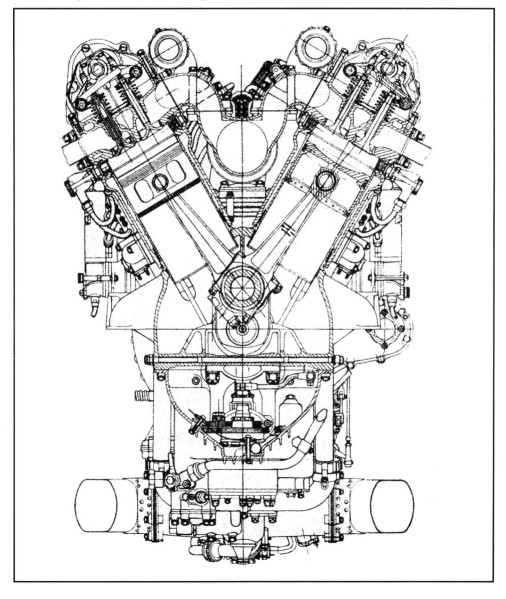

In 1939 the Wright Cyclone (R-1820) G-series rivalled the Pegasus as the best engine in the 1,000 hp class from the viewpoints of simplicity, economy and reliability. Note the 18 baffles which, when the engine was cowled, forced the air to flow between the cooling fins.

which gave both the configuration and the capacity in cubic inches), named Cyclone. This had excellent Heron-designed cylinders of 152 mm (6 in) bore and 175 mm (6.875 in) stroke. This engine was type-tested in 1927 at 500 hp, but by 1932 cylinder bore had been increased to 156 mm (6.125 in), giving capacity of 29,897 cc (1,823 cu in), and from that time on the R-1820 Cyclone was one of the world's most important engines. Thanks to ceaseless development, which brought in a forged crankcase, ever-greater cooling-fin area, dynamic crank-web counterweights and both geared and turbo-type superchargers, power settled at 1,200 hp for wartime B-17s and 1,525 hp for post-war aeroplanes and helicopters.

The top men left Wright because they believed they could design a better engine. This quickly materialized as the R-1340 Wasp, with the bold objective of 400 hp for a weight of 295 kg (650 lb). The first Wasp went on test just after Christmas 1925, and recorded 425 hp for a weight of just under the limit. Most features of its design can be guessed. Each cylinder of 146 mm (5.75 in) bore and stroke (22,042 cc/1,344 cu in for all nine) had a forged steel barrel machined with close-pitched fins. The well-cooled head was an aluminium casting, screwed and shrunk on. The two inclined valves were driven by completely enclosed gear, the rocker boxes being cast with the head. The two-piece crankcase was forged aluminium, so much lighter than a

casting that the engine could have greater capacity and keep within the 650 lb limit. The crankshaft was made in two parts so that a one-piece master rod could be used, calculated during design to allow 1,900 rpm instead of the limit with a split big end of only 1,650. The crankshaft had vibration dampers and ran in roller bearings.

In 1925 the big Pratt & Whitney machine-tool firm must have been troubled at the prospect of investing $1.25 million (today equivalent to about $90 million) in something as chancy as a new aviation engine. From the outset the Wasp was a success, and on it was built the company that today says it is the world's biggest builder of such engines. President Frederick B. Rentschler had gone ahead with the Wasp in the hope of big Navy orders, which he got. Indeed the Wasp and its later big brother, the R-1690 Hornet, practically monopolized Navy aircraft for many years. But at the 1928 National Air Races in Los Angeles the fastest aircraft were the latest pursuits (fighters), the Wasp-powered Navy XF4B and the Curtiss D-12 engined Army P-1B. In races the XF4B averaged 277.2 km/h (172.3 mph), against the 237.6 km/h (147.7

The Wright Cyclone crankshaft was made in two parts, joined by a Maneton coupling tightened by a pinch-bolt. This allowed the big end of the master rod to be in one piece. Note the dynamic vibration dampers in the counterweight, and the locking plate preventing the propeller shaft from unscrewing (the drive tended to tighten the joint).

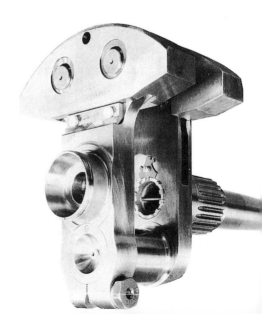

mph) of the water-cooled Army aircraft. Considered even more important was the race to 3,048 m (10,000 ft) and back, timed chock-to-chock. The P-1B took 7.08 minutes, but the XF4B needed only 5.92 minutes. The Chief of the Army Air Corps, General Fechet, was so impressed he placed a verbal order on the spot, so the Army got P-12s before the Navy got their almost identical F4B-1s.

By the start of 1930 Pratt & Whitney had 60 per cent of the total business reported by the nation's 25 chief aero-engine makers! The Hornet grew to 30,504 cc (1,860 cu in), and an odd water-cooled engine, with five banks each of four small cylinders, had come, run and been abandoned. Partly because of the growing prestige of Leonard S. 'Luke' Hobbs, who had been the Army carburettor expert at McCook Field and rapidly rose to be Pratt & Whitney's chief engineer, the company never really departed from the traditional air-cooled radial. It did not need to seek difficult solutions such as sleeve valves, because with two valves per cylinder a two-row engine was no problem. The first two appeared in 1932, both with 14 cylinders: The R-1535 Twin Wasp Junior and the R-1830 Twin Wasp. The former was developed for the Navy, which wanted a two-row engine not so much for higher power as to reduce diameter, mainly to improve pilot view ahead. By 1935 it had grown to 825 hp, but customers for this power could get a single-row engine, such as a Cyclone or Pegasus, for a lower price. One of the few who really made use of the R-1535's small diameter of under 1.12 m (44 in) was Howard Hughes, who used one in his 1935 monoplane in which he set a new world landplane speed record. But the 1535 was never important, and Hobbs stopped further development in 1936. In sharpest contrast, the Twin Wasp was one of the great engines of history. It passed its type test on 1 February 1933, at 760 hp. The 50th engine was shipped in October 1934, and from then on, while the power on 100-octane fuel climbed by 1938 to 1,200 hp, applications and demand kept on multiplying.

Whereas there was nothing really amiss with the R-1830 installation in the C-47 (the commercial DC-3 having invariably been powered by Cyclones), early R-1830 installations in fighters were generally unimpressive. In any case by 1940 even 1,200 hp was beginning to appear inadequate. In the Curtiss Hawk series the Twin Wasp had by 1940 been completely replaced by Allison or Packard

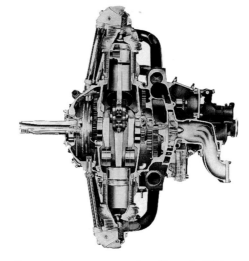

Cross-section cutaway of a Pratt & Whitney Wasp Junior, virtually a Wasp but with capacity reduced from 22,042 to 16,154 cc (1,344 to 985 cu in). Note the crankshaft counterweights, and the geared drives to the cam ring at the front (with separate tracks for the inlet and exhaust pushrods) and to the small supercharger.

(Merlin) liquid-cooled engines, and such fighters as the Swedish J22, Finnish Myrsky II and Australian Boomerang used the R-1830 only because no other engine was available. One could draw misleading conclusions from this, because by September 1935 Pratt & Whitney had begun work on a Twin Wasp with a two-stage supercharger. Much effort was expended investigating independent drive to the two impellers, and on the development of intercoolers (to increase the density of the charge) either ahead of or downstream of the second impeller. The Curtiss P-36 entered in the spring 1939 fighter competition was powered by a two-stage R-1830 rated at 1,050 hp at 6,858 m (22,500 ft), but the superchargers surged at altitude and the installation was very poor. Further effort led to the Navy accepting the world's first service-cleared, two-stage aircraft, the Grumman F4F-3 Wildcat, in July 1940. What received hardly any publicity was that in late 1941 Pratt & Whitney installed an R-1830-SSC7-G engine in their P-40 testbed. Designated simply as a Hawk 81A, it had an installation incomparably better than those of earlier Twin Wasps, and in 1942 this aircraft reached 626 km/h (389 mph) at 6,919 m (22,700 ft) and climbed to 4,572 m (15,000 ft) in 5.5 min and to 6,096 m (20,000 ft) in 7.54 min!

I am not pretending that this Hawk 81 might have been a cheaper substitute for such

Cutaway of the pioneer two-stage supercharger fitted to the Pratt & Whitney R-1830–76 Twin Wasp which powered the F4F-3, the initial production version of the Grumman G-36 (Martlet/Wildcat). The air was compressed first by the blower on the right.

much more powerful aircraft as the P-47 and F4U. What I do suggest is that, once designers had learned how to install them, air-cooled radials were fully competitive with liquid-cooled V and similar engines on the score of performance, and superior in all other respects, such as cost, moment of inertia (affecting manoeuvrability) and combat vulnerability. I have repeatedly commented on the unjustified conclusions drawn in the past from the many occasions when a low-powered radial was replaced by a high-powered liquid-cooled engine. My generation was strongly influenced by the Schneider Trophy contests, and when we drew a super-fast aeroplane in the back of a school exercise book it always had a long pointed nose, never a radial.

In the 1920s the only radial specially developed for the Schneider races was the Bristol Mercury, a short-stroke Jupiter which may have been the first engine to be knowingly designed to run faster than the principal torsional frequency of the crankshaft. All the other engines were large water-cooled designs, notably by Fiat, Isotta-Fraschini, Renault, Hispano-Suiza, Napier and Rolls-Royce. For the 1931 race there were only two serious contenders, the Rolls-Royce R (redesigned since the 1929 race) and Fiat AS 6. The former was a synthesis of all the latest technology in mechanical design, advanced materials, high-capacity superchargers (the impeller was double-sided, besides running at unprecedented speed) and totally new 'witches' brews' instead of any normal petroleum-derived fuel. For the 1931 speed record by an S.6B seaplane at 655 km/h (407 mph) the engine delivered something approaching 2,800 hp at 3,400 rpm at a boost pressure of nearly 21 lb/sq in. Nothing like this had been even approached previously, and — except perhaps for a few 'unlimited' racing engines — no subsequent piston aircraft engine has combined these figures. The nearest approach to the author's knowledge was an experimental Merlin (next chapter) run in 1944 at 2,640 hp. This was a much smaller engine than the R, and its BMEP appears to be an all-time record.

As for the Fiat AS 6, this was not in the same class, but obtained high power by sheer size. It comprised two AS 5 V-12 engines in tandem, built as one. The crankshaft of the front engine had a large gearwheel on the back driving a hollow propeller shaft lying between the cylinder blocks. The rear crankshaft had a similar gearwheel on the front to drive a second shaft down the centre of the first. At the front the two shafts drove contrarotating propellers, which removed the severe piloting problems caused by enormous residual torque transmitted to the aircraft. The AS 6 was almost three years late for the 1931 Schneider Trophy but it gave 3,100 hp in 1934 to set a seaplane piston-engined speed

record at 708.9 km/h (440.6 mph) that still stands.

Fiat's policy of just using a huge engine robbed the company, and country, of spin-off and experience that could be put to use in future engines. Fiat's ordinary (non-racing) water-cooled engines continued to be unimpressive (one powered the Fiat CR 32, page 134). By the Second World War Fiat had been left behind, and had to make the German DB 601 and 605 under licence in order to power Italian fighters. In contrast the Rolls-Royce R made the subsequent development of high-power engines much quicker. It also gave an enormous spur to the development of improved anti-detonation fuels and to the use of superchargers to boost power at low levels, instead of only to reduce the fall-off in power at high altitude. Naturally these advances were applied first and most strongly by Rolls-Royce, notably to the Merlin.

In the United States the Schneider Trophy was viewed with more long-range objectivity. The USA ceased to compete in this particular contest after 1926, but its own keenly contested races ensured plenty of input from speed competition. Sam Heron believed, 'Airplane racing ... has no useful effects upon either engine or fuel development. The gladiators (pilots) who are to be thrown to the

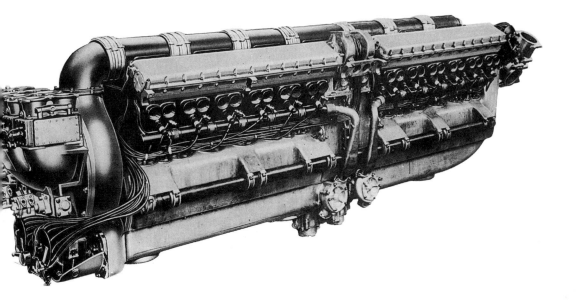

For 58 years the world seaplane speed record has been held by the Macchi MC.72, powered by the unwieldy Fiat AS 6. This comprised two massive V-12 engines joined into one, each half driving one unit of a coaxial propeller. Note the eight carburettor choke tubes feeding mixture to the huge supercharger. The induction system caused backfires violent enough to destroy the aircraft.

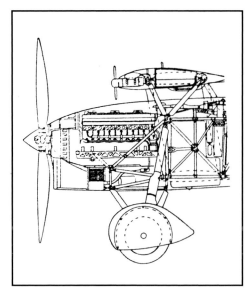

Typical technology of the 1930s is shown in this drawing of the Fiat CR 32, a particularly agile biplane fighter. The massive 600-hp Fiat A30 RA bis water-cooled V-12 sat on the front of the welded steel-tube fuselage truss, with the radiator underneath and the oil cooler above the reduction gear. Petrol from the tank between the engine and cockpit was pumped to the gravity tank in the upper wing, in front of which was the wind-driven generator.

lions and their backers fiddle around with inadequate facilities and, if anything, retard development by pestering the engine and petroleum industries with their problems . . .' This is a harsh and perhaps short-sighted view, though certainly the objectives and problems of racing are slightly different from those of service with a fighter squadron, and very different indeed from airline service.

By 1930 the US Navy had ceased to have any interest in water-cooled engines, while the Army had more reluctantly ceased to fund development of its only engines in this category, the Conqueror and the totally new P&W R-2060. Thus almost all high-power engine development was concentrated upon air-cooled radials, and by far the greatest spur to progress was the commercial rivalry between Wright and Pratt & Whitney. Leaving aside numerous engines which were eventually abandoned, the important engines by 1936 were: the P&W R-1830 Twin Wasp, already mentioned; the Wright 14-cylinder R-2600,

which began life at 1,400 hp and by 1942 gave 1,900; P&W's answer, the 18-cylinder R-2800 Double Wasp, which grew from 1,850 hp to 2,800; and the Wright 18-cylinder R-3350 Duplex Cyclone, aimed at 2,000 hp and developed after the Second World War to 3,700. None of these initially broke much new ground, and they achieved high power mainly by their large capacity. Conservatively rated, at least at the outset, they provided US and later Allied aircraft manufacturers with more installed power than was available anywhere else, and (with the exception of the early years of the R-3350) with acceptable reliability.

All this was externally obvious. What was not publicised at the time was that the US Army had been deeply impressed by the 1931 Rolls-Royce R, and, quite rightly, had formed the opinion that no air-cooled radial at that time could come anywhere near the same specific power (output per unit capacity). It was strongly reinforced in this view by experiments begun in 1930 by Heron at Wright Field, using single experimental cylinders. These began with an air-cooled version of the Liberty cylinder, with a water jacket round the barrel and a water spray on the head, and with sodium-cooled exhaust valves. Outstanding powers were soon achieved, and the Army began funding the development of a so-called Hyper cylinder, which could eventually be incorporated into a complete engine in the 1,000-hp class. This cylinder went ahead with the same 117 mm (4.625 in) bore as the Liberty, but with stroke reduced to 127 mm (5 in), so that a 12-cylinder engine would have only 16,531 cc (1,008 cu in). It was also decided that, instead of water, the coolant should be ethylene glycol (marketed in the USA as Prestone) at 149°C (300°F). Obviously the rate of heat transfer through the radiator depends on the difference in temperature, and the hotter the coolant, the smaller the radiator can be. A smaller radiator means significantly less weight and drag. Later it was discovered that at a coolant temperature of 300°F the engine transfers so much heat to the oil that the combined oil and coolant radiators must be at least as large as the total at 250°.

In 1932 the Navy suddenly felt it ought also to take an interest in liquid cooling, and contracted with Wright for the X-1800, a V-12 in the 800-hp class. This completed a 50-hour qualification test in June 1934, but had to be abandoned for lack of funds soon after. Meanwhile in 1932 the Army, thinking the Hyper cylinder almost fully developed, contracted with Continental to assemble 12 of them into a V engine with supercharger. It believed such an engine could run in short order, and perhaps be in production by 1935. What actually happened was a series of design changes. First the cylinder was made larger, though it was increasingly obvious that unless more than 12 were used the engine would still not be sufficiently powerful. The result was an engine of 23,452 cc (1,430 cu in) which was then changed to a horizontally opposed type so that it might fit inside the wings of bombers and even of fighters. By 1939 it was obvious that a 23,452 cc (1,430 cu in) engine was too small for bombers, and that fighter wings had become too thin for any 'buried' engine installation. The Army wanted to return to a V-12, but Colonel Charles Lindbergh had been so impressed by the Bf 109 that the final choice was an inverted IV-1430, supposedly because of better pilot view. Ironically, the only applications were in twin-engined fighters (XP-49 and XP-67) where the opposed engine might have been better and pilot view did not enter into the picture. Eventually the IV-1430 developed the outstanding power of 2,100 hp at 3,400 rpm with a manifold pressure of 87.8 in (28.5 lb/sq in), but it was too late and the costly 12-year effort was abandoned in 1944.

The sole American liquid-cooled engine that made the grade in time was the Allison V-1710. In his book Setright states, '. . . it was a dreadful engine.' This opinion can only result from unfamiliarity with it. Everyone knows that the P-51 Mustang was designed around the Allison, but achieved much higher performance when the Packard-built Merlin was substituted. This was simply because the supercharging system of the two-stage Merlin was in a different class from the Allison's gear-driven supercharger in the early war years. The basic engine was a beautiful design, with no obvious shortcomings. The 140 mm × 152 mm (5.5 in × 6.0 in) cylinders had pent-roof head with four inclined valves actuated by single overhead camshafts driven at the rear of each one-piece cylinder block. When Allisons began arriving in Britain in late 1940 our technical press was so ignorant it described the unfamiliar engine as 'at least two feet longer . . . than a Merlin' and as 'a new motor, quite undeveloped'. In fact a typical Tomahawk engine was just 76 mm (3 in) longer and 44 kg (98 lb) lighter than a Merlin XX. As for being undeveloped, the V-1710 first ran in August 1931, more than

two years before the Merlin, and in March 1937 passed a type test at 1,000 hp on 87-octane fuel, which was well beyond the reach of any Merlin at that time. I do not wish to suggest the V-1710 was some kind of super-engine, but it was tough, reliable and, in the P-51—in my opinion—a lot smoother to fly with than the crackling Merlin. Its short-coming at height was completely overcome by fitting a turbosupercharger, as was done to the prototype XP-39 Airacobra, Curtiss XP-37 and all P-38 Lightnings (except a handful built for Britain). This is commented on further in the next chapter, together with the big Pratt & Whitney liquid-cooled engines.

Having described how Mikulin developed the BMW VI into a far more powerful family of Soviet engines, it is only fair to see what his compatriot V. Ya. Klimov did with the Hispano-Suiza V-12s. The latter were developed continuously from 1919 until about 1952, but during the crucial 1930s, when France had need of a good fighter engine, they were in relation to their size pathetically under-rated. Of course, all had cast cylinder blocks with water cooling, almost all were geared, and several variants were equipped with the firm's patented *moteur canon* firing through the propeller hub. Fighters of around 1931 had the 12X series, with fork/blade con-rods, typically rated at 690 hp. By 1935 these had been super-

After two years testing totally new liquid-cooled cylinders, Pratt & Whitney began testing the 1,116-hp R-2060 in 1931. Funded by the Army, this had 20 cylinders in five banks, each bank having an overhead camshaft driving a magneto at the back. It was not a success (United Technologies Archive).

seded by the 12Y family, with much larger cylinders (150 mm × 170 mm, 36.05 litres/6 in × 7 in, 2,198 cu in) and master/link con-rods, typically rated at 860 hp. This performance can be compared with the Merlin's (admittedly later) achievement of 1,200 hp from 27 litres (1,646 cu in), and explains the inability of such fighters as the Morane-Saulnier MS.406 to fight on even terms with the Bf 109. All these Hispano engines had poor super-

chargers delivering air along enormous manifolds low down on each side to feed three carburettors for each block, each serving two cylinders. Klimov initially did nothing but make the VK-100 series easier to mass produce and easier to maintain, but he also managed by very painstaking refinement to get his VK-105 cleared to 2,700 rpm (one reason for the poor HS12Y performance being a limit to 2,400 rpm) and during the war

A selection of the 59 production versions of the Allison V-1710: top, the V-3420 double engine; next, in order, a typical F-series (made in by far the greatest numbers), with increased power, higher thrust line and reduced length; a C-series for the P-40; a direct-drive engine for an extension shaft; an F17 for a P-38 (remote turbo not shown); and (left) a D2 pusher with 5 ft extension shaft for the Bell YFM-1, and (right) an E11 with 8 ft tractor extension shaft for the Bell P-63A. Obviously the last two are to a smaller scale.

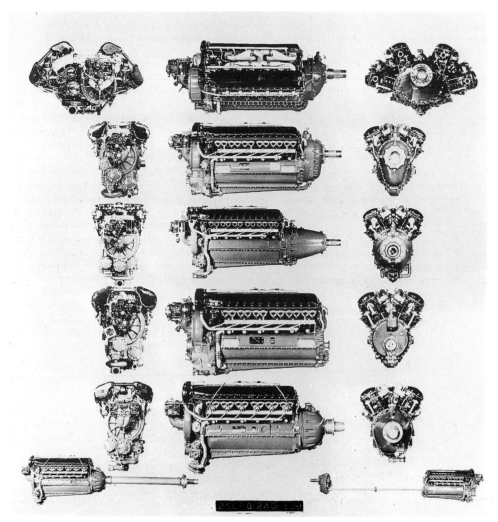

As far as mass-production engines are concerned the ultimate outcome of the Hispano-Suiza series was Klimov's VK-105PF. This example at Monino has the coolant header on top and three carburettors along each side (N. A. Eastaway).

over 101,000 of various VK-105 versions were produced at 1,260 or 1,280 hp.

As I pointed out in the foreword, this book of necessity concentrates on engines of technical interest. I have not referred to perhaps 90 per cent of the engines of the inter-war years, and in the case of small engines for light aircraft the proportion will jump to about 99 per cent, because there were over 500 makes. Many such engines were derived from already existing designs, some even intended for motor cycles. A few engines were of sufficient interest or commercial importance to merit brief mention.

One such family was the Cirrus/Gipsy series. Their genesis was unique. After the First World War Major Frank Halford (see previous chapter) worked at the Aircraft Disposal Co, which wondered how best to use at least 30,000 surplus engines and possibly about the same number of airframes. Not many engines found buyers, though Halford did effect a thoroughgoing redesign of the 9 litre Renault air-cooled V-8, including aluminium cylinder heads, larger valves, higher compression ratio and dual ignition (which was fast becoming mandatory for civil engines).

As a result, the power at 1,800 rpm was raised from 80 hp to 125, and Halford further got the Airdisco V-8 (as it was called) cleared to 144 hp at 2,000 rpm. This sounds fantastic,

but of course the original Renault only became acceptably reliable by virtue of its exceedingly modest rating. Trying to encourage private flying, the British Government organized a series of Light Aeroplane Competitions from 1923 to 1926. Had they just left designers to get on with it some good might have resulted, but organizers love to organize and they began by stipulating an engine size of 750 cc (45.7 cu in), which 70 years ago guaranteed useless aircraft. In a later competition the limit was raised to 1 litre (61 cu in). Geoffrey de Havilland wisely decided to ignore these competitions—despite enticing prizes—and instead to design a useful aeroplane.

He had known Halford well during the war, and together they schemed an upright four-in-line engine using the complete cylinders, connecting rods and crankshaft of the V-8 but with a new deep aluminium crankcase and direct drive to the propeller. The result, called the Cirrus, naturally had 105 mm × 130 mm cylinders, 4.5 litres (4 in × 5 in, 275 cu in), and with the very low compression ratio of 4.65 was rated at 64 hp at 1,800 rpm, with 68 hp at 2,000 rpm for take-off. It was fitted to the prototype DH.60 Moth, flown by de Havilland on 22 February 1925.

Halford went on to develop Cirrus engines with greater capacity, forged light-alloy conrods, bronze valve seats and other refinements. This is believed to have been the first

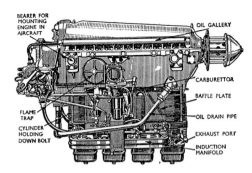

Of 27,654 Gipsy engines of all types no fewer than 14,615 were of the Major Series I type (used, for example, in Tiger Moths). This DH Engines drawing shows equipment on the right side. Cooling air flows past the cylinders from the left (far side) of the engine.

time aluminium alloy was used for connecting rods. In general light-alloy and steel rods are similar in mass, but the former are cheaper and have better thermal conductivity. Thus, by 1926 the Cirrus III was giving 95 hp, but de Havilland could see that even more power was really needed; and in any case a completely fresh design would be superior. The result was the de Havilland Gipsy.

Halford used a generally similar design of iron cylinder and aluminium head, bore and stroke being 114 mm × 128 mm (4.5 in × 5 in, 5.23 litres/319 cu in), the engine being made a left-hand tractor to avoid exhaust gas being blown into the cockpit. (In any case Moths invariably had exhaust pipes extending beyond the cockpits.) In the original Moth the cylinders had been completely exposed, the nose reminding one of German warplanes of a decade earlier. Various forms of cowling were progressively introduced, and with the Gipsy of 1927 the engine was fully cowled. A ram inlet was left at the front, on one side of the centre line, and the cooling air was forced to flow around the cylinders by a duct and baffles, and finally sucked out by making the rear edge of the cowling wider than the fuselage.

This arrangement was continued up to the abandonment of piston engines by de Havilland in the early 1950s.

The first Gipsy was a special engine for racing, cleared to 135 hp at 2,650 rpm, but the production engine had a compression ratio of

5.0 and was rated at 98 hp at 2,100 rpm. Subsequent Gipsies were enlarged, and in late 1929 an inverted Gipsy III was introduced, to improve pilot view and reduce drag whilst still preserving propeller ground clearance. Of course this meant a dry-sump lubrication system in which oil was pumped from an external tank to the hollow crankshaft, emerging from the big ends to be collected in channels surrounding the cylinder skirts, from where it was sucked by scavenge pumps connected to each end of the crankcase.

Using similar principles de Havilland went on to produce a range of uprated inverted four-cylinder Gipsies and also an important series of six-cylinder Gipsy Six and Gipsy Queen engines, some of which were supercharged and geared. The Six was naturally designed with the usual firing order, 153624, and with two carburettors each serving a group of three cylinders, the carburettors feeding alternately with this firing sequence. One of the first engines suffered a torsional vibration failure of the crankshaft. Investigation showed a large $4\frac{1}{2}$-order critical zone of the fundamental torsional vibration mode in the region of 2,200 rpm, which was that used for take-off. The solution was to change to an unusual firing order, 124653, which in turn resulted in an odd arrangement of the induction manifolds.

The final model, the geared and supercharged Queen 70 series, exhibited several

From the outset the six-cylinder Gipsies made the designers think again. Most banks of six cylinders fire in the sequence 153624, but the Gipsy Six and Queen had to change to 124653, needing an odd inlet manifold geometry (upper diagram). Rings indicate the carburettors.

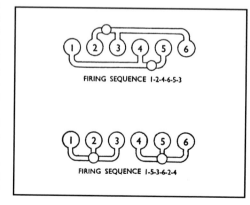

FIRING SEQUENCE 1-2-4-6-5-3

FIRING SEQUENCE 1-5-3-6-2-4

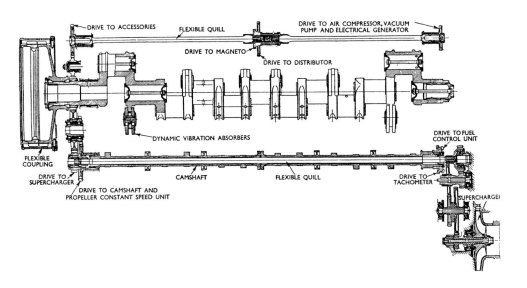

Long, thin engines tend to suffer from torsional vibration and fatigue. The ultimate Gipsy, the geared and supercharged Queen 70, was stuffed with palliatives. The crankshaft had dynamic dampers on every crankpin, the supercharger and accessories were all driven via flexible quill shafts from the front of the engine, and the propeller gearbox (not shown) was driven via a large Bibby flexible coupling.

unusual features. This engine used the bigger 120 mm × 150 mm (4 in × 6 in) cylinder standardized in post-war Gipsies, giving a capacity of 10.18 litres (621 cu in), with a compression ratio of 6.5. The Queen 70 series were rated at 380 hp at 3,000 rpm, at 7.5 lb/sq in boost. It was found that the fundamental torsional-vibration frequency was 4.8 kHz, corresponding exactly to the third order at 1,600 rpm. This appeared to be another critical combination of rpm and mode, and it was considered prudent to fit third-order pendulum vibration absorbers on six of the 12 crankshaft webs. So afraid was the company of this third-order vibration that it even inserted a flexible coupling between the crankshaft and the propeller reduction gear. This coupling was of the Bibby type, in which the drive is transmitted through a continuous grid spring, a flat spring zigzag formed into a ring. Besides damping the vibration this allowed the peripheral engine-driven annulus of the reduction gear to float on the springs, the load being shared equally by the five planet gears carried on the five-armed spider on the rear of the propeller shaft.

In virtually all Gipsy engines the accessories were at the back. In most variants the drive was naturally taken off the back of the crankshaft, but in the post-war six-cylinder engines it was taken off the front. A quill shaft—a small-diameter flexible shaft—ran the whole length of the engine to drive the airframe accessories, with an intermediate drive to the magneto and distributor. An intermediate pinion at the front drove the camshaft and propeller CSU. To relieve the long camshaft of the large torque required to drive the supercharger this drive was taken by a second, solid, quill shaft passing through the hollow camshaft. It was further found in these engines that the increased power would demand such large big ends that the crankcase would have to be widened; as an alternative the con-rods were redesigned in forged steel.

It will be obvious that these long and thin engines suffered more seriously from torsional vibration than most. Engines of higher power, for example, had much more rigid crankshafts, while the world's general aviation moved from Gipsy-type engines to the American horizontally-opposed type, which has inherently better balance and shorter lengths. There were many such engines in the 25 to 100 hp class in the 1920s, but none was really important until in 1930 Continental designed

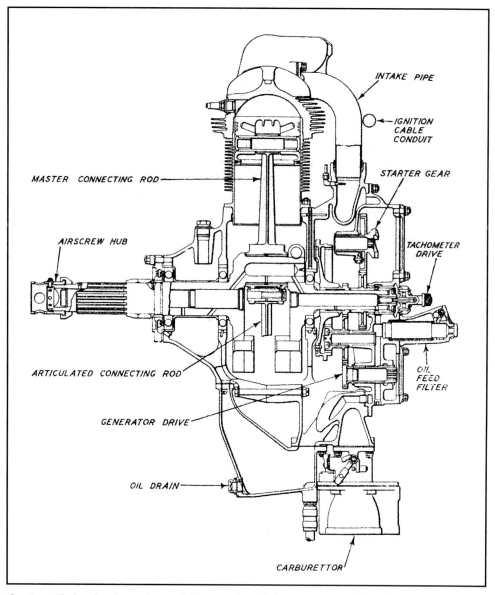

Continental, Jacobs, Lycoming and Kinner all made large numbers of simple and reliable low-powered radials. This cross-section shows the Continental W-670 of 220–250 hp, with seven cylinders and neither supercharger nor reduction gear.

the A-40, the number indicating the design horsepower. Continental Motors, at Muskegon, Michigan, had previously dabbled in various poppet-valve and sleeve-valve engines, and in 1928 produced a 170-hp radial that led to the important series of W-670 radials in the 200–300 hp category which competed against similar radials by Jacobs, Kinner and Lycoming. What was important about the A-40 was that it was a flat-four (four-cylinder horizontally-opposed engine) aimed at the light aviation market. It would be completely familiar to any private pilot today, and in fact was a neat and economical design which could even find a market in the 1990s.

Features of the A-40 included a large

aluminium crankcase cast in one piece, with deep internal ribbing for strength and with a wet (oil-filled) sump; iron cylinders cast in pairs held to the crankcase by six studs; aluminium alloy heads again cast in pairs and bolted to the barrels by 12 nickel-steel studs; single inlet and exhaust valves in the L-type head driven by pushrods from a camshaft directly below the crankshaft; and a one-piece forged crankshaft with three throws (the split big ends being arranged 1–2–1) held in only two plain bearings. As originally marketed, this classic engine even had single ignition. Bore and stroke were 79 mm × 95 mm (3.125 in × 3.75 in) (1.88 litres/115 cu in), CAA rating was 37 hp at 2,575 rpm and dry weight was 65 kg (143 lb). The weight/power ratio of 3.86 lb/hp would not have impressed an aviator of 1910, and the TBO (time between overhauls) of 200 hours was one-fifth of the TBO of the corresponding Gipsy. Yet, by adopting a 'Russian'-type approach and making the engine simple and tough, Continental sold so many A-40s, even during the Depression, that their next model, the A-50, did not appear until 1938. The A-50 was a 'real' engine, with heads screwed and shrunk on to forged steel barrels, completely enclosed valve gear with rockers driving overhead valves, a dry sump (but with an odd external sump looking like a bag pressed from thin steel sheet), and a four-throw crankshaft held in three steel-backed and cadmium-lined replaceable bearings. The A-50 gave (of course) 50 hp, and soon gave way to the A-65 of which many thousands were made during the Second World War as the O-170 for 'Grasshopper' observation aircraft.

In 1938 two rivals appeared. One was Aircooled Motors, whose engines, called Franklins, were small flat fours made like a big engine with beautifully balanced crankshafts, a host of exotic alloys and every advanced feature. The other was Lycoming, already producing the R-680 radial. Designer Morehouse planned his first lightplane engine, the O-145, to be if anything even simpler than the Continental. The entire crankcase and four cylinders were all a single piece of cast iron. The crankcase was enclosed by a top cover and a sump, both held by studs, and studs also secured the cast aluminium cylinder heads. Bigger than its rival with 92.06 mm × 89 mm, 2.38 litres (3.625 in × 3.5 in cylinders, 144.49 cu in), it was rated at 50 hp at 2,300 rpm and weighed (with single unshielded ignition) 69 kg (152 lb). By 1938 Lycoming had

developed the same engine with a crankcase split along the centre line and with ratings up to 75 hp at 3,100 rpm, this speed underlining the absence of vibration problems. There were over 180 other makes of engines for light aircraft between the wars, but the Lycoming and Continental were to be the chief survivors.

I suggested earlier that aircraft designers in the nineteenth century were handicapped by the absence of a powerplant of sufficiently good power/weight ratio, and that the crucial invention was the internal combustion engine. Accordingly, one might doubt the sanity of anyone who in 1930 began building a steam engine for aircraft! The fact that it got nowhere does not necessarily mean that the Besler brothers, George and William, were foolish. They had a very good try, and in June 1933 William Besler began a successful flight development programme with their engine installed in a Travel Air biplane.

Steam was generated in about 152 m (500 ft) of coiled pipe heated by an oil burner with an electrically driven blower. About one minute after ignition the steam was available at about 800°F (427°C) at 1,200 lb/sq in. All controls were automatic. The V-type compound engine had one HP cylinder of 76 mm (3 in) bore and stroke, from which the piston-type valves fed the steam to the 133 mm × 76

The O-235 is a post-war version of the O-145 designed by Lycoming's Harold Morehouse in 1939. It was one of the first American flat-fours to have the crankcase split along the centre line. Note the carburettor underneath, the valve pushrods above the cylinders and plugs above and below (O-145 photo: page 193).

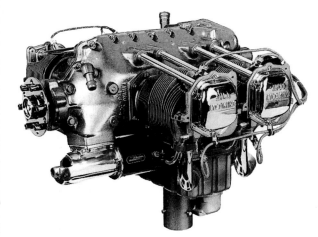

mm (5.25 in × 3 in) LP cylinder. It then passed through the condenser, from where about 99 per cent of the steam was returned as water to the boiler, heating the feed water on the way. At 1,200 lb/sq in the engine was said to give 150 hp at 1,625 rpm. The engine alone weighed 82 kg (180 lb), while the total installation was claimed to weigh 227 kg (500 lb). It was (probably rightly) said that a fully engineered installation would be much lighter.

The advantages claimed were mainly either nonsense or arguable, though there is no doubt the steam plant could use a wider range of fuels than other aero engines and was also very much quieter. Clearly, plenty of steam leaked out, and, in view of the fact that almost all the heat from the oil burner went straight out through a big exhaust pipe, the efficiency must have been very low. Perhaps the one advantage that William Besler had over other pilots was that immediately on touching down he could flick a switch and put the engine into

reverse, giving powerful braking with a traditional carved wood propeller!

Another rare type of engine was the diesel. We have already seen the basic problem: in order to compress freezing cold air from high altitude to such high pressure that heavy fuel oil will ignite instantly, on being injected into it, you must make the engine exceptionally massive. Thus it becomes uncompetitive except in the particular case of long-range aircraft, where the diesel's unrivalled fuel economy brings the total engines-plus-fuel weight down below that of a conventional petrol engine installation. It is surely remarkable that not one of the world absolute long-distance records was ever set by a diesel-engined aircraft.

The first and greatest name in aero diesels is Junkers. His FO3, exhibited in 1926, sparked off interest in many countries, as well as in Germany where Dipl-Ing Schwager masterminded the BMW-Lanova 114, virtually a BMW 132 nine-cylinder radial operating on

Schematic circuit diagram of the Besler steam aero engine, test flown in the 1930s. The burner was at the top of the sealed boiler box so that the hot flue gas could be discharged beneath the aircraft instead of into the windscreen.

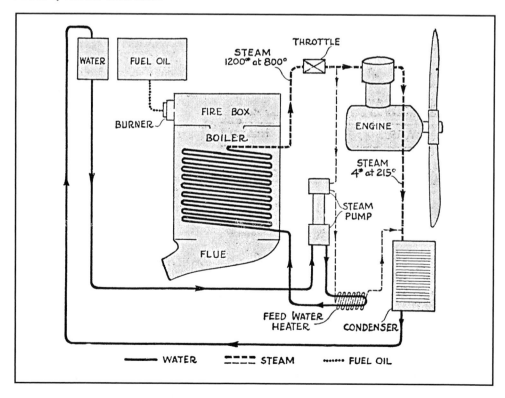

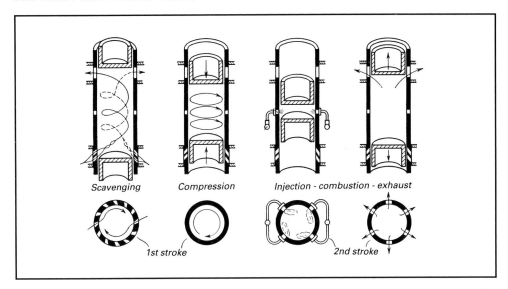

Schematic representation of the operating cycle of an opposed-piston two-stroke diesel. The cylinder and its upper and lower pistons are shown sectioned. In the text the sequence begins with the air compressed between the pistons and the injection of fuel, here called '2nd stroke'.

the four-stroke diesel cycle, with water-cooled cylinders and unusual individual radiators filling in the gaps between the cylinders. This 27.7 litre engine (the same capacity as the BMW 132, and the Pratt & Whitney Hornet from which the 132 was derived) was rated at 650 hp at 2,200 rpm. A much later German diesel was the Daimler-Benz DB 602, or LOF6, of 1934. More like a marine or locomotive engine, this water-cooled V engine had 16 cylinders of 175 mm and 230 mm (6.8 in and 9 in) bore and stroke (88.5 litres/5,396 cu in) and weighed 1,982 kg (4,370 lb). Unsupercharged but geared, it operated on the four-stroke diesel cycle and was rated at 1,320 hp at 1,650 rpm, with a cruise specific fuel consumption of about 0.373 lb/h/hp. Four were fitted to each of the airships LZ-129 *Hindenburg* and LZ-130 *Graf Zeppelin* (the second ship of that name). Consumption of all four engines of 1,200 lb/hr sounds trivial to a 747 pilot, but airships were so slow that crossing the Atlantic might burn 30 tons. Another airship diesel was the Beardmore Tornado, developed at great expense for the British R101. A four-stroke straight eight, it hardly merits inclusion here.

In contrast, the 1926 Junkers engine triggered off two much smaller diesels in the United States that had much to commend them. First off the mark, in 1928, was Pack-ard, whose DR-980 was qualified in 1930. A four-stroke, nine-cylinder, air-cooled radial, it weighed 231 kg (510 lb) and was rated at 225 hp at 1,950 rpm, but reputedly suffered severely from smell and vibration. On balance, the generally similar engines made by the Guiberson company seem to have been better. First to be qualified, in November 1931, the A-980 was rated at 185 hp at 1,925 rpm. More important was the A-1020, rated at 310 hp at 2,150 rpm for a weight of 295 kg (650 lb). Unlike its predecessor, the 1020, qualified in 1940, had enclosed overhead valve gear, with an inlet and exhaust valve in each cylinder. One could call it a near miss.

Most of the major aero engine firms built at least one experimental diesel between the wars, usually a compression-ignition version of an established engine. The only company to mass produce diesels was Junkers with the Jumo 205 and 207, and they settled on a type of engine which is not very common in surface applications and exceedingly rare in aviation. This is the opposed-piston two-stroke diesel, in which there is no cylinder head. Instead the air is compressed by the coming together of two opposed pistons inside an extremely long cylinder. When the two pistons have almost met in the centre, compressing the air to 'red heat', fine sprays of fuel oil injected between them burn immediately and completely, there

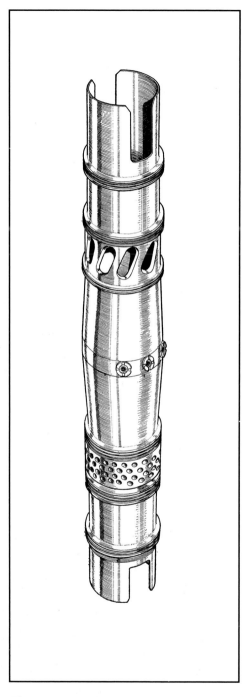

The machined steel liner of the Jumo 205 incorporated large exhaust ports in the upper part and rows of tangential inlet holes at the lower end. The ends were slotted for the conrods; in the centre were injector ports.

being a huge excess of air (albeit squeezed into a small space). The two pistons are thus driven apart, and near BDC one of them uncovers large exhaust ports through which the gas quickly escapes. Slight further travel to BDC allows the other piston to uncover a ring of inlet ports, angled tangentially, through which fresh air is blown at high velocity by an external blower (identical in form with a supercharger). This incoming air swirls rapidly up the cylinder cleaning out the exhaust gas, and to ensure good scavenging the blower manages to feed through the inlet ports 1.5 times the cylinder displacement, so that in theory nothing is left but clean air. The pistons come together again and the cycle is repeated.

Structurally the engine is exceedingly tall but narrow. The engine is tall not only because of the height of the double-ended cylinders, but also because there has to be a crankshaft at both the bottom and top of the engine, the two shafts being joined by a train of large gearwheels down the front. The inputs to the propeller shaft are not quite equal, because at the rear the lower crankshaft drives all the auxiliaries including the blower. Some diesels, including the dreadful Beardmore, suffered because long pipes joined the injection pumps to the actual injectors in the walls of the cylinders. This is the last thing you want, because to supply a microscopic but precisely measured quantity of fuel, at around 8,000 lb/sq in, about 40 times per second, demands control of a kind that in the 1930s was almost beyond the state of the available technology. There is no point in building a diesel if, because of inability to meter and inject the fuel doses with absolute precision, fuel consumption is no better than that of a much lighter petrol engine.

Obviously, it is essential to minimize the length of pipe between the injection pump plunger and the injector in the wall of the cylinder. Junkers placed a row of six pumps on each side of the engine, each pump feeding (via pipes only about 38 mm [1.5 in] long) two nozzles in the adjacent cylinder. Thus each cylinder had a pump close on each side feeding four nozzles spaced around the combustion chamber at 90°. Each nozzle ejected two microscopic jets of oil which impinged on each other to cause a fan of droplets of a few micrometres diameter. Of course, the fuel had to be carefully filtered, in the Junkers engines by a metal-disc filter followed by a filter with a large-area paper element. Many years of diesel experience were needed to make such engines as the Jumo 205 (600–880 hp) and turbocharged 207 (1,000 hp) work properly. This experience enabled the German industry to adopt direct petrol injection in the Luftwaffe's other high-power engines (see the next chapter).

It is important to add a note in this chapter about installations. At the end of the First World War it was an end in itself to bolt the engine in some way to the airframe so that the mountings could transmit the severe loads of engine and propeller weight, propulsive thrust, torque and vibration, and also incorporate proper fuel, exhaust, cooling and control systems. With air-cooled cylinders as much of the engine as possible was left out in the open, though often (as in the case of early DH Moths) it was found that the carburettor tended to freeze. Very gradually designers learned how to control the airflow around such cylinders to increase heat transfer and if possible reduce drag. Drag was an especially thorny question with radials, which after the advent of the Curtiss D-12 in the early 1920s appeared to be totally unstreamlined. In fact, one had to take into account the considerable weight and drag of the water radiator in the pointed-nose engines, though it became common practice between the wars to make the radiator retractable. Thus it would initially be concealed inside the fuselage or nacelle. As the coolant temperature rose, so would the radiator matrix be progressively extended into the airstream, by the pilot cranking a handle; in extremely cold air it might never be necessary to expose the whole matrix. Companies such as Rolls-Royce and (with radials) Bristol formed large and growing installation departments to help solve their customers' problems. In the USA installations were regarded as the preserve of the airframe manufacturer, with occasional disastrous results (extending up to recent times, a notable instance being the F-111).

Having cowled a long water-cooled engine efficiently, and fitted the best possible retractable radiator, there was little more that could be done where conventional installations were concerned. In racing aircraft drag could be reduced by fitting flush skin radiators. In several Schneider Trophy seaplanes the radiators covered much of the wings and the upper surfaces of the floats, while the oil radiators comprised arrays of pipes along the cowling or the sides of the fuselage. A more radical alternative solution was to allow the water to boil, and condense the steam back to water in condenser radiators very similar to the skin radiators of the S.6B. Apart from the hope of very low drag, evaporative cooling promised to be much more effective, in that the temperature difference between the coolant and the airflow was much greater than when water was used. Condensing the steam released 540 calories of heat per gramme, many times greater than the heat transfer from a gramme of hot water. Rolls-Royce tried harder than any other company to make steam cooling work, in the Goshawk V-12 of 1930–35. Sadly, it was found difficult to avoid steam leaks, the large-area surface condensers were obviously vulnerable in battle, and in combat manoeuvres the steam and water tended to swap places and cause great difficulty. Ultimately the best answers were found to be high-temperature ethylene glycol or pressurized water with glycol added as antifreeze (next chapter).

In the case of air-cooled radials the way ahead was less obvious, but the overall advances even greater. It is ironic that rotaries in the First World War single-engined tractor aircraft were by 1915 fully cowled within a tight-fitting casing. This was done purely to

From any aspect (this is the right side) the Jumo 205 looked very tall but narrow. Halfway down can be seen the row of fuel injectors, with the exhaust ports just above. At the top and bottom are the casings over the crankshafts, which drive the propeller and accessories via trains of gears up the front and rear.

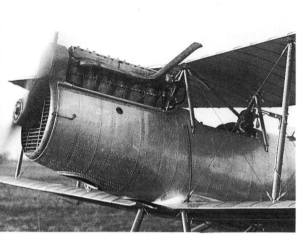

The Short Silver Streak of 1920 had a modern metal fuselage, but the Siddeley Puma water-cooled engine was still left with its cylinders out in the open as in the recent war. The heavy engine was mounted on a separate steel-tube truss, and a wartime frontal radiator was used.

Last of the Schneider Trophy biplanes, three Gloster IV seaplanes were built in 1926. Their 875-hp Lion VIIB was cooled by flush radiators in the surface of the upper wing and top of the floats (black areas). The oil cooler was flush with the bottom of the cowling.

catch castor oil sprays flung from the cylinders. After the war static radials were completely uncowled, or else the crankcase was cowled and the cylinders left exposed to keep them cool. Often the exhaust was collected in a ring round the front of the crankcase, from which one or two pipes carried it back under the fuselage or nacelle. Such a ring heated the air passing over the cylinders, but the effect was not serious. Drag, however, was high; this also caused little bother, partly because aircraft speeds were low and partly because the drag was hardly ever measured.

In a few fighters and racing aircraft the cylinders were to some degree streamlined by having light metal fairings added downstream, like the fairing behind the pilot's head on most biplane fighters. An even smaller number had the cylinders encased in a so-called helmeted cowling, though these were costly (being laboriously beaten out of flat sheet by hand) and tended to cause cylinder overheating. However, much better solutions were to hand. With hindsight it is obvious that an air-cooled engine ought to be inside a diffuser, a duct with a correctly profiled expanding inlet and a constriction at the exit, the source of heat (in this case the cylinders) being in the central portion where flow velocity is a minimum and pressure at its greatest. H. C. H. Townend did exhaustive research at the National Physical Laboratory which led to the ring cowl which bears his name. This was in

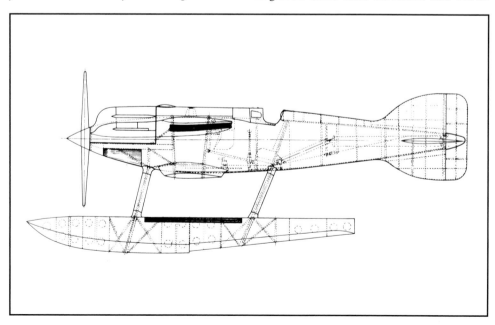

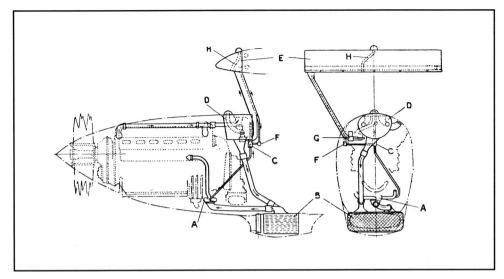

Composite cooling scheme for Rolls-Royce Kestrel: pump (A) circulates water through the cylinder blocks and via the header tank (D) to the radiator (B). Steam forms and is piped up to condenser (E) in the underside of the upper wing. Condensate is returned via ejector (C) which is energized by (A). (D) is not vented but sealed, but (E) is vented via (H). Valves (F) and (G) prevent water from running down into (E) during inverted flight. Despite these provisions, steam or composite cooling was abandoned, though Camm expected it to be used in the Hurricane (Charles Griffin).

Right The Gloster Gladiator was an interim wire-braced fabric biplane fighter with a simple Townend ring cowl over its Bristol Mercury engine. Exhaust was collected round the front of the cowl and then piped aft under the fuselage.

This was one of the few examples of a purely technical development which completely altered the appearance of aircraft. One has only to compare, for example, such airliners as the Handley Page 42 of 1930 (uncowled), the Boeing 247 of 1933 (Townend rings, always called anti-drag rings in the USA to avoid mentioning a foreign inventor) and the Short S.23 'Empire' of 1936 (NACA cowls) to see the rapid progress made in radial installations at this time. The Short boat had installations designed by Bristol, with all

effect a narrow-chord wing wrapped around the engine in such a way that it not only improved cooling but also generated a lift force that helped to pull the aircraft along. In the United States the NACA took the concept further, enclosing the engine in a long-chord cowl which began with an inward-curving inlet similar to the Townend to generate a force pulling forwards, continued with a parallel drum section and then ended with a ring of hinged gills, opened or closed to control the airflow. Usually the gills would be open under conditions of high power and low airspeed, as at take-off, and closed in cruising flight for minimum drag.

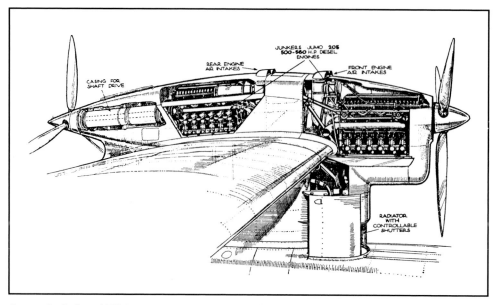

Strangely, before 1935 it was rare to see an aircraft with four engines in a row along the wings; push/pull tandem installations were the rule. In the Dornier Do 18 flying boat of 1935 the two diesel engines were mounted in a single tandem nacelle, with the air inlets on top and the coolant and oil radiators grouped in the front of the pylon. In fact the engines of the production Do 18G were 205Ds 880 hp.

exhaust piped forwards into a steel collector ring which formed the front (propulsive) part of the cowling. From here a single pipe took it back outside the cowling and then, oddly, into the leading edge of the wing to terminate in a plain hole in the wing upper surface. By late 1938 Bristol had recognized that such an arrangement significantly heated the air entering the cowling, and the collector ring was shrouded by a profiled ring of aluminium with air drawn through the gap. This again was hardly the best idea, as it sucked away the air needed to cool the hottest part of the cylinder, and a basic law of air cooling is that the mass flow past the cylinder must be a maximum. During the Second World War it was realized that the best answer is to take the exhaust away to the rear.

It is not easy to obtain meaningful comparative figures for the different types of cowling, if only because it is impossible to compare different types of engines or aircraft. One set of figures which are quite instructive refer to differently cowled engines in a Hawker Hart light biplane bomber used for engine testing by the Bristol company in 1933–6:

Once the full-length cowl with adjustable gills had been perfected, around 1936, little more could be done until more advanced schemes were introduced during the Second World War. As for liquid-cooled engines, again, once the engine itself had been closely enclosed in a streamlined cowling not much more could be done. On the other hand, quite a lot could be done to the cooling system. By 1931 the US Army was experimenting with

Hawker Hart flight test results

Engine	Full-throttle climb		Full-throttle level flight	
	Time to 17,000 ft	Cyl temp	Max speed	Cyl temp
Mercury VI uncowled	11 min 51 sec	205°C	180 mph	183°C
Mercury VI heads faired	11 min 3 sec	207°C	182 mph	184°C
Mercury VI Townend ring	9 min 30 sec	200°C	196 mph	180°C
Mercury VIII full cowl/gills	7 min 23 sec	185°C*	209 mph	190°C†
*Gills open; †gills closed.				

Prestone (pure ethylene glycol) at temperatures up to 320°F, while in Britain the best answer was found to be a 75/25 mixture of water and glycol maintained under pressure. All these schemes had the objective of keeping the cylinders below the desired maximum temperature whilst dissipating the heat through smaller radiators, reducing weight and drag.

Of course, a single-engined aircraft can have only a limited number of possible engine installations, but with a multi-engined aircraft the possibilities proliferate. Today a tandem push/pull nacelle is almost never seen, and with hindsight it seems remarkable that between 1918 and 1935 approximately 72 per cent of all four-engined aircraft had this type of arrangement. Detailed measurement of drag in wind tunnels was seldom done until the mid-1930s, and only then was it discovered that most of the under-wing or over-wing nacelle installations (simple tractor or push/pull tandem) were in approximately the worst possible place. In any case, in a tandem installation the rear propeller had to operate in the slipstream from the front propeller, which was already moving at high speed and had a powerful spiral component. This tended to make the rear propeller inefficient, caused severe aerodynamically induced vibration and led to very severe engine operating conditions. It was particularly difficult to achieve good cooling of air-cooled engines in tandem installations. Perhaps remarkably, tandem engines were chosen for the ultra-efficient Voyager of the 1980s.

In the special case of flying boats, the need to keep engines and propellers clear of waves and spray resulted in engines normally being mounted high up in nacelles carried on struts. The high thrust line usually resulted in major changes in longitudinal trim when the throttles were opened or closed. Streamlined wing-mounted engines had to await the development of larger aircraft with very deep hulls. An exception was the Dornier Do 26 (1938). This had pairs of push-pull tandem diesel engines, and the rear engines drove the pusher propellers via long pivoted shafts which could be angled upwards to keep the blades clear of spray.

7 The big-engine peak

During the 20 years between the two World Wars the piston aero engine developed more rapidly than at any other time before or since. This development was manifest in many ways. To the pilot by far the greatest advance was that forced landings through engine failure, commonplace in 1919, became almost unheard of. To the aircraft designer a major advance was to force the largest engines to give around 1,500 hp instead of 500, without changing their size or weight. Not least, aircraft speeds were significantly increased by learning how to install engines properly, and this applied equally to air-cooled and liquid-cooled engines.

Thus, when the Second World War began in the late summer of 1939, aircraft and engines had reached a plateau of technology that was not to change much subsequently. Of course, an exception must be made in the case of gas turbine engines, because in the postwar era these were to provide all the power and flight performance the aircraft designer could handle. In doing so they almost swept away the high-power piston engine, and for this reason it is convenient in this chapter to record the final era of the big piston engine right up to the mid-1950s, when development of this species finally ceased. This leaves the final chapter free to look at the smaller engines for general aviation which hold centre stage today.

It has always been a truism that engines take longer to develop than aircraft. Thus even though the Second World War lasted six years, every piston engine that played a part in that conflict was running before the war began. Indeed, some engines, such as the Bristol Centaurus, missed the war even though they were running in 1938. I have often drawn attention to the big role played in aviation (in former times, if not still) by personal preferences, personal jealousies, the ability of forceful characters to override people who might know more about the subject, and not least the whims of sheer fashion. The Centaurus was one of the engines that suffered in this way.

It was the last of Roy Fedden's great series of air-cooled radials to go into production, and so it had sleeve valves. Fedden's decision to change over from poppet valves to sleeves has already been mentioned, together with my belief that he would probably have done better merely to stick with the traditional valve and use two large ones per cylinder. I think if Fedden had had the slightest idea how hard it was going to be to perfect the sleeve-valve engine he would have agreed, and would never have started. There were several factors behind his decision. One was that he wanted to build an engine in the 1,000 hp class, which in the late 1920s meant 14 or 18 cylinders in two rows, and he found that the valve gear for such an engine, with four valves per cylinder, was hard to design.

In fact Fedden did seek other alternatives. One was an impressive 20-cylinder four-row radial. Another, which in 1933 was built and flown, was the Hydra. This was a double-octagon engine, with eight double (tandem) cylinders, each with two overhead camshafts. It was an interesting engine, but had two shortcomings. One was that Fedden thought the short and stiff crankshaft would not need a centre bearing, and he was wrong. The second was that it was rated at 870 hp, which meant 1,000 a few years hence, and this level of power could already be seen with the simple nine-cylinder Pegasus.

The Bristol Hydra was Roy Fedden's attempted alternative to sleeve valves. It had 16 cylinders in eight tandem pairs 25.74 litres (1,570.8 cu in), and ran at 3,620 rpm to give 870 hp. It was a near miss.

A further factor was that back in 1922 Harry Ricardo had said that the poppet valve was nearing the limit of its development. To wring greater power out of an engine of given capacity, which meant achieving higher BMEP, was thought by Ricardo to call for a switch to sleeve valves. Fedden was not the type to follow blindly, but Ricardo was perhaps the world expert on the advanced IC engine, and in any case nobody was really in a position to disagree. Fedden also liked the whole idea of the sleeve valve. The thin-walled yet very strong tube oscillated up and down inside the cylinder, with a simultaneous reciprocating and rotary motion, in an absolutely smooth manner, avoiding the poppet valve's hammer blows on its seat. Inside the sleeve the oscillating piston could be made to uncover inlet and exhaust passages of any desired shape and size to give perfect aerodynamic flow to the incoming mixture and outgoing exhaust.

There are various kinds of sleeve valve, some having two sleeves one inside the other. Fedden wisely picked the monosleeve, known as the Burt-McCollum type, driven by a simple crank at the base, so that in relation to the cylinder each point on the sleeve describes almost a perfect circle. The first research cylinder ran in 1927, and after building an inverted V-12 Fedden decided to go back to the more familiar ground of a nine-cylinder

radial. The sleeves caused endless trouble, but by 1934 it was possible to assemble an engine that would work properly. The result was the Perseus, with the same size of cylinder (146 mm/5.75 in bore and 165 mm/6.5 in stroke) as the Mercury. It began at 638 hp, and on 29 June 1935 entered service with Imperial Airways. Time between overhauls was a satisfactory 300 hours, and the Perseus impressed everyone with its uncanny smoothness and quietness. There was one small snag, however. Whilst each hand-built engine worked well, what was wanted was a mass production engine, assembled by taking any nine sleeves from thousands coming off production and building them into any nine cylinders in the sure knowledge everything would fit. This could not be done.

Fedden drove his team at Bristol night and day, as well as other teams, at High Duty Alloys at Slough, and at Firth-Vickers in Sheffield. After literally thousands of combinations of alloys and production methods a way was discovered to make flawless sleeves by centrifugal casting and then make them perfectly cylindrical. Final success came just in time for the Second World War. The first years of sleeve valve development had been funded entirely by Bristol, and even with Air Ministry help the costs nearly broke the company. Probably the American solution of a head-on attack with huge teams of engineers, with abundant funding, would have resulted in final success several years earlier. The

Each sleeve was driven by a simple crank, repeatedly bringing the inlet and exhaust ports opposite the appropriate holes in the cylinder barrel (Odhams Press).

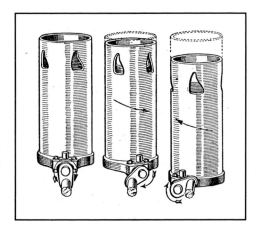

Instead Fedden spent 15 years struggling to perfect what finally became a great range of sleeve-valve engines. From right to left: cylinders of the Taurus, Hercules/Perseus (same), Centaurus and the sadly unbuilt Orion.

trouble is, once a big project has been started it is very difficult to stop, especially if it seems worth while and if final success appears to be just around the next corner. With hindsight we can see that Ricardo's belief that the poppet-valve cylinder was nearing the limit of its development was nonsense. New materials for exhaust valves and their seats, and especially the introduction of sodium cooling, greatly raised the limits on what could be achieved. Many other detailed improvements enabled the traditional species of engine to keep at least abreast of any sleeve-valve engine, and Fedden was only too keenly aware that by 1937 Pratt & Whitney and Wright could offer poppet-valve engines up to 2,200 hp.

Bristol tested cylinders from a Cyclone and a Twin Wasp, each with two poppet valves, and were favourably impressed. Some of their engineers must have wondered whether the agonizing and costly effort on sleeve valves had really been necessary. On the other hand, the sleeve-valve engines were beautiful in design, manufacture and performance. They comprised the Perseus, already mentioned, with nine cylinders the same size as the Mercury, which was later mass produced at 890 and 905 hp; the Aquila, with nine small cylinders giving around 500 hp; the Hercules, with 14 Perseus cylinders in two rows, over 57,400 of which were made during the war at 1,500–2,000 hp; the neat Taurus, with 14 small cylinders giving 1,000–1,200 hp, made in fair numbers; and the great Centaurus, with 18 large cylinders giving a capacity of 53,628 cc (3,270 cu in), first run in June 1938 at 2,000 hp and developed by 1950 to 3,220 hp. During

the war Fedden completed the design of his final engine, the Orion, with 18 even larger cylinders giving a capacity of 67,929 cc (4,142 cu in) and starting life at 4,000 hp. Very short-sightedly, this was thought to have been made obsolete by gas turbines, and to Fedden's intense disappointment it was never run.

Thus as far as the Western democracies were concerned, the late 1930s saw Pratt & Whitney and Wright on the one hand and Bristol on the other, the British firm's poppet-valve Pegasus and Mercury still being built in large numbers (about 17,700 and 21,993, respectively) but cut off from further development. All the poppet-valve engines, British and American, were the result of up to 15 years of relentless development, and it showed in their refinement and reliability. The American engines tended to be heavier, with specific weights of around 1.4 lb/hp compared with values very close to unity for the British engines. This was partly because the American engines had been type-tested (certificated) on fuel of lower octane number, and partly because they had been designed primarily for the airlines, where robust reliability was more important than performance. A further result of the different markets was that by 1939 every British high-power engine had variable-datum ABC (automatic boost control), as described in Chapter 3, whereas on all the American engines everything was left to the skill and experience of the pilot in reading rpm, manifold pressure and possibly even EGT (exhaust gas temperature) and adjusting the mixture, propeller and throttle levers repeatedly throughout each flight.

When the USA went to war in December 1941 there were very quickly some major changes in philosophy. Such long-established engines as the Cyclone and Twin Wasp were re-rated on fuel of much higher anti-knock value to give considerably more power. Perhaps the most outstanding example was the great R-2800 Double Wasp, which went into production in 1940 for the B-26 Marauder at 1,850 hp and by 1944 was in service in late-model P-47 Thunderbolts (and other aircraft) at a rating of 2,800 hp on 115-grade fuel with water injection. Of course, all engines naturally grow in power with development, but a major war demands the utmost performance from engines fitted to aircraft whose life in front-line service was unlikely to exceed 50 hours' flying, over a period of only a month or two. In peace time the call was for reliability over a period of perhaps a dozen years. And of course a pilot in combat has no time to fiddle endlessly with a fistful of engine controls in order to maintain the optimum engine operating conditions, and bearing in mind the rate at which aircrew had to be produced in wartime he probably did not have the knowledge of how to do this either.

Today we have airline captains with the experience of a lifetime in the job, and most of them could lecture at length on the design of high-bypass turbofans. Despite this, everything possible is automated. In a modern airliner the captain is really a supervisory manager. In an Airbus 320, for example, he does not have to tell the aircraft its take-off weight or the air density (a function of ambient temperature and runway altitude), and he certainly does not need to 'manage' the engines. Take-off can be selected by pushing a single button, and the thrust that will be selected will be exactly right for the circumstances, not the maximum available. In the Second World War life was harder. The pilot had to do everything by hand, and, either before releasing the brakes or during the early part of the run, he had to juggle throttles and possibly mixture and pitch to get the right readings on a set of what people today often call 'steam gauges'. To make life harder you often had to open up asymmetrically. I believe even today I could keep a Mosquito straight on take-off with my left hand held at an angle keeping the port throttle far in advance of the starboard. There was no way of automating such things, but you learned by experience. In other areas where the pilot had a free choice he often was not even told what to do. Air-

craft sometimes had ignition timing control, and a pilot would instinctively pick Advance in preference to Retard. There would certainly be a mixture control, and 100 per cent of pilots would pick Rich in preference to Lean. Only in the matter of propeller pitch would they know what to do, because the difference between Fine and Coarse is a matter of life or death. But not a few never did get the hang of radiator flap position on liquid-cooled engines and cowling gill position on air-cooled radials.

Getting these things wrong invariably meant sharply reduced engine performance and probably shortened engine life, or even pilot life. By mismanaging the engines—in a way that to the ignorant pilot seemed perfectly logical—it was possible to cruise with a fuel consumption from 250 to 300 per cent of the optimum! During the war the Air Ministry continually had to issue posters telling people basic facts about how aeroplanes flew. One day we were treated to, 'Reduce the revs and

Rear view of a Wright Cyclone G-series (front view, p. 130). Note twin magnetos, and downdraught carburettor feeding mixture along inlet manifolds marked '87 octane'. Powerful, efficient and reliable, such engines demanded constant skilled management from the pilot.

boost the boost, you'll have enough petrol to get home to roost.' This caused a storm of controversy, many pilots finding it hard to believe. Surprisingly, in Setright's book he considers low rpm and high boost a good way to wreck an engine, whereas it is actually the most efficient way to cruise.

Of course, miles per gallon is also greatly influenced by the way the engine is installed. We have already seen how great was the improvement made with air-cooled radials between the late 1920s and the early 1930s, with the introduction of full-length cowls with adjustable gills. By the late 1930s the designers of engine installations—who in most parts of the world were the designers of the aircraft—were ready to see whether the process could be taken any further. In 1939 several designers of radial installations experimented with tight-fitting cowlings which, at the front, exactly continued the streamlined form of the large propeller spinner. Examples of such installations included the Curtiss P-42 and Vultee Model 48 Vanguard, both of which required an extension shaft to place the propeller sufficiently far ahead of the engine, and the Deerhound-Whitley. In all these installations the cooling air entered through a seemingly quite small ram inlet at the bottom of the cowling immediately behind the spinner. The Deerhound installation was particularly attractive because this Armstrong Siddeley engine had 21 cylinders in seven straight rows of three, and cowled diameter was under 115 cm (45 in). All these installations were experimented with at length, to see the effect of increasing or decreasing air entry velocity or the velocity and pressure past the cylinders. Another variable was to add a cooling fan, which again offered limitless variation in aerodynamic form, position, ducting/baffle arrangement and power consumption.

Until June 1942, when a captured Fw 190A-3 was examined, official opinion in Britain was that radial-engined fighters were, as a class, inferior. This fixation on liquid-cooled (preferably V-12) engines stemmed almost entirely from Schneider Trophy racing. Certainly the Rolls-Royce Merlin was the most important British engine of the Second World War, and this was largely because the engineers at Derby relentlessly strove to wring from it the same level of power as the enemy obtained from engines half as large again. It has often been said that a good big engine will always beat a good little engine, but Rolls-Royce

appeared not to know this. With cylinders 137 mm × 152 mm (5.4 in × 6 in), giving a capacity of 26.99 litres (1,649 cu in), the Merlin gave Allied fighters the same order of power as the DB 603 of 44.45 litres (2,710 cu in) and the BMW 801 of 41.8 litres (2,548 cu in). For a more detailed history of the Merlin the reader is referred to this publisher's *Rolls-Royce Aero Engines*. The Merlin's early years were halting and disappointing, but with occasional glimpses of much greater potential. Notable among the latter was a specially prepared racing version which in 1937 reached 2,160 hp, and held 1,800 hp for 15 hours. This showed that, once the basic breathing and cylinders had been made to give double the power normally achieved at that time, the engine could hold together. In the racing engine the amazing power was achieved in the same way as in the bigger R engine in 1931, by using a special fuel (a mix of benzole, methyl alcohol and Romanian petrol, plus lead) and opening the throttle wide, letting rpm rise to 3,200 which in turn greatly increased boost from the supercharger. Six years of war were to bring the Merlin to the point where this kind of power was available to front-line pilots using regular fuel of 115/145 grade.

The Merlin had originally been designed to be cooled by water which was allowed to boil, and which left the engine as a steam/water froth. This called for a combined radiator and condenser. Flight testing showed severe problems, and before long (late March 1935) the decision was taken to switch to pure ethylene glycol, with no boiling. This system was used in several hundred early Battle and Hurricane aircraft, but the hot liquid always tended to seep through supposedly leakproof joints and catch fire. In August 1938 the cooling system was again redesigned to use water, with 30 per cent glycol added purely as an antifreeze, as is done in cars. The system was designed to operate at 18 lb/sq in pressure at all altitudes, so that the water did not boil even on being heated to 135°C (275°F). This eliminated the problems and, by keeping cylinders much cooler, greatly improved engine life. Not least, research by Rolls-Royce and by the RAE showed how the design of an installed liquid cooling radiator could be greatly improved, so that instead of severe drag the installation could actually impart modest thrust to the aircraft, and between 1937 and 1940 the weight of a Merlin radiator and coolant was cut by half.

By 1940 RAF fighters had mature Merlins

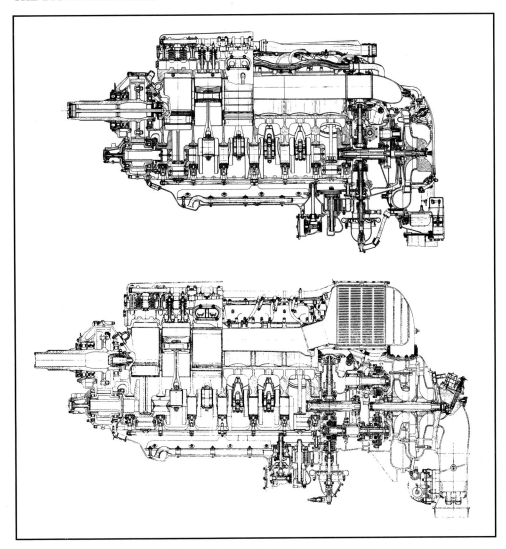

In depicting V-type engines in longitudinal section it is common to show the front half of the cylinder block as if it were vertical. These drawings contrast the Rolls-Royce Merlin II (upper) with the later Merlin 61, with two-stage supercharger delivering highly compressed mixture through an intercooler.

driving variable-pitch or constant-speed propellers, and with ejector exhausts which added about 68 kg (150 lb) to the propulsive thrust. At this time each ejector discharged the hot gas from two cylinders and ended in an expanding duct of C-section. Each engine had more accessories than people were used to, including not only oil, fuel and coolant pumps but also a DC generator, hydraulic pump, vacuum pump, tachometer and CSU (constant-speed unit, for controlling the propeller

pitch). An electric starter was fitted, though engines could also be started by arduous hand-cranking by two groundcrew. Not least, 100-octane fuel had become available (see Chapter 2), enabling maximum boost to be raised from 6 lb/sq in to 12, which at 3,000 rpm increased sea-level power from 1,030 hp to 1,310. As the RAF fighters were appreciably heavier than the Bf 109E this extra power was absolutely crucial. But one shortcoming had been overlooked. The 109 had direct fuel injection, so the engine operated normally in all attitudes and under negative g. The German pilots quickly learned that if they had an RAF fighter on their tail, they should simply push the stick forward and dive steeply. The sustained negative g going into the dive threw the fuel in the Merlin's carburettor to the top of the float chamber. None could reach the engine, which promptly stopped, the propeller going into fine pitch and acting as a brake. Once established in the dive, with the enemy now far out of reach, the fuel would again flow to the engine and rpm would immediately go 'off the clock' as a result of high airspeed and fine pitch. It seems amazing that four years of test and squadron flying had failed to draw attention to the problem. The elegant solution, by the RAE's Miss Tilly Shilling, was to insert a diaphragm in the float chamber with a small hole just large enough to pass take-off fuel flow. Later, injection-type carburettors were developed.

In 1938 most engine firms had a workforce of skilled and unskilled fitters, foundrymen, sheet metal 'bashers' and so forth, and possibly one or two technical staff who might be qualified stressmen or mechanical engineers but who were just as likely to 'design' on a basis of common sense, rule of thumb and past experience. Even Rolls-Royce had nobody brought up in the tradition of scientific research. At Bristol Fedden tried to attract young men of what he would have called 'the right type'; on his mantleshelf he had

a quotation from the American aircraft boss 'Dutch' Kindelberger: 'It may not always be the best policy to do what is best technically, but those responsible for policy can never form a right judgement without knowledge of what is right technically.' Very gradually engine companies recognized the need for a strong technical staff. In 1938 Rolls-Royce startled everyone by hiring an aerodynamicist, Dr Stanley Hooker. Most people wondered what he could possibly do for an engine firm. In fact, 'everything he touched turned to gold'. He began by transforming the air inlet and supercharger of the Merlin, improving pressure ratio and efficiency and, without altering the engine's weight or bulk, making it give more power and raising the full-throttle height. In 1941 a new version of the Merlin tailored to high-altitude flight was needed to power the pressurized Wellington VI. Rolls-Royce were reluctant to fit a turbosupercharger, so Hooker suggested using two mechanically driven superchargers in series, with an aftercooler to increase the charge density entering the engine. To say that the two-stage supercharger transformed the Merlin is an understatement, though of course this time the engine's weight and bulk were slightly increased. The performance gains were fantastic. The tandem superchargers enabled 9 lb/sq in boost to be maintained to 9,144 m (30,000 ft), at which height the maximum power was exactly doubled, from 500 hp to 1,000. Installed in a Spitfire, it raised combat

Cutaway Merlin 61 prepared for exhibition purposes. The blades of the Rotol propeller are cropped for convenience.

ceiling by more than 3,048 m (10,000 ft) and maximum speed by 113 km/h (70 mph)!

This version of the engine went into production in 1942, and at last Rolls-Royce were able to introduce a totally different form of cylinder block, made in two parts with a separate head. This had been designed in March 1938, but could not be introduced because of the intense pressure on maximum production. The two-piece block improved load distribution throughout the engine, stiffened the structure and eliminated the previous incessant coolant leaks. The two-stage Merlin was sufficiently different for one more design change to make no difference. In any case, the two-piece block was first introduced a year earlier, in 1941, by Packard Motor Co in the USA, who made more Merlins than any other factory (55,523 out of a total of 168,040). During the war Packard introduced their own features, apart from American accessories, one being the use of water injection in the V-1650–11 of 1944 to give a war emergency power of 2,270 hp at 90 in manifold pressure, or about 29.5 lb/sq in boost. Even this was eclipsed by the RM.17SM, which in 1944 was run at Derby on 150-PN fuel, plus water injection, at a boost pressure of 36 lb/sq in (103.2 in), the brake horsepower being 2,640. The BMEP was 404 lb/sq in, and IMEP (Indicated MEP) 535 lb/sq in. I have never heard of this having been exceeded.

Many Merlin histories just leave off at the end of the war, but in terms of engineering effort this was roughly half-way along a long road. The second half, 1943–65, began with the T24 transport Merlin, initially for Yorks and Lancastrians. These led to the civil Mk 500 series, in which for the first time performance took second place behind costs and long life (both total parts-life and TBO, time between overhauls). By 1946 a large team was working on the civil two-stage engines, the Mk 620 and 720 series for Tudors and DC-4Ms. Like the Mk 80 series in the Lincoln, these were installed in circular cowlings in the form of a self-contained 'power egg', with an almost circular radiator group under the reduction gear. The fantastic reputation of Rolls-Royce, and the Merlin in particular, tended to blind a small group of customers—such as BOAC and Trans-Canada—to the fact that the 27,044 cc (1,649 cu in) Merlin operating at high BMEP would not be able to compete economically with the R-2800 in similar aircraft. Almost non-stop operation at 58.5 in

boost resulted in very high costs, and also a lot of noise. Numerous modifications, including a full-depth intercooler and cross-over exhausts, eventually made the Mk 724 an acceptable engine, but the rewards did not justify the years of effort.

Alongside Merlins Rolls-Royce made Griffons, with larger cylinders giving a capacity of 36.69 litres (2,239 cu in), the same as the R. Like the Merlin the Griffon was later developed with two-stage superchargers, and eventually even with two stages with three gear ratios, which gave the Spiteful XVI a level speed in full combat trim of 795 km/h (494 mph). Oddly, the Griffon was generally of the same frontal area as the Merlin and actually shorter, yet despite its much greater size it was not very much more powerful. The camshafts were driven at the front, and length was reduced by putting the magnetos at the front between the blocks. For some reason the Griffon was designed to rotate in the opposite direction to the Merlin, and the firing order was 153624, instead of the Merlin's much less common 142635. Until July 1991 single-stage Griffons were still in service with RAF No 8 Sqn, possibly the last high-power piston engines in front-line duty anywhere. In radar early-warning Shackletons they drove six-blade contraprops in order to absorb the take-off power within the available diameter of 4 m (13 ft). Since 1965 both Merlins and Griffons have been carefully modified and tuned to give powers considerably in excess of 3,000 hp for racing purposes in both aircraft and power boats. I do not know what MEPs these engines reach, but the available hardware is becoming scarce.

The corresponding German engines were the DB 601, 603 and 605 by Daimler-Benz and the Jumo 211 and 213 by Junkers. All were inverted V-12 engines with cast blocks cooled by a water/glycol mixture, the usual mix being: water 47, Glysantin (a trade name for German ethylene glycol) 50 and anti-corrosion oil 3. All had poppet valves, the DB engines having two inlet and two exhaust per cylinder and the Jumos two inlet and one exhaust. Another common factor was that all had direct fuel injection, while yet another was that the supercharger was mounted on the side (on the left of the DBs and on the right of the Jumos), driven by a transverse shaft at the rear of the engine. This seemingly odd arrangement made it easy to feed the eye of the blower by a short curved duct from a ram inlet projecting from the side of the cowling,

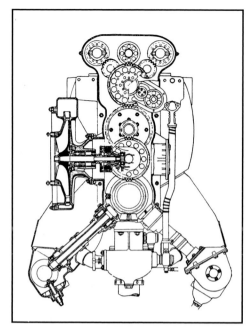

Cross-section through the rear of a Daimler-Benz DB 601A, the 1938 engine which powered the Messerschmitt Bf 109E. The upper wheelcase drove accessories, the inclined bevel shafts drove the camshafts, and the prominent drive in the centre turned the sideways-on supercharger via a hydraulic clutch (p. 79).

published photographs of the parts of a dismantled Merlin X carburettor (433 parts, of which 141 were different) and a Jumo 211 injection pump (1,576 parts, of which 327 were different). An accompanying release gave three reasons in favour of direct injection: slightly lower specific fuel consumption, somewhat better results on inferior fuels and total absence of any icing problems. Amazingly, since the Battle of Britain was over when this assessment was written, nobody mentioned the enormous air-combat advantage of indifference to negative g, except in one case when the journal *The Aeroplane* blandly stated that 'cutting-out problems can be avoided by careful design of the carburettor'. (This was true, of course, but not until two years after the crucial battle.)

When one examines the way the Germans developed their wartime engines one is forced to have even greater admiration for Rolls-Royce. Despite its sound design and beautiful execution the DB 601 never even approached the performance of the smaller Merlin. Instead the engineers at Stuttgart developed the DB 605, with capacity raised from 33.9 to 35.7 litres, to power the Bf 109 and 110 from 1942 onwards. I think it was fine in the twin-engined aircraft, which was nice to fly, but the 109G—made in greater numbers than all other 109s combined—was in my opinion a retrograde step and an aircraft that would never have got through Boscombe Down. Not content with this, Dr Nallinger pushed ahead with an even bigger engine, the 44.5 litre DB 603. He omitted to tell Berlin, which caused severe political problems, but eventually nearly 9,000 of these hefty engines were made for the Me 410, He 219, Do 217 and a wealth of prototypes which included a handful of Focke-Wulf Ta 152s and the unique push/pull Do 335. One of the features of the 603 was naturally a supercharger much larger than that of the 601, and a closely related version was used to pump more air into the 605. Moreover, by the mid-war years the Luftwaffe was so concerned at not being able to win by sheer engine power that it funded two power boosting systems which were fitted to virtually every German piston-engined fighter and fighter/bomber by 1944. One was MW50, a 50/50 mixture of methanol and water, and the other GM-1, liquid nitrous oxide. GM-1 in particular made a quite remarkable difference to aircraft performance at high altitude, by providing extra oxygen as well as postponing detonation, but the penalties of the installa-

and removed the need for a 90° elbow between the surrounding volute and the axial manifold feeding the cylinders. Most Jumos had a two-speed geared drive, but the DB engines had an infinitely variable hydraulic drive as described in Chapter 4. To make a sweeping generalization, the German engines were superbly designed and manufactured, but so conservatively rated that they appeared bulky and heavy compared with the rival Merlin.

Of course, during the war there was intense interest in enemy engines, on both sides. The British technical press naturally latched on to the German choice of direct fuel injection. It is fair to claim that in the late 1930s Britain could not have followed suit. The precision required for the injection pumps has already been emphasized, and the German Bosch company was able to mass produce such pumps only because of its long experience with diesels. In 1941 the British Air Ministry

The Daimler-Benz DB 601E of 1940 powered the Bf 109F. This shot-down example has been removed as a complete power unit with Glysantin header tank and piping, exhaust stubs and forged Elektron (magnesium alloy) mounting.

tion in weight and bulk were equally considerable.

The increasingly successful alternative to the Luftwaffe's liquid-cooled engines was the BMW 801. In 1929 the Munich firm had taken a licence for the Pratt & Whitney Hornet, which led to the mass-produced BMW 132 and also the Lanova 114 diesel mentioned in Chapter 6. To get into the power bracket beyond 1,500 hp two sets of BMW 132 cylinders were bolted to a single crankcase, producing the BMW 139 which powered early Do 217s and the first Fw 190. This rather uninspired engine was replaced by a completely fresh design, the BMW 801, with 14 smaller cylinders giving a capacity of 41.8 litres (2,549 cu in). The 801 was still a massive package, but it was a great engine. I had many chats with the former prisoner who mowed the grass at Thornhill in Southern Rhodesia, whose enormous experience made his views important. He said, 'At below 20,000 ft the 801 was an absolutely unbeatable engine. It made the Fw 190 and transformed the Ju 88.' He confirmed that a BMW-engined Ju 88

without radar or flame-damped exhausts could reach 650 km/h (404 mph).

The prototype Focke-Wulf Fw 190 began its flight test programme on 1 June 1939. It was considered remarkable because it had an air-cooled radial engine (at that time the massive BMW 139, of 55.44 litres/3,380 cu in). Even more remarkable was the installation, because

A prototype Daimler-Benz DB 605A, the 1,475-hp development of the 601 which powered the Bf 109G. It had cylinders of greater bore (154 mm), and later versions had a bigger supercharger.

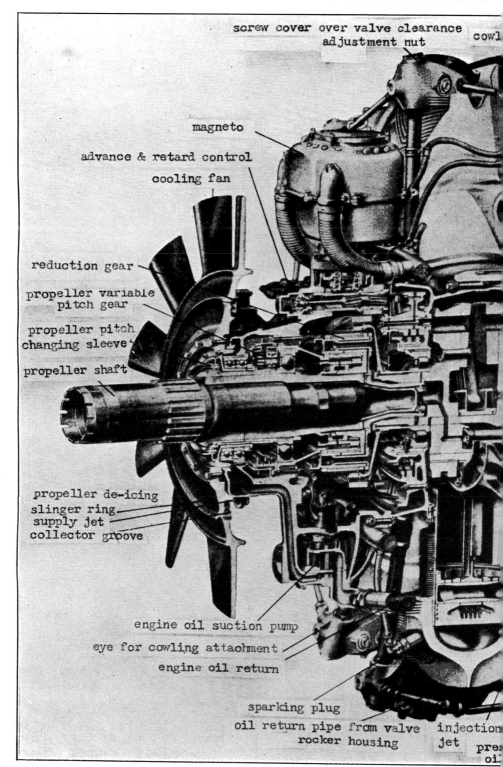

screw cover over valve clearance   cowl
         adjustment nut

magneto

advance & retard control

cooling fan

reduction gear

propeller variable
     pitch gear

propeller pitch
changing sleeve

propeller shaft

propeller de-icing
slinger ring
supply jet
collector groove

engine oil suction pump

eye for cowling attachment

engine oil return

sparking plug

oil return pipe from valve   injection
       rocker housing   jet   pres
                                                 oi

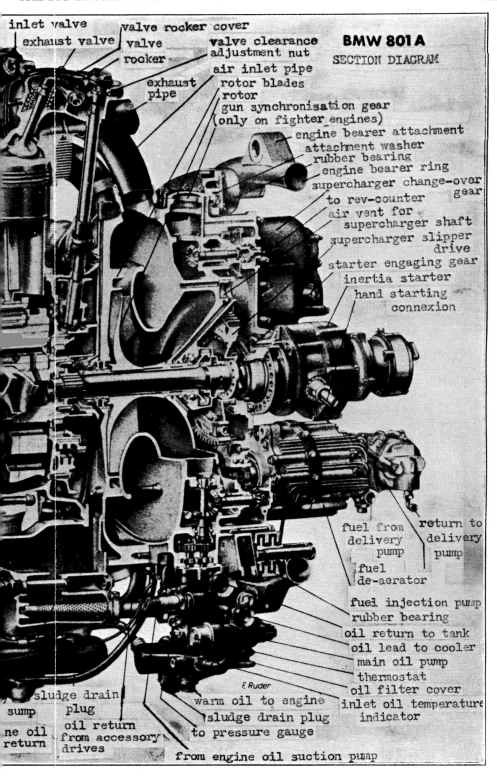

inlet valve
exhaust valve
valve rocker cover
valve
rocker
valve clearance
adjustment nut
air inlet pipe
exhaust
pipe
rotor blades
rotor
gun synchronisation gear
(only on fighter engines)

BMW 801 A

SECTION DIAGRAM

engine bearer attachment
attachment washer
rubber bearing
engine bearer ring
supercharger change-over
gear
to rev-counter
air vent for
supercharger shaft
supercharger slipper
drive
starter engaging gear
inertia starter
hand starting
connexion

fuel from
delivery
pump
return to
delivery
pump
fuel
de-aerator

fuel injection pump
rubber bearing
oil return to tank
oil lead to cooler
main oil pump
thermostat
oil filter cover
inlet oil temperature
indicator

F. Ruder

sludge drain
plug
sump
ne oil
return
oil return
from accessory
drives

warm oil to engine
sludge drain plug
to pressure gauge

from engine oil suction pump

the engine drove a conventional VDM propeller whose hub was surrounded by a spinner of the same diameter as the cowling, all cooling air entering through a central hole looking very like the inlet to a jet engine! The aircraft flew well enough, but the engine overheated, so that the test pilots complained of having their 'feet in the fire'. Even with fan-cooling the airflow was inadequate, so the ducted spinner was removed and replaced by one of normal size, with a conventional cowling inlet but fitted with a fan driven at 3.14 times propeller speed. This was the solution adopted on the BMW 801 engine which powered most production 190s. The exhaust pipes from the 14 cylinders were taken to the rear and used both to give modest propulsive thrust and also suck air through the cowling. There were many other interesting features; for example, the ring around the cowl inlet was armoured, and contained both the oil tank and the peripheral oil radiator. Quite apart from the impact made by the fighter itself, this was a landmark in the installation of radial engines, and it brought a swift and complete reappraisal of such engines in Britain, where such engines had from 1933 been increasingly regarded as suitable only for large, slow aircraft.

The BMW 801's only significant shortcoming was that it became less impressive at over 6,096 m (20,000 ft). The company's engineers, under Helmut Sachse, eventually decided the answer was turbosupercharging, and they set their sights very high. By 1943 the 801TJ was advanced in flight development. It was basically an 801D with a gigantic turbo at the rear, mounted on an almost vertical axis and discharging the gas above the nacelle centreline. The compressed air was delivered to the direct-injection cylinders through five large intercoolers between the engine and the turbo installation, resulting in a very long cowling. The TJ weighed 1,607 kg (3,542 lb) and gave 1,500 hp at 12,192 m (40,000 ft). This was impressive enough, but the 801TQ, a turbocharged version of the uprated 801E, did even better. Weighing precisely the same, it ran at higher speeds and pressures to give 2,270 hp for take-off and 1,715 hp at 12,192 m (40,000 ft). Rather surprisingly, neither tur-

bocharged version got into service; they would have been formidable.

Thus by the mid-war years Germany had three great engines, the 801, the DB 603 and, unquestionably, the Jumo 213. Their development thereafter suffered from being diluted by a host of other projects. It is fatally easy to become enthusiastic over something and launch off into its development. By 1942 the number of Daimler-Benz experimental and prototype engines had exceeded 50 different types. Junkers were not far behind, their best new engine being the 222 with 24 cylinders in six banks. Some of their creations included box-like engines looking rather like a garage open at both ends, because they consisted of four sets of opposed-piston diesel cylinder blocks driving crankshafts at the four corners! These massive engines thus had 24 double-ended cylinders containing 48 pistons and con-rods. Not to be outdone, BMW produced the 803, with 28 cylinders of 801 size but arranged in the form of two radial engines in tandem, each having seven tandem pairs of cylinders cast in an in-line block with liquid cooling. Even stranger, the rear 14 cylinders drove seven shafts passing between the cylinders of the front half of the engine, each 14-cylinder unit driving half a coaxial propeller. The 803 gave 4,000 hp on test.

Germanic size also showed in the remarkable two-stroke diesels produced during the war by KHD (Klöckner-Humboldt-Deutz). The basic Dz 710 was a 'flat-16' engine, with two horizontally opposed banks of eight liquid-cooled cylinders of 160 mm (6 in) bore and stroke, with compression ratio 15. It weighed 1,447 kg (3,190 lb) and gave 2,700 hp, with the very good specific consumption of 0.33. But by 1944 KHD were also running the Dz 720, a doubled-up H-32 version rated at 5,400 hp and weighing 2,900 kg (6,395 lb). Capacity was 103.04 litres (6,283 cu in), and the length and width were respectively 2.7 m (107 in) and 1.7 m (65 in). One was left thinking that, having omitted to look ahead at the start of the war, by the mid-1940s the Germans were looking 10 years ahead in engines, with the small oversight that none of these monster powerplants had any application.

Two further ideas could be described as 'one engine for the price of two' and 'two engines for the price of three'. The former was simply taking two existing and proven engines and bolting them to a common reduction gearbox to drive a single propeller. There may not seem much point in doing this, and in

Previous spread *A wartime cutaway of the superb BMW 801A, made up of a reproduced German drawing on which the British Air Ministry stuck English-language labels.*

Left *The BMW 801 TJ gave 1,500 hp at 12,192 m (40,000 ft)! At the front is the cooling fan; behind are the intercooler segments and exhaust from the oblique turbosupercharger (Heinkel).*

fact by the end of the war the Daimler-Benz company and several others had come to agree. It was all the fault of the Günter brothers (especially Siegfried), who were responsible for the fact that Heinkel aircraft

Below *Left rear view of a Junkers Jumo 222, with 24 liquid-cooled cylinders 135 mm × 135 mm, 46.5 litres (5 in × 5 in, 2,853 cu in) giving 2,500 hp at 3,200 rpm. Air entered via the rectangular inlets on each side at the rear and was then guided by variable-pitch vanes into the large supercharger. The two magnetos are obvious, while the mass of thin dark piping at the lower left shows the location of one of the three injection pumps.*

Below right *After languishing unrecognised in California for over 40 years the fifth prototype BMW 803A has been lovingly restored in Munich. This pinnacle of the piston aero engine has 28 liquid-cooled cylinders giving a capacity of 84 litres (5,126 cu in), and weighs 2598 kg (5,726 lb). Take off power was 4,000 hp, maintained by twin two-stage superchargers at 2,650 hp at 12 km (39,370 ft). The rear 14-cylinder unit drove its own 4-blade propeller via seven shafts passing between the front cylinders.*

Below *Here a BMW restorer is offering up one of the front double-cylinder units.*

When Allison joined two V-1710s together to make the V-3420 they did not know that Daimler-Benz had used exactly the same formula to produce the DB 610. This massive— 1,580 kg (3,483 lb)—engine had a take-off rating of 2,950 hp. It comprised two DB 605s geared to a single propeller, and powered most He 177s (Motor buch Verlag).

of the 1930s were things of beauty and exceptional aerodynamic efficiency. When the He 177 heavy bomber was planned, everything possible was done to reduce drag. Some ideas, such as steam cooling with skin condensers, had to be abandoned, but one idea that got through was that 2,000 hp packaged in one nacelle driving one large propeller was more efficient than two 1,000 hp engines in separate nacelles. To reduce drag still further, the cowling around the double engine was faired straight back into the wing, the four separate landing gears retracting sideways (two inwards, two outwards) into the wing like a fighter.

The engine company thought developing the DB 606 would be a simple job taking a few weeks. It consisted of two DB 601s joined by a common reduction gearbox, each half of the engine being tilted outwards so that the inboard cylinder blocks were almost vertical. Though a massive package, the 606 was installed like other German engines, supported by a big beam of forged Elektron alloy on each side and with a large circular coolant radiator at the front, the flow through which was controlled by gills. It was possible to start each half of the engine independently, with its own electric inertia starter. This double engine first flew in 1936, in a totally different installation in the 'single-engined' He 119. Maximum power was 2,700 hp and the dry

weight 1,565 kg (3,450 lb). Eventually well over 1,200 He 177s were built, most with the 2,950 hp DB 610, the power sections of which were DB 605s. Altogether the overall experience can be summed up as disastrous, mainly because of fires and other problems with the engines. The difficulties had nothing in particular to do with the coupling of the engines, but by 1944 Heinkel had switched to the He 177B, He 274 and He 277 with four separate engines. This was an ideal example of years of dangerous problems stemming from a wish to reduce drag by maybe 2 per cent.

So what about 'two engines for the price of three'? As noted in Chapter 4, in this scheme the aircraft is fitted with three engines, two on the wings driving propellers and the third in the fuselage doing nothing but driving a giant supercharger to boost the propulsion engines. In engineering you never get anything for nothing, but the converse is true also, and with this scheme you ought to get propulsive power that bears some relation to the rate of fuel burn of the three engines, not just the two on the wings. Called the Höhen Zentrale Anlage (high central system), it was studied by several German groups but put into practice by Daimler-Benz. Many different arrangements were experimented with, but the standard form used in such aircraft as the Hs 130E and Do 217P consisted of DB 603B propulsion engines, driving propellers with four very broad blades, supercharged by a DB 605T in the fuselage immediately aft of the wing. The central engine was geared up to a gigantic Roots-type blower, delivering the hot, compressed air through long but flat intercoolers under the inner wings. Under the fuselage were the very prominent inlets for the main supercharger and the ducted radiator for the engine that drove it. The DB 605 was rated at 1,435 hp up to about 6,096 m (20,000 ft), power falling off thereafter, but the overall result was that the wing engines each put out 1,750 hp for take-off and 1,860 hp at 6,900 ft (both figures quite ordinary) but a remarkable 1,440 hp at 45,000 ft. Like so many German wartime efforts the HZ Anlage gave a great deal of trouble and was eventually abandoned in February 1944, despite being perfectly sound in principle.

In the previous chapter we saw how the two giant US makers, Pratt & Whitney and Wright, gradually came to be world leaders. By ceaseless and painstaking development they saw their air-cooled radials sold in 66 countries, used by nearly three-quarters of the world's airlines and licensed to 22 countries. By the start of the Second World War they were in production with two-row engines of up to 2,200 hp, a power available from no other company, and with excellent gear-driven and exhaust-turbo superchargers. But the workhorses continued to be the Wright R-1820 Cyclone and the Pratt & Whitney R-1830 Twin Wasp, both available at up to 1,200 hp. During the war the production of these engines reached totals far surpassing anything seen previously. Pratt & Whitney's overall production of Twin Wasps amounted to 173,618, believed to exceed that of any other aero engine. Two major applications were the C-47 and, with a turbosupercharger, the B-24 Liberator. In the latter the engine cowlings were flattened ovals, because the ducting to the superchargers and intercooler passed on each side of the engine. The Twin Wasps themselves were familiar, but the aircraft was unbelievably complicated, and even managing the engines called for ceaseless attention to perhaps 60 indicators and 20 hand controls.

Before the war the American high-power two-row engines had hardly begun to make an impact, though the Wright R-2600 not only powered the very large and capable Boeing 314 and 314A flying boats but did so on the first 115-grade fuel ever to go into service. These aircraft were always underpowered, had a very poor rate of climb, flew nose-up and suffered from engine overheating. They opened an era in which large aircraft were exceedingly complex, and their pilots had to possess and constantly exercise deep know-ledge of how the entire propulsion system worked. Pan American was the airline which, after painstaking arithmetic, came to the con-clusion that the considerable extra cost of the very special fuel was justified. It allowed the huge boats to be fitted with the 709-C14 ver-sion of the engine, with higher compression ratio calculated to reduce fuel consumption by 5 per cent. There cannot have been much in it.

Unlike Pratt & Whitney, the Wright engines had steel crankcases. Again there can-not have been much in it. Numerous learned treatises have been written explaining why the best material for a crankcase is variously aluminium, steel or a magnesium alloy, and today a case can be made for some fibre-rein-forced composites. What it boils down to is that, give or take a few decimal points, if a material is stronger then you can use it in thin-ner sections which, when multiplied by the increased material density, means that the weight stays about the same. Just very occasionally you welcome high-strength steel because there are overriding geometric reasons why the part must be as small as poss-ible. Usually the deciding factor is the overall cost of material plus fabrication.

At the end of the war Wright offered a com-prehensive range of engines, all called Cyclones: seven-cylinder R-1300, up to 800 hp; nine-cylinder R-1820, up to 1,350 (later 1,525) hp; 14-cylinder R-2600, up to 1,900 hp; and 18-cylinder R-3350, up to 2,200 (later 2,800 and then 3,700) hp. Comparison with engines of the inter-war period showed that each 1945 engine appeared more solid and compact. There was no longer any significant space between the cylinders, which appeared to have got much larger. Each cylinder appeared to have expanded to fill the sector available to it. This was really only common sense. In the old days most of the cooling air passed between the cylinders several inches from the hot fins, and thus took away no heat whatsoever. The objective was to make all the air pass between the fins, and make the fins as

The HZ Anlage was a rather clumsy way of getting high power at high altitude. (A) DB 603B engines; (B) DB 605T engine; (C) two-stage Roots supercharger; (D) air for wing engines; (E) air for DB 605.

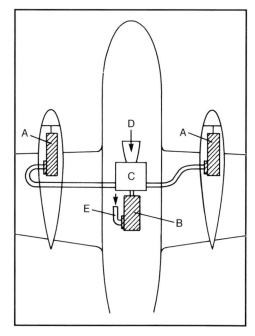

close together as possible. By the end of the war almost all Wright engines had cylinders with so-called W-type fins. Fine, closely spaced grooves were cut in the steel barrels, and thin aluminium sheet fins rolled and caulked in. The forged aluminium heads continued to be a large machining job, with roughly double the fin area of five years previously.

Like Pratt & Whitney, Wright had no engine with any form of fuel injection at the beginning of the war. As briefly traced in Chapter 3, such arrangements had been studied since 1919, but with no serious funding from the military, or from engine firms or customers. Despite this, one scheme worked on by Eclipse (which became part of Bendix) did attract some Army and Navy support. In 1936 TWA became interested, and in 1937 the

Wright Aeronautical (R-3350 engine), General Electric (twin B-11 turbosuperchargers), Hamilton Standard (5.055 m/16 ft 7 in four-blade Hydromatic propeller) and Boeing toiled for four years to bring the B-29 power plant to an acceptable standard. Here the front exhaust collector ring has been removed. The white-hot exhaust from front and rear cylinders was combined in the large pipe, taken back through the firewall and then split to discharge through the two turbos, one in each side of the nacelle (Aero Publishers Inc).

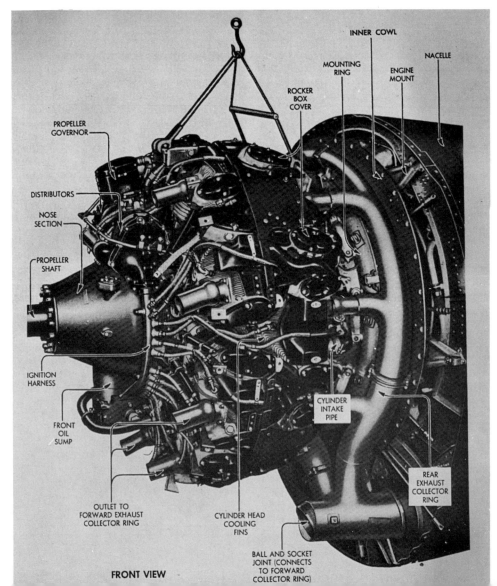

FRONT VIEW

airline did intensive testing with a Northrop Gamma powered by a Cyclone with an Eclipse nine-plunger injection pump. From 1939 the very slow pace of injector development gradually quickened, partly from the realization that some 95 per cent of the front line of the highly respected Luftwaffe had no carburettors. In 1941 Wright was into intensive testing of growing numbers of R-3350 Duplex Cyclones, the largest engine in production in the world at that time. It ran into unexpected problems. First, the injection of the fuel upstream of the supercharger resulted in reduced supercharger efficiency (strange, because in most engines addition of any volatile liquid increases charge density and blower efficiency). A second problem was that with the highly supercharged R-3350 which was under development for the B-29, its chief application, distribution of fuel vapour was unexpectedly bad, so that some cylinders received almost twice the mixture strength of others, the pattern of fuel distribution changing constantly. Perhaps most worrying of all, engines on the testbed suffered severely from backfires, which exploded the highly compressed mixture in the large induction manifolds. Had these engines been in B-29s they would probably have been blown clean off the wing.

This problem was so worrying that by late 1941 the US Army was insisting on direct fuel injection on the R-3350, and moreover saying it would like to see this method adopted on all engines. Obviously, direct injection would mean that the entire induction system would contain nothing but compressed air. It would also eliminate icing, ensure that each cylinder received exactly the correct mixture and improve performance generally. Unfortunately it was only just coming into use on the R-3350 at the end of the war, and on other engines it was later. In many respects the B-29 installation thrust beyond previous technology. The huge engine drove propellers to match, with a diameter of 5 m (16 ft 7 in) or 5.1 m (17 ft). On each side of the nacelle was one of the latest (B-series) General Electric turbosuperchargers, each driven by the exhaust from nine cylinders. The incoming hot compressed air was ducted through a large box-like intercooler, where it was cooled by a cross-flow of ram air at the $-50°C$ temperature appropriate to the 9,144 m (30,000 ft) level. Cooling the air increased the charge density and eliminated the likelihood of detonation. The air then passed the spray

of fuel from the injection-type carburettor (not to be confused with direct injection into the cylinders) and then entered the eye of the mechanically driven supercharger. This was driven from the crankshaft via a two-speed gearbox, and pumped the even more highly compressed mixture to the 18 cylinders. It was found that more mixture went to the front row of cylinders than to the rear, and this helped keep the US Army wedded to using two nine-plunger injectors eventually, so that the plunger stroke could be matched to the slightly different air supply. But, as noted, direct injection only entered service at the end of the war.

Hardly surprisingly, this large and complex installation suffered various other problems. The only dangerous one was that the upper cylinders in the rear row tended to receive inadequate cooling air. This caused exhaust valves to burn out, starting fires which quickly set fire to the magnesium aft casing around the supercharger. Burning magnesium is no joke, and it could easily result in loss of the aircraft. The cause was to add root cuffs to the propeller blades, to boost airflow through the cowling, and to add a special ram-air pipe which blasted cold air directly on to the affected exhaust valves. Even so, the enormous heat output inside the tight cowling was always a problem, and in tropical conditions it became standard practice to carry out all engine checks, including 'mag drop' testing, during the actual take-off run!

When the B-29 was designed an obvious requirement was to achieve the lowest possible drag. Boeing wanted to do even better than the Günter brothers with the He 177: they intended to put the engines—if possible—inside the wing. When it was recognized that the answer had to be giant nacelles, on an efficient slim wing, great efforts were made to reduce installation drag. Amazingly, no provision was made for access to the engine through hinged panels in the cowling. Every time the plugs were changed, the giant propeller had to be removed and the whole cowling pulled off to the front! This was the more surprising as Boeing's XPBB-1 Sea Ranger had R-3350 engines installed in accessible cowlings. Clearly, the wish to reduce drag, which had been prompted by the great advance in aircraft speed made possible by the streamlined monoplane, resulted in renewed interest in engines that could fit inside tight cowlings or even inside the wing. As explained in Chapter 4, some engines were

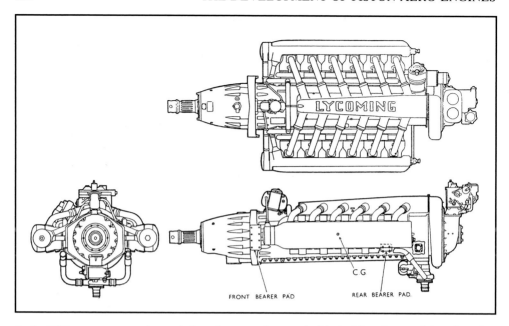

In the 1930s numerous engine and aircraft companies toyed with the idea of powerful engines that could be buried inside wings. One such engine was the Lycoming O-1230, rated at 1,200 hp and (ignoring the water pump and carburettor) 483 mm (19 in) high.

designed to be shallow enough to fit comfortably inside the profile of a wing, and these included an entire generation of high-power American engines. The 'Hyper' Continental IV-1430 was mentioned in the preceding chapter. The rival Lycoming company responded with the O-1230, a flat-12 engine with individual liquid-cooled poppet-valve cylinders. It ran in 1937 at 1,200 hp, which for a weight of 601 kg (1,325 lb), capacity of 20,238 cc (1,234 cu in) and overall height of 9.4 m (37 in) was encouraging. A year later it flew in the Vultee XA-19A (a pure testbed, making no attempt to use its shallow depth). Unfortunately by this time the Army had begun to see that buried engines were non-starters, and that 1,200 hp was in any case not enough. Lycoming doubled up their engine into the XH-2470, with two flat-12 units superimposed and driving a single propeller gearbox. This ran at 2,200 hp in July 1940, and powered the Vultee (later Convair) XP-54 which placed top in the Army's R-40C fighter contest which was meant to find the best new fighter to succeed the P-38 and 47. It was also intended for the Navy Curtiss XF14C, but by 1943 it was clear that this otherwise promising engine would be too late for the war.

Incidentally, Lycoming not only lost a lot of money on these big liquid-cooled engines but it also designed and built the biggest and most powerful aircraft piston engine of all time. The XR-7755 had 36 cylinders identical in form to those of the 'Hyper' opposed engines, but considerably larger: 162 mm × 171 mm/6.375 in × 6.75 in, giving capacity of 127,081 cc (7,755 cu in). Its configuration superficially looked like a radial, but it actually had nine banks each of four liquid-cooled cylinders. Maximum power on test in 1944 just exceeded 5,000 hp. With a unique two-speed reduction gearbox for contra-rotating propellers it weighed 3,198 kg (7,050 lb). No application was announced.

The biggest of all the programmes for advanced new engines launched in the 1930s was that of Pratt & Whitney. As described earlier, this firm had become number one in the world purely because of a handful of types of air-cooled radial, and had already had one unsuccessful brush with liquid-cooled engines. It launched into a totally new form of engine in 1936 partly because the Navy wanted a 2,300-hp engine, beyond the immediate capability of a two-row radial; the Army saw the Curtiss XP-37 as indicating that liquid-cooled fighters went faster; and both services had this bee in their bonnet about buried engines. The principle advocate within the company for liquid-cooled 'in-line' engines was its top engineer, Vice-President George Mead. In April 1937 he visited England, and returned convinced that the future lay not only with multiple liquid-cooled cylinders but also with sleeve valves. After dropping the Navy XL-3130 the company concentrated on two engines both with 24 liquid-cooled, sleeve-valve cylinders arranged in H form, the X-1800 of 36,736 cc (2,240 cu in) to give 1,800 hp, and the H-3730 (the original Navy XL-3130 enlarged to 61,172 cc/3,730 cu in) to give 2,900 hp and eventually, with exhaust turbos, 4,000 hp. These two engines were built and run in several forms. They were exciting engines, of great potential, and Mead got them accepted for various aircraft, including submerged wing installations for future Boeing and Douglas bombers.

This was one side of a multifaceted and complex picture. One of the other facets was that, even for a company as big and capable as Pratt & Whitney, developing these engines would take several (more than four) more years. The war was starting in Europe, and there was no point in costly development of an engine that would be too late. The new engines had nothing in common with the company's established radials, and would require different tooling in a different plant. The effort expended on them was slowing the pace of development of the established engines, notably the R-2800 Double Wasp. And there were further factors. From the outset 'Luke' Hobbs had been utterly unconvinced of the need for the unfamiliar breed of engine. He avoided open conflict with Mead, who was a sick man, but in mid-1939 Mead was forced to retire and Hobbs took over. Hobbs could now speak openly. He very quickly brought the Double Wasp to the production stage at 2,000 hp. A prototype, still rated at 1,850 hp, was fitted to the prototype XF4U Corsair Navy fighter, and in October 1940 this achieved 652 km/h (405 mph) in level flight. This was the first fighter in the world to exceed 644 km/h (400 mph), despite its great size and carrier gear, and Hobbs said, 'Who needs any other type of engine?'

Hobbs got Army permission to cancel the X-1800, returning the fees paid, but had to keep the H-3730 for the Navy because in 1940 this was more powerful than any radial. But Hobbs pointed out that nobody had ever actually set out to investigate the cooling problems of a radial with more than two rows. (He was unaware of Armstrong Siddeley's Deerhound and Boarhound.) Obviously, a multi-row engine tends to mean that each successive row is cooled by hotter air. At this time Wright began development of the R-2160 (see later)

Many engineers in Pratt & Whitney felt they were junking a superb engine, giving 3,300 hp and with 4,000 imminent, when they abandoned the liquid-cooled sleeve-valve H-3730. Note the giant intercoolers at the rear (United Technologies Archive).

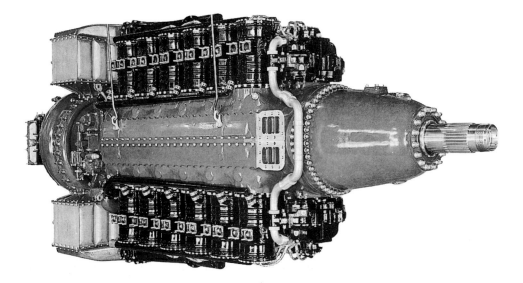

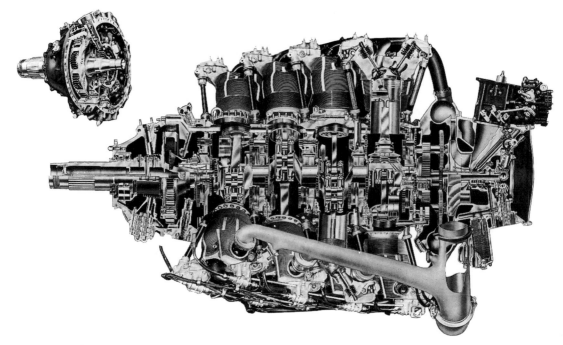

A beautiful cutaway of a typical Pratt & Whitney R-4360 Wasp Major. Note the geometry of the master and link rods, the geared drives to the cam rings and the projecting rocker-box covers. The injection carburettor and internal supercharger deliver compressed mixture via black pipes at top and bottom; the large pale manifold is exhaust (United Technologies Archive).

with the first row air-cooled but all the rest liquid-cooled! Hobbs discovered that by extremely careful design the cooling drag of a multi-row radial could be so low as to eliminate any advantage in drag of a liquid-cooled engine. He found the ideal arrangement to be four rows, each slightly rotated so that the rows were staggered. In late 1940 Hobbs completed the drawings of the R-4360 Wasp Major, with four rows of seven cylinders, each 146 mm × 152 mm (5.75 in × 6.0 in), 71,553 cc (4,363 cu in), aimed at 3,000 hp. He told General H. H. 'Hap' Arnold that the H-3730 would miss the war, but that the R-4360 might just make it. For the second time the Hartford company handed back all development moneys paid, and wrote off over $2m of its own funds, but set course on the R-4360 thinking it had probably done the right thing. The R-4360 missed the war, but became a very important engine in military, naval and airline applications.

The engine that had done most to captivate Mead had been the British Napier Sabre. Previously Frank Halford had designed for Napier the little Rapier and Dagger with large numbers of small air-cooled cylinders running at high rpm. These were of no importance

whatever, but the Sabre was something else. Though it was never intended for buried wing installation its cylinders were lying on their sides. Like several of the new US engines it had 24 cylinders arranged in the form of two opposed 12-cylinder engines mounted one above the other and driving a common front propeller gearbox. Despite its complexity the Sabre was quite compact. The cylinder design was naturally based on the long experience of Bristol, the light-alloy blocks having three inlet and two exhaust ports serving each cylinder, and the precision-ground steel sleeves having four ports. Bore and stroke were only 127 mm (5.0 in) × 121 mm (4.75 in) (36,703 cc/2,238 cu in), but by a combination of high speed (3,700 rpm) and high BMEP the Sabre was cleared in June 1940 to give 2,200 hp. It still needed three more years to become acceptably reliable, and never did develop as a suitable fighter engine with adequate performance at all altitudes, but in the low-altitude Typhoon and Tempest it was a useful engine in the final year of the war. Structurally the heart of the Sabre was the extremely complex crankcase. On each side was attached a light-alloy cast cylinder block containing an upper row of six cylinders and a lower row of six. The engine was held together by 48 tie bolts passing right across from one side to the other. At the front was a gear-train driven by the two crankshafts, driving (among other things) the compound helical gears to the propeller and a hollow shaft on each side, between the block and the crankcase, carrying the worm gears for the sleeve-drive cranks. Down the centres of these shafts ran torsionally flexible shafts driving the large double-entry supercharger at the rear, downstream of two pairs of twin-choke carburettors. The various pumps were underneath, and other accessories were on top, including the Coffman cartridge starter.

Eventually the Sabre was developed to give 2,340 hp in the Tempest VI, and Rotol and Napier together schemed interesting post-war installations, tested in a Warwick as well as in Tempests, not only with Germanic frontal annular radiators but also, in the case of Tempest NV768, a giant ducted spinner making the front end resemble that of the first Fw 190 of six years earlier. The annular radiator increased maximum speed from 700 km/h (435 mph) to 742 km/h (461 mph), but the Centaurus sleeve-valve radial was so much smoother and more reliable, besides being more powerful, it was standardized for post-war Tempests and Furies.

One engine which never got into production at all, despite great potential, was the Fairey P 24. This seemed to have everything going for it. It consisted of two independent left and right engines, each comprising upper and lower six-cylinder blocks with double overhead camshafts to poppet valves, and pressure glycol cooling. Beside each block was the supercharger, on a transverse shaft. Each half of the engine gave 1,100 hp, the opposite-rotation crankshafts each being geared to its own three-blade Fairey constant-speed propeller. The P 24 flew in Battle testbed K9370 in June 1939 and completed 87 hours' flying with no trouble whatever, the Battle having an excellent performance with either half-engine shut down and its propeller feathered (in other words, giving twin-engine safety in what looked like a single-engined aircraft). K9370 then flew some 250 hours at Wright

In the author's view the Fairey P 24 was a simpler and better engine than the Sabre, and, just like the Rolls-Royce Exe, it gave three years of trouble-free flying in a Battle after it had been cancelled (Fleet Air Arm Museum).

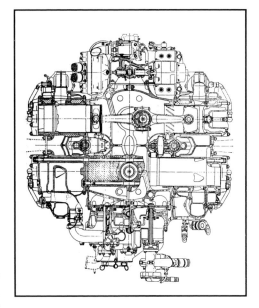

Despite the experience with the Dagger, Frank Halford persisted with the idea of a fast-running engine with numerous small cylinders in the Sabre. This differed, however, in having liquid-cooled sleeve-valve cylinders arranged horizontally. Between the two right-hand cylinders can be seen one of the sleeve drives.

Field in the USA, but Fairey was successfully kept out (as he had been in 1924) by the Mafia of the established builders.

Turning briefly to other wartime countries, I was fortunate to be able to look at almost all the Japanese engines, and formed the view, 'When you've seen one, you've seen them all.' Almost all were conventional radials, two showing signs of Bristol ancestry and the rest having a strong American flavour. The chief

Like the BMW 801 in the Fw 190, the Shvetsov ASh-82 in the La-5 was a major advance in the installation of an air-cooled radial. In fact both the engines and their installations were remarkably similar (N. A. Eastaway).

exception was a licensed copy of the Daimler-Benz 601, which in the Ki-64 prototype was used in a unique twin-engined installation, one engine in the nose and the other behind the cockpit, with steam cooling and wing/flap skin condensers. A small air radiator under the right wing cooled the oil. The Navy version of the same German engine was made by Aichi as the Atsuta, and the unfinished Yokosuka R2Y1 was to have been powered by two of these coupled side by side in exactly the same manner as the DB 606. This bulky engine was to be mounted amidships, with a long shaft passing between the two crew to the tractor six-blade propeller. The only other remarkable Japanese engine was the Nakajima Ha-505, very like a Wasp Major but even bigger, with four rows of nine cylinders and a target power of 5,000 hp. At least one Ha-505 was built, but I do not believe it flew.

In the Soviet Union the emphasis naturally tended to be on mass production in quantities great enough to overwhelm the might of Nazi Germany. One could have an enduring debate on how far quantity is better than quality. In the 1930s the official view of the RAF was that quality was everything. Better aircraft, it was held, would 'slice through enemy formations like a hot knife through butter'. That is a natural viewpoint to adopt if your quantity is non-existent. In the case of Soviet wartime aircraft and engines the astronomic numbers

tended to obscure the fact that their quality was not bad either. And the fact that 99 per cent of all front-line engines were of four types tended to obscure the wealth of interesting engines made in smaller numbers.

The four types were: the M-11 family, the AM-34 to 38 series, the VK-105 and the ASh-82 radial. The M-11 rates a mention partly because it was deliberately designed to be simple, and partly because, as a direct consequence, over 130,000 were built. A five-cylinder, air-cooled radial in the 100–150 hp class, it had two overhead poppet valves per cylinder, often with completely enclosed pushrods and rockers. Many versions were made by many factories, but all could run on any kind of petrol and be stripped without any special tools. The General Constructor was A. D. Shvetsov, who much later masterminded the ASh-82. This began life as a very tough and compact 14-cylinder engine using cylinders originally based on the R-1820 Cyclone but with numerous improvements and with stroke reduced to 155 mm (6 in), giving a capacity of 41.2 litres (2,514 cu in) despite holding overall diameter to 1,260 mm (49.6 in). This engine was qualified in 1940 at a conservative 1,250 hp on 87-octane fuel, and was subsequently developed not only in power (to 2,000 hp with direct injection and 100-grade fuel) but also in installation. The La-5 in December 1941 had an installation in some ways even better than the Fw 190, and certainly superior to anything in Britain and perhaps the USA either. Production exceeded 70,000, including versions for commercial transports and helicopters, the latter having the crankshaft at either 25° or 90° and with direct drive and a cooling fan, vital when hovering. The AM-34/38 and VK-105 were discussed in the previous chapter.

Of course there were many interesting Soviet experimental and prototype engines. Having just mentioned the ASh-82 it is logical to comment that in 1941 the first ASh-90 went on test, and was qualified at 1,500 hp, developing to 1,800 hp (at low priority) by 1943. Many Western accounts describe this engine as a copy of the Wright R-3350 Duplex Cyclone, but this somewhat bigger engine was unknown to Shvetsov until 1944, by which time the 90 had been dropped. What could be construed a 'copy of the R-3350' was Shvetsov's ASh-73, but even this was derived from the ASh-62, whose Cyclone ancestry went back to July 1933 in the M-25. One can trace the development from the M-25 through the

M-62 (later ASh-62), ASh-63, ASh-71 (basically two ASh-63 rows on one crankcase) and ASh-72 (qualified at 2,250 hp in 1943) to the ASh-73TK with turbochargers which powered the Tu-4. The latter was indeed a copy of the B-29, but its engines would have been just the same if the three B-29s had force-landed in Siberia without engines! There were various further developments, biggest of which was the ASh-2. Despite its confusing designation it was Shvetsov's last basic engine, and it comprised two ASh-82s in tandem on a common crankcase. Unlike the P&W R-4360 the cylinders were in straight rows of four, cooling being assisted by a large fan and tight-fitting baffles.

The ASh-2 was qualified at 3,600 hp in 1950 to power the Tu-85, but in fact the choice fell on the generally superior VD-4K designed for the job by V. A. Dobrynin. This was similar in bulk and weight, but gave greater power and promised lower installed drag. It had an X arrangement, the six banks being disposed at 60° and each comprising a straight row of four air-cooled cylinders (further details are given on page 216). In the Tu-85 it was neatly cowled as a radial, with a very large dorsal ram inlet behind the cowled engine to serve the giant turbosupercharger. Take-off power was 4,300 hp, and the turbo maintained this power up to 10,000 m (32,808 ft). This was probably the most powerful piston engine ever to fly.

Mention should also be made of the outstanding two-stroke diesels of A. D. Charomskii. Following much research he produced the AN-1 in 1933. A massive water-cooled V-12, this was tested at 850 hp, and later at 900 hp. From it Charomskii's KB (prototype construction bureau) developed the production version ACh-30, with cylinders 180 mm × 200 mm (7 in × 7.9 in), giving a capacity of 62.34 litres (3,804 cu in). This seems a large capacity for a two-stroke, and the weight was also naturally considerable, in the 1.2 tonne (2,645 lb) class. From the ACh-30, which was rated at 1,400 hp, came a series of impressive engines, with large turbochargers to ensure good scavenging and monobloc light-alloy cylinder blocks with pressure glycol cooling. Series production was achieved in 1942 by the 1,500 hp ACh-30BF and small series runs were achieved by other types including the 1,900 hp ACh-39BF. All used heavy fuel oil and had specific fuel consumption in the region of 0.365. Applications included the Yer-2 and Pe-8 long-range bombers, the latter ex-

periencing considerable trouble on operations.

Klimov developed the familiar VK-100 series in various ways. Whereas the mass-produced engines had two inlet and one exhaust valves per cylinder, the VK-107 family had one inlet, one air scavenging valve and two exhaust valves, actuated by three cams. Most 107s were cleared to 2,800 rpm and were rated at up to 1,800 hp with water injection. They had various features which differed from the 105 series, notably that exhaust was taken out from both sides of each cylinder, so that in addition to the usual six ejector stubs on each side of the cowling there were two more rows of six along the top. The VK-120 (M-120) was a straightforward attempt by Klimov to obtain more power by using three VK-103 cylinder blocks equally spaced at 120°, one being at the 12 o'clock position; it was developed during the war to 1,820 hp. Another General Constructor, A. M. Dobrotvorskii, used four of these blocks in X formation in the MB-100 and 102. These were almost two VK-103s, one inverted on top of the other, because there were two superimposed crankshafts. Rated at 3,200 hp, the MB-100 fitted a neat but very large circular cowling of 1,950 mm (77 in) diameter, installed in a Yer-2 in January 1945.

Thus by the Second World War the large, high-power, four-stroke engine had been taken to a very high degree of refinement, and most of the oddball ideas had fallen by the wayside. Some of these unsuccessful oddities are described by Herschel Smith in his book *Aircraft Piston Engines*. One group comprise the barrel-cam and swashplate engines, in which cylinders arranged like those of a six-shooter drive a central shaft by their axial force on a sloping surface. Most, such as the Avro (Redrup), Wooler and American Alfaro, were fairly low-powered, but the Soviet Sparost was rated at 600 hp and expected by the late 1930s to reach 1,200 hp.

Most of the oddities did nothing to help designers in their urgent quest for ever more power, and when long range was required the piston engine still had something to offer, because 50 years ago gas turbines were still relatively inefficient and suffered from high fuel consumption. Merely pressing ahead with detail refinement was one answer, but what many designers were looking for was some kind of major breakthrough. They sought a way of using the working fluid (basically air) so that less of the added heat energy was rejected back to atmosphere in the exhaust. One way of doing this, not mentioned by

Herschel Smith, was to use a gas generator of the free-piston type.

Since 1930 at least 28 companies, mainly in France, Germany and the USA, have developed free-piston engines. Some used opposed pistons oscillating linearly inside conventional straight cylinders, but quite a few designs have used pistons which move round a circular cylinder. In other words the cylinder is a hollow ring; there is no crankcase or cylinder head in the normal sense. The pistons are so arranged that as they move round the ring combustible mixture is drawn in through an aperture in the cylinder wall at one point, compressed between two adjacent pistons, and then fired, escaping through another aperture further on. Such a machine can be used as an engine in its own right, but in this case the pistons must be mechanically connected to the output shaft and this inevitably involves sealing problems where the radial arms pass through the cylinder. One of the few engines of this type developed for aircraft is on view at the Soviet Monino museum. The Constructor was I. A. Uvarov, who worked on it during 1933–40. The cylinder contained two groups each of six pistons, all 60° apart. It will be appreciated that a fundamental feature of all free-piston schemes is that the successive firings of mixture between pairs of pistons automatically compresses the next charge of mixture between the next pair of pistons. Uvarov's engine operated with a compression ratio of 8, and eventually gave 1,600 hp at 2,300 rpm with a specific fuel consumption of 0.19 kg (0.418 lb)/hp/hr.

Of course, if no shaft power need be extracted, then there is no need to cut a slot round the cylinder and the sealing problem vanishes. In this case the free-piston engine serves solely as a generator of hot compressed gas, which can then be used to drive either a separate piston engine or a turbine driving the output shaft. Compared with a conventional piston engine a free-piston unit can operate at higher temperature and pressure, and in most designs the pistons are cushioned by compressing additional air—in the circular type engine between the alternate pairs of pistons—which is then used to dilute and cool the gas. All the free-piston gasifiers used in aviation, by such companies and designers as Pescara, Alan Muntz, SIGMA, Lütz, Junkers, Anselm Franz (of Junkers and then Lycoming), Birmann and Pratt & Whitney (with the PT-1, their first gas turbine) operated with a thermal efficiency from 40 to 45 per cent. Thus, with a typical turbine efficiency, the overall efficiency could be around 37 per cent, which is a lot better than traditional piston engines. It was expected that a complete free-piston plus turbine powerplant would weigh more than a traditional engine, but this seemed of no importance. In 1940 Hobbs of Pratt & Whitney was discussing with Andrew Kaltinsky of the MIT the best way to power the future giant transatlantic bomber that matured as the B-36. Kaltinsky showed that, whereas the forthcoming R-4360 Wasp Major could not expect to better a specific fuel

Left *One of the few barrel engines on public view is the Sparost, in the Soviet air force museum at Monino. Its six large cylinders drove a sinusoidal cam ring. Sparost intended later to make his engine double-ended* (N. A. Eastaway). Right *Another oddball at Monino is Uvarov's ring-type free-piston engine. Such engines have never achieved success except as gas producers for shaft turbines* (N. A. Eastaway).

consumption of 0.42 (like, for example, the R-2800), a free-piston plant could cruise at better than 0.34 and possibly as low as 0.27. Assuming that 0.31 would be achieved, this would reduce the fuel required to carry 4,536 kg (10,000 lb) of bombs across the Atlantic from 58,968 kg (130,000 lb) to 43,546 kg (96,000 lb). Thus even if there was a slight increase in powerplant weight, the bombload could be quadrupled.

Pratt & Whitney put $3.3 million of their own money into the PT-1. The turbine caused few problems, but the free-piston (two-stroke diesel) gas generator, with afterburning, never did perform to satisfaction. The PT-1 was given up soon after the war, and never seriously affected the design of the B-36, mainly because conventional turboprops rapidly developed to give more power for much lower weight and with nearly as low a specific fuel consumption. Strangely, no turboprop ever powered the B-36, though the B-36C was designed to be powered by the R-4360–51, in which an exceptional fraction of the exhaust energy was recovered. The gases were expanded through an enormous General Electric CHM-2 two-stage turbine driving the largest supercharger blower ever used on a piston aero engine. The gas then escaped to atmosphere through a variable-area nozzle to give 'several hundred pounds of jet thrust'. At a cost of 408 kg (900 lb) in weight the maximum power was increased from 3,500 to 4,300 hp, and maintained at a high level to over 9,144 m (30,000 ft). In the B-36C these impressive engines would have been installed driving tractor propellers, whereas all other B-36 versions had a totally different installation with the R-4360s used as pusher engines behind the main wing structural box, fed by long flat ducts from the leading edge.

Whereas Pratt & Whitney got little return for their massive effort on the compound R-4360–51, rival Wright did achieve a colossal success with the corresponding development of the R-3350 Duplex Cyclone. Called the Turbo-Compound, a registered name, this was a family of related civil and military engines which stemmed from a prototype funded mainly by the US Navy which went on test in January 1949. The basic 18-cylinder engine was almost unchanged. The new part was at the back. Here were added three turbines spaced round the engine 120° apart, driven by the exhaust gas and—the new feature—putting their power into the crankshaft. The turbines were of the blow-down

This portion of the Pratt & Whitney PT-1 was just a turboprop. What made it unusual was that the hot gas was fed via the giant pipe in the rear from a free-piston two-stroke diesel engine (United Technologies Archive).

type, taking gas at 800–815°C at supersonic velocity. Each had a diameter of about 279 mm (11 in), with Stellite blades welded to the disc, rotating at full power at 23,200 rpm. Each drove a radial quill shaft, bevel reduction gear, hydraulic coupling and final spur reduction gear. The whole assembly was mounted on and in a rear extension of the crankcase, each turbine being fed by the shortest possible pipes from six cylinders. At a cost of some 245 kg (540 lb) in weight, the Turbo-Compound gave take-off power increased from 2,700 hp to 3,500 hp, or to 3,700 with water injection, and with specific consumption reduced by 20 per cent to about 0.39. This automatically meant aircraft range extended by at least 20 per cent, even if the extra power was not used to lift additional fuel (as in fact was done in such aircraft as the DC-7, 7B and 7C, and L-1049C to 1649). Adding the turbines required no extra control system, had no significant effect on cylinder conditions and had a useful silencing effect.

Wright began delivering Turbo-Compounds in 1950, and by the time production ran out in 1958 had delivered 12,000. But plenty of more complicated compound engines got nowhere. Some of the biggest were in the Soviet Union. At GAZ-501 V. M. Yakovlev (no relation to A. S. Yakovlev) produced the awesome M-501, with seven monobloc banks

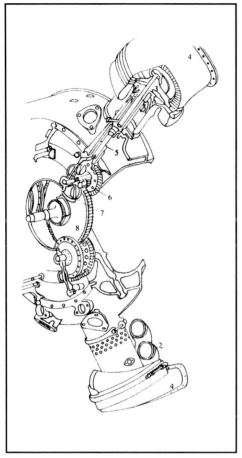

The Wright Turbo-Compound can in many ways be regarded as the pinnacle of the high-power piston aero engine. It was an R-3350 Cyclone plus three turbines spaced round the rear at 120° to extract energy from the exhaust and put it into the crankshaft. Gas from the 18 cylinders [(1) off to the left] was fed through two pipes (2) to each turbine (3), finally escaping through nozzles (4). Each turbine put about 270 hp into a quill shaft (5) which via a reduction gear (6) and hydraulic coupling (7) drove gear (8) connected to the rear of the crankshaft.

each of six four-stroke diesel cylinders (160 mm × 170 mm, 143.55 litres/6.2 in × 6.7 in, 8,753 cu in) with a double-sided, first-stage supercharger driven by an exhaust turbine and a second gear-driven supercharger. The M-501 was qualified in 1952 at 6,000 hp at 2,400 rpm. Even more colossal was the A-117,

developed in 1949–55 at GAZ-117 by M. A. Orlov. This used a free-piston gas generator to feed a turbine rated at 10,000 hp, with complex secondary flows and intercoolers. At least as complex, though of more manageable size, was the British Napier Nomad.

The Nomad passed through two major stages of development. In its first form, exhibited in 1951 and extensively flown in a Lincoln, it had a horizontally opposed, 12-cylinder, liquid-cooled, two-stroke diesel with valveless cylinders (A in the drawing), the capacity being 41,131 cc (2,508 cu in). This was geared down to the propeller (B). From the front of the crankshaft a quill shaft and step-up gears drove the supercharger (C). The exhaust drove the turbine (D), the gas energy being augmented on take-off by an extra combustion chamber (J) (there being plenty of spare oxygen in the exhaust from a two-stroke diesel). This turbine drove the axial compressor (F) and also the reduction gear to the propeller (G). The air compressed by (F) was cooled by the intercooler (H) (with various controls over the flow of both air and coolant) before being fed to the centrifugal compressor (C). Valve (L) enabled the second turbine (E) to be brought in when full-power operation was needed, with (J) in use, the gases finally escaping through the jet nozzle (K). This was a serious attempt to achieve the ultimate in low sfc, but in fact the achieved figure was never better than 0.36 and my memories of this version are of flames coming out of the jetpipe and exasperated engineers trying to explain the problems.

Chief engineer E. E. Chatterton was wise to get this version, the E 125, replaced by a rather simpler Nomad called the E 145. Among many other things this eliminated the centrifugal compressor, reheat chamber and auxiliary turbine, and added a Beier stepless variable gear to link both the axial turbine/compressor shaft and the crankshaft to a single propeller. Weight was reduced from 1,916 kg (4,225 lb) to 1,624 kg (3,580 lb), and power rose from 3,000 shp to a maximum with water injection of 4,095 ehp with sfc at the excellent level of 0.345. The only possible applications were the Shackleton (where it would have increased power by 67 per cent as well as lengthening range on the existing tankage by 35 per cent) and the Beverley (where the extra power really could have been put to use). Of course, nothing happened, so this pinnacle of the big piston aviation engine just ground to a halt in 1955.

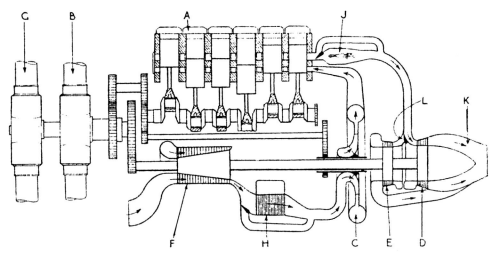

A less-successful 'pinnacle' was the Napier Nomad. This diagram of the original version is actually greatly simplified! See text for explanation.

Cutaway drawing of the de Havilland Gipsy Queen Series 50 inverted air-cooled six-in-line.

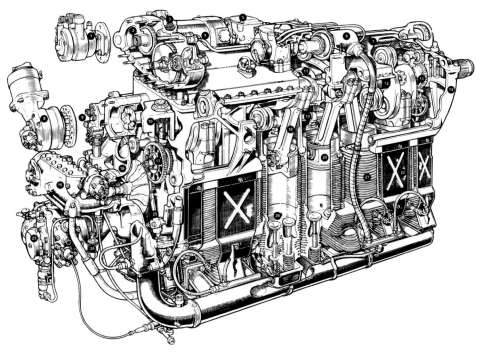

1. Vacuum pump.
2. Accessory-drive gearbox.
3. CSU oil filter.
4. Generator.
5. Port magneto. Rotating-magnet type.
6. Starboard distributor.
7. Top cover—light alloy.
8. Starter.
9. Engine speed indicator drive connection.
10. Oil suction filter.
11. Main bearings—lined with thin-wall bi-metal shells.
12. Crankshaft. Nickel-chromium steel forging fitted with rotating pendulum vibration absorbers.
13. Timing gears.
14. Crankcase—light alloy.

15. Oil-heated air intake.
16. Supercharger.
17. Supercharger drive.
18. Connecting rods. Aluminium-alloy forgings, big ends lined with bi-metal shells, small ends unbushed.
19. Camshaft.
20. Pistons—light-alloy, fully skirted, with fully floating gudgeon pins.
21. Cylinder barrels—machined from steel forgings.
22. Inter-cylinder baffles.
23. Fuel control unit.
24. Oil dilution valve.
25. Oil-pump drive.
26. Cylinder head with valves and valve springs.

8 Piston engines today and tomorrow

Like its predecessors, this chapter is made up of several rather distinct parts. The first story traces the gradual demise of the piston engine in fields other than what might loosely be called light aircraft. Another outlines the recent history of engines for light aircraft, and attempts to explain why so many advances in the technology failed to catch on. Another story concerns the rather unexpected emergence of the modern car engine as a force to be reckoned with. Yet another tale describes how, from a few generally crude motor cycle type engines, the smallest power category has grown to be big business, at least in terms of numbers of engines, such that 35 companies are today competing for it. This is divided into air-cooled and water-cooled sections. This still leaves to be reviewed the growing field of diesels, and the many unconventional kinds of engine, notably the RC (rotating combustion) species, which conclude the book.

When I was preparing a review of piston engines in 1970 I wrote down a list of types of fixed-wing aircraft designed since 1945 which fell between the big airline and cargo-airlifter transports on the one hand and sporting, private-owner and executive type aircraft on the other. Most were utility transports, STOL vehicles, agricultural aircraft and special-purpose machines (excluding helicopters). There were 244 names on the list. This shows that piston engines were 'a long time a-dying', though a different slant is provided by adding that of the 244 225 failed to sustain production into double figures. Among the most successful were the de Havilland Dove and Heron, de Havilland Canada Beaver, Otter and Caribou, Dornier Skyservant, Antonov An-2 and An-14 and, not in quite the same league,

the Scottish Aviation Twin Pioneer (because of sales to the RAF). Among the major mistakes were the Handley Page Herald (four Leonides Major), Agusta AZ-8 (four Leonides), PZL MD-12 (four WN-3) and Cessna 620 (four GSO-526). In the STOL utility field, Pilatus had a smash hit with the piston-engined Porter (despite an appearance reminiscent of the 1920s), whereas Shorts got nowhere with the Skyvan until they pulled out the piston engines and put in turboprops. Another machine in this class was the Bushmaster (three P&W Wasp), based on the Ford Trimotor of 1926 but the subject of repeated launch attempts in 1959–69.

The rule seemed to be established 35 years ago that the piston engine has no place in a passenger aircraft with more than 10 seats, but that it does have an enduring place in STOL utility transports with an unpressurized box-like fuselage with big cargo doors, and also in all forms of agricultural aircraft. These two classes undoubtedly provide an ongoing market for piston engines of up to 1,000 hp. In the larger sizes the turboprop is competing strongly, but it is a swings and roundabouts situation, with no evidence of either side being defeated. In a nutshell, the turboprop offers unlimited power (whereas 1,000 hp is the limit of power from new piston engines) with perhaps even less likelihood of inflight failure, whilst burning kerosene or diesel fuel that may be thought safer in a crash and is almost certainly cheaper than the now-rare high-octane petrol. The turboprop is also much lighter, so payload can be increased, but on the other hand it burns fuel rather faster, especially at low level, and, not least, is much more expensive to buy. I will discuss the RC engine later.

Before looking at this market in more detail, there are two further branches of general aviation where the piston engine is dominant, and they could hardly be more different, except in the fact that both are concerned with flight in close proximity to the ground. One is competition aerobatics, where among other requirements the engine must operate equally well under any vertical acceleration from +12g to −10g, respond instantly and unfailingly to rapid throttle movements and, if possible, have a very low moment of inertia about all axes. The other specialized field is fire-bombing, in which the aircraft drops the greatest possible load of water, with or without a chemical retardant, on to the edge of a forest fire. Some fire bombers can recharge their tanks in flight by making a slow run across any convenient stretch of water with a reasonably wave-free surface. In any event, fire bombing is a trucking job, calling for the maximum lifting power. More than 95 per cent of the world's fire bombers are retired military aircraft, formerly bombers or maritime patrol aircraft. They have been fairly effective, though they were never designed for such work. Today they are fast running out of airframe and engine hours, and nothing new in this category is being built except the CL-215T, which is powered by turboprops and is matched to various other tasks. A pure water bomber is perhaps the sole remaining requirement for really high-power piston engines, and it is surprising that this important market has so far not been addressed by an aircraft manufacturer.

Certainly, nobody in the immediate post-war era would have dreamt that by the 1990s the only source of fairly powerful piston engines would be Poland. This arose from the Kremlin decision of 1959 to transfer all general aviation manufacture, both aircraft (including helicopters) and engines, to Poland. Thus the Polish WSK-Kalisz factory went into production with the already extremely fully developed air-cooled radials which had previously been the responsibility of A. D. Shvetsov and Aleksandr G. Ivchyenko. There was no further application for the excellent ASh-82 in the 1,900 hp class, but no lack of demand for Shvetsov's ASh-62 in the 1,000 hp category, and Ivchyenko's AI-14 of one-quarter this power. Production began at Kalisz in 1960, and the factory was glad to have orders for over 100 engines in all. They hardly thought it worth changing the designation of the ASh-62 to ASz-62, and lit-

tle thought that by 1990 deliveries of one version of this engine alone, the ASz-62IR-16, would exceed 15,000! The smaller AI-14RA, of 256 hp, has also proved a staple product, with many thousands built, and to keep the production lines going both engines are now once again being further developed, with new factory designations. The K8-AA is a new aerobatic version of the AI-14P for the PZL-130 Orlik; like most current models it has a pneumatic (compressed-air) starter. The K9-AA is an ASz-62IR uprated from the previous rpm limit of 2,200 to 2,300, the power increasing to 1,170 hp. It powers the M-24 Dromader Super, the world's largest and most capable ag-aircraft, driving a four-blade constant-speed propeller, generator, hydraulic pump and, if necessary, a pump for spraying chemicals. Starting is electric.

An engine of intermediate power is the PZL-3S. This began life as Ivchyenko's AI-26W, in the 600-hp class. On the transfer to Poland it was assigned to another factory, WSK-Rzeszów. At first the Polish version was known as the LiT-3, but current production is designated PZL-3S. Whereas both the Kalisz

Shvetsov/PZL ASz-62IR, with cooling baffles fitted.

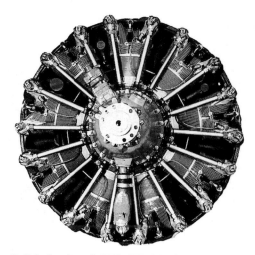

Polish-developed PZL K8-AA, based on the Soviet Vedeneyev Ivchyenko M-14Pm.

engines have nine cylinders, the PZL-3S has only seven. They are almost identical to those of the ASh-82 family (155.5 mm × 155 mm/ 6.12 in × 6.10 in), giving capacity just half that of the big engine at 20.6 litres (1,265 cu in). Of course, the general-aviation engine is nothing like so highly boosted, though it does have a supercharger, and instead of being cleared to 2,600 rpm it is redlined to 2,200, at which sea-level power is exactly 600 hp. It is available with a reduction gear as the PZL-3SR.

What perhaps even the Poles did not foresee is that because other sources of piston engines in the power category over 500 hp had dried up, a market for these engines would open up all over the world, despite the fact that all these engines were qualified in the 1940s and have ancestry going back even further. As yet this market is modest, but the number of customers is growing. Most are for ag-aircraft, which in the past have been able to rely on supplies of such engines as the 600 hp P&W R-1340 and 1,200 hp Wright R-1820. Now these are scarce, though various sources can provide zero-time spares. In the shorter term the only evident alternative to the Polish engines would be much more expensive turboprop power.

A growing market for the Polish engines is also opening up in the replacement of older engines in such aircraft as the DHC-2 Beaver, in which the R-985 Wasp Junior, of 450 hp, is replaced by the PZL-3S of 600 hp, and the DHC-3 Otter, in which the 600 hp R-1340

Wasp is replaced by the ASz-62IR of 1,000 hp. In each case the Polish engine drives a four-blade propeller in a very efficient installation engineered by Airtech Canada, and any pilot will immediately appreciate what the conversion does to aircraft performance. Indeed, Airtech has even put ASz-62s into a DC-3, though this results in a reduction in power. With the K9 engine the DC-3 is expected to have enhanced performance.

For all that, the over-500 hp engines are fighting a rearguard action, and turboprops are gradually increasing their penetration of the vast GA market, assisted by such companies as Soloy which specialize in conversions from piston engines. Whether RC engines, or diesels such as the Merlyn, described later, will make much impression remains to be seen. For the moment there is no shortage of engines in the under-500 hp category, and, as already noted, in the 20 to 200-hp bracket aircraft designers are spoilt for choice.

It has not always been so. It is getting on for half a century since the end of the Second World War, and for most of that time the under-200 hp market has been absolutely dominated by one type of engine: the traditional four-stroke with horizontally opposed, poppet-valve, air-cooled cylinders, made by either Lycoming or Continental. There is nothing particularly wrong with these engines, and indeed it is not often that a manufacturer gets the chance to mass produce essentially the same product, in constantly improved and refined forms, over a period which in this case exceeds 50 years. But competition and new ideas are healthy and to be welcomed, and not only the US lightplane engine but also the US lightplane itself is now having to meet new kinds of competition (quite apart from the appalling effect on the US lightplane industry of product-liability litigation). What it boils down to is that people all over the world are discovering that they can fly different kinds of aircraft, which may even bring greater pleasure, for less cost.

Of course, a considerable proportion of today's GA market is concerned with serious business and executive flying, using mainly engines of over 200 hp. Even here totally new competition is emerging, often with very powerful engines which also are well suited to the growing 'fighter replica' market. But the greatest revolution has been in what is on offer to the hundreds of thousands of private owners, many of whom are now building their

Agricultural aircraft are a remaining application for piston engines in the 300–1,000 hp class. The Brazilian Embraer Ipanema is at the lower end of this power category. This was the 600th to be built.

own aircraft. Unquestionably a central role in this development has been played by the EAA (Experimental Aircraft Association), which though a US organization now has members the world over. Thanks to the EAA a gigantic global market has opened up for lightplane engines, and a large number of engine designers are now competing to serve that market, and serve it better than the two traditional engine suppliers.

A flavour of the times is provided by this extract from an article in *Sport Aviation* in 1984:

> These points were vividly and enjoyably driven home to me when my German host took me flying in an older, but immaculately maintained, Limbach-powered motorglider. The two-place motorglider, with two somewhat 'over-standard' weight pilots, climbed out smartly at a solid 700 fpm. After levelling-off and levering the three-position Hoffmann propeller into cruise pitch, I was amazed at the performance. The low-drag motorglider, besides being a delightfully fun flying machine, was motoring along at about 120 mph and burning about 2.5 gallons of auto fuel per hour. I grimaced a little when I reflected that my relatively late model US-made, two-place production airplane (at home in its expensive hangar) normally cruises at no more than that speed on twice the horsepower while burning three times that amount of . . . not auto fuel . . . but avgas! At that point I was ready to send my For Sale ad to Trade-A-Plane and start looking for a motorglider.

> I guess the bottom line to these revelations is that maybe we here in the US ought to realize that most of the rest of the world has discovered the way, or at least a way, to diminish the economic pressures on flying without at all compromising safety, fun or even utility, of light two-place aircraft.

And there is more to the changing scene even than this economic revolution. A glance at the catalogue that concludes this book will underline the unprecedented variety of GA engines currently on offer. Not least of the surprises is the attractiveness of modified car engines. These range from half a VW (say, 35 hp) up to the 1,000-hp class. In the past the Unlimited Racers have been able to modify such existing engines as the Double Wasp, Wasp Major, Merlin, Griffon, Allison and Centaurus. Naturally, from time to time these have blown up or crashed, and today very few are left. Their replacements are increasingly highly rated automotive engines. By the time this book appears we may well see the name Nissan against all the major world piston-aircraft speed records, something that would have been unthinkable as recently as 1965.

Before running through the lengthy list of current engines it is worth adding a brief note on what they run on. The vast majority are conventional four-stroke, spark-ignition engines, and these all use some form of petrol (gasoline). A brief history of such fuels appeared in Chapter 2. This outline ended with the note that most GA aircraft today run on 100LL, a low-lead version of traditional 100/130 grade. A few use RON (research octane number) 96, still leaded. There are several reasons why we ought to do better. For one thing, 100LL Avgas (aviation gasoline) is by most standards expensive. Second, the fact that the lead (TEL) content has been reduced from around 4 cc/gal (as the specific gravity is near unity this can also be expressed as 4 grammes/gal) to only half this amount tends to give a false picture of good environmental acceptance. In the USA the EPA (Environmental Protection Agency) ruled that from the first day of 1986 the lead content of autogas (Mogas, ordinary car fuel) should be reduced from the previous 1.1 to only 0.1 cc/gal. In fact it is doubtful if such a low concentration of TEL would be worth adding.

What has naturally happened is that the world petroleum industry, and especially the companies that refine gasoline products, have multiplied their research efforts to find alternative additives which improve a fuel's octane rating. Some of the most obvious, such as methanol and other aromatic alcohols, are usable only after protecting plating of metal parts (especially aluminium and magnesium) exposed to the fuel, and a change in materials of gaskets and other seals. New additives are being tested every day, but it takes a long time for a new fuel to become a world standard.

The alternative is to qualify engines on unleaded fuel, as commonly used in cars (Mogas or autogas). Such fuel typically has an octane rating of 80 or slightly greater. The major manufacturers of GA engines have been reluctant to follow this path. In the mid-1980s Textron Lycoming, the largest volume producer of all, did experiment with various members of its O-360 and O-540 families modified with compression ratio reduced from 8.5/8.7 down to around 7.0, as well as with so-called O-245 and O-365 engines which were O-235 and O-320 engines whose stroke was increased (to give the capacities indicated) to maintain power unchanged, despite having lower compression ratio matched to 80-octane fuel. The point should be noted that both Continental and Lycoming make turbocharged engines, and these all have a modest compression ratio but need fuel of at least 100 octane to avoid detonation under the severe cylinder pressures and temperatures at high altitude. Unquestionably the leader in the movement towards cheap Mogas has been the EAA, which has such a vast global membership it can bring pressure to bear on manufacturers and even on legislators. It has achieved considerable success in clearing many types of light aircraft to fly on Mogas under an STC (Supplemental Type Certificate). There is a growing body of evidence that unleaded Mogas could power about two out of every three existing GA aircraft without causing operating difficulties or accelerated engine deterioration. Fuels for two-strokes, diesels and unconventional engines are discussed in the appropriate sections.

Lubrication was discussed in Chapter 3, but I said little about oil. The earliest aero engines usually used castor oil. This and other vegetable oils are in many ways excellent lubricants, but by the 1930s it was essential to switch to mineral (petroleum) based oils, partly because these were available in the enormous quantities needed and partly because they were produced to extremely tight specifications. Today most GA engines use 20W/50, which means a 20-weight (ie thin) oil at winter temperatures but containing VI (viscosity-index) improvers which make it behave like a 50-weight (thick) oil at high temperatures. Over a period of time the basic oil naturally becomes thicker, as might be expected from constant cooking, while the ceaseless shearing of the oil gradually breaks down the large polymer molecules of the VI improvers so that they become ineffective. In addition to this degradation the oil changes in more fundamental ways; most of us are familiar at least with the change in appearance from bright and clear to black and opaque.

Almost 40 years ago major suppliers began introducing totally synthetic oils for gas turbine engines, and especially for the very highly loaded gear teeth in turboprops. These lubricants were all based on esters, which enabled the finished oil to achieve the necessary thermal stability and resistance to oxidation. At that time nobody paid much attention to piston engine lubricants, and it was left to Mobil in the 1970s to decide to invest many millions of dollars in formulating a superior lubricant for the GA market. This was a calculated risk, but there seems little doubt that the resulting product, AV1, is not only worth its higher price but also offers many additional benefits. AV1 does contain a small proportion of esters, but the base liquid is an olefin hydrocarbon called polyalphaolefin. This is the first time a lubricant (certainly for piston engines) has been constructed from molecules tailored for the job from the outset. Thus no VI improver is needed, and AV1 maintains exactly the correct viscosity no matter what the temperature may be. Its deterioration is almost zero, and the growing number of users must find it very hard to follow the legally prescribed oil-change intervals (laid down when AV1 did not exist) and throw away what appears to be (and essentially is) perfect oil. Not only oil consumption but also fuel consumption is reduced, the fuel burn reduction being from 2 to 5 per cent.

One other topic deserves to be mentioned here: how to control the propulsion system. It seems to me odd that the vastly experienced captain of a wide-body can sit in state and watch Fadecs (full-authority digital engine controls) take care of every variable in engines putting out hundreds of thousands of horsepower, yet if his inexperienced son owns his own lightplane he has to keep juggling with throttle, mixture and propeller pitch in order to keep the right readings on fuel flow, cylinder-head temperature, rpm, manifold pressure, EGT (exhaust-gas temperature) and possibly other variables. Today a lightplane Fadec need not be much larger than a pack of playing cards, yet it could enable the pilot to exercise control with a single lever. Several different systems have now flown, beginning with just electronic control of the fuel-injection system. Electronic fuel injection is not complicated; a tiny computer monitors the engine variables and continually adjusts the individual nozzles on the cylinders to maintain precisely the desired EGT or turbocharger inlet temperature. The pilot can switch the system to *rich* for take-off and climb and *lean* for cruise. In the event of any electronic failure a manual (mechanical) mode takes over, the fuel being sent to a single jet which feeds mixture to the intake manifolds.

A complete Fadec is similar, but has additional functions. For example, the software would include a programmed engine-start sequence, feeding exactly the correct fuel flow to ensure a clean start from 120°F down to minus 40°F within one turn of the propeller, followed by a fast idle until the oil reaches a scheduled temperature, at which point the engine idling speed is reduced to (say) 600 rpm. Of course, the Fadec has to control the propeller, and (if fitted) turbocharger waste gate, and it also includes a pilot-alert function which warns of non-critical malfunctions (aural plus yellow light) or a serious problem requiring immediate attention (aural plus red, with reversion to manual control on the affected powerplant). Not least, experience to date with lash-up 'breadboard' systems shows that Fadec control reduces fuel consumption by at least 10 per cent and possibly 15 per cent, because of the much greater frequency of measurement of engine parameters and better precision of their control. There are also grounds for believing that a Fadec will enable a greater range of engines to operate successfully on unleaded Mogas.

The rest of this chapter is a necessarily brief review of GA engines in the final decade of the twentieth century. I have arranged it by alphabetical order of manufacturer within five main groups. The first, called simply Air-cooled, is the largest by a short head. The rest are Liquid-cooled, Derived engines (ie of basic automotive design), Diesels and Unconventional engines.

Air-cooled

This section includes both four-stroke and two-stroke engines. It also includes a number of small engines derived from, or related to, engines for such surface applications as motor cycles and snowmobiles. Most, however, have been designed for aircraft, and a high proportion are small engines for microlights, UMAs (unmanned aircraft) and to provide take-off power to sailplanes.

AeroMotion See AMI.

Advanced Engine Design (USA) AED makes the Spitfire range of air-cooled and liquid-cooled two-strokes, the chief air-cooled model being the 250FA. The upright cylinder measures 68.5 × 59.6 mm (2.7 × 2.35 in), giving capacity of 219.5 cc (13.4 cu in); output is 28 hp at 8,100 rpm, weight being 17 kg (38 lb). An optional oil-injection system enables plain petrol to be used.

Aerotechnik (Czechoslovakia) This company produces the Walter Mikron, designed in 1933. An inverted four-in-line four-stroke, of 2,440 cc (149 cu in) capacity, the Mikron is rated at 65 hp at 2,600 rpm. The Mikron IIIS(A) powers the Vivat motor glider, while

Czech L-13SV Vivat motor glider powered by 65-hp Aerotechnik Mikron III.

the IIISE(AE) adds an alternator and electric starter.

AMI (USA) AeroMotion Inc first ran their Twin in 1982. A horizontally opposed four-stroke of 1,650 cc (100 cu in) capacity, it initially used some off-the-shelf auto parts but was an original design. At first the cylinders were 102 mm (4 in) square, but today bore and stroke are respectively 105 mm and 95 mm (4.125 in and 3.75 in), capacity being unchanged. Rated at 53 hp at 3,100 rpm, the

AeroMotion Twin (rear left aspect).

Twin weighs 45 kg (100 lb), complete with dual ignition.

Arrow (Italy) This company produces a range of modular two-strokes with one, two or four cylinders of 74.6 mm (2.94 in) bore and 57 mm (2.24 in) stroke, all using 100-grade fuel plus 2 per cent oil. The single-cylinder GT250 is of 250 cc (15.25 cu in) and gives 34 hp at 6,800 rpm and weighs 26 kg (57 lb) complete with planetary reduction gear and electric starter. The GT500 twin is rated at 65 hp and weighs 36 kg (79 lb), while the twin-carb GT1000 gives 110 hp at 6,200 rpm and weighs 54 kg (119 lb). Arrow have developed an unusual installation in which two GT500s with cylinders vertical are geared to a single propeller. Arrow also make the GT654 V-twin four-stroke derived from the Moto Guzzi V65 motor cycle engine, rated at 55 hp and weighing 60 kg (132 lb).

Avia (Czechoslovakia) Various Czech aircraft are powered by the M137A and M337A, both derived from a design of the 1930s. Both are inverted six-in-line four-strokes, with cylinders 105 mm (4.13 in) by 115 mm (4.53 in) giving a capacity of 5.97 litres (364 cu in), with fuel injection (72–78 Mogas) and direct drive. The 337A has a supercharger, and gives 210 hp at 2,750 rpm for a weight of 148 kg (326 lb); the 137A is unsupercharged but fully aerobatic, and gives 180 hp for a weight of 142 kg (312 lb).

Bakanov (Russia) This newly opened KB (construction bureau) is based at Voronezh. Designer Bakanov has based a series of extremely attractive and advanced engines on a common design of cylinder. Largest is the M-16, with eight cylinders in a double-X 90° layout, rated at 300 hp. Splitting this in two yields the M-17, of 150 hp, with X-4 configuration. The flat twin version remains a project, but Bakanov has produced two further engines with cylinders of half the capacity. These are the two-cylinder M-18 of 40 hp and the four-cylinder M-19 of 75–80 hp. Most of these engines will be available from 1993.

Briggs & Stratton (USA) Made by the million, flat-twin engines of this make, rated at 18 hp at 3,600 rpm, are the low-cost choice of many microlight builders.

Camara See F.I. Sciences

CGS (USA) This company markets the Powerhawk 152, a two-stroke with two cylinders in line with capacity of 380 cc (23 cu in). It gives 20 hp at 5,500 rpm and weighs 27 kg (59 lb) with recoil starter and multi-V-belt reduction drive. The oil mix is 2.5 per cent.

Chotia (Weedhopper) (USA) The Model 460D is a microlight two-stroke with a single cylinder of 456 cc (28 cu in), giving 28 hp at 4,100 rpm using a 2.5 per cent oil mix. Weight is 15 kg (34 lb) including dual ignition and recoil starter.

Chrysler (USA) The Model 820 is another two-stroke (this time 4 per cent oil mix) with a single cylinder of 134 cc (8.17 cu in). Rating is 10 hp at 8,000 rpm (marginal for manned applications), the weight with reduction drive and recoil starter being 6.1 kg (13.5 lb).

Cicaré (Argentina) In the 1970s this company produced the 4C2T, the designation signifying four cylinders two-stroke. Capacity was 1,314 cc (80 cu in), and output 70 hp at 4,000 rpm using 2.5 per cent oil mix. Weight, with a propeller drive taken across the top of the engine from a rear gearbox, was 68 kg (150 lb).

Cuyuna (USA) One of the world's big producers, Cuyuna makes two-strokes using 2.5 per cent oil mix, with fan-assisted cooling, recoil starter and either Bosch flywheel magneto ignition or, in later models, capacitor discharge. The 215R has a single cylinder of 214 cc (13 cu in) capacity, giving 20 hp at 6,000 rpm for a weight of 18 kg (39 lb). The 340R has two cylinders in line of smaller bore giving 339 cc (20.7 cu in) capacity. Output is 25 hp at 5,500 rpm, for a weight of 28 kg (62 lb). The 430R has two 215 cc cylinders, giving 35 hp at 6,200 rpm for a weight of 65 lb. The latest production engine, the ULII-02, is an improved 430R, giving 35 hp at 5,200 rpm for a weight of 26 kg (58 lb). All Cuyunas have 12.5 compression ratio.

Dirk (Australia) The 2–500a is a four-stroke flat-twin with a capacity of 514 cc (31.4 cu in), the output being 41 hp at 6,400 rpm and the weight 20 kg (43 lb) with dual magneto ignition. A turbocharger can be added.

Emdair (UK) This company produces refined flat-twin four-strokes running on Avgas, with four-valve cylinders with 9.5 compression ratio, central and side plugs, direct injection, alternator, electric starter and a Fadec management system. The 077A of 1,261 cc (77 cu in) gives 60 hp at 3,600 rpm and weighs 47 kg (104 lb). The 077B adds a 2,500 rpm geared output with torsional damping. The 092A of 1,511 cc (92 cu in) gives 70 hp at 3,600 rpm and weighs 51 kg (112 lb), the 092B being geared. Largest Emdair is the 112 of 1,834 cc (112 cu in), rated at 85 hp for a weight of 58 kg (128 lb); the 112B is geared.

F.I.Sciences 509V2 (France) Alpha Camara, in the Riviera town of Biot, has developed this two-stroke V-twin, with cylinders 70 mm × 66 mm (2.8 in × 2.6 in, 508 cc/31 cu in) with the high compression ratio of 11. Even with epicyclic reduction gear (2.4, 2.6 or 3.1 ratio), carburettor, starter, silencer and battery it weighs only 21 kg (46 lb), take-off rating being 52 hp at 6,600 rpm.

Fichtel & Sachs (Germany) Among various piston and RC (Wankel type) engines the SA 340 is a popular two-stroke with a single cylinder of 336 cc (20.5 cu in), running on a 4 per cent oil mix to give 23 hp at 5,250 rpm for a weight of 22 kg (48.4 lb).

Fieldhouse (UK) This company produces a range of two-strokes based on a cylinder of 72 mm (2.835 in) bore and 64 mm (2.52 in) stroke, with compression ratio of 10 and using 2.5 per cent oil mix. The 260A (260 cc, 15.85 cu in) has direct drive and gives 25 hp at 6,000 rpm for a weight of 20 kg (44.1 lb). The

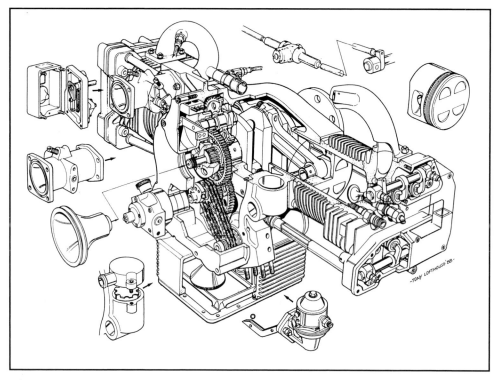

Cutaway and exploded view of a typical Emdair engine.

260AG is geared and weighs 26 kg (57 lb). The two-cylinder (in-line) 525A gives 45 hp and weighs 36 kg (80 lb); the fan-cooled 525AF is lighter at 75 lb, while the geared 525AG weighs 412 kg (90 lb).

Fuji (Japan) This company's aviation engines, called Fuji-Robin, exist in considerable numbers, and might be the second-best sellers in the under-100 hp category. Smallest current microlight engine is the EC25PS, of 244 cc (14.9 cu in), rated at 11 hp for a weight of 19 kg (41 lb). This is a single-cylinder engine, using 2.5 per cent two-stroke mix, available with dual ignition, electric starter, toothed-belt reduction and exhaust system. The EC34PM has two cylinders in-line (333 cc, 20.32 cu in) and gives 20 hp for a weight of 29 kg (63 lb). The EC34PL runs at 8,500 rpm to give 55 hp. The EC44PM and 2PM are two-cylinder engines of 432 cc (26.36 cu in), rated at 50–53 hp for a weight of 39 kg (86 lb) for the PM or 30 kg (66 lb) for the newer 2PM. The EC488 PM has two cylinders of 488 cc (29.78 cu in) and gives 65 hp. The EC51PL has a row of three cylinders of 500 cc (30.51 cu in), and

gives 75 hp at 8,000 rpm for a weight of 45 kg (99 lb).

Gemini (USA) Also known by the tradename Partner, the K1200 is a single-cylinder two-stroke using 2 per cent oil mix and rated at 8 hp.

Hirth (Germany) Gobler-Hirthmotoren is one of the more famous producers of aviation piston engines, covering the range from 3.5 to 130 hp. Except for the new and important F30, all are two-cylinder upright in-line two-strokes using 2 per cent or 4 per cent oil mix. There are too many models to list, a selection being: F22, 383 cc (23.37 cu in), 23 hp at 5,000 rpm for a weight of 20 kg (44 lb); F23A, 521 cc (31.79 cu in), 40 hp at 5,500 rpm for a weight of 24 kg (52 lb); and 2703, F23A with twin carburettors, 59 hp at 6,200 rpm. The F30 is a completely different flat-four using F23A cylinders. This gives capacity of 1,042 cc (63.58 cu in), the power being 110 hp at 6,500 rpm for a weight of only 36 kg (79.4 lb). A slightly larger cylinder is used in the 1,270 cc (77.5 cu in) version, which gives 130 hp at

6,500 rpm for the remarkable weight of 35 kg (77 lb).

Honda (Japan) This famous company appears under Derived engines, but also produces many smaller engines, including the CR125R single-cylinder two-stroke made and marketed by Bob Bowen in the USA. Capacity is 124 cc (7.57 cu in) and output 28 hp at 9,000 rpm for a weight of 13.6 kg (30 lb). A poly V-belt drive is essential.

Hunting (UK) Became Fieldhouse, which see.

IAME (Italy) This company makes the KFM (Komet Flight Motors) series, in two main series. The KFM 107 Maxi is a flat-twin two-stroke with cylinders of 64 mm (2.52 in) bore and 52 mm (2.05 in) stroke, giving capacity of 334 cc (20.38 cu in). Output is 30 hp at 6,300 rpm, for a weight of 19 kg (41.8 lb). The 107ER has a 0.5 toothed-belt reduction drive and weighs 22.5 kg (49.6 lb). The KFM 112 is a flat-four four-stroke, with cylinders 90 mm (3.54 in) by 64 mm (2.52 in), giving a capacity of 1,627 cc (99.4 cu in). The 112 can run at 3,400 rpm for 3 minutes, giving 62 hp, but normal limit is 60 hp at 3,200 rpm, the weight being 54 kg (119 lb).

IMAER (Brazil) See VW under Derived engines.

Janowski (Poland) The prototype Saturn 500 flat-twin two-stroke was run in 1969, with capacity of 500 cc (30.5 cu in) and output of 25 hp at 4,000 rpm for a weight of 27 kg (59.5 lb). Later the weight was slightly reduced and output increased to 30 hp.

JCV (Belgium) These two-strokes are made by the Butterfly Co, capacity being 274 cc (16.7 cu in) from two opposed cylinders, and output 22 hp at 6,800 rpm.

JPX (France) Using a two-stroke cylinder of 66 mm (2.6 in) bore and 62 mm (2.44 in) stroke, this company produces engines with one, two and three cylinders, designated by capacity in cc. The PUL 212 (212 cc/12.93 cu in) is rated at 15 hp at 6,500 rpm and weighs 7.9 kg (17 lb) complete. The twin PUL 425 (425 cc/25.89 cu in) gives 22 hp at 4,200 rpm and weighs 16.5 kg (36 lb) with silencer. With 0.5 belt reduction drive the weight is 21 kg (46 lb). The PAL 640 has three cylinders spaced radially at 120°, capacity being 636 cc (38.81

cu in), maximum output is 30 hp at 4,000 rpm and weight 21 kg (46 lb) without exhaust. The PAL 1300 has three radial cylinders of larger size giving capacity of 1,297 cc (79.2 cu in); output is 50 hp at 3,200 rpm, weight being 35 kg (77 lb). A VW-based engine is listed under Derived engines.

Kawasaki (Japan) This company's high-performance bikes have led to two-in-line two-strokes configured for aircraft use. Examples are the 340, of 339 cc (20.63 cu in) capacity, giving 28 hp at 6,500 rpm, and the more important TA440, with cylinders 68 mm × 60 mm (2.68 in × 2.36 in), giving a capacity of 436 cc (26.61 cu in), rated at 38.5 hp at 5,000 rpm, or with special carburettor and tuned exhaust 50 hp at 6,000 rpm, weight being 20 kg (44 lb) bare or 35 kg (77 lb) with every extra including belt reduction drive. The 440

Below *IAME KFM 107ER Maxi with belt reduction drive.*

Bottom *JPX PUL 425 with belt reduction drive.*

is also available with liquid cooling (which see).

KFM See IAME.

Kirk (USA) This company's X-4 is just what it says, a four-cylinder radial in the form of an X. The two-stroke cylinders measure 58.7 mm × 38.1 mm (2.31 in × 1.5 in), giving capacity of 413 cc (25.2 cu in), overall diameter being only 414 mm (16.3 in). With compression ratio of only 7 the rating is 25 hp at 5,000 rpm, weight being 27 kg (60 lb).

KKBM (USSR) In 1990 the Kuibyshyev engine design bureau exhibited the P-020 flat-twin two-stroke, with twin carburettors. Output is 20 hp at 7,300 rpm, the dry weight being 9 kg (19.8 lb).

In 1992 KKBM revealed the P-065 version, with left/right pairs of upright P-020 cylinders driving two crankshafts and contra-rotating propellers. Weight is 50 kg (110 lb) and output 65 hp.

König (Germany) Another specialist in two-strokes, this time recommending a 3 per cent oil mix, König uses a cylinder 66 mm × 42 mm (2.6 in × 1.654 in), with CD (capacitor-discharge) ignition, electric starter and the option (invariably taken) of a Powergrip belt drive of 0.637 ratio. The SC 430 has three cylinders spaced 120° apart, giving capacity of 430 cc (26.24 cu in); output is 24 hp at 4,200 rpm, weight being 16 kg (35.3 lb). This engine is used in the Fischer+Entwicklungen TOP (take-off power) retractable package for sailplanes which weighs 44 kg (97 lb). The SD 570 has four cylinders spaced at 90° (570 cc, 34.78 cu in), giving 28 hp for a weight of 19 kg (41 lb). The SF 930 is another X-4 but with bigger cylinders (70 mm × 60 mm/2.7 in × 2.4 in, giving capacity of 930 cc, 56.75 cu in); output is 48 hp at 4,200 rpm, weight being 36 kg (79.4 lb).

Limbach (Germany) One of the major producers, Limbach makes small opposed two-strokes and somewhat larger four-strokes, the latter originally using some VW parts but maturing into a family of original designs. Suffix E means single ignition (E for *ein*) and D means dual. The two-strokes include the L 90E (86 cc, 5.25 cu in) rated at 5.6 hp at 8,500 rpm for a weight of 4 kg (8.8 lb), and the L 275E (274 cc, 16.72 cu in) rated at 24 hp at 7,300 rpm for a weight with silencer (muffler) of only 7.5 kg (16.5 lb), both engines using a 4

per cent oil mix. There is also a four-cylinder version of the 275 which gives 43 hp for a weight of 15.5 kg (34 lb). Among the four-strokes the most numerous are the many variants of SL 1700, with cylinders 88 mm × 69 mm (3.46 in × 2.71 in), giving a capacity of 1,680 cc (102.5 cu in), rated at 60 to 68 hp at 3,600 rpm for weights around 72 kg (159 lb). Surprisingly, the L 2000 family, with increased bore and stroke to give 1,994 cc (120.26 cu in) capacity, are lighter, at around 70 kg (154 lb); they all give 80 hp at 3,400 rpm. The largest Limbach is the L 2400, with four 97 mm × 82 mm (3.82 in × 3.23 in) cylinders (2,424 cc, 147.9 cu in), rated at 87 hp at 3,200 rpm for a weight of 82 kg (181 lb) with accessories.

Lloyd (Germany) The chief Lloyd microlight engine is an inverted two-in-line two-stroke with cylinders 61.9 mm × 64 mm (2.44 in × 2.52 in), giving a capacity of 386 cc (23.55 cu in). Designated LS400, it has the low compression ratio of 6 and uses 2.5 per cent oil mix. Output is 22 hp at 5,500 rpm, and weight 21.7 kg (48 lb).

Lotus (UK) Lotus Cars marketed four-stroke flat-twin and flat-4 engines using cylinders 72 mm × 59 mm (2.83 in × 2.32 in). Each had capacitor-discharge ignition and a propeller drive off the camshaft at 2,500 instead of 5,000 max rpm. The Lotus 225 twin (480 cc, 29.3 cu in) was rated at 25 hp and weighed 14 kg (30.9 lb); the four-cylinder 450 gave 50 hp and weighed 25.2 kg (55.5 lb).

McCulloch (USA) This corporation sold rights in the mass-produced O-100 flat-four to Northrop, to power target drones (84 hp, weight 35 kg/77 lb). An important unit for micros and self-launching sailplanes is the Mc 101 two-stroke, with a single upright cylinder 58 mm × 45 mm (2.28 in × 1.835 in), capacity 123 cc (7.5 cu in), giving 12.5 hp at 9,000 rpm for a weight of 5.6 kg (12.3 lb).

Mosler Four-stroke MM two-cylinder engine for ultralights fitted to an N3 Wolfen Pup.

Nelson (USA) For many years Nelson Aircraft has marketed fully certificated flat-four two-strokes for aeroplanes (H-63CP) and helicopters (H-63C). Cylinder size is 68.3 mm × 70 mm (2.69 in × 2.76 in), giving a capacity of 1,030 cc (63 cu in). The fuel can be Mogas, but with the high addition of 6.25 per cent oil. The CP, cleared for sustained inverted flight, gives 48 hp at 4,400 rpm and weighs 30.8 kg (68 lb).

The 63C is rated at 43 hp at 4,000 rpm, and complete with centrifugal clutch, cooling fan and shroud weighs 34.5 kg (76 lb).

NGL (UK) Normalair-Garrett, part of the Westland Group, produces a variety of sub-types of the WAEL (Weslake Aeromarine Engines Ltd) 342 flat-twin two-stroke. These highly rated engines have simultaneous-firing, loop-scavenged cylinders 66 mm × 50 mm (2.6 in × 1.97 in), and use leaded fuel with 4 per cent oil to give 25 hp at 7,000 rpm, for weights from only 8.5 kg (18.7 lb).

OMC (USA) Produces several aviation-rated Cushman engines, including the Cushman 200 two-stroke flat-twin (200 cc, 12.2 cu in), rated at 18 hp.

Parodi See Honda under Derived engines.

Pieper See VW under Derived engines.

Piper (UK) This firm produces small two-strokes for RPVs, which have attracted the interest of manned home-builders. Features include lightweight generators and a microprocessor fuel control. The P 80 has a single 76.5 cc (4.67 cu in) cylinder and gives 7.8 hp at 7,200 rpm for a weight of 3.32 kg (7.3 lb). The P 80/2 has two even smaller cylinders (total 81 cc, 4.94 cu in), rated at 5.2 hp for a weight of 2.6 kg (5.8 lb). The P 100 has an upright cylinder of 99 cc (6.04 cu in) capacity, giving 8.8 hp for a weight of 3.6 kg (7.9 lb). The P 200 has two P 100 opposed cylinders and gives 16 hp at 7,200 rpm for a weight of 4.8 kg (10.5 lb).

Pong Dragon See Sadler.

Quickie (USA) This major producer of home-build aircraft kits modified the Onan flat-twin four-stroke to suit the original Quickie aircraft. Power was raised to 22 hp at 3,800 rpm, weight remaining at the ponderous level of 38 kg (84 lb).

Rebel (USA) The Twin 2–205 is a flat-twin two-stroke, running on 2.5 per cent oil mix. The cylinders are 67.5 mm × 57.2 mm (2.657 in × 2.25 in), giving a capacity of 410 cc (25.0 cu in). Output is 25 hp at 3,500 rpm (low for a two-stroke), weight being 16 kg (35.3 lb) complete with recoil starter, exhaust system and propeller.

Rectimo See VW under Derived engines.

The ruler shows the 16-hp Piper P200 is under 229 mm (9 in) wide.

Refrigeration Equipment (Poland) In 1975 Poland acquired all rights to the famous Franklin engines formerly produced in the USA by Aircooled Motors. Today known as PZL-F engines, three basic families remain available. All are horizontally opposed four-strokes with identical cylinders of 117.48 mm (4.625 in) bore and 88.9 mm (3.5 in) stroke. The 2A-120C (two cylinders) is rated at 60 hp at 3,200 rpm and weighs 75.8 kg (167 lb). The 4A-235B flat-four is rated at 125 hp at 2,800 rpm and weighs 117.6 kg (259 lb). The six-cylinder 6A-350C has compression raised from the 8.5 of the smaller engines to 10.5, though all models need 100/130 fuel; output is 220 hp at 2,800 rpm for a weight of 167 kg (367 lb). The 350A has a turbocharger, and compression reduced to 7.4; it holds 250 hp to altitude and weighs 189 kg (417 lb).

Rotax (Austria) This company became a global supplier of snowmobile engines, largely by having a worldwide network of dealers. Gradually they attracted the attention of the home-built aircraft market, and since 1987 several models have been added explicitly for aviation. Their success has been phenomenal. At a guess half the total sport-aviation market is shared by about 60 types of engine, while Rotax has the other half! Available engines fall into three groups: air-cooled two-strokes, air-cooled four-strokes, and liquid-cooled. In the first category are the mass-market models, all having piston-ported cylinders using a 2 per cent oil mix, with fan cooling. The 277 has one

Rotax 503, showing pull-start.

upright cylinder of 268.7 cc (16.397 cu in) capacity, rated at 25.5 hp at 6,500 rpm for a fully equipped weight of 24 kg (52.9 lb). The 377 has two smaller cylinders (62 mm × 61 mm/2.44 in × 2.40 in); rating is 34.9 hp and weight 32.5 kg (71.6 lb). The 447 has two cylinders of greater bore (67.5 mm/2.7 in) raising capacity to 436.5 cc (26.637 cu in); output is 39.4 hp and weight again 32.5 kg (71.6 lb). The 503 again increases bore (to 72 mm/2.8 in) to give a capacity of 496.7 cc (30.31 cu in); rating is 45.6 hp and weight 36.2 kg (79.8 lb). The twin-carb 503.2V still weighs 36.2 kg but puts out 51 hp, still at 6,500 rpm. The 508UL is a two-cylinder four-stroke with overhead valves; cylinder size is 71 mm × 64 mm (3 in × 2.5 in), giving a capacity of 507 cc (30.8 cu in), and rating is 43 hp at 7,800 rpm for an equipped weight of 48.5 kg (106.9 lb). See also under Liquid-cooled.

Sadler R1745U six-cylinder radial.

Sachs See Fichtel & Sachs.

Sadler (USA) William Sadler's American Microflight company produces the Vampire ultralight. He more recently took over the Pong Dragon engine and markets it as the R1745U. Though it incorporates some stock VW parts, including pistons, it certainly qualifies for separate mention. For one thing, it is a six-cylinder radial, arranged in two rows of three. The R1745U is bigger than Alex Pong's original Dragon, and it is very conservatively rated, the designation meaning 1,700 cc (103.7 cu in) and 45 hp, at a leisurely 2,450 rpm. The photograph shows the enclosed valve gear, and the successively smaller pipes at the back bringing inlet air, injection fuel and HT to the 12 plugs. Mogas can be used despite the compression ratio of 10.5.

Sauer (Germany) Sauer Motorenbau produces a flat-four four-stroke with two sizes of cylinder. The SS 2100 H1S has bore and stroke of 90 mm × 84 mm (3.54 in × 3.31 in), giving capacity of 2,135 cc (130.3 cu in). Output is 80 hp at 3,000 rpm, burning 100LL, the weight with starter and alternator being 76 kg (128 lb). The ST 2500 H1S has bore increased to 97 mm (3.82 in), raising capacity to 2,481 cc (151.3 cu in). Output is 92 hp, and weight 79 kg (174 lb).

Skylark (Australia) The Skylark II is made by Icarus Aviation for microlights. A flat-twin two-stroke, using 5 per cent oil mix, it has a capacity of 320 cc (19.53 cu in) and gives 24 hp at 5,200 rpm. Weight with toothed-belt drive is 14 kg (31 lb).

Solo (Germany) Several Solo engines are flying, with strangely small variations in cylinder size. For example the Type 209 has bore and stroke of 71.1 mm × 54.1 mm, giving capacity of 220 cc (13.4 cu in); maximum output on 4 per cent oil mix is 16.6 hp at 6,600 rpm. The 335 has a cylinder measuring 70 mm × 55 mm to give capacity of 210 cc (12.82 cu in), output being 19.9 hp at 6,900 rpm. The Solo Twin has two cylinders in-line, an intermediate size giving capacity of 430 cc (26.2 cu in); output is 22 hp at 5,500 rpm.

Spitfire See Advanced Engine Design.

Survol (France) Around 1969 Charles Fauvel assisted E. de Coucy to develop a flat-four four-stroke to power Fauvel self-launching sailplanes. Named Pygmée, it had a capacity of 1,160 cc (70.8 cu in) and gave 55 hp for a weight of 36.5 kg (80.5 lb).

Suzuki (Japan) Obviously derived from bike engines, the GT185 is a two-in-line two-stroke, with capacity of 185 cc (11.29 cu in), rated at 20 hp at 6,800 rpm.

Technopower (USA) The Technopower II Twin is a flat-twin four-stroke, with bore and stroke both 101.6 mm (4 in), giving a capacity of 1,647 cc (100.5 cu in). Output is 50 hp at 3,000 rpm, for a weight of 35 kg (77 lb).

TTL (UK) Target Technology, formerly associated with Piper, produces very small single-cylinder two-strokes, with electronic ignition and using 4 per cent oil mix. The T-70 has a capacity of 70 cc (4.27 cu in), and gives 6 hp at 7,200 rpm for a weight of 3.2 kg (7 lb) complete with tractor or pusher propeller. The P-100 has capacity increased to 99 cc (6.04 cu in), and gives 9 hp at 7,200 rpm for a weight of 3.6 kg (7.9 lb).

Teledyne Continental (USA) One of the two traditional giants of GA power, TCM (Teledyne Continental Motors) has made valiant efforts to find alternatives to supplement and possibly even to replace its established range of engines, all of which are horizontally opposed four-stroke units with four or six cylinders. It lost many millions of dollars in 1965–80 developing a new range of basically traditional engines called the Tiara series, noteworthy for their incorporation of a patented Hydra-Torque drive. This could be hydraulically locked to enable the propeller shaft (which was also the camshaft) to be driven directly via the 0.5 reduction gear. When unlocked this drive, also called VTC (vibratory torque control), interposed a slender quill shaft which eliminated torsional vibration resonance which otherwise occurred at high speeds around 2,800 rpm. The patented drive was claimed to eliminate torsional resonance from idling to 4,500 rpm, and without needing crankshaft dampers. Serious problems were encountered, and the whole programme was abandoned. Since then TCM has been even more adventurous, going into liquid cooling, RC (Wankel type) engines and a small turboprop. Except for the latter, these are covered in other sections. TCM's range of traditional engines is still very considerable, and large numbers are still flying of such small engines, long out of production, as the A40 (described by Herschel Smith as 'the direct

ancestor of every piston engine in production today in the free world' which is an overstatement), the bigger A-50, A-65 and A-75 (the numbers indicating horsepower), and various other engines up to 145 hp. Today the baseline engine is the O-200A. The four cylinders, 103.2 mm × 98.4 mm (4.0625 in × 3.875 in) giving capacity of 3,280 cc (201 cu in), are held by nuts around their flanged base to studs in the left and right halves of the cast aluminium alloy crankcase. The cast aluminium heads are screwed to the steel barrels, and have single inlet and exhaust valves side-by-side, sloping inwards in plan view. The crankshaft has two throws 180° apart and turns in three plain bearings. Underneath the engine is the updraught carburettor. Behind this is the pressed-steel oil sump, and at the back the twin magnetos. Rolls-Royce Motors at Crewe made Continental engines under licence in 1961–82, and also developed the O-200A into the O-240A by fitting O-360 size cylinders and making many other changes. The O-200A gives 100 hp at 2,750 rpm and weighs 99.8 kg (220 lb), while the O-240A gave 130 hp at 2,800 rpm and weighed 0.45 kg (1 lb) less. The O-360 series have six cylinders with bore enlarged to 112.7 mm (4.4375 in), increasing capacity to 5,900 cc (360 cu in). All current 360 models need 100/130 fuel and have direct injection, and several have a turbocharger and intercooler. One of the latter is the 360-MB, rated at 210 hp at 2,700 rpm

A Tiara 6–260 installed in a flight-test Cherokee Arrow. Most Tiaras had the fuel injection pumps on top of the air box feeding the six manifolds.

Teledyne Continental IO-550.

for a weight of 187 kg (412 lb). In contrast the older 360-C and 360-D (also with turbo) weigh only 136 kg (300 lb) and deliver 225 hp at 2,800 rpm. One of the older families still active is the O-470, with six bigger cylinders (127 mm × 101.6 mm/5 in × 4 in, 7,700 cc/471 cu in). These are rated up to 260 hp at 2,625 rpm. The most varied of all TCM families are the 520s, with six cylinders of the same 102 mm (4 in) stroke but bored out to 133 mm (5.25 in), increasing capacity to 8,500 cc (520 cu in). The two newest models use 100LL, all the rest needing 100/130. Output varies from 250 hp at 2,400 rpm all the way to 435 hp at 3,400 rpm. Weight varies from 172 kg (380 lb) to 272 kg (600 lb), these extremes happening to correspond with the extremes in rating. Largest of the range are the IO-550s, with stroke increased to 107.95 mm (4.25 in), capacity being 9,013 cc (550 cu in). These give 300 hp at reduced rpm of 2,700.

Textron Lycoming (USA) In terms of sheer output Lycoming has for many years been number one in the world, but it has been far less adventurous than Continental. Apart from an unsuccessful foray into the world of RC engines (see later) it has announced no departure from traditional horizontally opposed, air-cooled four-strokes. Basic construction differs little from Continental; valve pushrods are above instead of underneath the

cylinders, and the crankshafts have four plain bearings (except in the 720 family, which has five), whereas the Continentals have three bearings in four-cylinder engines and five in the others. A few obsolete Lycomings are flying, the most important being the O-290, with four cylinders 124 mm × 98 mm (4.875 in × 3.875 in) giving a capacity of 4,700 cc (289 cu in), and typically rated at 140 hp at 2,800 rpm for a weight of 118 kg (260 lb). Baseline modern engine is the O-235, with four cylinders 111 mm × 98.4 mm (4.375 in × 3.875 in), giving capacity of 3,850 cc (233 cu in). Oddly, the latest O-235s need 100-grade fuel, one being the 235N rated at 116 hp at 2,800 rpm for a weight of 98 kg (218 lb). The O-320 family have bore increased to 130 mm (5.125 in), giving capacity of 5,200 cc (319.8 cu in). These have compression from 7 to 9, matched to fuels from 87 to 100 grade. One of the high-compression models is the AEIO-320D, an aerobatic direct-injection engine rated at 160 hp at 2,700 rpm and weighing 123 kg (271 lb). Lycoming, like Continental, offers a range of O-360 engines, but with four cylinders instead of six small ones. Cylinders are of O-320 bore but with stroke lengthened to 111 mm (4.375 in), giving capacity of 5,920 cc (361 cu in). Most of this family need 100-grade fuel, and customers have the options of turbocharger, direct injection, geared drive, aerobatic provisions or helicopter installation.

Most give 180 to 200 hp at 2,700 rpm, for a weight near 132 kg (290 lb), but the turbocharged TIO-360C can hold 282 hp at 2,575 rpm to 3,048 m (10,000 ft), though it weighs 158 kg (348 lb). The O-540 series use six O-360 cylinders (8,860 cc/541.5 cu in), and are available for various fuel grades (usually 100), with fuel injection, turbocharger or vertical crankshaft for helicopters. Outputs range from 235 to 360 hp, usually at 2,575 rpm, weights ranging from 162 kg (357 lb) to 248 kg (547 lb). The TIO-541 series, all turbocharged, have the 540 cylinder dimensions but are completely redesigned to run faster and with higher efficiency. There are two production models, the TIO-541E, rated at 380 hp at 2,900 rpm and weighing 270 kg (596 lb), and the geared TIGO-541E, which can maintain 425 hp at 3,200 rpm to 4,572 m (15,000 ft), though it weighs 319 kg (704 lb). Biggest Lycoming, made in small numbers, is the direct-injection IO-720, with eight 540-size cylinders (11.84 litres/722 cu in), rated at 400 hp at 2,650 rpm and weighing around 257 kg (567 lb). Other families, no longer made, are the O-435s and O-480s. The former has six cylinders 123.7 mm × 98.4 mm (4.875 in × 3.875 in) giving capacity of 7,100 cc (434 cu in), giving up to 250 hp, while the 480 series have the same cylinder increased in bore to 130 mm (5.125 in) to give capacity of 7,860 cc (479.7 cu in) and powers of 260 to 320 hp at 3,200 rpm.

UP Arrow (USA) By mid-1991 this microlight builder was preparing for production with a four-stroke V-8 rated at 80 hp at 2,400 rpm, with an installed weight of 36.3 kg (80 lb).

Valmet/ABEC (Finland/France) The 2H 157 is a two-stroke with one upright cylinder 62 mm × 52 mm (2.44 in × 2.04 in), giving capacity of 157 cc (9.58 cu in). Output is 10 hp at 6,500 rpm with a 4 per cent oil mix, and weight 7.2 kg (15.8 lb).

Weslake See NGL.

Wheeler (Australia) The Pixie Major is another single-cylinder two-stroke, with capacity of 173 cc (10.56 cu in) and maximum output on 4 per cent oil mix of 14 hp at 6,500 rpm. Weight including exhaust unit is 8.6 kg (19 lb).

Yamaha (Japan) This company's engines for karts and bikes are becoming significant. The KT100S has a single two-stroke cylinder 52

The first Lycoming flat-four was the O-145, initially rated in 1938 at 50 hp. Crankcase and cylinders were cast in one piece.

mm × 46 mm (2.05 in × 1.81 in), capacity 97.6 cc (5.96 cu in), giving 15 hp at 10,000 rpm on 4 per cent mix, for a weight of 10.4 kg (22.9 lb). The standard 350 bike engine is a two-in-line with cylinders 64 mm × 65 mm (2.52 in × 2.55 in), capacity 347 cc (21.81 cu in), giving 39 hp at 7,500 rpm and weighing 40 kg (88 lb) complete with alternator and electric starter.

Yuhe (China) The Yuhe Machine Factory at Nanjing makes engines for models and RPVs, but the YH 280 is also suitable for piloted applications. A flat-four two-stroke, it has cylinders 46 mm × 42 mm (1.8 in × 1.65 in), giving capacity of 279.2 cc (17.04 cu in). It delivers 15 hp at 6,000 rpm.

Zenoah (Japan) The significant engine from this company is the G25B, another single-cylinder two-stroke. The upright cylinder measures 72 mm × 59.5 mm (2.835 in × 2.343 in), giving capacity of 242 cc (14.78 cu in). Rating is up to 22 hp at 6,500 rpm, for a bare weight of 17.5 kg (38.6 lb). The G50C flat-twin version was used only by a few aircraft builders.

Liquid-cooled

Included in this list are a variety of engines, some modified from automotive use (but so much so that they cannot properly be included under Derived engines) and others designed from the outset for aircraft. One of the more significant inclusions is the range of powerful and extremely efficient engines of TCM (Teledyne Continental). One of these was selected by Rutan/Yeager (see jacket illustration) for their non-stop flight round the world in *Voyager*, a name since made a trademark for these engines. After much testing TCM decided to use as coolant a mixture of 40 per cent water and 60 per cent ethylene glycol (Dowgard make is recommended), maintained at 200°F (93.3°C) in cruising flight, with the maximum set at 250°F (121°C). Despite the extra cost and bother of adding glycol, TCM has no doubt that this mix is superior overall to plain water. The glycol prevents corrosion or freezing, and enables the system to operate more efficiently at higher temperature. Many other engine companies are happy with plain water, which is in fact an extremely good heat-transfer medium.

The decision of TCM to invest many millions of dollars in developing and marketing a range of liquid-cooled engines is especially significant, because they were already a major producer of air-cooled engines. They could thus be regarded as having no axe to grind on behalf of liquid cooling; every Voyager engine sold might be regarded as one air-cooled engine unsold, so TCM's opinions carry a lot of weight. They list the advantages of liquid cooling as: improved cooling, reduced cooling drag, lower fuel consumption, better wear characteristics, longer life and TBO, and higher altitude capability. Improved cooling results from the even distribution of the dense cooling medium between all cylinders, whereas with air cooling there may be startling differences in flow around different parts of the cylinders, leading to local temperature variations exceeding 50°F (28°C). Reduced cooling drag may seem surprising; 50 years ago air cooling proponents pointed out the enormous temperature differences between a finned cylinder head and the air, claiming that to get rid of the same flow of heat by means of a water radiator inevitably involved enormous bulk and weight. Yet today TCM claim, and the aircraft conversions prove it, that a properly designed water/glycol radiator is more efficient than air cooling, needs a much smaller airflow and permits the basic cowling to be sealed. The small-flow radiator can be anywhere in the aircraft. In the RAM/Cessna 414AW (Chancellor) Series V the radiators

are in the extended tails to the nacelles (see Chapter 3). In the smaller and simpler British Super 2 it is inside the rear fuselage.

Lower fuel consumption stems from several factors, individually perhaps not large but generally valid and cumulative. One is an improved design of combustion space which squeezes the charge into a depression around the exhaust valve, generating high turbulence which mixes the air and fuel vapour thoroughly and results in complete combustion. A second and more important factor is that at climbing power (or at any high setting) traditional engines have to be operated at over-rich mixture, whereas TCM tell pilots at all times to fly a Voyager at the ideal fuel/air ratio. Another big reason for saving fuel is that the faster aircraft gets there quicker, so the engines run for a shorter time. Better wear results from the even cylinder cooling, which makes possible reduced piston/cylinder clearance and improves component life. Only the head is liquid-cooled, the pumped flow passing through at quite high velocity. The barrel is adequately cooled by a high-volume oil spray directed at the inside of the piston. The absence of any fins makes the cylinders easier to make and significantly lighter.

Other advantages, say TCM, include a marked reduction in noise level and a reduction in pilot workload, and each flight can hold cruising height longer (9,144 m/30,000 ft in the case of the Cessna 414 just mentioned) and then make a steep descent without subjecting the cylinders to the thermal shock they would get with air cooling. Critics would naturally ask about coolant leaks, and overall costs. The answer to the first is no problem, you can keep flying with all coolant lost, which you can't do if the fuel or oil supply fails. Unlike many cars, liquid-cooled aero engines, when properly installed, appear never to suffer from overheating during prolonged running when stationary. The severest test is to keep at fast idle when parked facing downwind on the hottest day; cylinder head and coolant temperatures have stayed at the optimum values. With coolant deliberately drained, head temperature rose from the normal limit of about 250°F (121°C) to settle at 500°F (260°C) without causing any damage to the engine. (Thinks: does that mean you can just leave the liquid out? Hardly!) As for price, all liquid-cooled makers offer prices strictly comparable with air-cooled engines.

Advanced Engine Design (USA) AED makes

the Spitfire range of engines, as noted under Air-cooled. The 220LC RV has the same size upright cylinder as the 250FA, but has pumped liquid cooling, with thermostat control. Like the air-cooled version it can run on fuel/oil mix or have an oil-injection option. It runs faster, at up to 9,300 rpm, to give 30 hp; the STD option gives 35 hp at 9,200 rpm, and the RPO option with compression ratio 10.5 is rated at 42 hp at 10,500 rpm, all versions weighing 19.5 kg (43 lb) without carburettor. The Spitfire 440LC is the corresponding flat-twin, with CDI ignition and options of dual ignition, electric start, oil injection and alternator. Rating is 60 hp at 8,500 rpm for a weight of 25 kg (55 lb). The Spitfire 880LC is doubled up again, with four cylinders; rating is 150 hp at 8,500 rpm for a weight of only 53.5 kg (118 lb).

AirDelta (Italy) This company produces two sizes of engine with a single upright two-stroke cylinder with pumped water cooling. Both run with only 2 per cent oil mix, both have electronic ignition and electric starter, and both have a reduction gear. The Hiro 22 has a cylinder 54 mm (2.125 in) square, giving capacity of 125 cc (7.62 cu in), the maximum output being 22.5 hp at 8,400 rpm. Weight without exhaust, radiator or propeller is 20 kg (44 lb), and reduction ratio 0.279. The Hiro 30 has bore increased to 74 mm (2.913 in), giving capacity of 220 cc (13.42 cu in). Maximum rating is 32 hp at 7,000 rpm, weight 24 kg (53 lb) and reduction ratio 0.4. Compression ratio in the larger engine is reduced from 7 to 6.

CAM (Canada) Canadian Airmotive Inc produces the CAM Turbo 90, a three-cylinder in-line four-stroke burning 92 RON or 100LL. Bore and stroke are 74 mm × 77 mm (2.91 in × 3.03 in), giving capacity of 993 cc (61 cu in), with compression ratio of 8.2. Cooling is by pumped water/glycol mix, ignition is dual CD electronic 'self-diagnostic', and the propeller is driven via a cam-action silent chain in an oil bath, ratio 0.448. Maximum power is 90 hp at 5,300 rpm, and dry weight 65 kg (144 lb) complete with starter, alternator and provision for controllable propeller.

Chaparral (USA) The main Chaparral engine used for aviation is a two-cylinder two-stroke with cylinder capacity of 460 cc (28.08 cu in). Maximum rating is 36 hp at 6,500 rpm, the weight with cooling circuit being 36 kg (79 lb).

Fuji (Japan) Most Fuji-Robin engines are air-cooled, but the EC51PL has a row of three liquid-cooled, two-stroke cylinders running on 2.5 per cent oil mix. Bore and stroke are 61.8 mm × 65.6 mm (2.433 in × 2.582 in), giving capacity of 500 cc (30.51 cu in). Maximum rating is 75 hp at 8,000 rpm, and the weight with electronic magneto ignition, three carburettors and 12V generator is 45 kg (99 lb).

Greth Working in Concord, CA, Gerry Greth has developed a V-8 specifically for aircraft. Cylinders are 95.25 mm × 105.54 mm (3.75 in × 4.155 in), giving capacity of 6,653 cc (406 cu in). Weight with accessories is 174 kg (384 lb) and maximum power 447 hp.

HAPI See Derived engines.

Hewland (UK) A major source of technology and parts for racing cars, Hewland produced the three-in-line two-stroke which powered the Super 2 aircraft. This attractive engine is now being produced by Mid-West.

Kawasaki (Japan) What could be described as a derived engine, the Invader 440 is an inverted two-in-line two-stroke with cylinders 68 mm × 60 mm (2.68 in × 2.36 in), capacity being 436 cc (26.61 cu in). Maximum rating is 65 hp at 7,800 rpm, weight with CD ignition, twin carburettors and belt drive being 25 kg (55 lb).

AED Spitfire 880LC.

Mid-West AE75

Mercury (USA) It is far from common to find marine outboards converted for aviation use, but Lyle Forsgren was an engineering manager with Mercury Marine when he built his LF-1 which won a major award at the 1984 EAA fly-in at Oshkosh. Its engine is a Mercury 25XD rated at 28 hp, water-cooled and driving a 60 W alternator.

Mid-West (UK) Mid-West Aero Engines, of Staverton Airport, took over the Hewland AE75 which powered the ARV/Island Super 2. It markets this engine, fully certificated to BCAR Section C, and a two-cylinder version. The AE75 is a two-stroke with three cylinders in-line, capacity 748 cc (45.5 cu in), weighing 50 kg (110 lb) with starter, generator and geared drive, and rated at 77 hp at 6,750 rpm. The AE45 has two cylinders (492 cc/30.2 cu in), weighs 38.5 kg (85.1 lb) with geared drive and accessories, and gives 50 hp at 6,750 rpm.

Rotax (Austria) A minor proportion of this company's gigantic output is liquid-cooled, including four of the five largest aircraft engines. The first three of these are two-in-line two-strokes. The Type 462 has bore and stroke of 69.5 mm × 61.0 mm (2.74 in × 2.40 in), giving capacity of 462.8 cc (28.242 cu in). Output is 51 hp at 6,000 rpm, for a weight of

27 kg (59.5 lb). The 532 has cylinders 72 mm × 64 mm (2.83 in × 2.52 in), giving capacity of 521.4 cc (31.81 cu in). Output is 64 hp at 6,500 rpm, for a weight of 28 kg (61.7 lb). The 582 has bore enlarged to 76 mm (2.99 in), giving capacity of 580.7 cc (35.44 cu in). Output is actually lower, at 63 hp at 6,500 rpm, for a weight of 28.4 kg (62.4 lb). These three engines are not piston-ported but have rotary valves. The fourth Rotax is not only the largest but also a completely different design, recently completed for aviation use exclusively. The 912 is a flat-four four-stroke, with overhead-valve cylinders with air-cooled barrels and liquid-cooled heads. Bore and stroke are 79.5 mm × 61 mm (3.13 in × 2.4 in), giving capacity of 1,211.2 cc (73.912 cu in). Output is 79 hp at 5,500 rpm, the weight with all accessories and exhausts being 60 kg (132 lb).

RotorWay (USA) RotorWay Aircraft developed the RW152 to power its own helicopters. A flat-four four-stroke, installed with crankshaft vertical, it has a capacity of 2,660 cc (162 cu in) and is rated at 152 hp at 4,400 rpm for a weight of 77.1 kg (170 lb) complete with starter. It has dual direct-fire electronic ignition, and though compression ratio is 9.6 it can run on 92-grade Mogas.

RotorWay RW-152.

Spitfire See Advanced Engine Design.

SPP See Sport Plane Power under Derived engines.

Teledyne Continental (USA) The philosophy of this great company was outlined in the introduction to this section. Commonly abbreviated to TCM, it has produced Voyager liquid-cooled engines which are direct counterparts of established air-cooled engines, as well as two new sizes, 300 and 370 cu in. The baseline engine, the Voyager 200, has the same size cylinder as the O-200A, but with compression ratio raised from 7 to 11.4. Accordingly the liquid-cooled engine needs 100/100LL fuel. Maximum output is raised from 100 to 110 hp at 2,750 rpm, weight with accessories being reduced from 100 kg (220 lb) to 88 kg (194 lb). A single Voyager 200 powered the *Voyager* aircraft on its non-stop flight around the world. Like the other Voyager engines it has an improved high-turbulence combustion space, which enables a specific fuel consumption of 0.375 lb/h/hp to be achieved over a broad operating range. Such a low sfc was previously possible only with complex compound engines or diesels. The Voyager 300 is a new size of TCM engine, with six identical cylinders giving capacity of 4.93 litres (301 cu in). Output is 170 hp at

2,700 rpm, for an equipped weight of 132 kg (291 lb). The 370 is another new size, being a four-cylinder version of the 550 with a capacity of 6,060 cc (370 cu in). The IOL-370 has compression ratio of 9 and is rated at 190 hp at 2,700 rpm, for a weight of 127 kg (280 lb). The turbocharged TSIOL-370 has compression reduced to 7.5 and is rated at 225 hp at 2,700 rpm, for an equipped weight of 142.4 kg (314 lb). Biggest of the range is the Voyager 550, with six cylinders the same size as the air-cooled 550, giving capacity of 9 litres (550 cu in). The basic engine gives 350 hp at 2,700 rpm for a weight of 229 kg (504 lb). The turbocharged T-550 gives 300 hp at 2,500 rpm and weighs 204 kg (450 lb). The turbocharged and geared GT-550 gives 400 hp for a weight of 249.5 kg (550 lb).

Westermayer (Austria) Oskar Westermayer has developed his W5/33 from the Continental O-200A by fitting cylinder heads cooled by pure ethylene glycol. The coolant pump feeds a separate pipe to each head, the return circuit passing through the air radiator. Compression ratio is raised to 8.6, and fuel consumption is reduced by about 25 per cent, sfc being around 0.42. Capacity and power are unchanged (100 hp at 2,750 rpm), weight being 85 kg (187 lb) bare or 102 kg (225 lb) with starter, alternator and silencer.

Derived engines

Many of the smaller engines already described have been based on designs originally marketed for various surface applications. This additional section outlines aero engines overtly based on types previously in production for automotive use, especially for cars. Whereas as recently as 1975 trying to replace a 'proper aero engine' with a car engine generally seemed ridiculous, today one could almost claim 'everybody's doing it'. We have seen already that such engines can be competitive on the scores of performance, weight and reliability. They also offer dramatically reduced first cost, even more startling reductions in the cost of replacement parts (with parts life certainly no shorter than before), the ability to use Mogas (if possible unleaded), and freedom from worrying about cracked cylinders caused by (for example) a long maximum-continuous climb followed by an idling descent through cold air. Most conversions also offer smoother and much quieter operation. Virtually all engines in the list have reduction gears or a belt drive. Dual ignition is usually mandatory, but in a few instances one ignition system is a stand-by for emergencies. The list includes both liquid-cooled and air-cooled engines, the latter category dominated by various modifications of VW engines.

Advanced Engine Design (USA) AED has already appeared in both the Air-cooled and Liquid-cooled sections. AED merits inclusion

AED (Kawasaki-derived) 91 hp.

in this section by virtue of a series of automotive-derived engines quite unlike the well-known Spitfire range. Two are based on Kawasaki models. One (illustrated) is a two-in-line upright two-stroke based on the liquid-cooled Kawasaki TC530-D. With capacity of 530 cc (32.34 cu in), it is rated at 91 hp. Complete with dual CD ignition, automatic oil injection, AED's anti-torsion control and 'floating' dual exhausts it weighs 39.5 kg (87 lb). AED also has several other engines under development. One is a four-in-line based on the air-cooled Kawasaki KZ-1000, weighing 64.8 kg (143 lb) and giving up to 150 hp. Another is a liquid-cooled flat-four using Subaru cylinder blocks; it weighs 61 kg (135 lb) and would be rated at 100 hp. Yet another liquid-cooled engine is a four-in-line being developed in collaboration with BMW, and in flight test in a Cessna 140. It weighs 74.8 kg (165 lb) and is rated at 110 hp.

Ardem See VW.

Auto Aviation See Oldsmobile.

Buick (USA) At least nine workshops (one being Mizell which see) have converted Buick engines for aircraft use, most picking the excellent water-cooled V-8 and adding a belt reduction drive. One of the first car engines to be converted for aircraft use, in the 1960s, was the air-cooled Corvair engine derated to 60 hp. Today's 'Chevvy' aero engines include the three-cylinder Sprint and, far more important, the 300 cu in (4,916 cc) V-6 typically rated at 250 hp at 4,000 rpm but giving 300 hp in the Sadler A-22 light attack aircraft. Many aircraft use V-8 engines, including the beautiful Morse 364P Prowler with a 350-hp engine using Rodeck cylinder blocks, and a Pawnee tug re-engined by Largent and Warren at Port Lincoln, South Australia. Most powerful of all was the Thunder Engines TE495 based on the Can-Am McLaren racing V-8 of 495 cu in (8,120 cc), with a continuous rating on 100/130 fuel of 700 hp at 4,400 rpm. Weight was 244 kg (537 lb) or 323 kg (711 lb) with turbocharger and 0.467 geared drive.

Citroen (France) Especially in Europe, the simple engines by this car manufacturer have proved popular. Conversions of the 2CV (602 cc, 29 hp) have generally proved unsuccessful, but the Ami and especially the Visa have been used as alternative powerplants by factory-builders and home-builders. The Visa, of 954 cc (58.2 cu in), is usually rated at about 40 hp.

Clutton See VW.

Custom See Ford.

DAF (Netherlands) Part of Volvo, this famous company has never marketed its engines for aeronautical use, but several home-builders have picked versions of the common flat-twin, air-cooled four-strokes. Probably the most common is the 850 cc (51.87 cu in), rated at 34 hp at 4,500 rpm and weighing about 40 kg (88 lb) with electric starter. Some builders, such as Wood Wing Specialty, use the 950 cc version, rated at 38 hp.

Diverse (USA) Diverse Mechanical produces the Hawk AE, derived from a British four-in-line water-cooled four-stroke. It is rated at 40 hp and typically weighs 49.4 kg (109 lb).

Electramotive The Pond Racer, designed to break all piston–engined speed records, is powered by two VG–30 racing–car engines. Running on methanol, these are V–6 four-strokes, with liquid cooling, turbocharger and intercooler, rated at a maximum of 1,000 hp each. See under Nissan.

FAM (France) Half-owned by Avions Pierre Robin, France Aero Moteurs has spent several years, and a lot of money, developing a fully optimized aero engine based on the PRV (Peugeot-Renault-Volvo) car engine. A 90° V-6 liquid-cooled four-stroke, it has a capacity of 2,850 cc (173.9 cu in) and is at present rated at 180 hp at 5,500 rpm, propeller speed being reduced to 2,430 rpm by reduction gear (early versions had a toothed belt). A notable feature is that complete and instantaneous control over fuel injection and electronic ignition is exercised by dual computers whose inputs are rpm, mixture ratio, throttle position, air temperature, water temperature, atmospheric pressure and manifold pressure.

Fisher See Ford.

Ford (USA/UK) At least 28 different conversions of at least six basic types of Ford car engine are currently flying, or in active development. Some of the simplest are based on Escort or even Fiesta engines, one example being engines from **Custom Aircraft** (Canada), all with toothed-belt drive. Most Ford conversions have been larger. Dave

Chevrolet 4,920 cc (300 cu in) V-6 (Bob's Special Products) ready for flight test in Velocity.

Blanton's **Javelin Aircraft** flew a Cessna 172 from 1976 until 1981 powered by a Mustang Cobra engine, basically a Ford 2,300 cc (140 cu in) engine plus turbocharger. It weighed 198 kg (437 lb) and gave 231 hp at 5,400 rpm. Much better results were then obtained with the Canadian-built 230 cu in (3,770 cc) 230V6, and results have been outstanding. This engine with belt reduction drive, two cheek radiators and all accessories, weighs 175.5 kg (387 lb), and in a typical installation the weight with two cheek radiators, coolant and propeller is 195.5 kg (431 lb). The 230V6 is conservatively rated at 230 hp, and Blanton has for a decade demonstrated his Cessna 175's ability not only to outperform the regular model but also to cruise faster at a

Javelin Ford 230V6 with 1.6 (0.625) drive ratio.

consumption of 6.8 US gal/hr, compared with 12 for the usual GO-300A engine. Javelin Fords are available with drive ratios of 1.6 (0.625), 2 (0.5) or 2.82 (0.355), to suit different applications. Over 1,000 sets of 230V6 plans have been sold. Blanton is now busy working on conversions of the tough 4,600 cc (280 cu in) Ford V-8, which he will rate at 360–550 hp, with 1,200 hp by 1995 (32-valve version). Another long-time Ford converter is Fred **Geschwender**. In the 1970s his company extensively tested Ford V-8 engines in a Funk 23B, starting with a 6,555 cc (400 cu in) engine rated at 270 hp, which was uprated by various modifications to 320 and finally to 400 hp, using a high-velocity chain drive. By 1980 work was concentrated on two Ford V-8 engines, the 5,752 cc (351 cu in), rated at 330 hp at 5,500 rpm and weighing 272 kg (600 lb) and the 7,538 cc (460 cu in), weighing 318 kg (700 lb) and rated at 430 hp at 5,250 rpm, or 600 hp with turbocharger. A massive 9,865 cc (602 cu in) is also offered. Since 1988 Geschwender has been concentrating on the same engine as Blanton, the 230V6. His chain-drive version weighs 172 kg (380 lb) and is flying a Piper Pawnee. (One is planned to power a full-size Spitfire replica.) Yet another 230V6 conversion is the **Fisher** Tornado, which uses a Kevlar-reinforced toothed belt. There are numerous internal modifications, resulting in a weight of 177 kg (390 lb) and power of 275 hp at 5,000 rpm, propeller speed being 3,125 or 2,500. Unlike the Javelin Ford the Tornado needs leaded fuel, though it too can cruise at around 7 US gal/h in a Cherokee with the 50/50 water/glycol radiator in the rear fuselage.

Geschwender See Ford.

HAPI See Honda and VW.

Honda (Japan) Various air-cooled and water-cooled engines have been adapted for aircraft use. In Germany Roland **Parodi** converted a four-cylinder air-cooled Honda engine in the 45-hp class as the HP 45 in the 1970s, and went on to develop the HP 60 of 60 hp. These had a new crankcase and lubrication system, dual ignition and belt drive. **Earthstar** Aircraft has developed the Laughing Gull II with a pusher conversion of the Honda Civic water-cooled engine, driving a three-blade propeller. **HAPI** Engines, basically a VW-based producer, has since 1986 added the HAPI 125-GRP Mini Merlin, a conversion of the four-in-line water-cooled Prelude. With capacity of

1,829 cc (111.6 cu in), the Mini Merlin has dual carburettors, dual electronic ignition and output of 125 hp at 2,500 rpm.

Hummel See VW.

IMAER See VW.

Jaguar (UK) Several organizations have produced aero engines based on the enviably smooth V-12 engine of 5,300 cc (323.4 cu in). A typical example, and one with considerable flight experience, is the Lightning Merlin, by **Thunder Wings**, rated at 300 hp, but no longer marketed.

Javelin See Ford.

JPX See VW.

Mazda (Japan) A small number of conversions are flying of the larger sizes of conventional piston engine, notably those by Don **Saunders** whose jet Hawk uses either a stock 2 litre or a 300 hp Turbo to drive a five-blade shrouded fan to produce a propulsive jet.

Mizell (USA) This company has converted several auto engines, concentrating since 1985 on the 125-hp Buick or the General Motors V-8 used in several Rover models. These are available with direct drive, geared drive or toothed belt.

Mudry See VW.

Nissan (Japan) Undoubtedly the most exciting piston-engined aircraft in the world today is the Pond Racer, designed by Bert Rutan's Scaled Composites Inc. Remarkable in almost every design detail, and likely to have exceeded 965 km/h (600 mph) long before this book appears, it is powered by two Nissan VG-30 engines. These are based on a standard automotive liquid-cooled V-6, but with the addition of turbochargers, intercoolers and reduction gearboxes to the advanced-technology four-blade propellers. Each engine is rated at 800 to 1,000 hp, burning methanol fuel.

ODA (Germany) The former East German Ostdeutsches Automobilwerk produced versions of the mass-produced Trabant car engine arranged to drive a pusher propeller for motorized gliders and other aircraft. An inverted in-line two-stroke, the Trabant has two cylinders 72 mm × 73 mm (2.834 in ×

2.874 in), 594.5 cc (36.3 cu in), with a rating of 26 hp at 4,200 rpm on unleaded fuel.

Oldsmobile (USA) A very limited number of groups have produced aero engines based on this GM division's products, notably **Auto Aviation** which marketed kits for the 3,500 cc (213.6 cu in) F-85 engine rated at 220 hp. In the Wittman Tailwind it is held to 125 hp.

Pieper See VW.

Porsche (Germany) This famous company's 911 engine has for many years been a standard power unit for airships. In 1980 Professor Porsche instructed his R&D staff at Weissach to produce an optimized engine for aeroplanes, and the 911 was used as a basis. The result, four years and many millions of Deutschmarks later, was the PFM 3200, certificated from late 1984 in various versions with reduced compression for unleaded fuel, increased compression for 100LL only, and with the option of a turbocharger. Remarkably, after such a large investment, the company withdrew from aviation in 1990. An exceedingly refined—and therefore expensive—four-stroke, the 3200 had six opposed air-cooled cylinders 95 mm × 74.4 mm (3.74 in × 2.93 in), giving 3,164 cc (193 cu in). Features included two independent electrical/electronic systems which controlled dual ignition and direct injection immediately upstream of the inlet valves, power/speed proportional fan cooling, 0.441 geared propeller drive, and twin 24V alternators. The basic 3200 was rated at 217 hp at 5,300 rpm and could use Mogas, weight being 181 kg (399 lb).

PRV See FAM.

Pulch (Germany) In the 1970s EAA member Otto Pulch developed and flew two types of engine using BMW air-cooled motor cycle cylinders. The 003A, first run in 1976, had six radial cylinders 90 mm × 70 mm (3.55 in × 2.76 in), capacity 2,700 cc (165 cu in), with 0.437 geared drive and the same Bosch K-Jetronic fuel injection as the Porsche 3200. Rated at 150 hp at 5,000 rpm, it weighed 110 kg (242.5 lb). The 003B had bore increased to 94 mm (3.71 in), raising capacity to 2.9 litres (177 cu in) and power to 180 hp at 5,500 rpm, weight being 120 kg (264.5 lb). Pulch also ran a version with three of the larger cylinders driving a vertical crankshaft with a 3:1 angle box on top driving the propeller in a retractable package rated at 75 hp.

Rectimo See VW.

Revmaster See VW.

Rollason See VW.

Ross (USA) Lou Ross has for many years produced conversions ranging from BMW motor cycle flat-twins up to 400-hp V-8s and various Wankel RC models.

SPP (USA) Though no longer trading, Sport Plane Power spent years developing an engine based on BMW motor cycle parts. A liquid-cooled four-stroke, the K-100A had four horizontal cylinders in line, with 10.2 compression ratio and twin overhead camshafts. The propeller drive can be 0.3125 planetary or 0.385 chain. Weight with the geared drive is 88.5 kg (195 lb) and output 100 hp at 8,000 rpm.

Stage II (USA) Joe Schubeck's Stage II Development Corporation has done a lot of work on high-power V-8 engines which are really original designs, though they incorporate many parts from the Chrysler 7,750 cc (473 cu in) V-8. Blocks, heads, reduction gear (based on that of the RR Merlin) and accessories are of Stage II design. The basic model is rated at 450 hp, but turbocharged derivatives have been run at powers up to 800 hp.

Stamo See VW.

Subaru (Japan) This company's mass-produced flat-four engines of 1,600 cc and 1,800 cc (97.6 cu in and 109.8 cu in) capacity feature electronically controlled ignition and fuel injection, and twin overhead camshafts. Both sizes have been used by Taylor Aero Inc, with ratings of 72 and 113 hp respectively.

Trabant See ODA.

VW (Germany) So numerous are the aero variations on this company's classic flat-four air-cooled car engines that there is no point in attempting to be comprehensive. Early converters used the original 'Beetle' engines, but since 1968 it has become common practice with microlights to use half a VW as being the cheapest possible way of getting power. In round figures a full engine gives 60–80 hp and a half engine 30–40 hp, but one can bear in mind that for racing and speedway use VW engines give as much as 200 hp for short periods. Over 70 different models are available as complete engines or conversion kits, the capacity of the four-cylinder engines including the following values in cc: 1,192, 1,200, 1,280, 1,400, 1,500, 1,550, 1,600, 1,650, 1,680, 1,700, 1,834, 1,835, 1,875, 1,915, 2,000, 2,017, 2,050, 2,074, 2,100, 2,180, 2,200, 2,450 and 2,498! I apologize if I have left out any size! The following are better-known versions.

Aeropower (Australia) concentrates on the 1,835 and 2,074 cc, the former giving 65 hp at 3,600 rpm and the bigger type 78 hp at the same speed. Either weighs 69–79 kg (152–174 lb) depending on the options, and can be tractor or pusher. **Ardem** (France) was one of the pioneer producers of a VW aircraft engine, the 4C02 being a conversion of the 1,500 cc (91.5 cu in) engine, rated at 45 hp at 3,300 rpm (see Rollason). In the 1970s Eric **Clutton** (UK) did much work on VW engines for his aircraft, including the refinement of a 1,500 cc (91.5 cu in) version with 0.5 toothed-belt drive, dual ignition and carb heat, maximum power rising to 66 hp at 4,800 rpm. **Flight Specialties** (USA) is a major supplier of complete VW-based engines. **Global** Machine Tool (USA) makes a range of flat-twins with either 85 mm (3.34 in) or 92 mm (3.62 in) bore, which with 69 mm (2.716 in) stroke gives capacity of 783 cc or 819 cc (47.79 or 50 cu in). Compression ratio is 9.5, but Mogas can be used, output being 25 or 35 hp at 3,250 rpm for a weight of 33.5 kg (74 lb). **HAPI** (USA) offers the biggest range, from the Hornet (two 94 mm × 78 mm/3.7 in × 3.0 in cylinders, 1,100 cc/67 cu in, 40 hp) up to the 82–2DH Magnum Plus (four similar cylinders, 82 hp at 3,400 rpm). In between come versions with capacity 1,680–1,915 cc, rated at 55–75 hp at 3,200 rpm. Morry **Hummel** (USA) is a major producer of half-VW engines, typically rated at 35 or 37 hp and weighing about 34.9 kg (77 lb), marketed also as a kit or (for $18) drawings. **IMAER** (Brazil), formerly called Retimotor, has developed two VW-based engines with cylinders 90.4 mm × 78.4 mm (3.6 in × 3.1 in), the 1000 (63.8 hp at 3,600 rpm, 39 kg/86 lb), and the 2000 (2,017 cc/123.08 cu in, 80 hp at 3,400 rpm, 78 kg/172 lb). It is ironic that, whereas Retimotor tried to certificate these engines on alcohol from sugar-cane waste, they are today confined to Avgas 100/130! **JPX** (France) has backed up its range of two-strokes (see under Air-cooled) by the completely different four-stroke 4T60/A, which powers the ATL. The four cylinders are 93 mm × 75.4 mm (3.7 in ×

3 in) (2,050 cc/125 cu in), and rating 65 hp at 3,200 rpm, weight being 73 kg (161 lb) with starter and alternator. A version for microlights weighs 61 kg (134 lb). **Kite Industries** (USA) is another big supplier of kits and plans. **Monnett** (USA) was the famed designer of the Sonerai family of sporting aircraft, which became INAV and then HAPI. Monnett's engines included 1,600 cc (97.5 cu in) and 1,700 cc (103.7 cu in) versions and the Aero Vee 2,180. **Mosler Motors** (USA) makes the MM series of half-VWs, 92 mm × 78 mm (3.6 in × 3.1 in) (1,039 cc/63.4 cu in) which have much in common with HAPI since both use Hummel parts. The Mosler crankcase incorporates redesigned oil passages in an improved oil circuit with larger pump and separate cooler. Standard rating is 35 hp at 3,250 rpm on Mogas for a weight of 39 kg (86 lb). Auguste **Mudry** (France) appears to produce the biggest variant, his MB-4-80 having many original parts. A cylinder size of 93 mm × 92 mm (3.66 in × 3.62 in) gives capacity of 2,498 cc (152.4 cu in), output being 80 hp at only 2,750 rpm, weight being 83 kg (183 lb). Cal **Parker** (USA) markets vast quantities of plans and kits for his aircraft and their engines of 1,500 cc to 1,835 cc (91.5 cu in to 112 cu in), rated at 40, 42 or 65 hp. Ladislao **Pazmany**'s latest production type, the PL-4A, is normally to be powered by a VW 1,600 cc (97.5 cu in) conversion rated at 50 hp (Revmaster optional). **Pieper** (Germany) manufactures the Stamo MS 1500–1, based on the VW of that capacity and rated at 45 hp on Mogas for a weight of 52 kg (115 lb). **Rand Robinson** (USA) market kits and plans for aircraft, but Ken Rand has done a lot of development on VW conversions, especially including Rajay turbocharged installations which hold 90–100 hp to high altitude. **Rectimo** (France) has manufactured over 500 Type 4AR 1200 engines, smallest of the VW four-cylinder derivatives, with 1,192 cc (73 cu in), rated at 40 hp for a weight of 61.5 kg (136 lb). The 4AR 1600 weighs little more 64 kg (141 lb) and is rated at 61 hp. **Revmaster** (USA) was probably the first to offer a refined factory-built VW-based engine, fully certificated. The most important Revmasters are at the top end of the range, 2,100 cc (128 cu in), typically rated at 64 hp, or 75 hp with turbocharger. **Rollason** (UK) produced the Ardem 4C02, of 1,500 cc (91.5 cu in) (cylinders 83 mm × 69 mm/3.3 in × 2.7 in) as the Mk X, and also developed the 1,600 cc (97.6 cu in) Mk XI (bore increased to 85.5 mm/3.4 in), rated at 55

hp at 3,300 rpm for a weight of 71.6 kg (158 lb). For **Stamo**, see Pieper. In 1979–86 Gary **Watson** (USA) sold well over 1,000 kits and plans for his delightful Windwagon, including its 900 cc (55 cu in) half-Beetle rated at 30 hp.

Diesels

The point has been made repeatedly in this book that diesel engines have made almost no impact on aviation, even in aircraft intended for the longest range possible. On the face of it, to persist in developing compression-ignition engines, which (one might expect) to be heavier and therefore more costly to make than Otto-cycle engines, would seem to be foolish in today's world of aviation, especially as the only available markets would appear to be smaller aircraft not requiring long range. This gives only one facet of the picture, however, and there are others.

One is that, as fuel becomes much more expensive, it pays to use an engine of greater thermal efficiency, and thus lower fuel consumption, even if it weighs slightly more. Second, and again related to the price of fuel, it is an advantage to be able to operate safely and without loss of performance on a wide range of fuels (and at many major airports Jet A-1 is the only fuel readily available). Third, though I personally doubt this, it is a plausible argument to claim that diesel fuels are less likely than gasolines to catch fire outside the engine. Fourth, if you have no ignition system, you cannot interfere with radio reception. Fifth, absence of ignition or a carburettor could be held to result in increased reliability, and today's diesel promoters claim that their engines will soon achieve TBOs beyond those of existing GA piston engines and turboprops. On top of these real or hoped-for advantages, some of the engines which follow are expected to achieve superior power/weight ratio, superior power/frontal area, lower vibration, lower first cost, longer parts-life, reduced maintenance and lower installed drag. Some designers also make the point that their engine, unlike equivalent turboprops, provides an adequate number of drive pads for accessories. We must wait and see. Certainly the old image of the diesel—as something ponderously huge, that clanks and clatters even when idling and can be identified from a distance by its smell— is no longer appropriate.

CRM (Italy) One of the most unexpected engines in this book is the CRM 18D/SS.

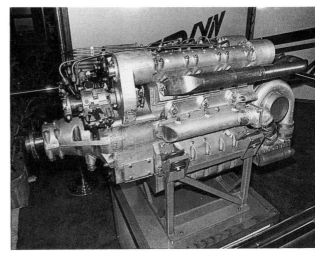

Merlyn 650 hp three-cylinder diesel.

CRM has for many years been one of the world's major producers of large high-speed diesels for marine and rail-traction applications, most of their engines being distant derivatives of the Isotta-Fraschini Asso 1000 of 1928. Biggest of that company's aero engines, the Asso (Ace) 1000 had three monobloc banks each of six cylinders measuring 150 mm × 180 mm (5.91 in × 7.09 in), giving the considerable capacity of 57.26 litres (3,494 cu in). In the giant Ca 90 bomber this engine was rated at 900 hp, yet 60 years of refinement have brought today's CRM diesel version to the point where it can be rated at 1,850 hp at 2,100 rpm, with supreme reliability in applications which often call for 30 or 40 hours non-stop. Two 18D/SS engines provide cruise propulsion for the US Navy's YEZ-2A Sentinel 5000 surveillance airship. These engines are mounted internally but drive vectored-thrust shrouded propellers carried on long pylons. Each engine exactly follows the original Asso cylinder size, but with two turbochargers and intercoolers, and with compression ratio of 16.25. The 18D/SS is 1,304 mm (51.33 in) high and weighs 1,700 kg (3,745 lb).

In-Tech (USA) In the 1970s Machen Inc identified a need for a new aviation engine in the 500–700 hp bracket, able to burn any fuel with maximum economy. The result was a remarkable two-stroke diesel called the Merlyn, which in 1985 was taken over by In-Tech. It is remarkable because of its simplicity and high power/weight ratio. The Merlyn has three cylinders 130 mm × 86 mm (5.125 in × 3.388 in), giving a capacity of 3,470 cc (210 cu in). Cooling is by water/glycol mix, compression ratio is 15.3, and features include twin overhead camshafts for four exhaust valves per cylinder, an offset crankshaft, a geared supercharger at the front feeding the Garrett turbocharger at the rear, with an aftercooler in the intake manifold, and eight accessory drive pads. At a BMEP of 236 lb/sq in the take-off power is 650 hp at 4,800 rpm for an engine weight of only 263 kg (580 lb). Since its first run in January 1984 the Merlyn has been tested on Jet-A1, JP-4, JP-5 and Nos 1 and 2 diesel fuels.

Rybinsk DN-200 (Russia) DN stands for Diesel Novikov, Aleksandr S. Novikov being Chief Designer of the Rybinsk bureau (concerned mainly with big gas turbines). Planned as the most efficient engine possible for light aircraft, it has three double-ended cylinders of 72 mm (2.8 in) bore, the six opposed two-stroke cylinders each having 72 mm (2.8 in) stroke. Capacity is thus only 1,758 cc (107 cu in). Take-off and cruising ratings are respectively 200 and 160 hp, and dry weight 165 kg (364 lb). Specific fuel consumption of the five single-cylinder test engines built by 1991 averaged 0.27. Novikov expects certification of this very advanced twin-crankshaft unit in 1995.

Mock-up of the DN-200, with the wheelcase and propeller drive at the left and scavenging blower at the right.

SCOMA-Énergie (France) This company, which specializes in diesel R&D, decided around 1980 to study the development of an aviation engine with multi-fuel capability, multi-fuel being taken to include petrols, kerosenes, jet fuels, diesel oils, LPG and ethanol. To gain a background of experience a research engine, the GMA 140TK, was built and flown in a Cessna L-19 from June 1987. This engine has four in-line two-stroke cylinders, leaning to starboard (the left as seen from the front), with liquid cooling, turbocharger, air/air intercooler and geared drive. With a capacity of 2,068 cc (126 cu in) the GMA 140TK gives a take-off power of 136 hp for a weight of 180 kg (397 lb). Cruising at 88 hp the fuel consumption is 20 litres (4.4 gal)/hr. This research is underpinning the development of the Comète range of engines, with from one to 16 cylinders of 94 mm (3.7 in) bore and stroke, giving a cylinder displacement of 652 cc (39.79 cu in). Except for the single-cylinder Comète these will be 170° V engines, in other words virtually with opposed cylinders. Other features follow closely the GMA 140TK. Output will vary from 46.9 hp for the single-cylinder engine to 750.7 hp for the 16-cylinder, in all cases at 4,191 rpm.

SECA (Belgium) In 1977 the Société d'Entreprises Commerciales et Aéronautiques began developing a diesel prototype which could equally well be included under Unconventional engines. Known as the GK, this engine comprised an aluminium block which, complete with four double-ended cylinder sleeves, weighed only 19 kg (41.9 lb). The four cylinders were arranged axially, housing opposed pistons driving swash plates on a central output shaft. The advantage of this arrangement, claimed designer James Kenny, was that the engine could be started at a compression ratio of 22 and then, once running, be quickly adjusted to the compression ratio for best economy, around 14. Other advantages claimed included perfect balance and absence of any torque reaction, but nothing has been heard of the GK since 1986.

VM (Italy) In complete contrast, VM Motori appear to have said, 'How can we make diesels that look like Lycomings and Continentals?' The company have a long track record with high-speed diesels, and provide a 2,500 cc (152 cu in) turbocharged engine for one version of the Range-Rover. For aviation they are developing three sizes of four-stroke

VM TPJ-1304HF.

engine, all with opposed cylinders 130 mm × 110 mm (5.1 in × 4.33 in), with compression ratio of 18, propylenic glycol cooling and camshaft-driven pumps injecting JP-4, Jet-A, JP-5 or various other fuels. The three engines, using standard modular parts, are: the TPJ-1304HF, four cylinders, 5,840 cc (356 cu in), 206 hp at 2,640 rpm (same rpm for all models), 185 kg (408 lb); TPJ-1306HF, six cylinders, 8,760 cc (535 cu in), 315 hp, 243 kg (536 lb); and the TPJ-1308HF, eight cylinders, 11.68 litres (713 cu in), 424 hp, 298 kg (657 lb). These engines, claimed to offer cruise sfc '40 to 80 per cent lower than for a petrol engine', are designed for operation to 8,839 m (29,000 ft) and with TBO of 3,000 hr.

Zoche (Germany) Michael Zoche in Munich began running his first prototype aero engine in 1984, and has subsequently maintained a good pace of development. His basic engine, the ZO 01A, has four air-cooled, direct-injected, two-stroke cylinders arranged at 90°, giving perfect balance. Cylinder size is 95 mm × 94 mm (3.74 in × 3.70 in), giving capacity of 2,665 cc (163 cu in). By 1990 the injection pump and its feed pump, fuel filter and all plumbing were all integrated into the crankcase. Charge air pressure is generated by a mechanically driven blower and a turbocharger, and an unusual feature is that the engine is started by compressed air (fed from a football-size container recharged by the engine) fed to impinge on the mechanically driven supercharger, taking the engine from rest to 2,500 rpm in one second. Other features include tungsten crankpin counterweights and fully aerobatic pressure lubrication. Take-off rating is 150 hp at 2,500 rpm, for a weight of 84 kg (185 lb) with all accessories. Zoche is also running the ZO 02A, basically two 01A cylinder banks staggered on a common crankcase. This is one of the lightest and most compact 300 hp engines available, with a weight of 'under 120 kg' (264 lb) and diameter of 635 mm (25 in) and length of 910 mm (36 in). Both engines have cruise sfc of about 0.36, so in theory there should eventually be a lot of Zoche engines.

Unconventional engines

Throughout this century probably 99.999 per cent of all 'piston aero engines' have been of the traditional type in which a piston oscillates up and down a cylinder to drive a crank on an output shaft. Yet over the same period, hundreds of inventors and designers have tried to find alternative arrangements. There have been almost as many arrangements as there have been inventors, but in recent years only two have attracted much interest. One is the so-called barrel engine. The author knows of only one such engine to have made an impact on aviation, and this could even yet start

The Dyna-Cam's double-ended pistons contain large rollers which drive the sinusoidal cam.

replacing conventional engines. It is the first type discussed below. The other unconventional form might be argued not to be a piston engine at all, because there is absolutely no reciprocating motion in the RC (rotating combustion) engine. On the other hand, such engines—most modern forms of which are derived from the Wankel—do induce combustible mixture into a space which first enlarges and then contracts, compressing the mixture, which is then fired, the combustion pressure driving round the movable wall of the chamber in exactly the same way as in an Otto engine. RC engines have their own introduction after discussing the remarkable Dyna-Cam.

Dyna-Cam (USA) This California company owns the rights to an engine with a long history. In principle the Dyna-Cam resembles dozens of other barrel engines, at least 23 types having been developed for aircraft. Most of them arrange their cylinders axially round a drum, like the chambers in the cylinder of a six-shooter. In fact, this particular barrel engine has six cylinders at each end. Pistons oscillate in the cylinders, and barrel inventors have used various ways to connect this motion to a useful output. The Dyna-Cam uses what is by far the commonest arrangement: a swash-plate drive. In this the axial motion is made to apply forces to oblique surfaces which translate the axial force into a tangential force tending to rotate a shaft arranged down the centre of the engine. Most barrel engines of the past used central pistons with a rod projecting at both ends terminating in a slipper or roller driving a swash-plate at each end. The Dyna-Cam instead has six

double-ended pistons, each cut away at mid-length to accommodate two rollers. These bear on each side of the rim of a single cam, a thick steel disc which curves sinusoidally first one way and then the other. This disc cam is in the centre of the output shaft. To assemble the engine the six pistons, with their rollers, are arranged around the cam and this assembly is lowered into the six-cylinder block forming one end of the engine. Then a centre section is added around the cam, and the engine is completed by adding the other block containing the six cylinders at the opposite end. The simplicity is self-evident. The pistons float freely, being constrained only by the cylinder liners and the rollers riding on the rotating cam. Conventional poppet valves are driven by a face cam disc in each end. Shaft speed is half that of conventional engines, each piston makes four strokes per shaft revolution, and the number of firing strokes per revolution is 12. This, combined with essentially perfect balance, makes for extremely smooth running.

This engine had its origins in a design by the Blazer Brothers, who worked for Studebaker, in 1916. In 1936 the Blazers sold the rights to Studebaker's head of engineering, Karl Herrmann. He managed to get a US Army prototype contract, and he ran the first engine in 1940. The war intervened, and after 1945 no investor was interested in a 'new piston engine'. Herrmann kept going on a shoestring budget, and by 1950 had built an improved engine weighing 286 lb (130 kg) with starter and generator, which gave up to 200 hp at 1,800 rpm, and with a supercharger was run at 270 hp at 1,500 rpm for 50 hours without measurable wear. In 1957 he put one of two completed engines through a 150-hour test and received FAA certification. In 1961, aged 80, Herrmann sold up to one of his employees, Dennis Palmer. Everything sat in a warehouse until 1980, when Palmer decided to revive the project. With his son and daughter Palmer worked on the engine in fits and starts, and at last in 1987 a 210 hp version flew seven hours in a Piper Arrow. Despite an unsuitable propeller, the rate of climb was increased from 274 to 457 m/min (900 to 1,500 ft/min). Meanwhile, another engine with twin carbs replaced by fuel injection developed 285 hp for slightly reduced weight. In 1988 Dyna-Cam failed to agree with Piper on questions of money and control of the project, but Piper remains interested in seeing this radical engine reach the production stage.

RC Engines No designer of traditional Otto-type engines needs to be reminded that they suffer from fundamental shortcomings. One is that by their very nature they are full of large masses which either reciprocate in a linear manner or, like con-rods, oscillate in a complex way. Various rotating parts suffer variable angular velocity. With conventional poppet valves the effective port area climbs from zero, as the valve opens, very briefly reaches a maximum and immediately starts falling back to zero. There are many other problems, such as the promotion of detonation by the hot spot around the exhaust valve. Various forms of RC (rotating combustion) engine had been proposed since the nineteenth century, but it was Felix Wankel who in 1954 proposed the configuration that has since become very widespread.

Right *Two views of the Mid-West AE90R engine, derived from a design by Norton.*

Below *Textron Lycoming artwork emphasizing the apparent simplicity of an RC engine compared with a traditional reciprocating engine.*

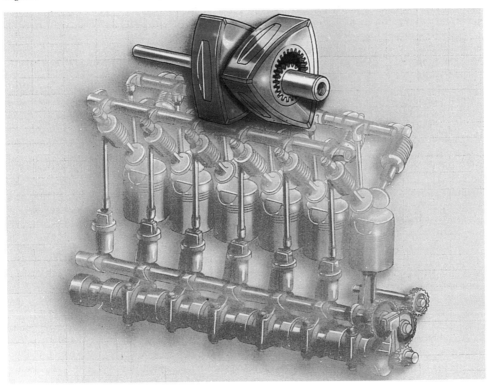

Basically, it comprises a rotor in the form of an equilateral triangle with convex curved sides which rotates inside a housing shaped rather like a figure 8. There are very many other arrangements, but this is the most common. In the centre of the rotor is an internal gear which meshes with a gear on the output shaft in the centre of the housing. At any given moment the rotor is offset eccentrically. Each of the three faces of the rotor is equivalent to a piston, and combustion pressure acting on each face in turn drives the rotor round. This in turn drives the output shaft, but at three times the rotor speed. The three corners of the rotor, and the edges of its sides, are sealed with flexible apex seals pressed (by springs and by combustion pressure) against the housing. In most RC engines a carburettor is used to feed mixture, but in the series of five diagrams the more efficient stratified-charge method is shown, as described later on this page.

Each operating cycle begins as one apex seal slides past the intake port (1). From this point (in the engine shown) high-pressure air from the turbocharger enters the combustion chamber (outlined by a dotted line) downstream of that apex seal. (Of course, not all RC engines have turbochargers.) In (2) the rotor has moved through 120°, turning the output shaft through one revolution. At this

A typical apex seal.

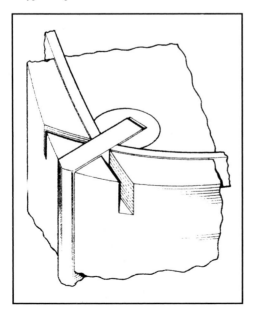

point the next apex seal has just closed off the inlet port, ending the intake 'stroke'. Further rotation compresses the air as the space between the rotor face and the housing shrinks. At (3) the air is compressed to its minimum volume, and fuel is injected (in this engine, by the stratified charge method). This is the beginning of the power stroke, in which the very high combustion pressure acts on the face of the rotor to drive round the rotor and output shaft. At (4) the power stroke is about half completed, providing the output power and simultaneously compressing the air above the next rotor face. The power stroke is completed when the leading apex seal has uncovered the exhaust port. In (5) the charge is escaping through this port, the trailing apex seal sweeping all of the residual gases out of the housing.

Most RC engines use this form of rotor and housing, but on the intake stroke draw in mixture from a carburettor. The so-called stratified-charge system was developed by NSU-Audi, followed by NASA Lewis Laboratory, taken further by Curtiss-Wright, and then adopted by John Deere and Lycoming (at the time, Avco Lycoming). The idea has much in common with that of the same name used in the Jameson FF-1, a 110-hp piston engine developed in Britain in 1945–9 and used to power the prototype Skeeter helicopter. The objective is to establish combustion with a normal or even rich mixture and then sustain it with a very weak mixture. In the RC engine the initial burning takes place immediately the leading apex seal sweeps past the small pilot injector, which sprays past the spark plug to create a flame front. The main injector then sprays into this flame, holding the flame front stationary as the compressed air is swept through it by the rotor. Stratification is claimed to minimize fuel consumption and make the engine able to run perfectly on almost any fuel. If combined with pressurizing the incoming air (for example, by a turbocharger, which is efficiently driven by exhaust from an RC engine) the result is a dramatic increase in power from a given engine, but at the cost of putting a severe strain on the moving parts, especially the seals. See the enlarged drawing on page 210.

Aerotek (USA) This company supplied single-rotor engines based on the mass-produced Mazda RX-7, one application being the original Wind Dancer. Capacity 655 cc (40 cu in), rating 120 hp.

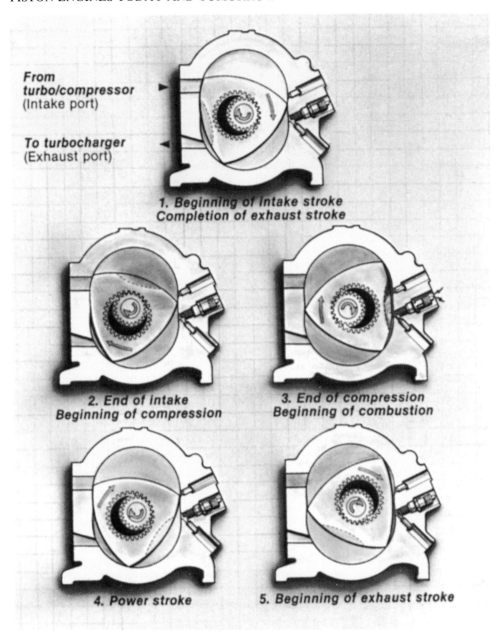

From turbo/compressor
(Intake port)

To turbocharger
(Exhaust port)

1. Beginning of intake stroke
Completion of exhaust stroke

2. End of intake
Beginning of compression

3. End of compression
Beginning of combustion

4. Power stroke

5. Beginning of exhaust stroke

The operating cycle of a typical RC engine (turbocharger need not be present).

Alturdyne (USA) This San Diego firm is funding development of two sizes of advanced RC engine for aircraft propulsion, the larger being rated at 250 hp. Testing of complete engines began in December 1984, most of which has been on diesel fuel and using a reduction gearbox.

Duncan (USA) This Oklahoma company began developing RC aero engines in 1984, basing their work initially on Mazda RX-7 technology. Today they are marketing five engines. The SR-40A is an air-cooled single-rotor engine rated at 40 hp at 6,000 rpm, weighing 30 kg (66 lb) complete with centrifu-

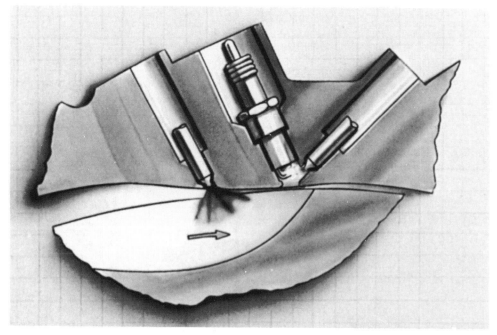

Stratified-charge injection by pilot (left) and main injectors (see text).

gal cooling fan. The SR-60D is a direct-drive, water-cooled, single-rotor engine rated at 60 hp at 4,000 rpm, weighing 50 kg (110 lb) complete with IR-beam triggered dual ignition. The SR-120R is another water-cooled single-rotor engine rated at 120 hp at 9,000 rpm and weighing 74.8 kg (165 lb) with turbocharger and toothed-belt drive. The DR-200R is a dual-rotor engine with output held anywhere from 125 to 200 hp by limiting the rpm (max 8,100). With belt drive and accessories it weighs 109 kg (240 lb). The DR-240R is the same engine allowed to deliver 240 hp at 9,000 rpm, installed weight being 127 kg (280 lb). Duncan is testing a Dual-Pac coupling two dual-rotor engines to give 700 hp, the whole package being 'smaller and lighter than any available 300 hp conventional engine'.

Fichtel & Sachs (Germany) This versatile company was one of the pioneers of RC aviation engines, concentrating on the smallest sizes. First came the KM 48, flown on a Schleicher sailplane in 1968. This 160 cc (9.76 cu in) air-cooled engine was rated at 10 hp at 5,000 rpm, and had an installed weight of 8.5 kg (18.8 lb) complete with 5 litres (1.1 gal) of fuel. The Sachs RC 30E is a 303 cc (18.49 cu in) air-cooled engine rated at 23 hp at 5,000

rpm and with an equipped weight of 18 kg (39.9 lb) including 0.5 belt drive and alternator. Other single and dual-rotor engines are rated at 35 and 50 hp.

Grünig (Germany) Ernest Grünig has developed his own conversion of the RX-7, initially for a Long-Eze, rated at 200 hp and with a total weight, with fixed-pitch propeller, of 135 kg (298 lb). Vibration is 'not detectable'.

Jongbloed (USA) Bill Jongbloed (pronounced Youngblood) has spent his life mainly with racing cars, but his first love has always been aviation and in recent years he has devoted much effort to RC aero engines. He picked the twin-rotor Mazda 3B 'for its compactness and turbine smoothness', and after much research decided to use a geared drive. He suggests that a 750-hp belt would have to be 22 in (559 mm) wide! His 1,311 cc (80 cu in) engine is rated at 200 hp at 6,500 rpm, propeller rpm being 2,850. Total installed weight, complete with cooling water, is 150 kg (330 lb).

Mazda (Japan) At least 18 groups or workshops have already produced aero conversions of Mazda automotive RC engines. Those listed here—Aerotek, Duncan, Grünig and Jongbloed—are only a selection.

Mid-West (UK) This firm (see Liquid-cooled section) markets single and twin-rotor rotary engines, specially developed for manned aircraft. Using a core manufactured by Norton Motors, they have dual spark ignition, liquid cooling of the housing and air cooling of the rotors. Precise control of internal temperature gives a long life, and the rotor air passes through a coalescing and separating filter to recover any entrained lubricating oil. Notable features are exceptionally low frontal area, vibration and noise (the exhaust system has two stages). The installation can be tractor or pusher. The single-rotor AE50R has capacity of 294 cc (18 cu in), weighs 30 kg (66 lb) with gearbox, starter, generator and exhaust system, and is being certificated to E/JAR-22 and FAR-33 at 45–50 hp at 7,000 rpm. The twin-rotor AE90R has a capacity of 588 cc (35.9 cu in), weighs 54 kg (119 lb) and is being certificated at 90–100 hp at 7,000 rpm.

Moller (USA) Moller International specializes in VTOL technology, but it also has consider-

Duncan DR-240R.

Moller RC engine nudging 2 hp/lb.

12"

Norton NR 731, 38 hp for 10 kg (22 lb).

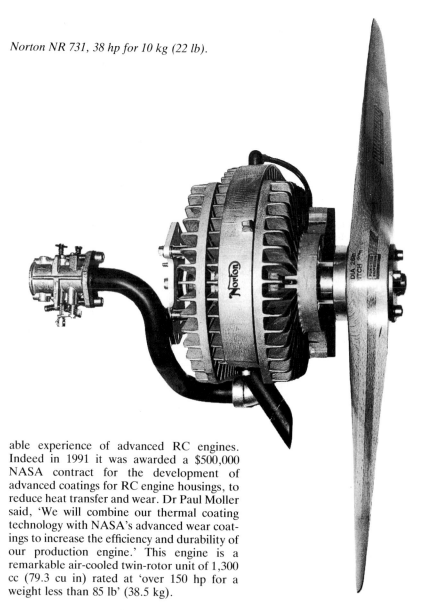

able experience of advanced RC engines. Indeed in 1991 it was awarded a $500,000 NASA contract for the development of advanced coatings for RC engine housings, to reduce heat transfer and wear. Dr Paul Moller said, 'We will combine our thermal coating technology with NASA's advanced wear coatings to increase the efficiency and durability of our production engine.' This engine is a remarkable air-cooled twin-rotor unit of 1,300 cc (79.3 cu in) rated at 'over 150 hp for a weight less than 85 lb' (38.5 kg).

Norton (UK) A forerunner of this company, BSA Motorcycles, began to investigate the Wankel engine in 1969. In 1978 Norton took the Fichtel & Sachs KM 914 single-rotor engine as a starting point and developed 50–60 hp engines for motor cycles. Subsequently a much wider range of engines has been produced in quantity for aero applications. Aircraft cruise at a higher percentage of maximum power than road vehicles, so water-cooled housings predominate. Advantages claimed include multi-fuel capability, power/weight ratio better than a two-stroke, sfc competitive with a four-stroke, extreme compactness, zero vibration and very low maintenance requirement. Current research includes turbocharging to sustain power at high altitude (mainly for unmanned aircraft). The first to be certificated was the NR 642, a heavy-duty version of a basic twin-rotor type with helical reduction gearbox. Rating is 90 hp, and the weight, complete with water cooling for the housing and a large exhaust ejector to cool the rotor, is 64 kg (140 lb). The slightly smaller NR 622, of 588 cc (35.9 cu in), has a rating of 82 hp at 7,500 rpm and with 0.5 or 0.33 geared drive weighs 52 kg (115 lb). The NR 602 is basically a 622 with direct drive, reducing weight to 48 kg (105 lb). The NR 801 is a direct-drive single-rotor engine with liquid-cooled housings, rated at 52 hp at 7,500 rpm and weighing 22.7 kg (50 lb). The remarkable NR 731 is claimed to be the lightest RC engine in the world and to have the highest ratio of power to weight. A single-rotor engine with air cooling throughout, it has a width of 236 mm (9.3 in), length of 188 mm (7.4 in) and weight in running order of only 10 kg (22 lb), yet output at 7,500 rpm is 38 hp. Chamber capacity is 208 cc (12.7 cu in).

Ross (USA) Lou Ross has tested single and twin-rotor conversions, including examples with his own geared drives.

Teledyne Continental (USA) In 1983 TCM, famous for its reciprocating engines, decided to enter the field of RC engines. Its Aircraft Products Division took a licence for the use of Norton designs and technology, and the immediate result was two excellent engines using identical rotors. At the time of writing (1992/3) these had not been certificated for piloted applications, though both were in production for UAV/RPV applications before 1986. The GR-18 is a single-rotor engine of 294 cc (17.9 cu in), rated at 45 hp at 7,500 rpm, with output rpm selectable by gearbox ratio from 2,000 to 4,000, basic engine weight being 22.7 kg (50 lb). Features include a carburettor, dual electronic CD ignition, air-cooled rotor, liquid-cooled housing and total-loss metered lubrication. The twin-rotor GR-36 is basically identical, and gives 90 hp at 7,500 rpm, but usually is held to 6,900 rpm at which 85 hp is available. Basic weight is 50 kg (110 lb). It was TCM's intention to clear both engines on a wide range of fuels, though most running has been on Mogas.

Textron Lycoming (USA) The other giant among engines for general aviation announced in 1985 that it had entered into an agreement with John Deere (best-known for agricultural machines and tractors) under which they would jointly spend $30m by 1990 in developing and certifying what Lycoming later called Score, from Stratified-Charge Omnivorous Rotary Engine. The effort had its roots in the original Wankel and NSU technology, which in 1958 was picked up by Curtiss-Wright. Once a giant among aero engine builders, this company purchased a licence from NSU and carried out years of research, eventually working with NASA Lewis Laboratory on the stratified-charge concept. Among a host of projects, the one taken furthest for aero use was the RC2–75, typically rated at 340 hp at 7,000 rpm and with a total installed weight of 167 кg (368 lb). In the early 1980s Curtiss-Wright gave up, and John Deere bought not only all the rights and hardware but also the vast factory at Wood-Ridge. Deere undertook to develop RC engines for non-aviation applications, while Lycoming concentrated initially on a Score of 400 hp, maintained by turbocharger to 6,096 m (20,000 ft), with continuous cruise power set at 300 hp at 7,620 m (25,000 ft), the engine burning any aviation piston or jet fuel and being outstandingly light and compact. Lycoming announced its intention to market Score engines from 50 to 500 hp, and to get the initial 400-hp model certificated by 1989. Unfortunately, two years short of that date the work was stopped, and the agreement with Deere terminated. Sad to end the book on this note, especially as the Score seemed to have everything going for it.

VAZ The Togliatti (Fiat) car plant in Russia has developed the VAZ-430 twin-rotor engine specifically for aircraft. First run in 1991, it is liquid-cooled, has a clutch-driven centrifugal dynamic inlet compressor and electronic control. Weight is 135 kg (298 lb) and power 230 hp (take-off) or 270 hp (contingency), running on Mogas or any other petrol. It has been chosen for the Mil Mi-34V helicopter, to fly in late 1993.

In front of a mock-up Mi-34 helicopter, the VAZ-430 shows twin electronic boxes and, on top, the huge air filter feeding to the centrifugal compressor at left.

Update to
New Edition

This book was first published in 1993. It was so well received that a new edition is now offered, with this extra section of eight pages. In the reviews of the original book the only criticism offered was that it would have helped if a table of data had been provided. In fact, it only needs a minute or two to see that such a table would occupy more than this extra eight pages. The author considers the space can be better used.

Thus, this extra section is devoted to two topics. One is the present scene in which new piston aero engines continue to appear. The big question is: will anything really shake the seemingly unassailable position of Lycoming and Continental, who sell traditional types of engine all over the world? In the smaller power class, under 100hp, by 1997 the Austrian firm of Rotax had achieved the even more difficult task of capturing about 80 per cent of the world market, leaving over 40 firms to compete for the other 20 per cent.

The other topic is that the Russian magazine *Aviastsiya i Kosmonavtika* published in its March 1997 issue, a comprehensive article by Vladimir Rigmant on the subject of the last Soviet heavy bombers powered by piston engines. He has for many years been the archivist of the A. N. Tupolev design bureau. Unlike many aircraft people, he has a strong interest in engines, and his article contains much new information on the impressive super-powerful piston engines which were developed in the USSR in 1940–50. The following information is extracted from Vladimir's text. I have arranged it in alphabetical order by engine designation.

ASh-2K This was the ultimate engine developed at OKB No. 19 by A. D. Shvetsov, one of the pioneer Soviet engine designers.

Derived from the ASh-2TK (see text), it had both a geared supercharger and a single enormous TK-2 turbosupercharger, as well as seven impulse (blowdown) turbines driven by exhaust gas, all geared to the crankshaft. These increased the dry weight to 2,550 kg (5,622 lb), but raised take-off power to 4,500 hp at 2,800 rpm at a manifold pressure of 1,430 mm Hg (13 lb/sq in). Specific fuel consumption was 0.19 kg (0.42 lb)/hp/hr. Prototypes ran in early 1949, but there were many difficulties. Moreover, the proportion of the engine's power expended in driving the cooling fans reached 30 per cent at 13 km (42,650 ft), and an unacceptable 50 per cent at 15 km (49,213 ft). Though it was earmarked for the 85/2 heavy bomber, driving the five-blade AV-55 propeller, and was the engine favoured by Tupolev, the ASh-2K flew only in a Tu-4LL testbed, in October 1950. It was the most powerful piston engine ever to fly.

ASh-2TK This was the original super-power piston engine (predecessor of the ASh-2K), developed at OKB No. 19 under Arkadiya D. Shvetsov. It was an air-cooled radial, with 28 cylinders in four rows. As it was in effect two ASh-82s back-to-back, the cylinders in the four rows were one behind the other (not helical, as in the Pratt & Whitney R-4360), and capacity was 82.4 litres (5,028 cu in). The diameter was 1.28 m (50.4 in), and length 2,911 mm (114.6 in). Complete with its gear-driven supercharger and two TK-19F turbosuperchargers it weighed 2,080 kg (4,585.5 lb). Take-off power was 4,000 hp at 2,620 rpm, with 1,310 mm (10.7 lb/sq in) manifold pressure. At the same rpm at an altitude of 9 km (29,528 ft) the power was still 3,070 hp, with a manifold pressure of 1,090 mm (6.4 lb/sq in). The ASh-2TK was to have been flown in a Tu-4LL testbed, but – possibly before the start of flight testing (documentation has not been found) – was overtaken by the ASh-2K.

ASh-73TK As noted on p.173, this was simply a big air-cooled radial of traditional form, with 18 cylinders in two rows. It was the standard engine of the Tu-4, the Soviet copy of the B-29. Capacity was 58.1 litres (3,545.5 cu in), which for example compares with the 3,350 cu in of the Wright Duplex Cyclone used in the B-29. Dry weight was 1,275 kg (2,811 lb), or 1,355 kg (2,987 lb) with its two TK-19 turbosuperchargers. At 2,400 rpm and 1,080 mm Hg (6.4 lb/sq in) manifold pressure, a power of 2,200 hp was maintained up to 8.7 km (28,543 ft). At nominal power, with 980 mm manifold pressure, 2,000 hp was maintained to 9.3 km (30,512 ft). At a 60 per cent cruise setting the specific fuel consumption was 0.225-0.2442 kg (0.496-0.539 lb)/hp/hr.

ASh-73TKF This uprated version was provided with direct fuel injection. Take-off rating was 2,720 hp, and nominal power was 2,360 hp. Another variant was the ASh-73TKFN. Both versions were used in the Tu-80 bomber prototypes, installed in new low-drag cowlings with cross-section area reduced by 1.9m² (20.45 sq ft). In March 1951, the inboard engines were fitted with AV-16U reversing propellers.

M-35 This was the last oil (semi-diesel) engine to be tested by the brigade of Charomskii (p. 173).

M-51 This was a compound engine developed by the bureau of M. M. Maslennikov. The author has no information on this, beyond the fact that it was a candidate engine for the Type 487 bomber, which became the Tu-85.

M-222 Under this designation, development of the German Jumo 222 (see pp. 162-163) was continued for two years in the USSR. It never had an application.

M-224 Having discovered plans and a few parts intended for the Junkers Jumo 224 (which was never built) the Soviet VIAM assembled and tested at least one example. It was assigned to GAZ (aviation factory) No. 500, under V. M. Yakovlev (no relation to the aircraft designer). The massive direct-injection diesel looked like an enlarged Jumo 222, having X-24 configuration. Dry weight with a turbosupercharger was 2,750 kg (6,063 lb). The length was 3,128 mm (123 in) and height 1,897 mm (74.7 in). Take-off power was 4,400 hp at 3,000 rpm, with sfc of 0.193 kg (0.425 lb)/hp/hr. At cruise setting of 2,400 hp at 2,600 rpm at 9 km (29,528 ft) the sfc was 0.18 kg (0.397 lb)/hp/hr.

M-250 Designed in 1939-40 by the bureau of G. S. Skubachevsky, this massive engine had six banks each of four liquid-cooled

Originally designed by the bureau of Skubachevsky, the M-250 was later developed by Dobrynin into the VD-4K. The six banks of cylinders were liquid-cooled.

cylinders. It is briefly described and illustrated on pp. 56-57 of my book *World Encyclopaedia of Aero Engines*. The first M-250 was first run at GAZ No. 16 in Voronezh on 22 June 1941, the day the Soviet Union was invaded by Germany. (See next).

M-251TK During what the USSR called *The Great Patriotic War*, Voronezh fell to the invaders, and – like nearly all the other aeronautical design bureaux – Skubachevsky's OKB was evacuated. The M-250 was developed into the M-251TK by Skubachevsky's assistant Vladimir A. Dobrynin, who soon succeeded his boss at OKB No. 36 as General Designer. Under the new scheme, this engine was redesignated for Dobrynin as the VD-3TK. Compared with the M-250, it had capacity increased from 50.98 to 59.43 litres (3,627 cu in). With a length of 2.86 m (112.6 in) and the remarkably small diameter of 1.19 m (46.9 in), the dry weight was 1,520 kg (3,351 lb), or 1,900 kg (4,189 lb) complete with the two TK-19 turbosuperchargers. Take-off power was 3,500 hp at 2,850 rpm, while the 75 per cent cruise rating at 10.7 km (35,105 ft) was 1,875 hp, with sfc of 0.22 kg (0.485 lb)/hp/hr. (See next).

M-253 In January 1949, OKB No. 36 submitted a proposal to develop the M-251TK into this engine with greater power and efficiency. This was agreed, and the first of 24 prototype engines, fitted with three blowdown (impulse) exhaust turbines, first ran in January 1950. For the Tu-85 heavy bomber a neat installation was devised, complete with an enormous TK-36 turbosupercharger. Two such installations were flight tested in the inboard positions of a Tu-4LL between September and December 1950. State Acceptance testing was completed in February 1951, whereupon the engine was redesignated VD-4K. Dobrynin and his assistant, P. A. Kolesov (later famous in his own right with turbojets for VTOL) received a Stalin Prize. (See VD-4K).

M-501 Despite its impressive 6,000 hp, this diesel (pp. 175-176) was quite compact, fitting into a cube with sides of 1.64 m (64.5 in). At cruise setting of 3,260 hp (plus 55 kg, 121 lb, thrust from the turbo exhaust) at 2,000 rpm at 11 km (36,089 ft) the sfc was as low as 0.16 kg (0.353 lb)/hp/hr.

VD-4K Originally designated M-253K, this was rapidly and successfully developed with the Tu-4LL testbed, one of the few changes necessary being to add a cooling fan. OKB No. 120 developed the four-blade AV-44 propeller, of 4.5 m (14 ft 9¼ in) diameter, with reversing capability. Like the original M-251, this engine had six banks each of four liquid-cooled cylinders, with a capacity of 59.43 litres. Diameter of the engine was 1.27 m (50 in), and that of the cowling complete with exhaust turbines was 1.598 m (62.9 in). Without the turbosupercharger the length was 3.02 m (118.9 in) and dry weight 2,065 kg

In the Tu-85 heavy bomber the VD-4K engines were able to put out 4,300 hp at 32,808 ft. Exhaust from the 24 cylinders initially escaped through three turbines geared to the crankshaft. The hot gas then drove the TK-36 turbosupercharger (top right) before escaping through a nozzle giving propulsive thrust. Air rammed in at the main inlet was compressed in the turbosupercharger, passed through a heat exchanger (lower right) and finally compressed again by the shaft-driven supercharger on the back of the crankcase. Note the cooling fan round the propeller shaft (left).

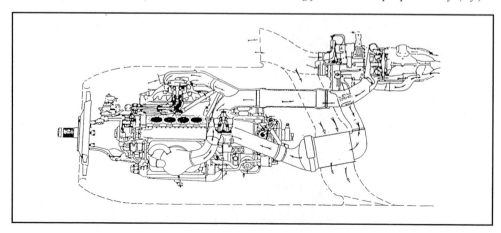

(4,552 lb). Maximum rating at 10 km (32,808 ft) was 4,300 hp at 2,900 rpm, with a manifold pressure of 1,625 mm Hg (16.7 lb/sq in). The corresponding sfc was 0.185 kg (0.408 lb)/hp/hr. In the Tu-85 all four engines and propellers were controlled and synchronised by 'a special electronic system'. It seems fair to claim that by the end of the piston era, the propulsion system of the Tu-85 was more advanced than that of any other aircraft in the world. Despite this, the aircraft was rejected in favour of the Tu-95, which had engines not of 4,300 hp but of 14,795 hp!

Today's general aviation engines

To say the piston engine for light aviation is alive and well is a considerable under-statement. In all parts of the world, attractive and potentially important new engines are running on the testbed and being flight tested. Some of these are already sparking off corres-ponding developments by the previously rather relaxed giants, Lycoming and Continental.

In a nutshell, apart from the traditional quest for higher reliability at lower costs, today's designers are striving to make engines simpler, burn less fuel and meet the demands of the growing environmental lobby. Though noise has not been an issue in general aviation's light aircraft, it is fast becoming one. Slower and more efficient propellers will almost eliminate traditional forms. Even more importantly, as a route to burning less fuel, the diesel is not just making a comeback, it is likely to become the norm. Perhaps most important of all, new engines – especially the diesels – are showing every sign of gradually eliminating Avgas and other gasolines as the universal fuel of light aircraft. Jet fuels do not discharge lead into the atmosphere, they offer reduced flammability, they are cheaper (in Europe roughly half the price of Avgas) and more universally available at airfields.

There are far too many new engines to mention, but two of the most important are to be found in Canada and France.

Orenda Once the famous name of Canadian turbojets, this is making a comeback in aircraft propulsion thanks to the efforts of the new company Orenda Recip, of Toronto. They have had the courage to design an all-new engine, called the OE600, which in principle is exactly the same as thousands of Lycomings and

The Orenda OE-600 has a geared drive (in this demo exhibit, to a propeller with cropped blades).

Continentals in being a four-stroke engine with spark ignition burning 100LL gasoline in poppet-valve cylinders. So what's new? First, it is very well designed in the latest materials, most of the structure being aluminium, Second, it is a liquid-cooled V-8 with fuel injection and twin turbochargers and a geared drive. Above all, it is being certificated at 600 hp.

Thus, while for 50 years we have watched turboprops taking over from piston engines, Orenda intend the OE600 to start replacing not only old piston engines but also turboprops!

Brief specification:
Cylinder bore 112.6 mm (4.433 in); stroke 101.6 mm (4.00 in); capacity 8.111 litres (495 cu in); compression ratio 8.
Dimensions: length 1,511 mm (59.5 in); width 812.8 mm (32.0 in); height 825.5 mm (32.5 in)
Dry weight, with accessories: 340.2 kg (750 lb).
Maximum output: 600 hp at 4,400 rpm, with sfc 0.2 kg (0.44 lb)/hp/hr; reduction gear ratio 0.4675, giving propeller speed of 2,057 rpm.
Continuous power: 500 hp; cruising propeller rpm 1,683, with fuel burn at 325 hp of approximately 94 litres (25 US gal, 20.8 Imp gal)/hr.

Stevens Aviation of Greenville, South Carolina, installed the first pair of flight-test engines in a Beech King Air C90. Flight development at Spokane, Washington, began on 11 July 1997, and FAA certification has now been granted. In the King Air the OE600 replaces the PT6A turboprop, and Orenda have published curves showing dramatic improvements in performance. Compared with the original aircraft with PT6A-20 engines, cruising speed at 20,000 ft is plotted at 270 mph, compared to 218, while the curves of engine-out rate of climb are a case of 'no contest'. Of course, the author has to stay on good terms with Pratt & Whitney Canada, and emphasizes that these curves are plotted by Orenda Recip!

The first aircraft designed for the OE600 is the Lancair Tigress, a composite two-seater expected to reach 644 km/h (400 mph). Among many targeted retrofit applications, in the Cessna 400, StarKraft 700 and various Aero Commanders, the OE600 would replace horizontally opposed piston engines, in the Ag-Cats it would replace various types of engine including turboprops, and in the venerable Beaver it would replace a radial engine designed in 1926! Orenda has been so encouraged by the reception given to the OE600 that work is now in hand on the naturally aspirated OE500, to be rated at 500 hp.

Morane Renault Though this is the brand name, a conjunction of two of the most famous names in French aviation, the MR engines are actually products of a company called SMA. In turn SMA, Société de Motorisations Aéronautiques, is a new joint venture with stock held 50/50 by Renault-Sport and the aircraft constructor (subsidiary of Aérospatiale) Socata.

The Orenda-engined King Air C90B about to land after its first flight on piston engines on 11 July 1997.

In the author's opinion, the MR family are, in the long term, likely to prove the first ever to provide real competition for Lycoming and Continental. This is because they are not only outstandingly well designed, with the very latest technology, but they are diesels designed for the lowest possible consumption of any aviation kerosene, particularly Jet A1. This is dramatically cheaper than 100LL, and unlike gasoline is available at virtually every licensed airport. One could suggest it is probably also a safer fuel.

There are currently three MR models on offer, with at least 90 per cent commonality. The MR 250 (250 hp) was certificated in April 1998. The MR 300 was to follow in August, followed by the MR 180 in November. All have four horizontally opposed cylinders of 5 litres (305 cu in) capacity. The cooling is by a mix of air and oil; 'to reduce weight and risk of engine failure due to a liquid cooling system'. Air for combustion enters a ram inlet under the engine from where a short pipe takes it to the eye of the supercharger. From here it is piped through the two diagonal heat exchangers behind the engine, emerging at the top to enter the four cylinders from above. Fuel is injected directly into the cylinders. Exhaust is piped away underneath to escape through the turbine driving the supercharger. Valve pushrods are under the cylinders. Control is fully digital, with manual backup. All parameters are automatically optimised according to the position of the single cockpit lever.

The MR 180 has a direct drive to the propeller. Power at sea level is 180 hp at 2,000 rpm, falling away with altitude much more slowly than in competitor engines, so that 130 hp is still available at 20,000 ft (6,096 m). Fuel consumption is throughout much lower than that of a *moteur traditionnel*, being about 38 litres/hr at sea level instead of 62-63. The MR 250 has a reduction gear driving a Hartzell three-bladed propeller at 2,000 rpm with a crankshaft turning at 3,000 rpm. This engine is controlled to give a constant 250 hp from sea level to 15,000 ft (4,572 m), at which point a 250-hp competitor would give 149-150 hp. Fuel consumption at sea level is about 54 litres/hr, compared with the competitor's 77. The MR 300, with the same reduction gear, is controlled to give a constant 300 hp to 10,000 ft (3,048 m); at 25,000 ft (7,620 m) power is still about 230 hp, whereas a 300-hp competitor would be down to 150. At sea level the MR 300 is shown as

The Morane Renault MR 250 is now being test-flown. One of the heat exchangers is prominent.

burning 64 litres/hr at full power, compared with the 92 of a *traditionnel*. TBO for all three of the Morane Renaults is to be 3,000 hours, and the overall saving on direct operating cost is reckoned to be 35 per cent (fuel 60, TBO 34, spares and man-hours 10).

SMA do not wish to be too specific about certain factors which are subject to change, but they describe the MR 180 as 'about the same length and width as the Lycoming IO-360' and the length as 'about 150 mm (6 in) shorter than the Lycoming IO-540'. Luc Pelon, programme manager, says 'The height is around 550 mm (21.65 in) from the top of the plenum to the bottom of the turbocharger. This is based on the free space we have on the Socata Trinidad. With a shallower cowling we

Under the Morane Renault can be found the turbosupercharger.

can put the turbo on the back of the engine'. He comments that castings, forgings, machining and accessories are the subject of contracts with 'various European suppliers'. Bench testing began in January 1997, and by September had demonstrated predicted powers with equal to or better than the calculated fuel consumption. Flight testing in Socata aircraft will have begun long before this new edition appears.

In the face of competition like this, the two US giants are hardly sitting on their hands. The firm which for many years has been in the No. 1 spot, Textron Lycoming, has – again for many years – been studying how best it can stay there, but is not yet ready to announce anything other than new models of established engines. When Cessna wanted to relaunch the Model 206 Stationair it asked Textron Lycoming and Teledyne Continental to come up with new engines that made less noise (for example for environmentally sensitive Germans). Lycoming offered an IO-540 version with larger cylinders, the IO-580-A1A and TIO-580-A1A, with the same 300 and 310 hp ratings as the 540 cu in versions. Cessna has not bought the 580 cu in engine, but a single AEIO-580 is flying in the new Extra 330 aerobatic aircraft, the designation reflecting the horsepower of this new engine.

Lycoming's immediate rival, Teledyne Continental, burned its fingers with the all-new Tiara range (p. 191), but is now embarking afresh on a wholly new range of engines. This time they are diesels. The following is the complete text of a release issued on 18 November 1997 by a British company:

'Perkins Technology Ltd, the engineering consultancy of diesel-engine manufacturer VarityPerkins, has won a contract in America to design a new two-stroke internal-combustion engine for light aircraft.

US engine manufacturer Teledyne Continental Motors, of Muskegon, Michigan, has selected Perkins Technology as design consultant on the two-stroke compression-ignition direct-injection light-aircraft engine. A team led by Teledyne was awarded a co-operative agreement by NASA to develop the new engine under its GAP (General Aviation Propulsion) programme.

The engine, being developed under the three-year GAP programme, will be flight-demonstrated near the end of the programme. The engine will burn Jet-A (aviation kerosene) fuel.

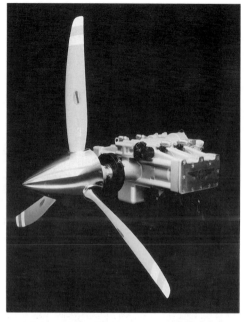

The only released illustration of the new Teledyne Continental diesel being developed in the UK by Perkins.

NASA's and Teledyne's objectives are to reduce the acquisition cost of a new engine, improve reliability, lower maintenance costs and meet current and future noise and emissions requirements.

Perkins Technology's ability to provide state-of-the-art engine designs, using advanced technologies and CAE (Computer-Aided Engineering) processes, enables its engineers to provide low-noise and low-emissions designs.

The consultancy provides cost-effective production engine design solutions to many sectors worldwide. Its success is due largely to its ability to develop advanced designs that are capable of being put into production. The ability stems from 65 years' knowledge and experience of volume engine manufacture, coupled with continuous investment in diesel-engine research.'

The consultant has been permitted to issue a single photograph, which doubtless shows a mock-up. Apart from the advanced design of Hartzell propeller, this shows that the engine – at least in one version – is a four-cylinder horizontally opposed unit with liquid cooling. The exterior is amazingly 'clean'. Fuel-injection pipes appear to be above the

Testing the remarkable propulsion system of the Grob Strato 2C.

cylinders, and under the rear of the engine it is just possible to make out the expected turbosupercharger. This particular engine appears to be in the 200-hp class. It is interesting that Perkins claim 'reduced acquisition cost', but say nothing about the cost of fuel.

Teledyne Continental are also prime propulsion contractors for a unique aircraft, the German Grob Strato 2C. Designed to fly for 48 hours at 18 km (59,055 ft) – for example on weather reconnaissance over the Poles – it has two pusher engines mounted above its amazing carbon-fibre wing with a span of 56.5 m (185 ft 4½ in). The huge (6 m, 19 ft 8¼ in) five-bladed propellers are driven via reduction gears from generally unmodified 402-hp Teledyne Continental TSIOL-550 engines each with six opposed liquid-cooled cylinders (predecessors are described on p.197). What makes the propulsion system unusual is that the engine exhaust is really made to give up as much energy as possible. First, it drives an AlliedSignal turbocharger with a pressure ratio of 3.0. The still energetic gas is then expanded through a second turbine driving a two-stage compressor based on the core of the PW127 turboprop. Total airflow at sea level is 10 kg (22 lb)/sec, and at altitude the overall pressure ratio is 54. The exhaust is finally made to give jet thrust, adding an extra 12 per cent to the propulsive power. There are three intercoolers and two further radiators.

Though in Britain it is particularly hard to obtain financial backing, especially for anything really worthwhile, several little

The Walter M202.

groups are toiling away on new or improved engines. One designer who has obtained backing from the Department of Scientific and Industrial Research is former Cosworth engineer Mark Wilksch, at Buckingham, who has taken a diesel to the flight stage. Another is John Ashton, working in the Isle of Wight. A third diesel, so far developed on the proverbial shoestring, is a 100 hp two-stroke running at Diesel Air, of Hastings.

Among many other new developments, there are so many enthusiastic builders of experimental, replica or scaled aircraft who have wished for a small radial engine that a US firm has developed one. HCI Aviation, of New Haven, Missouri, are marketing the R180, based on five air-cooled cylinders of 85.5 mm Volkswagen type. The R180 is supercharged but has direct drive. It is rated at 75 hp at 2,150 rpm, with a dry weight of 55.3 kg (122 lb). Apart from the few accessories, almost everything about it is traditional – 'We have chosen the best features of LeBlond, Viele, Kinner, McClatchie and Szekeley'. The

Sketch by HCI Aviation of the R180, for replica enthusiasts, which uses five Volkswagen 85.5 mm-bore cylinders.

A newly released section drawing of the Russian D-200 rotary engine.

R180 is offered as a kit of finished parts at $9,600.

In 1995 the famous old Czech firm of Walter, which makes jet and turboprop engines, went into production with the M 202, a neat flat-twin with air-cooled cylinders, each with its own carburettor, of 676 cc (41.25 cu in) capacity. This attractive engine weighs 36 kg (79.4 lb) and has a take-off rating of 48 kW (65 hp) at 6,300 rpm, the propeller being geared down to 2,350 rpm. So far it powers five types of ultralight, one (the ZA-1) being a pusher.

Finally, the author has always wondered why the Wankel-type rotary engine has appeared to be, at the same time, better than anything else and yet rejected by the markets. One of his friends was delighted with his rotary-engine Audi Ro 80 car, which in over ten years, never suffered from rapid wear, increasingly high fuel burn or any of the other supposed problems with such engines. In Perm, Russia, the mighty Aviadvigatel (means 'aircraft engine') firm has taken the VAZ-430

family (the last engine in this book) and brought it to the production stage as the D-200. In its first form this is a geared fixed-wing engine, initially for the Yak-112. Take-off rating is 220 hp at 2,700 rpm output speed, with fuel consumption of 111 lb/h (sfc, 0.507). Dry weight is 145 kg (320 lb).

Meanwhile, Wankel Rotary GmbH have done the obvious thing and developed some of their wide range of engines to have multifuel capability. The first two to be offered are the LOCR-407 (single 407 cm^3 rotor, 45 hp) and the LOCR-814 (twin rotors, 90 hp). Both are being qualified on diesel F-34 or Jet-A F-54 kerosene. Slightly further off are the VIP (variable installation position) series, again to be qualified on Jet-A and diesel. The largest of this family is the four-rotor VIP-4200, which for a weight of 69 kg (152 lb) puts out 260 hp. In the UK Mid-West Engines)p. 211) were delighted to exhibit their first engine actually running on Jet-A kerosene at the Berlin airshow in May 1998.

Piston engine aircraft speed

The following are the fastest aircraft to have flown with piston engines:
de Havilland DH.103 Hornet prototype (RR915), 485 mph
Dornier Do 335 V8, 479 mph
Focke-Wulf Ta 152H-1, 472 mph
Grumman F8F Bearcat, as modified by Darryl F. Greenamyer, 482.46 mph
Hawker Fury LA610, 'about 485 mph'
Messerschmitt Me 209 VI, 469.22 mph (26 April 1939)
Mikoyan MiG I-250, 513 mph (boosted by auxiliary compressor/jet)
Montagne Mach-Buster, designed to exceed Mach 1 (not yet completed)
Napier–Heston racer, designed (1939) for 520 mph; a replica is planned
North American P-51 Mustang, as modified by Frank Taylor, 517.06 mph (30 July 1983)
Pond Racer, designed for 535 mph, flown 1991 but no record by mid-1998.
Republic XP-47J, alleged 504 mph (unconfirmed), 6 August 1944
Republic XP-72, designed for 520 mph (reached 490)
Supermarine Spiteful XVI, 494 mph in combat trim

Appendix of abbreviations

ABC Automatic boost control
ADI Anti-detonant injection, such as methanol/water
BDC Bottom dead centre, position of piston furthest from top of cylinder
bhp Brake horsepower, power actually available at propeller shaft
BMEP Brake mean effective pressure, MEP calculated from measured bhp
CD Capacitor discharge
CI Compression ignition
CR Compression ratio, ratio of volume in cylinder above piston at BDC (clearance volume + swept volume) to that at TDC (clearance volume)
CS Constant-speed (propeller)
CSU Constant-speed unit, controls CS propeller
cu in Cubic inches, 1 cu in = 16.387 cc
EGT Exhaust-gas temperature
FS Full supercharge gear ratio
G Geared type engine
GM-1 Nitrous-oxide injection
H Engine layout with four parallel cylinder banks driving two crankshafts
hp Horsepower
HP High pressure
HT High tension (electrical)
HZ German abbreviation for a central supercharger driven by a separate engine providing compressed air for propulsion engines
I Direct injection into cylinders
ihp Indicated horsepower, derived from measures taken of cylinder MEP (IMEP)
IMEP Indicated mean effective pressure

kW Kilowatt, standard SI unit of power, 1 kW = 1.341 hp
lb/sq in Pounds per square inch
LP Low-pressure
LT Low tension (electrical)
MEP Mean effective pressure inside the cylinder
METO Maximum except take-off power
MMA Mono-methyl aniline
MS Medium supercharge gear ratio
MW50 50/50 mix of methyl alcohol and water
NACA US National Advisory Committee for Aeronautics, became NASA National Aeronautics and Space Administration
O Opposed-cylinder type engine
OAT Outside air temperature
OEI One engine inoperative
PN Performance number of fuel (octane numbers over 100)
R Radial type engine
RC Rotating combustion
rpm Revolutions per minute
S Supercharged type engine
sfc Specific fuel consumption, rate at which fuel is burned for a given power output
shp Shaft horsepower
T Turbosupercharged type engine
TBO Time between overhauls
TDC Top dead centre, position of piston closest to top of cylinder
TEL Tetra-ethyl lead, anti-knock fuel additive
V Vee type engine, two cylinder banks meeting at an angle driving one crankshaft
VP Variable-pitch (but not CS) propeller
WM Water methanol or weak mixture

Bibliography

Readers are referred to the following books for additional information, as well as to the Engines section of *Jane's All the World's Aircraft* (which from 1969 has been compiled by the author), to the Smithsonian *Annals of Flight* monographs, to articles in the sadly discontinued *Shell Aviation News*, and to valuable publications by numerous engine manufacturers and such professional organizations as the Royal Aeronautical Society, Institution of Mechanical Engineers, and American Institute of Aeronautics and Astronautics (and its predecessor the IAS).

Angle, Glenn D., *Aircraft Engine Cyclopedia* (Otterbein Press, 1921) and *Aerosphere* (Otterbein Press, 1939).

Burls, G. A., *Aero Engines* (Griffin, 1916).

Von Gersdorff, Kyrill, and Grasmann, Kurt, *Flugmotoren und Strahltriebwerke* (Bernard u Graefe Verlag, Munich, 1981).

Molloy, E. (Gen Ed), *Engines Pts 1, 2 and 3* (Vols 5, 9 and 13 of Aeroplane Maintenance and Operation Series, Newnes, 1940).

Nahum, A., *The Rotary Aero Engine* (HMSO, 1987).

Rubbra, A. A., *Rolls-Royce Piston Engines* (RR Heritage Trust, 1990).

Schlaifer, Dr R., and Heron, S., *Development of Aircraft Engines and Fuels* (Harvard, 1950).

Setright, L. J. K., *The Power to Fly* (Allen & Unwin, 1971).

Smith, Herschel, *Aircraft Piston Engines* (McGraw-Hill, 1981).

Staff of *The Motor, The Aero Manual* (reprint of 1910 book by David & Charles, 1972).

Wilkinson, Paul H., *Aircraft Engines of the World* (Wilkinson in US, Pitman in UK, annually from 1941).

Gunston, Bill, *Faster Than Sound* (Patrick Stephens Ltd, 1992).

—, *The Development of Jet and Turbine Aero Engines* (Patrick Stephens Ltd, 1997).

—, *Rolls-Royce Aero Engines* (Patrick Stephens Ltd, 1989).

—, *World Encyclopaedia of Aero Engines* (Patrick Stephens Ltd, 1986, 1989 and 1998).

Index